Thomasine Traditions in Antiquity

Nag Hammadi and
Manichaean Studies

VOLUME 59

Thomasine Traditions in Antiquity

The Social and Cultural World of the Gospel of Thomas

Edited by

Jon Ma. Asgeirsson, April D. DeConick,
and Risto Uro

BRILL

LEIDEN • BOSTON

2006

This book is printed on acid-free paper.

Library of Congress Cataloging-in-Publication data

Thomasine traditions in antiquity : the social and cultural world of the Gospel of
Thomas / edited by Jon Ma. Asgeirsson, April D. DeConick, and Risto Uro.
    p. cm. — (Nag Hammadi and Manichaean studies, ISSN 0929–2470 ; v. 59)
    "A Collection of papers . . . presented to the Society of Biblical Literature
Thomasine Traditions Group"—Pref.
    Includes bibliographical references (p.) and indexes.
    ISBN 90–04–14779–9 (alk. paper)
    1. Gospel of Thomas (Coptic Gospel)—Criticism, interpretation, etc.
I. Asgeirsson, Jon Ma. II. DeConick, April D. III. Uro, Risto. IV. Society of
Biblical Literature. Thomasine Group. V. Nag Hammadi and Manichaean
studies ; 59.

BS2860.T52T46 2006
29'.8—dc22

2005054210

ISSN 0929–2470
ISBN 90 04 14779 9

© Copyright 2006 by Koninklijke Brill NV, Leiden, The Netherlands.
Koninklijke Brill NV incorporates the imprints Brill Academic
Publishers, Martinus Nijhoff Publishers and VSP.

PRINTED IN THE NETHERLANDS

CONTENTS

PREFACE

This volume is a collection of papers that were presented to the Society of Biblical Literature Thomasine Traditions Group. The Group was preceded by a Consultation on Thomasine Traditions launched at the Annual Meeting of the Society of Biblical Literature in Washington, DC, in November of 1993. Its work lasted for three years at which juncture the program unit was expanded into a Group (1996) that continued through the year 2001. The program units on Thomasine traditions attracted huge enthusiasm by Society members from around the world. No less than two sessions were organized for each of the Annual Meetings for the duration of the two program units—on a few occasions in collaboration with other program units (the Q Section, the Nag Hammadi Section and the Christian Apocrypha Section).

The Steering Committees of the two program units consisted of six members, each with equal numbers of European and North American scholars. For the Consultation, the following members were appointed by the SBL Program Committee: Jon Ma. Asgeirsson (Iceland), Chair; Tjitze Baarda (The Netherlands); Ron Cameron (USA); Karen King (USA); Gregory J. Riley (USA); and Risto Uro (Finland). For the Group the following members served on the Steering Committee: Jon Ma. Asgeirsson, Chair; Tjitze Baarda; Ron Cameron; April D. DeConick (USA); Gregory J. Riley; and Risto Uro. Elaine Pagels (USA) joined the committee during its last three years.

The preparation of the initial proposal took place at the Institute for Antiquity and Christianity in Claremont, California. A visiting scholar from Helsinki, Finland, Risto Uro, together with Jon Ma. Asgeirsson, then Associate Director of the Institute, met with several specialists on Thomasine traditions from southern California along with another visiting scholar, from South Africa, Patrick J. Hartin, for the planning and eventual drafting of a proposal that was subsequently submitted to and approved by the SBL Program Committee.

Numerous scholars have since contributed to the work of the Thomasine Traditions program units. Their research has appeared in various publications during the work of the program units (such as doctoral dissertations; the *SBL Seminar Papers*; Nag Hammadi and

Manichaean Studies; journals; collected essays; and monographs). At
the end of the work of the SBL Group on Thomasine Traditions,
the Steering Committee made plans to publish a selection of studies
by several members of the Group. The result of this effort is the
present volume.

Research on Thomasine Traditions continues and will continue
for a long time. The Steering Committe of the Thomasine Traditions
Group is convinced its work has improved and furthered studies in
this very important aspect of early Christian development. It has
placed in focus a tradition whose accessibility has been increased
immensely through the find of the Nag Hammadi Library in the
year 1945. The *Gospel of Thomas* (NHC II,2), the *Book of Thomas*
(NHC II,7), and the *Acts of Thomas* are a corpus of texts showing
clear relations of an intertextual nature (if they are not the products
of a single community) of unparalleled importance for the understanding of a small and now lost branch of Christianities. While the
Group did expand the focus of its intertextual research to include
other writings attributed to St. Thomas (the *Infancy Gospel of Thomas*
and the *Apocalypse of Thomas*) as well as such writings as the *Odes of
Solomon*, those of Valentinus and even Islamic literature, the *Gospel
of Thomas* remained the main focus of the work of the two program
units. Even within the context of the *Book of Thomas* and *Acts of Thomas*,
the gospel securely retained its place as *primus inter pares*, as is reflected
in the number of articles on the *Gospel of Thomas* in this volume.
Indeed, relations with the more distant relatives of the *Gospel of Thomas*
were found to be indecisive, and, thus, for the most part they were
not pursued by project members (but see on Valentinus and Islam
below). As for the closer relatives of the gospel, the need for establishing a solid picture of the *Gospel of Thomas* proved to be most
urgent, before attempting to identify the topics linking the *Book of
Thomas* and the *Acts of Thomas* with those of the gospel (the notable
exception being the persona of Thomas himself; see below).

For the most part, research into the *Gospel of Thomas* has been
characterized by comparisons with the New Testament gospels on
the one hand and with gnostic literature on the other. The Society
of Biblical Literature's program unit on Thomasine literature (1993–
2001) was established for the very purpose of looking at the *Gospel of
Thomas* and related literature in its own right rather than looking at
it from the point of view of a given framework outside of these texts.

This idea, of Thomasine literature having come of age, evolved in several directions in the work of the program unit. While the Steering Committee made sure to make room for this varied tenor within the program unit, certain aspects were carried out in still other program units of the Society of Biblical Literature (for instance the unit on Christian Origins and the one on Jewish Mysticism).[1]

One of the most disputed questions within the Thomasine program unit had to do with the criteria for disengaging from the New Testament framework. Just how is it possible to look from the Thomasine literature to the outside world? Does the framework collapse by viewing the sayings of Jesus in the *Gospel of Thomas* from a Thomasine perspective? Can a Thomasine uniqueness be established through an alleged metaphoric expression of the resurrection in the *Gospel of Thomas*, considered to be of a different nature than the expression(s) found in the New Testament gospels, or to represent a unio mystica over against faith?

Another approach characteristic for the work of the Thomasine program unit had to do with the application of social critical methods, whether based on historical or contemporary models. Yet, the prominence of this approach did not go uncontested. Just to what extent is it possible to view religious texts as a window into past societies? Does a myth reflect social realities or an ideological aspiration?

---

[1] Examples of the variety of the recent Thomasine studies may be found e.g. in the following works: Tjitze Baarda, *Essays on the Diatessaron* (CBET 11; Kampen: Pharos, 1994); Gregory J. Riley, *Resurrection Reconsidered: Thomas and John in Controversy* (Minneapolis, MN: Fortress, 1995); April D. DeConick, *Seek to See Him: Ascent Mysticism in the Gospel of Thomas* (VCSup 33; Leiden: Brill, 1996); John D. Turner and Anne McGuire eds., *The Nag Hammadi Library after Fifty Years: Proceedings of the 1995 Society of Biblical Literature Commemoration* (NHMS 45; Leiden: Brill, 1997); Jon Ma. Asgeirsson, "Doublets and Strata: Towards a Rhetorical Approach to the *Gospel of Thomas*" (Ph.D. Diss.; Claremont Graduate University, 1998); Stephen J. Patterson and James M. Robinson eds., *The Fifth Gospel: The Gospel of Thomas Comes of Age* (Harrisburg, PA: Trinity Press International, 1998); Risto Uro ed., *Thomas at the Crossroads: Essays on the Gospel of Thomas* (Studies of the New Testament and Its World; Edinburgh: Clark, 1998); Elaine Pagels, "Exegesis of Genesis 1 in the Gospel of Thomas and John," *JBL* 118 (1999): 477–496; April D. DeConick, *Voices of the Mystics: Early Christian Discourse in the Gospels of John, Thomas and Other Ancient Christian Literature* (JSNTSup 157; Sheffield: Sheffield Academic Press, 2001); Risto Uro, *Thomas: Seeking the Historical Context of the Gospel of Thomas* (London: Clark, 2003); Ron Cameron and Merill P. Miller eds., *Redescribing Christian Origins* (SBLSymS 28; Atlanta, GA: Society of Biblical Literature, 2004) (the pertinent articles on the *Gospel of Thomas*).

What does it take to place an ancient text in an alleged social context?

Yet another prominent feature of the Thomasine unit's work was the issue of the ideological background of the Thomasine literature. How does the *Gospel of Thomas* portray the Judaism of its day? Is it under the influence of Philo of Alexandria or Jewish mystics? To what extent is the gospel under the influence of Greek ideology and tradition (for instance rhetorical) in its presentation of the sayings of Jesus? And just how does this scenario relate to the *Book of Thomas* and the *Acts of Thomas* and various presentations of Gnosticism?

Lastly, comparison with topics within the Thomasine traditions themselves and other early Christian literature was periodically undertaken during the work of the Thomasine program units, with the emphasis on the *Gospel of Thomas* noted above. Examples of this research are to be found in the last three contributions to this volume.

*   *   *

The contributions collected in this volume are reflective of the Thomasine program units' results and, indeed, of the state of the art of Thomasine studies at the dawn of the twenty-first century. Stephen J. Patterson draws attention to the fact that the *Gospel of Thomas* remains largely ignored by scholars working in the field of Christian beginnings. Patterson argues that the people using the *Gospel of Thomas* in the first century had no use for a story of origins, due to its social construct of an itinerant model. Yet, the gospel has become a source for writing a new story of Christian beginnings by scholars today, a story promising to be much different from that of the dominant view perpetuated in the writings of Luke and adopted by biblical scholars of the New Testament, for the most part, until now.

Risto Uro takes on the problem of describing the social environment of the *Gospel of Thomas*. He rejects ideas about myths reflecting social circumstances or some specified function within a society, such as is argued by Patterson in his application of the itinerancy theory to the *Gospel of Thomas*. On the one hand, information about the social milieu must be gained from "other relevant data" (being, for instance, the gospel at large, or external sources). On the other hand, a myth may have a totally different function than that of portraying the "existing social reality" (by, for instance, formalizing a new world of symbols in a given society). Philip H. Sellew provides an excellent insight from an "external" source and undertakes an investigation into the meaning of the briefest saying of Jesus attested in the *Gospel*

of Thomas (logion 42). Sellew advocates an approach to the gospel
in which the logion must be understood "in and of itself." Indeed, the
nature of the language of the sayings draws attention to the "cultural
setting" and the "challenge it represents." Adducing abundant funerary
epigraphic evidence (epitaphs) from the Graeco-Roman world, in which
are found such sentiments that contrast the world of the living with
that of the dead, Sellew notes how these epitaphs reflect the general cultural environment, in which logion 42 can be interpreted.

Milton Moreland argues that logion 52 in the *Gospel of Thomas* offers
an insight into the rejection of the Hebrew epic contrary to what
was conventional among other early varieties of Christianity. The process is revealing at the same time of the community's search for
identity and self-authentification. While Moreland finds strong evidence
for the rejection of Jewish traditions in the *Gospel of Thomas*, April
D. DeConick seeks to establish an original Christian-Jewish core of
materials there through tradition-historical analysis. It is on the basis
of rhetorical composition that she identifies the "kernel gospel," which
she argues is identical with ("most similar to") "Christian Judaism." The
intertextual setting of the oldest core of the *Gospel of Thomas* thus
appears to be characterized by "apocalyptic expectations" and prophetic
motifs typical of an Old Testament matrix for Christianity. Petri
Luomanen provides yet another angle for viewing the *Gospel of Thomas*
against Jewish traditions. He discusses four specific logia in the *Gospel
of Thomas* in relation to and with parallels to a set of Jewish-Christian
gospels. Thus, he is interested in actual literary dependence rather
than tradition per se. Common elements between the *Gospel of Thomas*
and the Jewish Christian gospel fragments over against the Synoptic
tradition and the *Diatessaron* in particular point him in the direction
of a common gospel harmony preceding the *Diatessaron* of Tatian. This
reconstruction is an alternative to concluding that there are, in each
given case, two independent sayings behind each of the gospel traditions under comparison.

The application of Greek epic and ideology as well as Hellenistic
rhetoric provides for still a different approach to the relationship of
the *Gospel of Thomas* to Judaism. Jon Ma. Asgeirsson attempts in his
contribution to establish intertextual links between Platonic traditions
of creation as found in Plato's *Timaeus* and the *Gospel of Thomas*. The
rhetorical composition is seen as secondary in this very context. Thus
Platonic traditions, framed with Dioscuri motifs and the *paideia* of
acquiring knowledge, constitute the Greek gospel par excellence,

augmented by the gospel's direct rejection of the ethos of Judaism. Vernon K. Robbins explores one of the most prominent features of rhetoric, enthymemic structuring, in a selection of logia in the *Gospel of Thomas*. Sayings consisting of "assertions" and "argumentative rationales" in a gospel text Robbins labels "enthymematic logia."

Comparison of various topics within the Thomasine literature to its relatives, other early Christian literature (canonical and non-canonical) and beyond is a theme that combines the last four contributions to this volume. Antti Marjanen argues that most studies on the persona of Jesus in the *Gospel of Thomas* have focused on its relevance for the "historical Jesus." Having explored the sayings of *Thomas* about Jesus, Marjanen concludes that the Thomasine Christology is, for its early age, mature in comparison to other early attempts at such a description, being much like that of Paul and John. On the other hand, Marjanen argues not only for the similarity but also for the dissimilarity of *Thomas* to the canonical authors, emphasizing *Thomas*' "egalitarian type of Christology."

Ismo Dunderberg observes that a particular fragment from the writings of Valentinus has been variously discussed in comparison with wisdom literature, Paul and John, as well as in view of its possible gnostic proclivity. Noting that the fragment has been understood as a likely interpretation of Genesis, Dunderberg directs attention to its possible relationship with the *Gospel of Thomas*. What does constitute a link, above all, is the idea of a human "dominion over all things," more specifically, as Dunderberg maintains, the rule of a "sage" over everything—a tradition attested in Philo among others.

Patrick J. Hartin demonstrates how the author of the *Acts of Thomas* applies the genre of a narrative for getting across a "specific understanding of the Christian message." Hartin focuses in particular on the manipulation of the character of Thomas in the narrative construction and how it is used to affect the "reader's self-awareness." Learning from the example of the apostle, the readers are challenged to look into themselves and to examine what controls their way of "life."

Marvin Meyer ventures to trace possible vestiges of the *Gospel of Thomas* in Islamic literature through an investigation of logion 42. He ponders over this enigmatic logion in Coptic and its rendering in translations, as well as conflicting interpretations. In a final section, Meyer proceeds to examine how "similar themes" in Islamic literature may shed light on the understanding of this cryptic saying in the *Gospel of Thomas*.

* * *

The Steering Committee is profoundly thankful for the understanding and interest expressed in its work by the SBL Program Committee and the SBL Executive Staff. It is equally thankful to all the many participants in the work of the said program units and in particular to those who have contributed to this volume.

Lastly, but not least, the editors would like to express their gratitude to Professor Stephen Emmel, editor of Nag Hammadi and Manichaean Studies, for recommending the volume for publication by Brill. Emmel has further provided invaluable insights for stylistic improvement and aided in correcting the text in various ways. The staff of Brill Academic Publishers are to be commended for their enthusiasm and collaborative efforts to see this volume to its published end. Two research associates of the University of Helsinki have diligently worked on the bibliography under the supervision of Risto Uro. Many thanks to Kristel Nyberg and Sanna Ingo.

* * *

The contribution by Marvin W. Meyer has previously appeared in his *Secret Gospels* (Harrisburg, PA: Trinity Press International, 2003). An earlier version of the contribution by Vernon K. Robbins appeared in *SBL Seminar Papers* 36, Part II (Atlanta, GA: Scholars Press, 1998).

The article by April D. DeConick provides a summary of the ideas developed in her *Recovering the Original Gospel of Thomas: A History of the Gospel and Its Growth* (JSNTSup 286; London: T & T Clark International, 2005).

The editors have in general adapted the style of the *SBL Handbook of Style: For Ancient, Near Eastern, Biblical, and Early Christian Studies* (Peabody, MA: Hendrickson, 1999). The subdivision of the individual logia in the *Gospel of Thomas* follows the custom of Robert J. Miller, ed., *The Complete Gospels: Annotated Scholars Version* (rev. and exp. version; San Francisco, CA: HarperSanFrancisco, 1994).

> Reykjavik, Bloomington, Helsinki,
> St. John's Mass, 2005,
> Jon Ma. Asgeirsson
> April D. DeConick
> Risto Uro

ABBREVIATIONS

AASF	Annales Academiae scientiarum fennicae
AB	Anchor Bible
Acts	Acts of the Apostles
Acts John	*Acts of John*
Acts Thom.	*Acts of Thomas*
An.	*De anima*
AnBib	Analecta biblica
ANF	*The Ante Nicene Fathers*
ANRW	*Aufstieg und Niedergang der römischen Welt: Geschichte und Kultur Roms im Spiegel der neueren Forschung*
AP	*Anthologica palatina*
2 Apoc. Jas	*Second Apocalypse of James*
1 Apol.	*Apologia 1*
Barn.	*Barnabas*
BETL	Bibliotheca ephemeridum theologicarum lovaniensium
BJS	Brown Judaic Studies
b. Sanh.	*Babylonian Talmud: Sanhedrin*
BZNW	Beihefte zur Zeitschrift für die neutestamentliche Wissenschaft
CBET	Contributions to Biblical Exegesis and Theology
2 Clem.	*Second Clement*
Cod. NT	Codex Novi Testamenti
Col	Colossians
Comm. Ezech.	*Commentariorum in Ezechielem libri XVI*
Comm. Isa.	*Commentariorum in Isaiam libri XVIII*
Comm. Jo.	*Commentarii in evangelium Joannis*
Comm. Matt.	*Commentarium in evangelium Matthaei*
Comm. Mich.	*Commentariorum in Michaeum libri II*
Comm. Ps.	*Commentarii in Psalmos*
ConBNT	Coniectanea biblica: New Testament Series
Contempl.	*De vita contemplativa*
1 Cor	*First Corinthians*
2 Cor	*Second Corinthians*
CSCO	Corpus scriptorum christianorum orientalium
CurBS	*Currents in Research: Biblical Studies*

Dial.	*Dialogus cum Tryphone*
Diatr.	*Diatribai (Dissertationes)*
Ebr.	*De ebrietate*
Eccl	Ecclesiastes
Ecl.	*Eclogae propheticae*
EKKNT	Evangelisch-katolischer Kommentar zum Neuen Testament
Ench.	*Enchiridion*
Eph	Ephesians
Exod	Exodus
ExpTim	*Expository Times*
FF	Foundations and Facets
ForFasc	Forum Fascicles
FRLANT	Forschungen zur Religion und Literatur des Alten und Neuen Testaments
Fug.	*De fuga et inventione*
Gal	Galatians
GBS	Guides to Biblical Scholarship
Gen	Genesis
Gos. Thom.	*Gospel of Thomas*
Gos. Phil.	*Gospel of Philip*
Haer.	*Adversus haereses*
H. Ceres	*Hymnus Homericum ad Cererem*
HDR	Harvard Dissertations in Religion
HeyJ	*Heythrop Journal*
Hist.	*Historiae*
Hist. eccl.	*Historia ecclesiastica*
HR	*History of Religions*
HTR	*Harvard Theological Review*
HvTSt	*Hervormde teologiese studies*
IG	*Inscriptiones graecae*
Ign. *Eph.*	Ignatius, *To the Ephesians*
Ign. *Smyrn.*	Ignatius, *To the Smyrnaeans*
Ign. *Trall.*	Ignatius, *To the Trallians*
Isa	Isaiah
JAAR	*Journal of the American Academy of Religion*
JBL	*Journal of Biblical Literature*
JECS	*Journal of Early Christian Studies*
JHS	*Journal of Hellenic Studies*
John	Gospel of John

JSNT	*Journal for the Study of the New Testament*
JSNTSup	Journal for the Study of the New Testament: Supplement Series
JTS	*Journal of Theological Studies*
1 Kg	First Kings
LCL	Loeb Classical Library
Leg.	*Legum allegoriae*
Luke	Gospel of Luke
Mark	Gospel of Mark
Mart. Pol.	*Martyrdom of Polycarp*
Matt	Gospel of Matthew
Migr.	*De migratione Abrahami*
MTSR	*Method and Theory in the Study of Religion*
NHC	Nag Hammadi Codex/Codices
NHMS	Nag Hammadi and Manichaean Studies
NHS	Nag Hammadi Studies
NovT	*Novum Testamentum*
NovTSup	Novum Testamentum Supplements
NRSV	New Revised Standard Version
NTAbh, n. F.	Neutestamentliche Abhandlungen, neue Folge
NTS	*New Testament Studies*
Od.	*Odyssey*
Off.	*De officiis*
On Euch. A	*On the Eucharist A*
On Euch. B	*On the Eucharist B*
Opif.	*De opificio mundi*
Pan.	*Panarion*
Pel.	*Adversus Pelagianos dialogi III*
1 Pet	First Peter
PGM	*Papyri graecae magicae*
Phaed.	*Phaedo*
Phil	*Philologus*
Phil	Philippians
PO	Patrologia orientalis
P. Oxy	Papyrus Oxyrhynchus/Papyri Oxyrhynchi
Ps	Psalms
Ps.-Clem. Hom.	*The Pseudo Clemintine Homilies*
Ps.-Clem. Rec.	*The Pseudo Clementine Recognitions*
Q	"Quelle"/The Synoptic Sayings Source (Q)/Q Gospel

RelSRev	*Religious Studies Review*
Resp.	*Respublica*
Rhet.	*Rhetorica*
RHR	*Revue de l'histoire des religions*
Rom	Romans
RSV	Revised Standard Version
SAC	Studies in Antiquity and Christianity
2 Sam	Second Samuel
SAQ, n. F.	Sammlung ausgewählter Kirchen- und dogmen-geschicht- licher Quellenschriften, neue Folge
SBL	Society of Biblical Literature
SBLDS	Society of Biblical Literature Dissertation Series
SBLMS	Society of Biblical Literature Monograph Series
SBLSBS	Society of Biblical Literature Sources for Biblical Study
SBLSP	Society of Biblical Literature Seminar Papers
SBLSympS	Society of Biblical Literature Symposium Series
SBLTT	Society of Biblical Literature Texts and Translations
SBT	Studies in Biblical Theology
SE	*Studia evangelica*
SEÅ	*Svensk exegetisk årsbok*
SecCent	*Second Century*
SEG	Supplementum epigraphicum graecum
SHR	Studies in the History of Religions
Sir	Sirach
SNTSMS	Society for New Testament Studies Monograph Series
Somn.	*De somniis*
Spec.	*De specialibus legibus*
SPhilo	*Studia philonica*
StPatr	Studia patristica
Strom.	*Stromata*
TGH	Three Gospel Hypothesis
Theaet.	*Theaetetus*
1 Thess	First Thessalonians
Thomas	*Gospel of Thomas*
Thom. Cont.	*Book of Thomas the Contender*
Tim.	*Timaeus*
1 Tim	First Timothy
2 Tim	Second Timothy
TLZ	*Theologische Literaturzeitung*
Treat. Seth	*Second Treatise of the Great Seth*

Tri. Trac.	*Tripartite Tractate*
TRu, n. F.	*Theologische Rundschau, neue Folge*
TU	Texte und Untersuchungen
TUGAL	Texte und Untersuchungen zur Geschichte der altchrist-lichen Literatur
USOR	*Union Seminary Quarterly Review*
Val. Exp.	*A Valentinian Exposition*
VC	*Vigiliae christianae*
Vir. ill.	*De viris illustribus*
Wis	Wisdom of Solomon
WMANT	Wissenschaftliche Monographien zum Alten und Neuen Testament
WUNT	Wissenschaftliche Untersuchungen zum Neuen Testament
ZTK	*Zeitschrift für Theologie und Kirche*

CHAPTER ONE

THE *GOSPEL OF THOMAS* AND
CHRISTIAN BEGINNINGS

STEPHEN J. PATTERSON

The *Gospel of Thomas* has been with us now for more than 50 years. What impact has this very different new text had on our understanding of Christian beginnings? In 1991 Ron Cameron wrote of the state of this question:

> It is difficult to avoid the suspicion that *Gos. Thom.* has been treated in isolation, if not actually ignored, by most biblical scholars because its account of Christian origins does not square with the conventional picture gathered from the writings of the New Testament.[1]

Ten years later, regrettably, it must be said that Cameron's suspicions are still warranted today. Even though there is now a considerable body of research on *Thomas*, and a good bit of it of a revisionist nature, in the wider discussion of Christian origins the *Gospel of Thomas* still is not making much of an impact. A quick survey of the several major works devoted to Christian origins that have appeared in the last decade is, on the whole, discouraging. Ekkehard and Wolfgang Stegemann do not mention *Thomas* at all.[2] Luise Schottroff and Gerd Theissen both make small, though magnanimous gestures toward *Thomas*,[3] but have not allowed their overall conception to be affected by it. Even Gregory J. Riley, whose investigations into *Thomas* are significant in their own right, does very little to integrate *Thomas* into his later project on

---

[1] Ron Cameron, "The *Gospel of Thomas* and Christian Origins," in *The Future of Early Christianity: Essays in Honor of Helmut Koester* (ed. Birger Pearson et al.; Minneapolis, MN: Fortress, 1991), 388.

[2] Ekkehard W. Stegemann and Wolfgang Stegemann, *The Jesus Movement: A Social History of Its First Century* (trans. O. C. Dean; Minneapolis, MN: Fortress, 1999).

[3] Luise Schottroff, *Lydia's Impatient Sisters: A Feminist Social History of Early Christianity* (trans. Barbara and Martin Rumscheidt; Louisville; KY: Westminster John Knox, 1995), 87; Gerd Theissen, *The Religion of the Earliest Churches: Creating a Symbolic World* (trans. John Bowden; Minneapolis, MN: Fortress, 1999), 284–85.

Christian origins, *One Jesus, Many Christs*.[4] The one exception to all
of this, of course, is John Dominic Crossan's *The Birth of Christianity*,[5]
to which I will turn shortly. While each of these works makes a creative new contribution to our view of Christian beginnings, the *Gospel
of Thomas* and other extra-canonical literature still remain as pieces
to be accounted for in a redrawn landscape of earliest Christianity.

In this essay I wish to sketch out some of the basic areas in which
this task of broadening the textual base of our historical work to
include *Thomas* might proceed, even while acknowledging the work
that has been done so far.

1. *The Diversity of Christianity at the End of the First Century*

There is first of all the task of understanding *Thomas* in itself, as a
text of early Christianity at the end of the first century. With *Thomas*
more fully described we shall have a richer sense of the diversity of
Christianity during that very crucial period. Happily, a number of
very fine studies of *Thomas* that have appeared during the last decade
or so have greatly enhanced our understanding of *Thomas* in itself.[6]
One may note here the work of Lelyveld,[7] Davies,[8] Pagels,[9] Sellew,[10]

---

[4] Gregory J. Riley, *One Jesus, Many Christs: How Jesus Inspired Not One True Christianity, but Many* (New York: Harper, 1997); cf. his earlier work, *Resurrection Reconsidered: Thomas and John in Controversy* (Minneapolis, MN: Fortress, 1995).

[5] John Dominic Crossan, *The Birth of Christianity: Discovering What Happened in the Years Immediately after the Execution of Jesus* (New York, NY: HarperCollins, 1998).

[6] Recent surveys include Gregory J. Riley, "The *Gospel of Thomas* in Recent Scholarship," *CurBS* 2 (1994): 227–52; and Philip H. Sellew, "The *Gospel of Thomas*: Prospects for Future Research," in *The Nag Hammadi Library after Fifty Years: Proceedings of the 1995 Society of Biblical Literature Commemoration* (ed. John Turner and Anne McGuire; NHMS 44; Leiden: Brill, 1997), 327–46. Earlier see Francis T. Fallon and Ron Cameron, "The *Gospel of Thomas*: A Forschungsbericht and Analysis," in *ANRW* 25.6: 4195–251 and Ernst Haenchen, "Literatur zum Thomasevangelium," *TRu*, n.F. 27 (1961–62): 147–78, 306–38.

[7] Margaretha Lelyveld, *Les logia de la vie dans l'Évangile selon Thomas: À la Reserche d'une tradition et d'une rédaction* (NHS 34; Leiden: Brill, 1987).

[8] Stevan L. Davies, *The Gospel of Thomas and Christian Wisdom* (New York, NY: Seabury, 1983); and more recently "The Christology and Protology of the *Gospel of Thomas*," *JBL* 111 (1992): 663–82.

[9] Elaine H. Pagels, "Exegesis of Genesis 1 in the Gospels of Thomas and John," *JBL* 118 (1999): 477–96.

[10] Philip H. Sellew, "Death, the Body, and the World in the *Gospel of Thomas*," in *Proceedings of the XII International Patristics Conference, Oxford, 1995* (ed. E. A. Livingstone; StPatr 31, Leuven: Peeters & Leuven University Press, 1996), 530–34.

DeConick,[11] Zöckler,[12] Valantasis,[13] and the studies by the Finnish school collected and edited by Risto Uro.[14] Now, not all of this work is similarly oriented. Lelyveld, for example, locates *Thomas* within a Jewish apocalyptic milieu, while Davies and Pagels place *Thomas* in the world of Jewish exegesis of Genesis associated especially with Philo of Alexandria, and DeConick stresses evidence for the practice of ascent mysticism among its readers. Each of these studies is, in my view, helpful in explaining some of the sayings in *Thomas*— sometimes astonishingly so. Nevertheless, I find it difficult to press all of the sayings of *Thomas* into one or another of these interpretive schemes. This may mean that we will look in vain for a single theological framework that will successfully hold the whole book together. It is, after all, most certainly a cumulative piece of literature gathered over several years, perhaps decades. A unified theological perspective may not be a realistic expectation from such a text. Or it may mean that the thing holding the whole collection together is not a set of ideas or a consistent theology, but, as Valantasis has suggested, a common agenda: the refashioning of a new self through *askesis*[15]—an agenda that is quite compatible with all the various theological tastes in evidence here.

The broadly redefined concept of asceticism Valantasis has brought to this discussion[16] raises once again the issue I sought to highlight in my first attempt to understand *Thomas* in 1988, viz. the social radicalism that seems to be promulgated by this text.[17] Most aspects

---

[11] April D. DeConick, *Seek to See Him: Ascent and Vision Mysticism in the Gospel of Thomas* (Supplements to Vigiliae Christianae 33; Leiden: Brill, 1996); also *Voices of the Mystics: Early Christian Discourse in the Gospels of John and Thomas and Other Ancient Christian Literature* (JSNTSup 157; Sheffield: Sheffield Academic Press, 2001).

[12] Thomas Zöckler, *Jesu Lehren im Thomasevangelium* (NHMS 47; Leiden: Brill, 1999).

[13] Richard Valantasis, *The Gospel of Thomas* (New Testament Readings; London: Routledge, 1997); and "Is the *Gospel of Thomas* Ascetical? Revisiting an Old Problem with a New Theory," *JECS* 7 (1999): 55–81.

[14] Risto Uro, ed., *Thomas at the Crossroads: Essays on the Gospel of Thomas* (Studies of the New Testaments and Its World; Edinburgh: Clark, 1998) with essays by Risto Uro, Ismo Dunderberg, and Antti Marjanen. See also Uro, *Thomas: Seeking the Historical Context of the Gospel of Thomas* (London: Clark, 2003).

[15] Richard Valantasis, "Is the *Gospel of Thomas* Ascetical?," 78–79.

[16] For the theoretical framework proposed by Valantasis, see his "Constructions of Power in Asceticism," *JAAR* 63 (1995): 775–821.

[17] Stephen J. Patterson, *The Gospel of Thomas and Jesus* (FF: Reference Series; Sonoma, CA: Polebridge Press, 1993), see esp. 121–57 for the social radicalism of Thomasine Christianity.

of this thesis remain undisputed, with many of them appearing in
Valantasis' work, now helpfully redefined under a new theory.[18] I
say "most," for one very important aspect of this social radicalism
has been widely challenged in Theissen's work, from which I had
drawn my own theoretical orientation, viz., itinerancy.[19] And more
recently William Arnal ("The Rhetoric of Marginality") has criticized
my own work along these same lines.[20] In spite of these critiques, I
remain convinced that itinerancy was indeed an important part of
the socially radical ethos promulgated by the *Gospel of Thomas*, as I
have recently indicated.[21] I persist for two reasons:

First, as Theissen argued, many of the socially radical sayings one
finds in the Jesus tradition—and now in *Thomas*—are simply incompatible with normal village life. For example, no one could embrace
Gos. Thom. 55 ("Whoever does not hate his father and his mother . . . his
brothers and his sisters . . . cannot become a disciple of mine.") and
remain comfortably in place in an ancient agrarian village, where
one's entire social world begins and ends with stable family structures. It is not just those sayings that recommend or presume itinerancy that are important here, but also those sayings which would
have necessitated it, if they had been embraced.

Second, neither Theissen's thesis nor my own appropriation of it
rested primarily on an analysis of Q (as many have assumed), but
on a variety of texts and traditions where itinerant practice seems
to be reflected, including the *Didache*, 3 John, James, Acts, the Pauline
epistles, and now *Thomas*. I thought, and still think I see itinerancy

---

[18] See Valantasis, *The Gospel of Thomas*, passim.

[19] For Theissen's theory see his "Wanderradikalismus: Literatursoziologische Aspekte
der Überlieferung von Worten Jesu im Urchristentum," *ZTK* 70 (1973): 245–71,
and the other essays gathered and reprinted in Gerd Theissen, *Studien zur Soziologie
des Urchristentums* (2. Aufl.; WUNT 19; Tübingen: Mohr, 1983). Burton L. Mack has
challenged Theissen's itinerancy thesis in "The Kingdom That Didn't Come," *SBL
Seminar Papers, 1988* (SBLSP 27; Atlanta; GA: Scholars Press, 1988), 620–21; as has
Richard A. Horsley in *Sociology of the Jesus Movement* (New York, NY: Crossroad,
1989), 13–64. John S. Kloppenborg, ("Literary Convention, Self-Evidence, and the
Social History of the Q People," in *Early Christianity, Q, and Jesus* [Semeia 55; ed.
John Kloppenborg and Leif Vaage; Atlanta, GA: Scholars Press, 1992], 89–90) has
challenged Theissen's understanding of early Christian itinerancy, but not the pres-
ence of itinerant radicals.

[20] William E. Arnal, "The Rhetoric of Marginality: Apocalypticism, Gnosticism,
and Sayings Gospels," *HTR* 88 (1995): 480–82.

[21] Stephen J. Patterson, "*Askesis* and the Early Jesus Tradition," in *Asceticism and
the New Testament* (ed. Leif Vaage and Vincent Wimbush; London: Routledge, 1999),
54–56.

in *Thomas* not just because of my reading of *Gos. Thom* 42, 12, or 14, but because of the way its trajectory stands in relation to other trajectories running through the last decades of the first century. Following the work of Georg Kretschmar and Erik Peterson,[22] especially, it seemed to me that the path leading from Palestinian Christianity to Syrian Christianity was an itinerant one, marked on one end by the early Jesus tradition, and on the other by the itinerant, ascetical practices in evidence in texts associated with Edessa and the east. *Thomas'* content connects it to both ends of this journey, as simple aphorisms and parables from the early Jesus tradition sit side by side with and enclosed on either end by sayings that connect *Thomas* to Syrian Christianity—connections reinforced again recently by Alexei Sivertsev.[23] I thus concluded that *Thomas* was quite likely a key text in that journey, both figuratively and literally. As Thomasine Christians wandered to Syria, they brought with them their itinerant habits and their correlate theology.[24]

However, there are two aspects of the critique of Theissen that must be taken to heart.[25] The first, from Mack, is that the notion of a "mission" in the early Jesus tradition seems to be rooted in the specific apocalyptic urgency of Q, which may not have characterized the whole of early Christianity.[26] This is borne out by an examination of the *Thomas* parallels to the "mission discourse" in Q. *Gos. Thom.* 14 (= Q 10:8–9) offers no hint of a mission.[27] And the harvest saying used in Q to introduce the entire discourse as a "mission" (Q 10:2) occurs in *Thomas* as an independent logion (*Gos. Thom.* 73)

---

[22] Georg Kretschmar, "Ein Beitrag zur Frage nach dem Ursprung frühchristlicher Askese," *ZTK* 61 (1964): 27–67; Erik Peterson, "Einige Beobachtungen zu den Anfängen der christlichen Askese," in his collected essays, *Frühkirche, Judentum, und Gnosis: Studien und Untersuchungen* (Freiburg: Herder, 1959), 209–220.

[23] Alexei Sivertsev, "The *Gospel of Thomas* and the Early Stages in the Development of Christian Wisdom Literature," *JECS* 8 (2000): 319–40.

[24] See my discussion in *The Gospel of Thomas and Jesus*, 166–68, 210–12.

[25] I restrict myself here to those aspects of the discussion that have a direct bearing on the earliest period of Christian beginnings. I will not take up, for example, the firestorm of critique occasioned by Theissen's notion of "Liebespatriarchalismus" in the second-century church, which is another aspect of the discussion to be taken to heart.

[26] "The Kingdom That Didn't Come," 620–23.

[27] Ron Cameron, "Alternate Beginnings—Different Ends: Eusebius, *Thomas*, and the Construction of Christian Origins," in *Religious Propaganda and Missionary Competition in the New Testament World: Essays Honoring Dieter Georgi* (ed. Lukas Bormann, Kelly Del Tredici, Angela Standhartinger; NovTSup 74; Leiden: Brill, 1994), 521.

with no connection to the mission speech.[28] The second, from
Kloppenborg, is that the wandering folk of the mission discourse in
Q are not presumed to be leaders, but enjoy rather a weak position with respect to those who might take them in.[29] This is so in
Thomas as well, where those who wander are not themselves leaders, but are counseled about how they might regard others who
would lead them (see *Gos. Thom.* 3 and 12, for example). These are
valid criticisms of Theissen's hypothesis, and by extension, my own
views on *Thomas*. The question, then, is: if these itinerants who promulgated the Thomasine tradition were not on a mission, what were
they doing? And if they were not leaders, what was their role in the
circles they frequented?

In a recent essay[30] I have tried to answer these questions with the
use of Valantasis' theory of asceticism, to which I have alluded above.
Valantasis describes ascetic practice as a set of "performances . . .
intended to inaugurate a new subjectivity, different social relations,
and an alternative symbolic universe."[31] A more apt description of
the practices advocated in the *Gospel of Thomas* one will not find.
Gaining a new sense of self, a new "subjectivity," is at the heart of
the *Gospel of Thomas*. And yet this centering on self is not a private
thing. It involves interrupting and creating new social relations; it
has a public side. As such, the practices and attitudes promulgated
in its sayings bring one into a *performative* mode. And not only the
practices advised in these sayings, but also the very act of collecting
sayings itself presumes their later delivery in some kind of *performance*.
The sage must hold forth—in the synagogue, in the agora, at table.
And these performances of word must be followed by deeds to match:
more performance in *praxis*. And what does one expect from a performance in antiquity? An ancient expects a performer to be engaged
in *mimesis*, in the *imitation* of life—life not as it is, but better than it
is (comedy), or worse (tragedy).[32] To Aristotle's categories we might

---

[28] For the independence of the Thomasine version of this saying and its tradition-historical implications see my *Gospel of Thomas and Jesus*, 56–57.

[29] "Literary Convention," 89–90.

[30] "*Askesis* and the Early Jesus Tradition."

[31] Richard Valantasis, "Constructions of Power in Asceticism," 797. For Valantasis'
own more recent attempt to apply this theory to the *Gospel of Thomas*, see his "Is
the *Gospel of Thomas* Ascetical?"

[32] See Aristotle, *Poetics* 2.7. For fuller discussion see Patterson, "*Askesis* and the
Early Jesus Tradition," 59–61.

add the performative life of the religious ascetic. An ascetic imitates life, not as it is, but as it might be in some imagined ideal. This describes, in my view, what the Thomasine folk were about. Those who cultivated the traditions of the *Gospel of Thomas* were not leaders of a movement with a mission. They were performers of an existence and a self-understanding that is understood as an ideal. "When you know yourselves, then you will be known, and you will understand that you are children of the living Father" (*Gos. Thom.* 3:4).

Whether or not one accepts these arguments about itinerancy, one of the most important tasks before us now is to understand better the relationship between the socially radical ethos of Thomasine Christianity and the various theological impulses contained in its sayings. This constitutes a program for pursuing a "thick description" of Thomasine Christianity in order to determine its distinctive contribution to and place within the diversity of Christianity at the end of the first century. Such a program is necessary regardless of how one finally resolves the much-debated question of *Thomas*' relationship to the synoptic tradition.[33] For there is so much in *Thomas* that bears no relationship at all to the synoptic tradition, and the interpretive strategy for presenting those materials that are held in common is so distinctive, one would at any rate need to account for the Thomasine *perspective* and the distinctive *practices* it entertains, as part of the theological and social-historical landscape of early Christianity. Just as one could not overlook, say, "Johannine Christianity" in a complete accounting of Christian beginnings, so also one cannot now overlook "Thomasine Christianity" in its distinctive characteristics.

---

[33] This question has proven to be a thorny problem in the history of the *Thomas* discussion. For a review of the literature see my "The *Gospel of Thomas* and the Synoptic Tradition: A Forschungsbericht and Critique," *Forum* 8:1–2 (1992): 45–97. More recent proposals have made the discussion even more complex, including especially that of Hans-Martin Schenke, "On the Compositional History of the *Gospel of Thomas*," *Forum* 10:1–2 (1994): 9–30. Schenke argues on the basis of a series of apparent narrative spurs in *Thomas* that its sayings were drawn from a narrative work, but not one of our known gospels. Risto Uro ("*Thomas* and the Oral Gospel Tradition," in *Thomas at the Crossroads*, 8–32) has revived the idea of "secondary orality," first promulgated by Klyne Snodgrass some years ago ("The *Gospel of Thomas*: A Secondary Gospel," *SecCent* 7 [1989–90]: 19–38), as a way of arguing for *Thomas*' dependence on the synoptic gospels, while acknowledging evidence in *Thomas* of a certain freedom over against the synoptic text themselves. Similarly, Jens Schröter argues that the synoptic formulation of sayings has influenced *Thomas* in specific instances, but rejects the direct literary dependence of *Thomas* upon the synoptic gospels (*Erinnerung an Jesu Worte. Studien zur Rezeption der Logienüberlieferung in Markus, Q und Thomas* [WMANT 76; Neukirchen-Vluyn: Neukirchener Verlag, 1997], *passim*).

In pursuing this program, however, one must be very careful not
simply to work *Thomas* into the existing model for Christian origins
that, as Cameron has suggested, relies overly much on the myth of
origins provided by Luke in the Acts of the Apostles, and adopted
by Eusebius as the *Historia ecclesiastica*.[34] This will always be a temptation because *Thomas* does not provide its own alternative myth of
origins to rival the story told by Luke (*contra* Cameron). To the contrary, as a sayings collection, this absence of story is one of the most
distinctive and challenging aspects of *Thomas*. Indeed, *Thomas* does
not need a story, a myth of origins, for it has no need of establishing
the antiquity or uniqueness of its traditions.[35] Those who made use
of this gospel were convinced that the insights they enjoyed from
the *living Jesus* (*Gos. Thom.* Prologue) could now pour forth from *them*
just as authentically as it did, or does, from Jesus himself (*Gos. Thom.*
13 and 108). Those who understand these sayings are themselves
said to be full of life and light. This revelatory multiplicity is itself
a challenge to the tendency to tell the story of Christian origins with
a singular point of departure at its core. *Thomas* seems to presuppose
a movement with Jesus at its center, but still a *movement*, not a cult.

2. Some Elements of a New Story: Crossan and "Ethical Eschatology"

The people who found the *Gospel of Thomas* useful did not need a
story. If *we* want or need one, we will have to author it ourselves.
How will the *Gospel of Thomas* help us to write that story differently?
One way, of course, will be through a thick description of this gospel
and the life it prescribes, and accounting this as part of the diversity of Christianity as it existed at the close of the first century. But
Thomas can help us in other ways as well. One of the most interesting things about the critical discussion of *Thomas* has been the
way it has helped us to see things in the Jesus tradition whose presence or significance had been overlooked before. The best instance
of this is the presence of an aphoristic core in *Thomas*, much of
which overlaps the synoptic tradition, in which, however, the apoc-

---

[34] Ron Cameron, "Alternate Beginnings."
[35] Cf. Cameron's analysis of the Eusebian tradition and its motivations in "Alternate Beginnings," 507–11.

alyptic framework of the synoptic gospels is absent. This helped us
to see in early Christianity an aphoristic tradition in which the oper-
ative theological perspective was sapiential, not apocalyptic. Understanding this as an important part of the diversity of Christian
beginnings changes everything. No one has seen this more clearly than
John Dominic Crossan, who has built these insights first into his work
on the historical Jesus, and more recently into his quite revolution-
ary account of Christian beginnings, *The Birth of Christianity*. His discovery and description of "ethical eschatology" as "non-violent
resistance to systematic violence"[36] is a development with implications reaching beyond the discipline of Christian origins, into the
very heart of Christian theology itself. What would it mean for theology to take seriously the eschatological possibility of non-violent
transformation, and to forswear once and for all our western Christian
predilection to looking for divine activity in the chaotic and indis-
criminate violence of apocalyptic?

But Crossan's description of this early Christian theology associated with the aphorisms of Jesus raises another question of origins—
or more precisely, of disappearances. If Crossan's ethical, or "sapiential"
eschatology existed, say, at mid-first century, by the end of the century it had passed from the scene. The parables and aphorisms that
conveyed that perspective had been absorbed into the synoptic gospels,
which reframed them in apocalyptic mythology, or into the *Gospel of
Thomas*, which presented them as esoteric teaching to transform the
self in preparation for the heavenly journey home. In neither instance
was this sapiential core retained to inspire non-violent cultural transformation. It was absorbed and washed over with perspectives interested less in transformation and more in culture's violent destruction
(apocalyptic) or in abandoning the world altogether in favor of a heavenly home (speculative wisdom theology or gnosis). Why was this?

Part of the answer to this question must surely lie in the unfolding
events that engulfed the eastern Empire, and the Jews especially, in
the last decades of the First Century. As events spiraled ever closer
to outright revolt and open warfare, chaos and violence would have
become the dominant experience of Christians living in the eastern
part of the Empire, most of them still Jews. As they, their families,
and their friends were swept up into the violence of the Jewish War

---

[36] Crossan, *Birth of Christianity*, 287.

and the hardships of its aftermath, profound questions would have arisen among those committed to the reflective and non-violent processes of personal and cultural transformation cultivated in the aphoristic wisdom of the early Jesus movement. What happens when resistance to violence is rendered irrelevant by the overwhelming violence of war—not seen from a distance, but raging through one's own communities? In the face of such grave circumstances only those of 'Ghandian' fortitude persist. Most are moved, either to embrace a mythic framework within which violence can be reconciled to some overall divine plan for justice and the triumph of God (apocalyptic), or, to withdraw into the inner realm of mysticism or cosmic speculation with the hope of personal transformation and, ultimately, translation out of this world of woe (speculative wisdom theology or gnosis). Of these alternatives, the synoptic gospels represent the former, *Thomas* and John represent the latter. I can see no Christian Ghandi at the end of the first century.

The question of the disappearance of Crossan's "ethical eschatology" by the end of the First Century, together with the ascendancy of apocalyptic and speculative wisdom theology or gnosis, raises a related question, namely, the overwhelming influence the experience of war must have had on the texts of the New Testament and their various dominant ideas. With the exception of the earliest letters of Paul, all of the writings of the New Testament would have been profoundly affected by this peculiar cultural situation. To what extent, then, is "New Testament Christianity" a wartime religion? How does this context determine the topics that emerge as important in the texts of the New Testament—such as martyrdom, loyalty (*pistis*), or resurrection as vindication? And what does it mean that these topics have been given a normative role in shaping the Christian religion, even apart from the immediate experience of war? These are broad sweeping questions, but they are the kind of question that the project of re-charting the landscape of the first Christian century will ultimately occasion.

3. *Some Elements of a New Story*: Thomas, *Paul, and Jewish Mysticism*

With recent studies taking us deeper into the nature of Thomasine Christianity in itself, one might anticipate that there are many more such discoveries to be made. How will the peculiar details of the

Thomasine trajectory help us to see other aspects of the story of Christian beginnings in a new light, or new episodes in that story we have overlooked entirely?

No one can know the answer to this question. Nonetheless, the possibilities might be illustrated with an example. April D. DeConick's study of the *Gospel of Thomas* and her more recent study of the Gospel of John and *Thomas*, [37] have demonstrated anew that certain of *Thomas'* sayings are best understood within the context of Jewish mysticism. Some of these sayings are among the most mysterious of *Thomas'* gems (e.g., *Gos. Thom.* 15, 84, 53) and generally have been regarded simply as part of the exotica to be expected from such a strange new text. But in recent years Jewish mysticism has emerged once again as an important topic in the history of early Judaism, with New Testament texts forming part of the basis for this discussion. [38] Of particular importance in this respect is Alan Segal's work on Paul. [39] Paul was clearly part of this tradition, and drew others into it as well.

This evidence for Jewish mysticism in both Paul and *Thomas* gives us a context for understanding the oft-noted parallel between 1 Cor 2:9 and *Gos. Thom.* 17: "I will give you what no eye has seen, and what no ear has heard, and what no hand has touched, and what has not occurred to the human mind." What Jesus promises in *Thomas*, Paul claims to have received already "through the Spirit" (1 Cor 2:10). The result of this revelatory experience for Paul might well be termed "illumination." So we may conclude from the way in which Paul typically describes his encounters with the divine, as, for example, in 2 Cor 4:6: "For it is the God who said, 'Let light shine out of darkness,' who has shone in our hearts to give the light

---

[37] See note 11, above.

[38] See, e.g., Jarl Fossum, "Jewish-Christian Christology and Jewish Mysticism," *VC* 37 (1983): 260–87; *idem*, "*Kyrios Jesus* and the Angel of the Lord in Jude 5–7," *NTS* 33 (1987): 226–43; *idem*, "Colossians 1.15–18a in the Light of Jewish Mysticism and Gnosticism," *NTS* 35 (1989): 183–201; Gedaliahu Stroumsa, "Forms of God: Some Notes on Metatron and Christ," *HTR* 76 (1985): 269–88; Christopher Rowland, *The Open Heaven: A Study of Apocalyptic in Judaism and Early Christianity* (New York, NY: Crossroads, 1982); James Tabor, *Things Unutterable: Paul's Ascent to Paradise in its Greco-Roman, Judaic, and Early Christian Contexts* (Lanham, MD: University Press of America, 1986); Christopher R. A. Morray-Jones, "Paradise Revisited (2 Cor 12:1–12): The Jewish Mystical Background of Paul's Apostolate, Part 1: The Jewish Sources," *HTR* 86 (1993): 177–217, and "Part 2: Paul's Heavenly Ascent and Its Significance," HTR 86 (1993): 265–92.

[39] Alan F. Segal, *Paul the Convert: The Apostolate and Apostasy of Saul the Pharisee* (New Haven, CT: Yale University Press, 1990), esp. 34–71.

of the knowledge of the glory of God in the face of Christ."[40] Paul
is describing here the inner illumination he has received as a result
of seeing the "glory of God in the face of Christ" in a visionary
experience.[41] Moreover, Paul believes that his own illumination is
intended to shine forth as a light to others, whose unbelief or ignorance has kept them from "seeing the light of the gospel of the glory
of Christ, who is the image of God" (2 Cor 4:4).

These or similar ideas are all thoroughly at home in the *Gospel of
Thomas*. *Thomas* also speaks of the image of God, in which there is
light, and from which those who encounter it may also receive illumination (*Gos. Thom.* 83; 61:5). What is more, a "person of light" is
not to conceal the light, but to let it illuminate the whole world.
This is the sense of *Gos. Thom.* 24:

> His disciples said: "Show us the place where you are, because it is
> necessary for us to seek it." He said to them: "Whoever has ears should
> hear! Light exists inside a person of light, and he shines on the whole
> world. If he does not shine, there is darkness."[42]

In this saying the disciples wish to follow Jesus, the true light person (cf. *Gos. Thom.* 77) to his place, the heavenly realm of light, "the
place where the light has come into being by itself, has established
[itself] and appeared in their image" (*Gos. Thom.* 50). But Jesus refers
them instead to their own place, the world, where they shall illuminate the "whole world."

Segal has shown that in Paul, as in Jewish mysticism generally
speaking, illumination and ecstatic religious experience is accompanied by a profound sense of transformation, from earthly to heavenly, from mortal to immortal. Moses, Jacob, Enoch: these mortals
all became immortal after ascending to the heavens and encountering the *kavod* (glory) of God. For Paul this is true as well, only—
astonishingly—more so even than Moses. In contrast to Moses, who
wore a veil over his face so that no one would notice that his vis-
age, initially illuminated by the beatific vision, soon faded, "we," says

[40] All biblical quotations in this chapter are taken, unless otherwise indicated,
from *The Holy Bible: Containing the Old and New Testaments with Apocryphal/Deuterocanonical
Books: New Revised Standard Version* (New York, NY: Oxford University Press, 1989).
[41] Notice the context, 2 Cor 3:18–4:6; for discussion see Segal, *Paul the Convert*, 59–62.
[42] The translations of the *Gospel of Thomas* are from Stephen J. Patterson, James
M. Robinson and Hand-Gebhard Bethge, *The Fifth Gospel: The Gospel of Thomas Comes
of Age* (Harrisburg, PA: Trinity Press International, 1998).

Paul are different: "... we all, with unveiled faces, seeing the glory of the Lord as though reflected in a mirror, are being transformed into the same image (εἰκόνα) from one degree of glory to another" (2 Cor 3:18). What is most striking here is the idea, common in Jewish mysticism, that one who beholds the glory of God will be transformed by the experience into the likeness, or "image" (εἰκών) of God—God's human form.[43] For Paul, of course, the human form of God, the Son of Man, the "Lord," is Jesus Christ. Thus, Paul thinks of himself as being "in Christ," or even having the "mind of Christ" (1 Cor 2:16). And he speaks of a future resurrection in which the followers of Jesus will shed the "image of the man of dust," which all have inherited from Adam, and bear the "image" of the "heavenly man," Christ (1 Cor 15:49). They, Paul says, have been "predestined to be conformed to the image of his Son, in order that he might be the first born of a large family" (Rom 8:29). Thus, Paul looks forward to the day when the Lord "will change our lowly body to be like his glorious body, by the power which enables him even to subject all things to himself (Phil 3:20–21).

DeConick has shown that this same set of ideas about personal, even bodily transformation through mystical experience are present in the *Gospel of Thomas* as well. She argues, for example, that this is the proper framework for understanding the enigmatic *Gos. Thom.* 22:

> Jesus said to them: "When you make the two into one and when you make the inside like the outside and the outside like the inside and the above like the below—that is, to make the male and female into a single one, so that the male will not be male and the female will not be female—and when you make eyes instead of an eye and a hand instead of a hand and a foot instead of a foot, an image (ϩΙΚШΝ) instead of an image (ϩΙΚШΝ), then you will enter [the kingdom]."

Strange as this saying may seem, its ideas are not all that different from ideas we find scattered throughout Paul's letters. Paul, for example, more than likely knows the Jewish tradition of exegeting Genesis 1–2, in which Adam's fall is taken to result in the sexual differentiation of humanity into male and female—a rift now to be mended in Christ.[44] And *Thomas*' description of part-by-part bodily transformation

---

[43] This idea may be explicitly expressed in *Gos. Thom.* 61:5, if the Berlin group is correct in their emendation from ЄЧШΗЧ (destroy) to ЄЧШΗШ (be like), and adding the word ΠΝΟΥΤЄ: "If someone becomes <like> (God), he will become full of light" (see Patterson et al., *The Fifth Gospel*, 22).

[44] Cf. Gal 3:28 and the treatment of this early baptismal formula by Dennis

is only a more vivid statement of what Paul speaks of as being transformed gradually, "from one degree of glory to another," until finally
the believer comes to share the same glorious "image" as Christ (2
Cor 3:18), exchanging "an image for an image."[45] Finally, *Thomas* is
familiar with the idea, seen also in Paul, that the transformation one
seeks is ultimately, to become like Jesus himself. This is what *Gos.
Thom.* 108 is speaking of, albeit using metaphors that are distinctive
to *Thomas* over against Paul: "Jesus says, "Whoever will drink from
my mouth will become like me. I myself will become he and what
is hidden will be revealed to him" (*Gos. Thom.* 108). This is, in *Thomas'*
own distinctive parlance, "having the mind of Christ."

To these ideas about spiritual transformation and identification
with Christ (or Jesus) we should probably add the closely related
idea from Jewish mysticism that those who experience God by ascending to the heavens will themselves become divine, or "children of
God." This is how one should probably understand Paul's statement
in Romans 8:14–16:[46]

> For all who are led by the Spirit of God are children [lit.: 'sons'] of
> God. For you did not receive the spirit of slavery to fall back into
> fear, but you have received the spirit of adoption. When we cry 'Abba!
> Father!' it is the Spirit itself bearing witness with our spirit that we
> are children of God, and if children, then heirs, heirs of God and fel-
> low heirs with Christ. . . .

Paul is speaking here of a moment of religious ecstasy in which it
becomes clear to the ecstatic that he/she is a child of God. *Gos.
Thom.* 3 presents this same basic notion of religious awakening, though
in this case not clearly associated with pneumatic ecstasy: "When you
know yourselves, then you will be known, and you will realize that
you are children [lit: 'sons'] of the living father" (*Gos. Thom.* 3:4).

R. MacDonald in his study *There Is No Male and Female: The Fate of a Dominical Saying
in Paul and Gnosticism* (Philadelphia, PA: Fortress, 1987). On the role of speculative
Jewish exegesis of Genesis 1–2 and its role in *Thomas'* theology, see Pagels, "Exegesis
of Genesis 1," 477–96, and Stevan L. Davies, "Christology and Protology" 663–83.

[45] That Valantasis ("Is the *Gospel of Thomas* Ascetical?" 71–72) regards this saying as key to understanding *Thomas'* asceticism should not trouble us here. The
connection between asceticism and mysticism is well known, and Paul himself would
be a second example of the coordination of these two phenomena in early Christianity
to set along side the example of *Thomas*.

[46] Segal (*Paul the Convert*, 249–50) suggests this is how to understand the passage.

The realization that one is a child of God was not without its detractors in early Christianity, especially when it was linked to the practice of baptism, as it likely was in both Pauline and Thomasine Christian circles,[47] and understood as the achievement of immortality already in the present life. It was probably this idea of premature transformation, of becoming immortal already, among the Corinthians (1 Cor 4:8) that caused Paul to distance himself from baptism in 1 Corinthians (1 Cor 1:14–16), for it had, in his view, led to excessive claims of exalted status among the "strong" at Corinth. This is probably also the reason Paul follows the claim to "child of God" status in Romans 8 with the caveat in 8:17b: "provided we suffer with him in order that we may also be glorified with him." The exalted, glorified Christ of Paul's vision was also Jesus, the crucified messiah, whose fate as a martyr was inextricably linked to his exaltation as the Son of God. Sharing in Christ's glory meant also sharing in his inglorious fate (2 Cor 4:7–18).

And yet these problems did not lead to the abandonment of this idea in Pauline circles. It persisted as an element in Paulinism, where we encounter it near the end of the century in Luke, whose author was the great admirer and rehabilitator of Paul. It occurs in Luke's version of Jesus' reply to the Sadducees who try to stump him with a question about a woman's marital status "in the resurrection" age to come:

> Jesus said to them, "Those who belong to this age marry and are given in marriage; but those who are considered worthy of a place in that age and in the resurrection of the dead neither marry nor are given in marriage. Indeed, they cannot die anymore, because they are like angels and are children [lit: 'sons'] of God, being children [lit: 'sons'] of the resurrection" (Luke 20:34–36).[48]

David Aune rightly argues that this saying speaks of persons who have *already* been deemed worthy (note the aorist participle, κατα-ξιωθέντες) in this life and elevated to the status "sons of God."[49] He

---

[47] For Paul see Segal, *Paul the Convert*, 249 (in reference to Romans 6); for *Thomas* and baptism see Jonathan Z. Smith, "The Garments of Shame," *HR* 5 (1965–66): 217–38 (in reference esp. to *Gos. Thom.* 37).

[48] Cf. Mark's version, which Luke has modified: "For when they rise from the dead they neither marry nor are given in marriage, but are like angels in heaven."

[49] David Aune, "Luke 20:34–36: A 'Gnosticized' Logion of Jesus?" in *Geschichte—Tradition—Reflexion: Festschrift für Martin Hengel zum 70. Geburtstag* (ed. Hubert Cancik, Hermann Lichtenberger and Peter Schäfer; Tübingen: Mohr, 1996), 191–92.

locates the saying in the context of early Syrian Christianity and the practice of "Christian baptism in a quasi-gnostic setting,"[50] where, of course, the *Gospel of Thomas* was also quite at home. But one should not overlook the roots of this idea in Christian circles evident already in Paul, whose own grounding in Jewish mysticism and speculative eschatology places him in this very same trajectory within early Christianity.

There is much more to be said here, of the way these ideas were grounded biblically through exegesis of Genesis 1–2, of the correlate practices that were worked out around these ideas, ascetical ideals, and of course, of difference and sameness, of overlaps and departures. Nevertheless, the point I am trying to make is this: understanding *Thomas* in itself, as part of the diversity of Early Christianity, will help us to see and understand aspects of other, better known ways of being "Christian," that we had not noticed before. The idea of mystical transformation, present in Paul's letters, and continuing on a trajectory in the Pauline school tradition, and even nominally present in the Gospel of Luke at the end of the century, is an example of how the presence of something in *Thomas* might serve to draw our attention to that same odd something elsewhere in the more familiar texts of early Christianity. This underscores once again the importance of not allowing later distinctions of "canonical" versus "non-canonical" to influence our thinking about where *Thomas* might fit into the landscape of early Christianity. Placing *Thomas* and other lesser known texts into the mix will change things by helping us to see phenomena we had never seen before, which nevertheless may have been very important for those who counted themselves as the followers of Jesus.

4. *Concluding Remarks*

It is clear from the current literature on Christian origins that the *Gospel of Thomas* still has not made the kind of broad impact that one might have expected at its discovery some 50 years ago. Among those who have begun to take it seriously, however, the landscape of earliest Christianity has begun to take on some striking new fea-

---

[50] Aune, "Luke 20:34–36," 196–99 (the quotation is from his conclusion, 200).

tures. And old features, previously overlooked or perhaps just mis-understood, have been seen in a new light. Eventually, *Thomas* may necessitate the drawing up of a new map of Christian beginnings, and a new story to account for this uncharted geography will have to be told. In this retelling there will be new episodes, and the famil-iar episodes we thought we knew so well may appear unfamiliar in the new light cast upon them by *Thomas* and other rediscovered or newly appreciated texts. Luke's metanarrative will have to be eval-uated against all the actual experiences and their interpretations that filled the diversity of earliest Christianity in its historical particular-ity. It is a large agenda, but the charting of this diversity in early Christianity has been underway now for more than a generation, beginning with Walter Bauer's *Orthodoxy and Heresy in Earliest Christianity*,[51] and developing through Robinson and Koester's programmatic essays in *Trajectories through Early Christianity*,[52] and continuing more recently in the subtle historical work of Schüssler Fiorenza,[53] Mack,[54] and Crossan.[55] That Luke's vision of a seamless story with a single strand, a clear path in the history of salvation, was an artificial construct has for many years been widely recognized. Nonetheless, that tidy ver-sion of things has a powerful appeal that makes it difficult really to abandon. The *Gospel of Thomas* is one of the texts that is forcing us now to come to grips with the reality that earliest Christianity was not tidy. Its history was just as messy as history always is, and just as rich. The more we take *Thomas* seriously as part of that diversity of interpretation and experimentation that followed Jesus, the more we will appreciate the richness of Christianity's complicated origins.

---

[51] Originally published in German in 1931, translated by the Philadelphia Seminar on Christian Origins in 1971 (*Orthodoxy and Heresy in Earliest Christianity* [ed. Robert Kraft and Gerhard Krodel; Philadelphia, PA: Fortress, 1971]).

[52] James M. Robinson and Helmut Koester, *Trajectories through Early Christianity* (Philadelphia, PA: Fortress, 1971).

[53] Elizabeth Schüssler Fiorenza, *In Memory of Her: A Feminist Theological Reconstruction of Christian Origins* (New York, NY: Crossroad, 1988).

[54] Burton L. Mack, *A Myth of Innocence: Mark and Christian Origins* (Philadelphia, PA: Fortress, 1988).

[55] *The Birth of Christianity*.

CHAPTER TWO

THE SOCIAL WORLD OF THE *GOSPEL OF THOMAS*

RISTO URO

In 1972 Wayne Meeks published an article on "The Man from Heaven in Johannine Sectarianism," which was a pioneering study on the social context of John's christological language and inaugurated a vivid interest in the use of the social sciences among New Testament scholars.[1] Meeks criticized earlier studies for having one-sidedly analyzed John's Christology as a "problem in the history of ideas." Says Meeks, "Mythical language tends to be reduced to theological categories, and *historical* judgments are then made on the basis of the presumed *logical* priority of one or other of these categories."[2] In contrast to such reduction to theological categories, Meeks raised the question of what "social function" the Johannine myth may have had. Drawing on the theory of the sociology of knowledge advanced by Peter Berger and Thomas Luckmann,[3] which was to become a standard theoretical framework in the study of the social world of the New Testament, Meeks argued that the Johannine myth and the whole gospel provided "a symbolic universe which gave religious legitimacy . . . to the group's actual isolation from the larger society."[4] The Johannine myth of a descending and ascending redeemer figure "defines and vindicates the existence of the community that evidently sees itself as unique, alien from its world, under attack,"[5] and separated from the synagogue.[6]

---

[1] Wayne A. Meeks, "The Man from Heaven in Johannine Sectarianism," *JBL* 91 (1972): 44–72.

[2] *Ibid.*, 46–47 (Meeks' emphasis).

[3] Peter L. Berger and Thomas Luckman, *The Social Construction of Reality: A Treatise in the Sociology of Knowledge* (London: Lane, 1967).

[4] Meeks, "Man from Heaven," 70.

[5] *Ibid.*

[6] *Ibid.*, 55.

1. *Myth Is Not a Map*

After Meeks' seminal study, much has been written on the social
context of the gospel traditions and on what social functions these
traditions may have had in the communities that produced the gospels.
The *Gospel of Thomas* has also been a subject of such investigation.
Before I go into the analysis of *Thomas'* social world, though, I would
like to dwell for a moment on more general issues concerning the
risks and problems in taking a similar approach to Meeks in analyzing
the social function and setting of the gospel traditions. Meeks' article is much-acclaimed, but it has also received substantial criticism.[7]
I will concentrate here on two methodological issues Meeks' study
raises. To begin with, there is the vexed question of the relationship
between myth (or any symbolic presentation) and social order. The
conclusion that the social function of John's christological myth was
to legitimate the social alienation and separation of the Johannine
group may be a valid observation, provided we have enough social
data for such a social context of the gospel, but the symbolic language
cannot be taken as a proof of that context. Myth is not a map of
the social location. Rather the social situation gives a clue to the
function of the myth. This means that the idea of the social function
of the myth does not really add to our knowledge about the social
situation in which this myth was originally cultivated. The knowledge
must be inferred from other relevant data, either from the gospel
itself or other sources.[8]

Scholars have also taken notice of the problems inherent in a functionalist sociological analysis.[9] Functionalism has been criticized for,

---

[7] According to Jonathan Z. Smith, Meeks' conclusions are the "results of a happy
combination of exegetical and sociological sophistication." "The Social Description
of Early Christianity," *RelSRev* 1 (1975): 19–25, esp. 21. For an illuminating review
of the reception and critical discussion of Meeks' article, see Bengt Holmberg,
Sociology and the New Testament: An Appraisal (Minneapolis, MN: Fortress, 1990), 125–28.

[8] Holmberg, *Sociology*, 128.

[9] See, e.g., John H. Elliott, "Social-Scientific Criticism of the New Testament:
More on Methods and Models," in *Social-Scientific Criticism of the New Testament and
Its Social World* (Semeia 35; ed. John H. Elliott; Decatur, GA: Scholars Press, 1986),
1–33, esp. 10–25; Richard A. Horsley, *Sociology and the Jesus Movement* (New York,
NY: Crossroad, 1989), 30–42 (both focusing on Gerd Theissen's study on *Sociology
of Early Palestinian Christianity* [(trans. John Bowden; Philadelphia, PA: Fortress, 1978)];
David G. Horrell, *The Social Ethos of the Corinthian Correspondence: Interests and Ideology
from 1 Corinthians to 1 Clement* (Studies of the New Testament and Its World; Edinburgh:
Clark, 1996), 33–38.

among other things, adopting an essentially static view of society.[10] Thus, the focus on the legitimating or explanatory function that the christological myth had in the Johannine community assumes a social system in which the symbolic universe "fulfils" the need (legitimation) created by the social setting so that the system can work properly. This kind of analysis ignores the other socially relevant functions the myth may have had, for example, those of challenging the existing social reality or creating a new symbolic universe which does not so much legitimate the existing social order as envision a new world.[11] To be sure, Meeks formulates his position very cautiously arguing that there was a continual dialogue between social experience and the group's social situation. According to him, "the christological claims of the Johannine Christians resulted in their becoming alienated" and this alienation is "in turn 'explained' by further development of the christological motifs (i.e., the fate of the community projected onto the story of Jesus)."[12] In spite of this emphasis on the dialectical process, Meeks' main interest is in the actual social and historical circumstances which he thinks to have been "explained" by the Johannine myth. In other words, his article is based on a traditional exegetical approach in which the text is analyzed "backwards," with the social world as something which is basically "behind" the text.[13]

The analysis of the social world of the *Gospel of Thomas* involves similar problems to Meeks' article. *Thomas* contains very little direct information about the social situation in which its sayings were compiled. Most of the social data must be inferred from the religious

---

[10] Horrell, *Social Ethos*, 37.

[11] This recalls Paul Ricoeur's approach to the biblical myths. According to him, such texts "do not exhaust their meaning in some functioning which is purely internal to the text. They intend a world which calls forth on our part a way of dwelling there." Paul Ricoeur, "Naming God," *USQR* 34 (1979): 215–27, esp. 226. The Ricoeurian pespective is applied by Anne McGuire to her analysis of the myth of Norea's confrontation with the Archons in the *Hypostasis of the Archons*. According to to her, the mythic narrative "invites the reader to dwell in the imaginative world depicted in the text." Anne MacGuire, "Virginity and Subversion: Norea Against the Powers in the *Hypostasis of the Archons*," in *Images of the Feminine in Gnosticism* (ed. Karen L. King; SAC; Philadelphia, PA: Fortress, 1988), 239–58, esp. 257.

[12] Meeks, "Man from Heaven," 71.

[13] Cf. Horrell (*Social Ethos*, 37–38), who contends that functionalist analysis tends to "read backwards" and fails "to incorporate the temporal nature of social interaction." With reference to Anthony Giddens' structuration theory, Horrell prefers an approach in which "considerable attention will be given to the potential impact of various texts upon social groups and relationships within the early Christian communities" (*ibid.*, 38).

teaching of the gospel, the nature of which is mainly symbolic and mythic. However, if myth is not a map of the social location, how can we make any implications about the social world from *Thomas'* symbolism? The issue of the "function" is also pertinent in the context of Thomasine studies. As I will argue in this paper, scholars' suggestions about the social world of *Thomas* often address different social functions and this methodological difference is not always clearly spelled out. For some scholars, the social world is clearly something "behind" the text, while others, applying new literary, semiotic or other reader-oriented strategies, are more interested in the world the text promulgates or creates for the receiver.

2. *Itinerant Thomasine Christians?*

The most thorough argument for the social setting "behind" the *Gospel of Thomas* has been presented by Stephen J. Patterson. In his 1988 dissertation, published five years later,[14] Patterson provided a socio-historical description of the "Thomas Christians" which is built on Gerd Theissen's influential theory of the role of the wandering radicals in the early Jesus movement.[15] According to Patterson, "the persons who used and championed"[16] the Thomasine traditions were the wandering radicals (*Wandercharismatiker*) proposed by Theissen, homeless vagabonds and beggars responsible for transmitting early sayings traditions and practising the ethical radicalism promoted in these traditions. These wandering radicals had given up possessions and family ties, rejected conventional piety, and resisted stringent organization.[17] However, whereas Theissen had based his case of *Wanderradikalismus* mainly on the synoptic sayings tradition and *Did.* 11–13, for Patterson it is the *Gospel of Thomas* which most clearly

[14] *The Gospel of Thomas and Jesus* (FF: Reference Series; Sonoma, CA: Polebridge Press, 1993).

[15] Gerd Theissen, "Wanderradikalismus: Literatursoziologische Aspekte der Überlieferung von Worten Jesu im Urchristentum," *ZTK* 70 (1973): 245–71 (English translation: "The Wandering Radicals: Light Shed by the Sociology of Literature on the Early Transmission of Jesus' Sayings," in Theissen, *Social Reality and the Early Christians* [trans. M. Kohl; Minneapolis, MN: Fortress, 1992], 33–59); and *Soziologie der Jesusbewegung: Ein Beitrag zur Entstehungsgeschichte des Urchristentums* (Theologische Existenz heute 194; Munich: Kaiser, 1977) (English translation: *The First Followers of Jesus: A Sociological Analysis of the Earliest Christianity* [trans. John Bowden; London: SCM 1978] = *Sociology of Early Palestinian Christianity* [Philadelphia, PA: Fortress, 1978]).

[16] Patterson, *Gospel of Thomas*, 121.

[17] *Ibid.*, 163.

represents the untamed tradition of wandering radicalism. In his seminal essay, Theissen had referred to *Thomas* only briefly and noted
that in the gospel the concrete demands of the synoptic tradition
"have lost their edge and have been translated into the realm of the
speculative."[18] Patterson makes the opposite claim that precisely "in
Thomas Christianity the wandering radicalism of the Jesus movement continued to define its way of living in the world."[19]

Patterson builds his case for itinerancy both on sayings in *Thomas* that
according to him imply a wandering existence and on a more general
description of the conflicts between itinerant radicals and settled communities reflected in such writings as *Didache*, the Epistle of James, and
Second and Third John.[20] His analysis of these last-mentioned documents independently develops Theissen's overall theory, but in this
paper I will concentrate on the Thomasine sayings alone. Whatever evidence we have for wandering radicalism in other early Christian sources,
the assumption that this phenomenon featured in *Thomas'* social world
needs to be grounded on the analysis of that gospel itself.

Among the few sayings that speak directly of wandering is the terse
saying *Gos. Thom.* 42. According to Lambdin's translation it reads:
"Become passers-by."[21] Scholars have proposed a great variety of
interpretations of this enigmatic saying. It has been understood, to
mention a few examples, as a gnostic exhortation to "come into
being as you pass by,"[22] as an echo of funerary epigrams,[23] and, by

---

[18] "Wandering Radicals," 118 n. 53. Compare, however, a later comment on
the *Gospel of Thomas* by Gerd Theissen and Annette Merz, which is open to Patterson's
social description of the gospel: "The *Gospel of Thomas* suggests an original itinerant
charismatic movement, if we do not understand the instructions contained in it in
a 'spiritualized way.'" *The Historical Jesus: A Comprehensive Guide* (trans. J. Bowden;
London: SCM, 1998), 41.

[19] Patterson, *Gospel of Thomas*, 168.

[20] For Patterson's analysis of the external evidence for itinerancy, see *ibid.*, 171–95.

[21] English translation by Thomas Lambdin, "The *Gospel According to Thomas*," in
Gospel According to Thomas, Gospel According to Philip, Hypostasis of the Archons, and Indexes
(vol. 1 of *Nag Hammadi Codex II, 2–7 together with XIII,2*, Brit. Lib. Or. 4926(1), and
P.Oxy. 1, 654, 655*; ed. Bentley Layton; NHS 20; Leiden: Brill, 1989), 53–93, esp.
71. Unless otherwise noted, translations of the Thomasine sayings in this chapter
are from Lambdin's translation.

[22] This interpretation was prevalent in early translations of *Thomas*. See, e.g.,
Johannes Leipoldt, "Ein neues Evangelium? Das koptische Thomasevangelium übersetz und bescprochen," *TLZ* 83 (1958): 482–96, esp. 488; Bertil Gärtner, *Ett nytt
evangelium? Thomasevangeliets hemliga Jesusord* (Stockholm: Diakonistyrelsens bokförlag,
1960), 225; Robert M. Grant and David Noel Freedman, *The Secret Sayings of Jesus*
(With an English Translation of the *Gospel of Thomas* by William R. Schoedel;
London: Collins, 1960), 147.

[23] See Bentley Layton, *The Gnostic Scriptures: A New Translation with Annotations and*

means of ingenious philological maneuvers, as a command to "be Hebrews" (cf. John 8:30–47).[24] Patterson, taking his cue from Jeremias and Quispel,[25] sees here clear evidence for a wandering lifestyle and translates the saying as a concrete admonition to "become itinerants."[26] Yet scholars often admit that the saying is strikingly ambiguous and it is difficult and probably useless to seek a single authoritative reading of it. Arthur Dewey, for example, has taken notice of the aphoristic nature of the saying, which has an "ambiguous edge" and invites the reader/hearer to a variety of interpretations.[27] The aphorism could fit countless situations just like we can use the saying "a rolling stone gathers no moss" for various reasons and in many kinds of situations. The wandering life of ascetics is an imaginable context, but the saying itself or its immediate surroundings in the gospel give very little guidance on whether it should read literally as a concrete exhortation to become itinerant or in some other less concrete way. The saying on the homeless son of man (*Gos. Thom.* 86), which also evinces itinerancy to Patterson,[28] is similarly ambiguous. In fact, there is very little material in *Thomas* which is unambiguous in this regard.[29]

Introductions (Garden City, NY: Doubleday, 1987), 387, and especially Philip H. Sellew, "Jesus and the Voice from beyond the Grave: *Gospel of Thomas* 42 in the Context of Funerary Epigraphy," Chapter 3 in this volume.

[24] Titzje Baarda, " 'Jesus Said: Be Passers-by:' On the Meaning and Origin of Logion 42 of the *Gospel of Thomas*," in *idem, Early Transmission of Words of Jesus: Thomas, Tatian and the Text of the New Testament* (A collection of studies selected and edited by J. Helderman and S. J. Noorda; Amsterdam: VU Boekhandel/Uitgeverij, 1983), 179–205.

[25] Joachim Jeremias, *Unbekannte Jesusworte* (3rd ed.; Gütersloh: Mohn, 1963), 107–10; Gilles Quispel, *Makarius, das Thomasevangelium und das Lied von der Perle* (NovTSup 15; Leiden: Brill, 1967), 20–21. April DeConick admits that the Greek expression behind "passers-by" may be translated from the Hebrew עבר ("move through," "travel," "pass over"), but she believes that it did not originally evoke the image of a traveler or wanderer. Rather it was "the notion to pass by or turn away from someone or something such as we find in Psalm 119:37." See DeConick, "On the Brink of the Apocalypse: A Preliminary Examination of the Earliest Speeches in the *Gospel of Thomas*," Chapter 5 in this volume.

[26] Patterson, *Gospel of Thomas*, 131.

[27] Arthur A. Dewey, "A Passing Remark: Thomas 42," *Forum* 10:1–2 (1994): 69–85, esp. 84. Dewey focuses on the setting of the saying in the ministry of the historical Jesus. Marvin Meyer stresses the ambiguousness of the saying in the Thomasine context: ". . . there may be no single authoritative interpretation of *Gos. Thom.* 42. Readers of the *Gospel of Thomas* are to discover for themselves what it means to be passerby." See his " 'Be Passersby': *Gospel of Thomas* Saying 42, Jesus Traditions, and Islamic Literature," Chapter 12 in this volume.

[28] Patterson, *Gospel of Thomas*, 133.

[29] Patterson thinks that *Gos. Thom.* 12:2 ("No matter where you are, you are to

An explicit reference to traveling is, however, found in *Gos. Thom.* 14:4: "When you go into any land and walk about in districts, if they receive you, eat what they will set before you, and heal the sick among them." This unit has a close parallel in the synoptic Mission Charge, especially in Luke 10:8–9, which similarly contains entering some place and instructions to eat what is set before one and to heal the sick. At least part of these instructions derive ultimately from "Q," which contained an arresting set of instructions to those who are sent "like sheep in the midst of wolves" and who, relying on the support of friendly houses, travel without protection from one place to another to preach the kingdom and to heal the sick (Q 10:2–16). Q's Mission Charge has played a dominant role in the discussion of wandering radicalism and many, including the present author, have argued that these traditions go back to the itinerant charismatic preachers of the early Jesus movement.[30] This discussion has had some biasing impact on the perspective from which scholars have interpreted the saying in *Gos. Thom.* 14. Unlike Q's Mission charge, the cluster of sayings in *Thomas* is not a set of instructions about wandering from house to house without equipment,[31] but a thematic unit focusing on the value of such religious practices as fasting, praying, almsgiving, and purity rules. In the view of *Thomas*, Jesus' attitude to these pious activities is very unresponsive.[32] Fasting would only give rise to sin, praying to condemnation, and almsgiving

---

go to James the Just") supports his itinerancy hypothesis, since the use of Coptic ⲉⲓ ("go") indicates that the Thomas Christians are dispersed. The saying may indeed imply that the disciples go to different parts of the world (cf. *Acts of Thomas* 1), whereas James resides in Jerusalem; see Risto Uro, *Thomas: Seeking the Historical Context of the Gospel of Thomas* (London: Clark, 2003), 84–88. It is uncertain, however, whether one should infer from this "historical" feature that Thomas Christians were itinerant.

[30] Sayings from Q's Mission Charge played an important role in Theissen's essay ("Wanderrakalismus"). Already before Theissen, Paul Hoffmann had traced the Q instructions back to the prophetic-charismatic mission of a Jewish-Christian group in Palestine before 70 BC; see Paul Hoffmann, *Studien zur Theologie der Logienquelle* (NTAbh 8; Münster: Aschendorff, 1972), 287–334. For the Mission Charge and itinerancy, see also Risto Uro, *Sheep Among the Wolves: A Study on the Mission Instructions of Q* (AASF: Dissertationes humanarum litterarum 47; Helsinki: Academia Scientiarum Fennica, 1987), 124–34 and Leif E. Vaage, *Galilean Upstarts: Jesus' First Followers according to Q* (Valley Forge, PA: Trinity Press International, 1994), 17–39. For a recent thoroughgoing criticism of itinerancy in Q, see William E. Arnal, *Jesus and the Village Scribes: Galilean Conflicts and the Setting of Q* (Minneapolis, MN: Fortress, 2001).

[31] Cf., however, Patterson, *Gospel of Thomas*, 145.

[32] For a similar emphasis, see Sellew, "Jesus and the Voice beyond the Grave," Chapter 3 in this volume.

would harm the spirits of the giver (14:1–3).[33] The food taboos are
rejected with almost the same words as in the synoptic gospels (cf.
Q/Luke 10:8b and Matt 15:11). The command to heal can also be
seen as being related to the purity rules, since many sicknesses, most
notoriously "leprosy,"[34] were believed to be sources of impurity.

Of course the idea of traveling is there, but it is subordinated to
the discussion of religious observances. "Going into any land" signifies
crossing cultural boundaries and thus exposing oneself to the risk of
impurity. This must have been an imaginable possibility for Thomasine
Christians, but one cannot conclude from it that they were itinerants. Mobility does not necessarily mean itinerancy.

An important part of Patterson's argument is a group of sayings
on abandoning family ties.[35] Many of these sayings come very close
to what we have in Q and the synoptic gospels. The disciple must
"hate" his father and mother, and his brothers and sisters (*Gos. Thom.*
55; 101; cf. Q 14:26–27). *Thomas* also provides a succinct version of
the story of Jesus' rude response to his own family who are "standing outside" (*Gos. Thom.* 99; cf. Mark 3:31–35parr.). This tradition
contains the idea of the surrogate kinship group: Jesus' true family
is those "who do the will of my father."[36] The saying on the dissension in the family brought by Jesus (*Gos. Thom.* 16; cf. Q 12:51–53)
is usually also mentioned in this context. In addition to these synoptic-type sayings, *Thomas* has material which promotes more distinctive ideas about the true (divine) family lineage (101:2–3 and 105)
and about the "solitary" (*monachoi*; 16:3; 49; 75).[37]

These sayings are not particularly strong indications that Thomas
Christians were itinerants. Hating one's father and mother can mean
many things from challenging the parental will to abandoning the
family inheritance and disgracing the family honor. It is by no means

---

[33] See Antti Marjanen, "*Thomas* and Jewish Religious Practices," in *Thomas at the Crossroads: Essays on the Gospel of Thomas* (ed. R. Uro; Studies of the New Testament and Its World; Edinburgh: Clark, 1998), 163–82.

[34] For a recent helpful discussion on "leprosy" in early Christianity, see Susan R. Holman, "Healing the Social Leper in Gregory of Nyssa's and Gregory of Nazianzus's 'περὶ φιλοπτωχίας,'" *HTR* 92 (1999): 283–309.

[35] See Patterson, *Gospel of Thomas*, 134–37.

[36] For the history of this idea, see Joseph H. Hellermann, *The Ancient Church as Family* (Minneapolis, MN: Fortress, 2001).

[37] For an analysis of these sayings, see Risto Uro, "Is *Thomas* an Encratite Gospel?," in *Thomas at the Crossroads: Essays on the Gospel of Thomas* (ed. R. Uro; Studies of the New Testament and Its World; Edinburgh: Clark, 1998), 140–62.

obvious that obedience to Jesus' command to dispense with the family would have resulted in a vagabond life, even though it certainly created severe problems and suffering in societies which were strongly oriented towards maintaining the descent group and family honor. The dissension in the family (*Gos. Thom.* 16) and "taking up one's cross" (55) describe this experience. The fact that the idea of the surrogate family appears in *Thomas* indicates that some kind of alternative family group is assumed in place of the biological family.[38] We can imagine, therefore, that if there were those who broke off family ties, they could rely on the help of other Christians and were not forced to beg (cf. also *Gos. Thom.* 48).

Thomas has a special honorary title, *monachoi*, for those who have renounced family ties and been chosen by Jesus (*Gos. Thom.* 16; 49; 75). Much has been written on this term and its relationship to the history of the ascetic movements.[39] There are different opinions about whether the appearance of *monachoi* in the gospel shows that those who were engaged in transmitting and putting the Thomasine traditions down in writing were celibate. I have argued against the clear-cut encratite interpretation and suggested that *Thomas* is much more ambiguous in its relationship to sex and marriage than is usually assumed.[40] Arland Jacobson, on the other hand, has recently presented a trajectory from the "proto-ascetic ethos" of Q to the more developed ascetic practice in the Thomasine community based on his reading of Q's prohibition of remarriage (Q 16:18).[41] According to Jacobson, the people behind the *Gospel of Thomas* formed "some kind of community or at least association of [celibate] solitaries."[42]

This kind of difference of opinion underlines the difficulties in reconstructing the social context of the gospel. *Thomas*' ethical teaching

---

[38] Richard Valantasis argues similarly: "The gospel . . . fosters new social associations of people imaged as a group of solitaries . . . standing together with power as a new kind of family and living in a world full of light and immortality." "Is the *Gospel of Thomas* Ascetical? Revisiting an Old Problem with a New Theory," *JECS* 7 (1999): 55–81, esp. 76. See also Arland D. Jacobson, "Jesus Against the Family: The Dissolution of the Family Ties in the Gospel Tradition," in *From Quest to Q: Festschrift James M. Robinson* (ed. Jon Ma. Asgeirsson, Kristin De Troyer and Marvin W. Meyer; BETL 146; Leuven: Peeters & Leuven University Press, 2000), 189–218, esp. 216–17.

[39] For a discussion of the sayings on *monachoi* and further literature, see Uro, "Is *Thomas* an Encratite Gospel?" 156–60.

[40] *Ibid.*, esp. 160–62.

[41] Jacobson, "Jesus Against the Family."

[42] *Ibid.*, 217.

is often loaded with symbolic expressions and language and therefore open to multiple, often equally plausible interpretations. There
is, of course, no reason to deny that *Thomas* presents a version of
ethical radicalism which is similar to the one we find in the synoptic
gospels, especially in Q. But the problem is, how to define the relationship between the radical sayings and the social reality of the
Thomasine Christians. Theissen's basic argument is that this radicalism
could be passed on in oral tradition only "on the fringes of society"
and "under extreme conditions."[43] Had no one taken it seriously,
the traditions would have died out. However, the application of this
principle to the analysis of *Thomas'* social world is problematic in
two respects. First, as I have argued in other contexts, it is quite
unrealistic to assume a "pure" oral trajectory from the earliest sayings tradition to the *Gospel of Thomas*.[44] Unless we suggest a very early
date for *Thomas* (cf. Davies' contention that the gospel was composed
in the 50s),[45] there must have been written gospels and notes around
by the time the gospel was composed and hence some sort of intertextuality has to be assumed (true even if the author had not directly
copied his text from other documents). Secondly, oral or written ethical radicalism similar to that of the synoptic gospels and *Thomas* was
demonstrably used and transmitted in circumstances that were not
"extreme" and "on the fringe of society." Chriae about Diogenes and
other Cynics were used as exercise material in educational contexts.[46]
Cynic traditions were idealized and interpreted by the aristocratic
elite, who often praised "Cynics of old" and despised contemporary
itinerant philosophers.[47] Philo admired the Therapeutae, who had

---

[43] See Theissen, "Wanderradikalismus," 247, 252 (ET: "Wandering Radicals,"
35, 40).

[44] For orality in the *Gospel of Thomas*, see Risto Uro, "'Secondary Orality' in the
Gospel of Thomas? Logion 14 as a Test Case," *Forum* 9:3–4 (1993): 305–29 (reprinted
with the title "*Thomas* and the Oral Gospel Tradition," in Uro, *Thomas at the Crossroads*,
8–32), and *idem, Thomas*, 106–33.

[45] Stevan L. Davies, *The Gospel of Thomas and Christian Wisdom* (New York, NY:
Seabury, 1983), 146–47. For the date of *Thomas*, see Uro, *Thomas*, 134–36.

[46] Ronald F. Hock and Edward N. O'Neil, *The Progymnasmata* (vol. 1 of *The Chreia
in Ancient Rhetoric*; SBLTT 27: Graeco-Roman Religion Series 9; Atlanta, GA: Scholars
Press, 1986).

[47] R. Bracht Branham and Marie-Odile Goulet-Cazé, "Introduction," in *The Cynics:
The Cynic Movement in Antiquity and Its Legacy* (ed. R. Bracht Branham and M.-O.
Goulet-Cazé; Berkeley, CA: University of California Press, 1996), 1–27, esp. 15. This
is not to say that aristocrats did not occasionally convert to Cynicism. Demonax
and Peregrinus, the most prominent Cynics of the second century AD, are known
to have come from well-to-do families.

left "their brothers, their children, their wives, their parents . . . the fatherlands in which they were born and reared,"[48] even though he himself did not follow their example. I am *not* arguing that Philo's writings and the *Gospel of Thomas* arise from a similar social background or that early Christians did not take seriously the ethical radicalism of Jesus' sayings. Neither do I argue that there were no wandering charismatics in early Christianity. My point is that itinerancy and the practice of rigid asceticism are not the *only* prerequisites for the survival of the sayings on homelessness and abandoning family ties. Thomasine Christians may have felt like "standing behind"[49] these traditions, even though they did not necessarily put them into full practice.

3. Thomas *as an Ascetic Text*

The problems in drawing reliable conclusions about the people "behind" the text have probably been one reason why many scholars have changed their focus from the transmitters and producers of the text to the text itself and its implied audience. Fundamental to this change is the insight that such texts as the *Gospel of Thomas* do not just reflect the world as it exists, but they also envision the world as it is *wished* to exist. In Thomasine studies, Richard Valantasis is the scholar who has most vigorously brought to the discussion the literary perspective and the function of the reader of the gospel.[50] His interest is not in reconstructing a homogeneous community behind the *Gospel of Thomas*. In contrast, Valantasis contends that

> [t]he sayings genre leaves ample room for diversity, disagreement, alter-
> native and resistive interpretations, and even subversive readings by
> people within the various groups of readers who may not agree with
> one another. Moreover these sayings could be used in a variety of
> organized communities: fourth-century monks could have found in
> them rich ascetical teaching; gnostic Christians would have found pro-
> found esoteric meaning; orthodox Christians might have thrilled to
> hear parables without allegorical interpretation. Many people in many

---

[48] *Contempl.* 18 (trans. F. H. Colson; LCL). In *Fug.* 33–35 Philo expresses an explicit distaste for the Cynic lifestyle.

[49] This expression is used by Patterson (*Gospel of Thomas*, 122).

[50] Richard Valantasis, *The Gospel of Thomas* (New Testament Readings; London: Routledge, 1997); *idem*, "Is *Gospel of Thomas* Ascetical?"

different kinds of communities could, and did, read these sayings and interpret them, but they cannot be assumed to share one common theology, perspective, or even interpretation of the sayings.[51]

The text is not, however, only a mirror which reflects back the various religious ideas of the readers.[52] Valantasis insists that the *Gospel of Thomas* exhibits "a strong ascetical orientation."[53] Asceticism should not be defined in a narrow sense as a practice of particular acts of self-denial, for example, fasting, prayer, alms and attention to ritual purity. In terms of such traditional categories, the *Gospel of Thomas* is not ascetical, as the saying cited earlier in this chapter clearly shows (*Gos. Thom.* 14).[54] For Valantasis, however, such specific acts of renunciation do not describe the heart of asceticism, but rather asceticism should be understood as "the intentional reformation of the self through specific practices."[55] The ascetical refashioning of the self consists of both negative and positive actions: a rejection of the existent self and the reconstruction of a new self. It is "the articulation of two selves, one rejected and one sought after" that "provides the strongest evidence for the ascetical orientation of the *Gospel of Thomas*."[56] Thus, for example, *Gos. Thom.* 47, which emphasizes the impossibility of mounting two horses, stretching two bows, serving two masters, and the incompatibility of "old" and "new" wines and garments, speaks precisely of the incompatibility of the two selves of a person who is engaged in the ascetical process promoted in the gospel.

The contest of the two selves in *Thomas* is the starting point for Valantasis' general definition of asceticism "as performances within a dominant social environment intended to inaugurate a new subjectivity, different social relations, and alternative symbolic universe."[57]

---

[51] Valantasis, *The Gospel of Thomas*, 26.

[52] The difference between historical criticism and literary criticism has sometimes been described with the metaphors of a window and a mirror. According to Mark Allan Powell, "[l]iterary criticism . . . regards text as a mirror; the critic determines to look at the text, not through it [as in historical criticism], and whatever insight is obtained will be found in the encounter of the reader with the text itself." *What is Narrative Criticism? A New Approach to the Bible* (London: SPCK, 1993), 8.

[53] "Is the *Gospel of Thomas* Ascetical?," 66. In his commentary, Valantasis is more temperate in introducing the language of asceticism into the explanation of the gospel ("I have resisted making it the heart of my own reading," *Gospel of Thomas*, 27).

[54] "Is the *Gospel of Thomas* Ascetical?," 61–64.

[55] *Ibid.*, 61.

[56] *Ibid.*, 63.

[57] *Ibid.*, 64. For Valantasis' theory of asceticism, see his articles on "Constructions of Power in Asceticism," *JAAR* 63 (1995): 775–821 and "A Theory of the Social

Valantasis demonstrates that *Thomas* advances manifold such performances, the goal of which is the production of a new subjectivity: for example, the search for interpretation and discovery (e.g., *Gos. Thom.* 2), the reconstruction of a new family (e.g., 55; 99; 101), and disengagement from the world (e.g., 42; 56). In his most recent works, Patterson has utilized Valantasis' idea of ascetic performances to support his own description of the social history of *Thomas*.[58] There is much in common between these two scholars,[59] but that should not obscure their different perspectives. Patterson's social description is still mainly about those "who cultivated" the traditions of the *Gospel of Thomas*, wandering Thomasine Christians,[60] whose lifestyle is documented in the gospel's urge for public and social performances. Valantasis, on the other hand, is consistent in his literary approach and contents himself with showing how the text "promulgates" or "promotes" these performances.[61] This leaves room for imagining various serious responses to the gospel. As Valantasis notes, "it does not matter here whether the new self is gnostic or whether the practices align with modern understanding of encratism. Only the positive agenda for creating a newly refashioned self in conflict with the old self matters in describing the gospel as ascetical."[62]

Function of Asceticism," in *Asceticism* (ed. V. L. Wimbush and R. Valantasis; New York, NY: Oxford University Press, 1995), 544–52.

[58] Stephen J. Patterson, "*Askesis* and the Early Jesus Tradition," in *Asceticism and the New Testament* (ed. L. E. Vaage and V. L. Wimbush; New York, NY: Routledge, 1999), 49–70 and "The *Gospel of Thomas* and Christian Beginnings," Chapter 1 in this volume.

[59] Valantasis refers approvingly to Patterson's description of the social history of the movement behind the *Gospel of Thomas* ("Is the *Gospel of Thomas* Ascetical?," 67 n. 42).

[60] See "The *Gospel of Thomas* and Christian Beginnings."

[61] These verbs are used throughout the article.

[62] "Is the *Gospel of Thomas* Ascetical?," 63. Valantasis' broad definition of asceticism can be criticized and some scholars would prefer more narrow ways of defining the phenomenon. See, for example, Mary Ann Tolbert, "Asceticism and Mark's Gospel," in *Asceticism and the New Testament* (ed. Leif E. Vaage and Vincent L. Wimbush; New York, NY: Routledge, 1999), 29–48, esp. 30. My understanding is that Valantasis' theory, though based on literary criticism, captures some essential features of a universal human predisposition which lies *behind* the ascetical actions and behavior. This predisposition may or may not produce actions that are in common language understood as ascetic, for example, the renunciation of sex, reduction of food, and avoidance of social relations. It is a moot question whether this universal "ascetic instinct" (Johannes Bronkhorst) should define asceticism proper or whether "asceticism" and "ascetic" should be used in the more traditional senses of the words. For an attempt at the universal theory of asceticism, see Johannes Bronkhorst, "Asceticism, Religion, and Biological Evolution," *MTSR* 13 (2001): 374–418.

In addition to these possible readings of *Thomas* mentioned by
Valantasis, such as the gnostic and encratite interpretations, I would
like to offer one more reading, which I think is plausible in the contemporary historical context of the gospel. My suggestion is that
Thomas' language of the human body and the world could quite
smoothly be read from the Stoic point of view.[63] Consider, for example, how a Stoic-minded person would have understood Jesus' saying about children living in a field:

> Mary said to Jesus, "Whom are we disciples like?"
> [2]He said, "They are like children who have settled in a field which is
> not theirs. [3]When the owners of the field come, they will say, 'Let us
> have back our field.' [4]The children are naked[64] in their presence in
> order to let them have back their field and to give it back to them."
> (*Gos. Thom.* 21:1–4.)[65]

As with many other parables in *Thomas*, this saying is open to multiple
interpretations and I would like once again to emphasize that I am
not looking for a single authoritative reading of *Thomas'* symbolic
language. However, the basic idea of the saying, namely that the
disciples are compared to little children who have settled in a field that
is not theirs which they then give back to its owners, would have
easily found acceptance with a person who had adopted a similar
philosophy of life to that promoted by Epictetus in his *Handbook*:

> Never say about anything, "I have lost it," but only "I have given it
> back." Is your child dead? It has been given back. "I have had my
> farm taken away." Very well, this too has been given back. "Yet it
> was a rascal who took it away." But what concern is it of yours by
> whose instrumentality the giver called for its return? So long as he
> gives it to you, take care of it as of a thing that is not your own, as
> travelers treat their inn.[66]

For Epictetus, everything outside *prohairesis*, moral purpose or the
inner faculty of choice, is neither good nor bad, and is something
that should be treated with indifference. One's own body is also con-

---

[63] The reading of *Gos. Thom.* 21 presented here summarizes my interpretation in
Uro, *Thomas*, 65–70.
[64] The verb ϹⲈⲔⲀⲔⲀⲎ̄Ⲩ should probably be understood as a qualitative form,
but most translations ignore this. For the correct grammatical definition, see Stephen
Emmel, "Indexes of Words, Catalogues of Grammatical Forms," in Layton, *Nag
Hammadi Codex II, 2–7*, 1:267.
[65] Translation modified from Lambdin.
[66] *Ench.* 11. Translation modified from Oldfather (LCL).

sidered to be outside this moral purpose. The body "is not yours but is clay ingeniously mixed."[67] In the parable, the reference to the body is made by means of the metaphor of "being naked," which easily evokes the common metaphor of the body as a garment (cf. also *Gos. Thom.* 37, in which those who "will see the son of the living one" will "disrobe without being ashamed"). *Thomas'* attitude to the human body and the world is often understood in terms of extreme asceticism or at least of emphatic rejection of the social world. A Stoic reader may have felt differently. One may compare *Thomas'* gloomy words about the world as "a corpse" (*Gos. Thom.* 56; cf. 80) with Epictetus' similarly pessimistic statement: "The paltry body, which is not mine, which is by nature dead." It does not really matter whether one speaks of the body or the world, since both are, in the Stoic view, outside one's control and not part of the real self, that is, the faculty of a person's moral choice.

Stoics did not reject marriage or involvement in the city life. They did not favor life outside society, except perhaps as a special Cynic calling.[68] The Stoics' attitude to ascetic practices is summarized by James Francis:

> Because of Stoicism's fundamental emphasis on interior disposition, it defined asceticism less as a discipline of the body than that of the mind. Physical practice is certainly required, but gained meaning only as it related to the development of internal discipline. Once such mental discipline was attained, all externals became indifferent and physical exertions, for the most part, lost their significance.[69]

According to Judith Perkins, the basic tenet of Stoicism was self-mastery in which "pain, poverty, exile, prison, loss of status were all indifferent and could not affect the real self."[70] *Thomas* envisions "ruling over the all" and immortality as the ultimate goals of the human life (see *Gos. Thom.* 1–2). These may not be completely congruent with the teachings of Stoicism. But the psychological step from Stoic philosophy to *Thomas'* pessimistic world view[71] is not overwhelmingly

---

[67] *Diatr.* 1.1.2 Translated by Oldfather (LCL).
[68] See Epictetus, *Diatr.* 3.22.
[69] James A Francis, *Subversive Virtue: Asceticism and Authority in the Second Century Pagan World* (University Park, PA: The Pennsylvania State University Press, 1995), 19.
[70] Judith Perkins, *The Suffering Self: Pain and Narrative Representation in the Early Christian Era* (London: Routledge, 1995), 83.
[71] Cf. Phil Sellew's assessment of Thomas' view of the world "as deeply pessimistic." See "Jesus and the Voice Beyond the Grave," Chapter 3 in this volume.

long. A Christian, whose "plausibility structure" (Berger and Luckmann) had been influenced by Stoic ideas, would have found many salient features of the gospel familiar, such as *Thomas'* "individualistic" stance, its "pantheistic" view of the kingdom (e.g., *Gos. Thom.* 113), ambiguous (or indifferent) attitude towards religious authority (cf. 3;12–13),[72] and even the Cynic-type social radicalism, if understood idealistically or as a special calling.

4. *Social World Sophisticated*

It is difficult to say how many of *Thomas'* first hearers would have shared the kind of social location the Stoic interpretation presented here suggests. Nonetheless, if *Thomas* is to be dated to the early second century (as both I and Valantasis date it), Epictetus' teaching activity (late first and early second century) overlapped with the writing of the gospel (or preceded it, if one suggests a later date for *Thomas*) and some sort of cultural intertextuality is possible. Stoicism was the ethical *koine* of the second century empire[73] and therefore a comparison between *Thomas* and Epictetus, an eminent and contemporary representative of Stoicism, is relevant for the analysis of *Thomas'* social world.[74] In terms of historical development, Stoicism may well bring us closer to the time of *Thomas'* writing than, for example, the Gnostic demiurgical systems, which do not yet appear in *Thomas*.[75] There are "Gnostic-pleasing" elements in *Thomas*, to be sure, just as there are "Stoic-pleasing" features. Both lenses provide valid historical readings. But the analysis of *Thomas'* social world should not restrain itself from asking questions about the *primary* hearers of the gospel and its more immediate historical context.

---

[72] For *Thomas* and religious leadership, see Uro, " 'Who Will Be Our Leader?' Authority and Autonomy in the *Gospel of Thomas*," in *Fair Play: Diversity and Conflicts in Early Christianity: Essays in Honour of Heikki Räisänen* (ed. Ismo Dunderberg, Kari Syreeni and Christopher Tuckett; NovTSup 103; Leiden: Brill, 2002), 457–85, reprinted in *idem, Thomas*, 80–105.

[73] Francis, *Subversive Virtue*, 1.

[74] This is not to say that Stoicism constitutes the most important ideological background of *Thomas*. The cosmology of *Thomas* is unmistakably Platonic. See Jon Ma. Asgeirsson, "Conflicting Epic Worlds" Chapter 7 in this volume.

[75] Valantasis regards both gnostic and encratite perspectives as rather late from the point of view of *Thomas'* original setting, since he dates the gospel earlier than the emergence of these movements. "Is the *Gospel of Thomas* Ascetical?," 60–61. For a criticism of the view that *Thomas* promotes demiurgical beliefs, see Uro, *Thomas*, 40–45.

If "social world" is characterized with Richard Rohrbaugh's words as "the context in which other ideas are interpreted and understood as realistic possibilities,"[76] then comparison with other texts and sources is the only way to delineate the social world of *Thomas*. It is not possible to construct a social world only "from within the text and its sayings,"[77] since the *Gospel of Thomas* does not give us enough information about its social location. It is by means of other "inter-texts" that the "social world" in this broad sense can be constructed. Such examination need not be limited to the reconstruction of a hypothetical "community" behind the *Gospel of Thomas*.[78] It is rather a search for plausible readings and contexts by means of which the world of *Thomas* can be described and interpreted. The search includes the producers of the text as well as its early receivers. We can hardly make a sharp distinction between these two, but it would be unwarranted to assume that the author(s) and the early readers/hearers would have consisted of a homogeneous group without different opinions and social backgrounds and hence without partially different social worlds. We may, therefore, ask whether the social radicalism of the gospel conveys a unified social experience or just a (sub)culturally conditioned topos, which could have been variously received depending on the social location of the hearer. The sayings on leaving one's family would probably have meant quite different things

---

[76] Richard Rohrbaugh, "'Social Location of Thought' as Heuristic Construct in New Testament Study," *JSNT* 30 (1987): 103–19, esp. 114. I have somewhat inaccurately merged "social world" with what Rohrbaugh calls "social location of thought." Rohrbaugh defines the latter as "the common structural position occupied by a number of individuals in relation to a larger social whole" (*ibid.*, 115).

[77] This is how Valantasis describes his approach; see his *Gospel of Thomas*, 26. To be sure, Valantasis does not intend to examine the social world of *Thomas*. Rather he states that his commentary "was designed to lay the foundation for subsequent research in the biblical and theological intertextuality of the *Gospel of Thomas*" (*ibid.*). In an earlier study, Valantasis formulates his stance with reference to the issue as to whether the experience finds expression in the language or the language of the texts forms the experience: "My position is that the literary creation of the text is itself the experience and the fullest expression. Although some experience may lie behind the text, the text as a complex literary construction, refers not to the experience, but to itself." Richard Valantasis, *Spiritual Guides of the Third Century: A Semiotic Study of the Guide-Disciple Relationship in Christianity, Neoplatonism, Hermetism, and Gnosticism* (HDR 27; Minneapolis, MN: Fortress, 1991), 150 n. 5.

[78] For a good analysis of the problems in reconstructing a Thomasine community or Christianity, see Philip Sellew, "Thomas Christianity: Scholars in Quest of a Community," in *The Apocryphal Acts of Thomas* (ed. Jan N. Bremmer; Leuven: Peeters, 2001), 11–35. See also Uro, *Thomas*, 20–26.

if the hearer was a man or a woman, a master or a slave, a craftsman
or a member of the elite class.[79] To take another example, Jesus'
words that "businessmen and merchants [will] not enter the places
of my father" (*Gos. Thom.* 65:12) would have made sense for both
upper and lower class audiences, but for at least partially different
reasons. For an aristocrat like Cicero, small-scale business was "mean"
and "not liberal," hardly to be done "without much outright lying."[80]
For others, traders and merchants may have simply represented those
rich who were blinded by their wealth and did not renounce the
world to become spiritually rich (cf. *Gos. Thom.* 110).

Adopting a literary critical or reader-oriented approach to the
Gospel of Thomas does not mean that the critic is simply asking different
kinds of questions than the one who is doing traditional historical
criticism. We cannot go back from literary studies to the traditional
issues of the Thomasine community and Christians as if nothing had
changed. For one thing, a scholar who is informed by the literary
approaches will probably be much more cautious about arguing for
a single authoritative interpretation of the Thomasine sayings or suggesting a harmonious Thomasine community in which everybody
agreed on how the sayings should be understood and acted accordingly. Such descriptions of *Thomas'* social background are of course
unrealistic and psychologically naïve, and it would be needless to
remind anyone of it, were it not for the fact that Thomasine scholarship
is replete with debates about the *right* interpretations. Many of *Thomas'*
symbols and parables are open-ended and it is natural to assume
that people debated about their interpretations as they do now.[81]

---

[79] Patterson argues firmly that "Thomas Christianity was not a conclave of med-
itating elites." See "Gospel of Thomas: Introduction," in John S. Kloppenborg
et al., *Q Thomas Reader* (Sonoma, CA: Polebridge Press, 1990), 77–123, esp. 100. This
can hardly be contested. But it is difficult to exclude the possibility that at least
some of the primary hearers of the gospel came from the privileged classes. As an
analogy, one may refer to the recent discussion about the social composition of the
Pauline communities. See, e.g., Dale B. Martin, *The Corinthian Body* (New Haven,
CT: Yale University Press, 1995).
[80] Cicero, *Off.*, 1.150–51. See Moses I. Finley, *The Ancient Economy* (2nd ed.;
London: Penguin, 1992), esp. 41–42. For further references to the criticism of
"traders" and "merchants" in the Greco-Roman literature, see Ron Cameron, "Parable
and Interpretation in the Gospel of Thomas," *Forum* 2:2 (1986): 13–39, esp. 18
n. 39. Cameron notes that "wholesalers . . . and retailers . . . were regularly referred
to as wheelers and dealers, hucksters and hustlers bent on greed and corruption,
trafficking in sophistry, pandering to deceit" (*ibid.*, 18).
[81] One method of searching the social experience reflected in the Thomasine sayings is to analyze the body symbolism of the gospel. Following the insights pre-

Thus, what I am suggesting is that we continue to search the social world of *Thomas* while being more sensitive to the literary approach promoted by Valantasis and others.[82] We may narrow our scope by focusing on the primary hearers of the gospel and its more specific cultural context using all the possible fragments of knowledge we can get from the gospel itself and other relevant sources.[83] At the same time, we have to accept that there may not have been one "original" hermeneutical key by means of which *Thomas* was read, one "social world" shared by all of its primary hearers, nor a uniform response to its ethical demands.

To sum up, I have evaluated and compared some recent attempts to delineate the social world of the *Gospel of Thomas*. Some scholars have been keen to reconstruct a social world *behind* the gospel, making hypotheses about the transmitters of the Thomasine sayings and about the community in which and for which the gospel was written. These hypotheses are, however, often built on a rather simplistic reading of *Thomas'* religious symbolism and ethical teaching. Those scholars who have moved towards literary-oriented reading strategies have focused on the text and the function of its readers. They are not so

---

sented by Mary Douglas, it is possible to take *Thomas'* body symbols as "condensed statements about the relation of society to the individual," see her *Natural Symbols: Explorations in Cosmology* (2nd ed.; London: Barrie & Jenkins, 1973 [1970]), esp. 195, and my application of Douglas' model to *Thomas* in Uro, *Thomas*, 77–79. The symbolistic approach is not however, without problems. Its fundamental assumption that body symbols or symbols in general form a kind of encoded language has been strongly criticized by anthropologists and theorists of religion. At least in its simplistic form, Douglas' model involves the idea that body symbols can be decoded into overt messages about the relationship between the individual and society. But if there is such a one-to-one relationship between the symbols and their "implicit meanings" (Douglas), why use symbols, which are characteristically cryptic or open to multiple interpretations? Whose interpretation is the authoritative one? For a theoretical discussion of symbolism, see, e.g., Dan Sperber, *Rethinking Symbolism* (trans. A. L. Morton; Cambridge: Cambridge University Press, 1975) and Ilkka Pyysiäinen, *How Religion Works: Towards a New Cognitive Science of Religion* (Cognition and Culture Book Series 1; Leiden: Brill, 2001), 33–44.

[82] Cf., e.g., Philip Sellew, "The *Gospel of Thomas*: Prospects for Future Research," in *The Nag Hammadi Library after Fifty Years: Proceedings of the 1995 Society of Biblical Literature Commemoration* (ed. J. D. Turner and A. McGuire; NHMS 44; Leiden: Brill, 1997), 327–46. Sellew encourages to read *Thomas* "with a more literary sensibility" (*ibid.*, 335).

[83] Perhaps the clearest clue for determining a more specific cultural setting for *Thomas* is the appearance of "Judas Thomas or the Twin," the hero of the Syrian Christians. For recent comparisons between *Thomas* and early Syrian literature, see Alexei Sivertsev, "The *Gospel of Thomas* and the Early Stages in the Development of the Christian Wisdom Literature," *JECS* 8 (2000): 319–40, and Uro, *Thomas*, 26–30.

interested in reconstructing a hypothetical community or group that produced the gospel,[84] but their interpretations about what the text "promotes" or "promulgates" include social dimensions and issues (for example, how ascetical is *Thomas*?) and occasionally come close to the communities reconstructed by other scholars. Sometimes these two approaches are confused so that literary inferences are taken at face value as statements about the social world behind *Thomas*.

The future study of the social world of the *Gospel of Thomas* should pay more attention to the insights achieved in the literary critical reading of the gospel. The two perspectives may not be easily combined since they ask different questions and are based on divergent philosophical models.[85] Yet it may not be fruitful to let them go their own ways without intersection.[86]

---

[84] "Cf. Valantasis' somewhat restrained comment on the Thomasine community behind the gospel: "*If* a community exists behind these sayings . . ., it consists of those who have taken the interpretation of these sayings as their primary duty," *Gospel of Thomas*, 26.

[85] That is, should we interpret *Thomas* in terms of its origin and process of development or in terms of what the text communicates between its author and the reader? Cf. Powell, *What is Narrative Criticism*, 10.

[86] See especially Vernon K. Robbins, "Social-scientific Criticism and Literary Studies: Prospects for Cooperation in Biblical Interpretation," in *Modelling Early Christianity: Social-Scientific Studies of the New Testament* (ed. Philip F. Esler; London: Routledge, 1995), 274–89, and Kari Syreeni, "Wonderlands: A Beginner's Guide to Three Worlds," *SEÅ* 64 (1999): 33–46. Syreeni's hermeneutical "three-world model" combines literary and sociology-of-knowledge approaches.

CHAPTER THREE

JESUS AND THE VOICE FROM BEYOND THE GRAVE:
GOSPEL OF THOMAS 42 IN THE CONTEXT OF
FUNERARY EPIGRAPHY

Philip H. Sellew

The *Gospel of Thomas* calls us to interpret the words of Jesus in a process that leads to salvation. The opening of the text informs us that we are about to read secret teachings of the "living Jesus" recorded by Judas Thomas the Twin. "Whoever discovers the meaning of these statements will not taste death!" Life and death are clearly at issue; but salvation will come not, apparently, through the suffering and death of Christ on the cross, memorialized in the Eucharist, nor through his revivification and resurrection from the dead on Easter morning. Neither of those events is even mentioned in this gospel. Instead, redemption is found through a spiritual and intellectual process of scrutiny, mystical exploration, and self-discovery. Through Jesus' words, we are offered God's life, light, and enlightenment as counterweight and cure to the pervasive death, darkness, and obscurity of our world. These terms both reflect and challenge basic and widespread ancient notions of how light and life relate to this world and the world of the dead.

In this chapter I shall discuss the briefest and perhaps the most enigmatic saying spoken by Jesus in *Thomas*, logion 42: ϢⲰⲠⲈ ⲈⲦⲈ-ⲦⲚ̄ⲠⲀⲢⲀⲄⲈ, "Become passers-by." The literary character of the *Gospel of Thomas* puts a premium on close reading, use of paradox and contrast, and deliberate mystification. Yet one of the great challenges for interpreters of *Thomas* is its lack of overt narrative structure, coupled with its restraint in providing verbal clues to the meaning of the various parables, aphorisms, questions, or brief anecdotes that it has Jesus present, one after the other. Even the *Q Gospel* provides a more meaningful sequence and narrative thrust than does *Thomas*. This has meant that scholars approaching *Thomas* in the past often did so not to understand or explain the text in its own terms, but rather to dissect it and ransack its contents in service of other questions.

Even this briefest of statements, "become passers-by," has served this function. In contrast, much of the recent work on *Thomas* attempts to interpret the gospel within its own literary, rhetorical, and ideological context first and foremost.[1]

1. *Previous Scholarship on* Gos. Thom. *42*

The first question typically asked about *Thomas* was its potential connection or relationship with other early gospels, especially those now in the Bible.[2] A second line of inquiry has been to position *Thomas* within the developing literary and theological genre of the gospel form itself.[3] Naturally its structural and soteriological peculiarities have left *Thomas* on the margins of that discussion. A more fruitful approach has been to track the history of religious ideas reflected in *Thomas*, with scholars proposing to label the book as 'gnostic,' or expressing a 'wisdom' perspective, or an 'encratite' theology, that is, preaching a life of radical renunciation.[4] Finally, and most provocatively, some

---

[1] I have discussed this issue more fully in Sellew, "The *Gospel of Thomas*: Prospects for Future Research," in *The Nag Hammadi Library after Fifty Years: Proceedings of the 1995 Society of Biblical Literature Commemoration* (ed. John D. Turner and Anne McGuire; NHMS 44; Leiden: Brill, 1997), 327–46. Quotations of gospel texts generally follow the Scholars Version printed in *The Complete Gospels* (ed. R. J. Miller; Sonoma, CA: Polebridge Press, 1994).

[2] For an early and insightful survey of research see Ernst Haenchen, "Literatur zum Thomasevangelium," *TRu* 27 (1961–62): 147–78, 306–38. Of more recent treatments I would mention Francis T. Fallon and Ron Cameron, "The *Gospel of Thomas*: Forschungsbericht and Analysis," *ANRW* 25.6:4195–251; Gregory J. Riley, "The *Gospel of Thomas* in Recent Scholarship," *CurBS* 2 (1994): 227–52; Stephen J. Patterson, "The *Gospel of Thomas* and the Synoptic Tradition: A Forschungsbericht and Critique," *Forum* 8:1–2 (1992): 45–97.

[3] James M. Robinson and Helmut Koester, *Trajectories through Early Christianity* (Philadelphia, PA: Fortress, 1971); John Dominic Crossan, *Four Other Gospels: Shadows on the Contours of Canon* (Minneapolis, MN: Seabury, 1984); Patterson, *The Gospel of Thomas and Jesus* (FF: Reference Series; Sonoma, CA: Polebridge Press, 1993); William E. Arnal, "The Rhetoric of Marginality: Apocalypticism, Gnosticism, and Sayings Gospels," *HTR* 88 (1995): 471–94.

[4] These three options are explored by Ernst Haenchen, *Die Botschaft des Thomas-Evangeliums* (Theologische Bibliothek Töpelmann 6; Berlin: Töpelmann, 1961); Gilles Quispel, *Makarius, das Thomasevangelium und das Lied von der Perle* (NovTSup 15; Leiden: Brill, 1967); "L'Évangile selon Thomas et les origines de l'ascèse chrétienne," in *Gnostic Studies II* (Istanbul: Nederlands Historisch-Archaeologisch Instituut te Istanbul, 1975), 98–112; and "The *Gospel of Thomas* Revisited," in *Gnostic Studies II*, 218–66; Jacques – É. Ménard, *L'Évangile selon Thomas* (NHS 5; Leiden: Brill, 1975); Stevan L. Davies, *The Gospel of Thomas and Christian Wisdom* (New York, NY: Seabury, 1983);

scholars have plumbed *Thomas* to find information about the teachings and even the intentions of the historical Jesus of Nazareth.[5]

Brief as it is, *Gos. Thom.* 42 has been deployed in all these debates.[6] To be sure, in no other text do we find Jesus giving this particular command to "become passers-by"; still, gospel scholars influenced by the theories of Gerd Theissen[7] have been able to find connections with Jesus' postulated style of itinerant ministry, evidenced most clearly in passages of the *Q Gospel* where the Lord commands his followers to abandon their homes and families to travel on special journeys without food, extra clothing, or even simple protection from the elements, wild animals, or bandits. Some have seen a connection with the command, ὑπάγετε ("get going!") that opens that Q

Margaretha Lelyveld, *Les Logia de la vie dans l'Évangile selon Thomas: À la recherche d'une tradition et d'une rédaction* (NHS 34; Leiden: Brill, 1987); Stephen J. Patterson, "Wisdom in Q and Thomas," in *In Search of Wisdom: Essays in Memory of John G. Gammie* (ed. Leo G. Perdue, Bernard Brandon Scott and William Johnston Wiseman; Louisville, KY: Westminster John Knox, 1993), 187–221; Arnal, "The Rhetoric of Marginality"; April D. DeConick, *Seek to See Him: Ascent and Vision Mysticism in the Gospel of Thomas* (Supplements to Vigiliae Christianae 33; Leiden: Brill, 1996); Thomas Zöckler, *Jesu Lehren im Thomasevangelium* (NHMS 47; Leiden: Brill, 1999). For incisive surveys of the 'gnostic' and 'encratite' interpretations of *Thomas* see Antti Marjanen, "Is *Thomas* a Gnostic Gospel?" and Risto Uro, "Is *Thomas* an Encratite Gospel?" in *Thomas at the Crossroads: Essays on the Gospel of Thomas* (ed. R. Uro; Studies of the New Testament and Its World; Edinburgh: Clark, 1998), 107–39 and 140–62.

[5] The parables included in *Thomas* have been of special interest for this question since the beginning: Hugh Montefiore, "A Comparison of the Parables of the *Gospel According to Thomas* and of the Synoptic Gospels," *NTS* 7 (1960–61): 220–48; Joachim Jeremias, *The Parables of Jesus* (2nd ed.; New York, NY: Scribners, 1972); Norman Perrin, *Rediscovering the Teaching of Jesus* (New York, NY: Harper, 1967); Helmut Koester, "One Jesus and Four Primitive Gospels," *HTR* 61 (1968): 203–47; repr. in Robinson and Koester, *Trajectories*, 158–204, and *idem*, "Three Thomas Parables," in *The New Testament and Gnosis* (ed. A. H. B. Logan and A. J. M. Wedderburn; Edinburgh: Clark, 1983), 195–203; John Dominic Crossan, *In Parables: The Challenge of the Historical Jesus* (New York, NY: Harper, 1973); more recently, Bernard Brandon Scott, *Hear Then the Parable: A Commentary on the Parables of Jesus* (Minneapolis, MN: Fortress, 1989).

[6] Arthur J. Dewey provides a helpful survey of interpretations of *Gos. Thom.* 42 in his article "A Passing Remark: Thomas 42," *Forum* 10:1–2 (1994): 69–85.

[7] Gerd Theissen, "Wanderradikalismus: Literatursoziologische Aspekte der Überlieferung von Worten Jesu im Urchristentum," *ZTK* 70 (1973): 245–71, and *Sociology of Early Palestinian Christianity* (trans. John Bowden; Philadelphia, PA: Fortress, 1978). Theissen in turn was influenced by Georg Kretschmar's study of Syriac Christian ascetics in relation to the gospels: "Ein Beitrag zur Frage nach dem Ursprung frühchristlicher Askese," *ZTK* 61 (1964): 27–67. Arnal has a critical and methodological discussion of Theissen's hypothesis and reactions to it in his important book *Jesus and the Village Scribes: Galilean Conflicts and the Setting of Q* (Minneapolis, MN: Fortress, 2001), 23–65.

discourse (Luke 10:3//Matt 10:6).[8] Is that what is meant in *Gos. Thom.* 42 when Jesus tells his audience to "become passers-by"? Is this an exhortation to give up house and home and become radical itinerant prophets or missionaries?

Some have attempted to bolster this interpretation by pointing to the statement imbedded within the complex logion at *Gos. Thom.* 14, "When you go into any land and walk in a district, if they welcome you, eat the food that people serve you and heal the sick among them."[9] As deployed in the narratives of both Mark 6:7–13 and Q 10:2–12, this sort of advice does refer to Jesus' messengers being sent out on some sort of special journey.[10] Yet the thematic context within the *Gospel of Thomas*—as is shown by the surrounding bits of logion 14 itself—is focussed not on 'missionary' work but instead on the relative value of food purity rules.[11] Additional evidence that *Thomas* supports the itinerancy model is supposedly found in *Gos. Thom.* 86: "Foxes have their dens, birds have their nests, but the Son of Man has no place to lay his head and rest." Though as cited in its canonical parallels in Matt 8:20 or Luke 9:58, this Q logion could refer to wandering preachers, in *Thomas* it is more likely meant as a philosophical comment on the place of humanity stuck between the realms of heaven (the birds) and earth (dens of foxes).[12]

---

[8] See James M. Robinson, Paul Hoffmann, and John S. Kloppenborg, eds., *The Critical Edition of Q* (Hermeneia Supplement; Minneapolis, MN: Fortress, 2000), 162–63.

[9] Patterson, *Thomas and Jesus*, 128–33, arguing that *Gos. Thom.* 42 supports a model of itinerancy modeled after Jesus' practice; his suggestion has been received favorably by DeConick, *Voices of the Mystics: Early Christian Discourse in the Gospels of John and Thomas and Other Ancient Christian Literature* (JSNTSup 157; Sheffield: Sheffield Academic Press, 2001), 100; Arland D. Jacobson, "Jesus Against the Family: The Dissolution of Family Ties in the Gospel Tradition," in *From Quest to Q: Festschrift James M. Robinson* (ed. Jon Ma. Asgeirsson, Kristin De Troyer and Marvin W. Meyer; BETL 146; Leuven: Peeters & Leuven University Press, 2000), 189–218, but critiqued by Sellew, "*Thomas*: Prospects for Research," 333; Zöckler, *Jesu Lehren*, 150–51 n. 55; and more thoroughly by Arnal, *Jesus and the Scribes*, 34–38.

[10] Sellew, "Early Collections of Jesus' Words," (Th.D. diss., Harvard University, 1986), 59–162; Risto Uro, *Sheep among the Wolves: A Study of the Mission Instructions of Q* (AASF: Dissertationes humanarum litterarum 47; Helsinki: Academia Scientiarum Fennica, 1987).

[11] On this point see Sellew, "Pious Practice and Social Formation in the *Gospel of Thomas*," *Forum* 10:1–2 (1994): 47–56; cf. Marjanen, "*Thomas* and Jewish Religious Practices," in *Thomas at the Crossroads*, 163–82.

[12] Cf. Richard Valantasis: "The contrast dramatizes the homing instincts of animals and the homelessness of humans. Unlike these animals, humans live as aliens in the world into which they are born. . . ." (*The Gospel of Thomas* [New Testament Readings; London and New York, NY: Routledge, 1997], 166).

An earlier and more plausible version of this line of interpretation was to explain *Gos. Thom.* 42 in the context of Syrian asceticism, that is, the encratite Christianity known from the *Liber Graduum*,
Bardasanes, or the *Acts of Thomas*, among other texts. Gilles Quispel
and Jacques – É. Ménard, for example, following Kretschmar and
Vööbus, connect the command to "pass on by" with encratite demands
to abandon family life and worldly entanglements.[13] This suggestion
is more reasonable than a supposed link with the Q instructions for
messengers, because of its compatibility to a theme of central importance to *Thomas*: readers are called repeatedly to be or become 'solitary' or 'single,' to 'make the two one,' terminology which in turn
is very much at home in Syrian ascetic movements (e.g., *Gos. Thom.*
4; 22–23; 49).[14]

The dominant interpretation given *Gos. Thom.* 42 in earlier scholarship was to connect the statement with the gnostic myth of salvation,
in which reading, perhaps, our souls are called to pass by or through
the planetary spheres guarded by the evil archons to reach their true
heavenly home in the Pleroma and with the Father.[15] Once again,
though a gnostic reading of *Thomas* is certainly possible, and just as
plausible as a gnostic interpretation of the Gospel of John,[16] one
needs to pick and choose among the words of *Thomas* to construct

---

[13] Quispel, *Makarius*, 20–21, and "*Gospel of Thomas* Revisited;" Ménard, *L'Évangile
selon Thomas*, 143; Georg Kretschmar, "Ein Beiträg," 27–67; Arthur Vööbus, *History
of Asceticism in the Syrian Orient*, Vol. 1 (CSCO 184; Leuven: van den Bengt, 1958).
On this topic see further Sellew, "Thomas Christianity: Scholars in Search of a
Community," in *The Apocryphal Acts of Thomas* (ed. Jan N. Bremmer; Leuven: Peeters,
2001), 11–35.

[14] For a balanced and well-informed discussion of this topic see Uro, "Is *Thomas*
an Encratite Gospel?" Uro makes the significant point that while *Thomas* clearly
demands separation from one's parental family and disparages childbirth, there is
no explicit condemnation of marriage as such. This interesting observation suggests
to me that *Thomas* or its readers may connect somehow to early Christian debates
about sex and 'continent' marriage, visible in such writings as Clement's *Stromateis*
or the so-called *Protevangelium of James* (a topic discussed in my forthcoming article
with the tentative title "Heroic Biography, Continent Marriage, and the *Protevangelium
Jacobi*").

[15] Bertil Gärtner, *Theology of the Gospel of Thomas* (trans. Eric J. Sharpe; London:
Collins, 1961), 243–44; Haenchen, "Literatur zum Thomasevangelium," 328; and
still Michael Fieger, *Das Thomasevangelium: Einleitung, Kommentar und Systematik* (NTAbh,
n.F. 22; Münster: Aschendorff, 1991), 139.

[16] M. F. Wiles, *The Spiritual Gospel: The Interpretation of the Fourth Gospel in the Early
Church* (Cambridge, MA: Cambridge University Press, 1960); Elaine H. Pagels, *The
Johannine Gospel in Gnostic Exegesis* (Nashville, TN: Abingdon, 1973); A. H. B. Logan,
Gnostic Truth and Christian Heresy (Edinburgh: Clark, 1996).

the gnostic story from its contents, and ultimately, just like the radical itinerancy model, one must import significant elements crucial to the interpretation from outside the text. Nonetheless these are the leading interpretations of the logion on offer in scholarship today: those interested in second-century Christian Gnosticism employ *Gos. Thom.* 42 as part of their data-base, while the more recent move on the part of some to give *Thomas* a central role in the modern construal of Jesus has led to revival of the itinerancy model, originally proposed in connection with later Syrian Christianity.

My primary interest here is not to use *Thomas* to track gnostic or encratite ideology, or to reconstruct what the historical Jesus was all about, though these are worthy tasks that can find some enlightenment in this gospel, but instead to find the meaning of the text in and of itself. We should begin by considering any particular passage within the more general literary and thematic framework of *Thomas* as a whole.[17] How does this enigmatic command connect to the overarching ideology of the text?

2. *Life and Light versus Death and Darkness*

One of the most striking aspects of the *Gospel of Thomas* is its deeply pessimistic view of the world in which we live.[18] We are called to turn away from the entanglements of the world to find God within

---

[17] Tjitze Baarda's attempt to explain *Gos. Thom.* 42 as a command to "become Hebrews" in view of the disparaging reference to "the Jews" in *Gos. Thom.* 43, though improbable on other grounds, has the virtue of seeking to explain the logion within its close literary context, " 'Jesus Said: Be Passers-By:' On the Meaning and Origin of Logion 42 of the *Gospel of Thomas*," in *idem, Early Transmission of the Words of Jesus: Thomas, Tatian and the Text of the New Testament* (ed. J. Helderman and S. J. Noorda; Amsterdam: VU Boekhandel/Uitgeverij, 1983), 179–205. Dewey also uses the surrounding thematic context to suggest helpfully that "becoming a passer-by" means avoiding the "discrepancy, division, and disharmony of this world," and that the command expresses "an invitation to enter into this unfinished revisioning of lifestyle and society" ("A Passing Remark," 75, 82).

[18] I have discussed this theme more thoroughly in Sellew, "Death, the Body, and the World in the *Gospel of Thomas*," in *Proceedings of the XII International Patristics Conference, Oxford, 1995* (ed. E. A. Livingstone; StPatr 31, Leuven: Peeters & Leuven University Press, 1996), 530–34. Haenchen has a similar view of *Thomas*' perspective on the world, though he connects the text's gloomy picture of the cosmos with an asceticism motivated by gnosticism (*Botschaft des Thomas-Evangeliums*, 49–62) rather than encratism. For further discussion of Haenchen see Marjanen, "Is *Thomas* a Gnostic Gospel?," 116–18.

us, and to reject the world so as to return home to true divinity above. This cosmos is a dark and gloomy place of death (*Gos. Thom.* 56; 80), while our real home is the very source and essence of life and light (*Gos. Thom.* 50). Indeed our true nature and character, if we are among those chosen and called "children of the living Father" (*Gos. Thom.* 3), is itself light and life. Thematizing the values of the gospel in just this way—the contrast between life and light on one side with death and darkness on the other—is a fascinating and powerful challenge not only to the biblical view of creation, but also to the standard Greek and Roman understanding of the character of our world, the nature of our life within it, and our most likely fate after death.

Thomas portrays Jesus as sent into the cosmos to shine light in the darkness, to carry the message of his Father about the true life found only with God in his spiritual abode above our world. Readers are urged to recognize the divine light within themselves and then follow Jesus' model and example and return to its source. In *Gos. Thom.* 24, for example, Jesus says, "There is light within a person of light, and it shines on the whole world. If it does not, it is dark." That is to say, "If the light does not shine, the world remains dark." Here and elsewhere *Thomas* reflects and elaborates on the familiar biblical image of the divine light that first shone into the vast cosmic darkness (Gen 1:1–5).[19] *Thomas* is not alone: in the opening verses of the Gospel of John, the narrator tells us that in the divine word "was life, and this life was the light of humanity. Light was shining in the darkness, and darkness did not master it" (John 1:4–5). Nonetheless, for *Thomas*, as we shall see, and perhaps even for John, the inherent darkness of the world endures and retains its potency.

Both *Thomas* and John present Jesus as the divine wisdom who has appeared in human flesh to enlighten the world: in John 1:9 we read that "the true light that enlightens every person was coming into the world," while in *Gos. Thom.* 28 Jesus says, "I took my stand in the midst of the world, and in flesh I appeared to them."[20] Here Jesus continues with the metaphors of blindness, emptiness, and drunkenness

---

[19] See the different treatments of Stevan L. Davies, "The Christology and Protology of the *Gospel of Thomas*," *JBL* 111 (1992): 663–82; April D. DeConick, *Seek to See Him*, 21–24; and Pagels, "Exegesis of Genesis 1 in the Gospels of Thomas and John," *JBL* 118 (1999): 477–96.

[20] On this theme see most recently Ismo Dunderberg, "*Thomas'* I-Sayings and the Gospel of John," in *Thomas at the Crossroads*, 33–64.

so frequently found in wisdom literature: "I found them all drunk, and I found none of them thirsty. My soul ached for the children of humanity, because they are blind in their hearts and do not see. They came into the world empty, and they also seek to depart from the world empty. But meanwhile they are drunk. When they shake off their wine, then they will change their ways."

These metaphors of awakening, sobering up, and departure, though possibly 'eschatological' in import, are not deployed in the apocalyptic direction familiar from the Apostle Paul[21] as well as from the Jesus tradition at large. Nor does the distinction of light from darkness in *Thomas* function in the typically apocalyptic fashion as a mere symbol or label for insiders and outsiders: 'children of light' and 'children of darkness' (meaning 'us' and 'them'). In fact, at several points in *Thomas*, Jesus can be seen criticizing the apocalyptic scenario familiar from the Synoptic Gospels and Q (though absent from John), and frequently traditional apocalyptic imagery is re-directed. In *Gos. Thom.* 18, for example, the disciples ask Jesus when "their end will come." This sort of question by the disciples is part of a widespread pattern in *Thomas* of incomprehension on their part, a stubborn inability to get the point or see the bigger picture of what Jesus is trying to say.[22] In the Gospel of Mark, this narrative theme of the incomprehension of the disciples is made to serve the apocalyptic drama: the world, including Jesus' own circle, is divided into insiders and outsiders, first and last, those given the 'mystery' or 'secret' of God's kingdom and those left to muddle through in ignorance and misunderstanding.[23] None of the apocalyptic imagery of the coming of the Son of Man or the cosmic crisis involved in God's judgment of Israel or the nations is found in *Thomas*. Jesus' response in

---

[21] Cf., e.g., 1 Thess 4:13–17; 5:4–11; Rom 13:11–14; see further Dunderberg, "*Thomas*' I-Sayings and John," 59, who also points to John's use of the light/darkness contrast to characterize "good or bad actions" as part of "a certain way of life" (John 3:20–21; 8:12; 11:9–10; 12:35).

[22] I have discussed this theme at length in Sellew, "*Thomas*: Prospects for Research," 340–46; see also Uro, "'Who Will Be Our Leader?' Authority and Autonomy in the *Gospel of Thomas*," in *Fair Play: Diversity and Conflicts in Early Christianity: Essays in Honour of Heikki Räisänen* (ed. Ismo Dunderberg, Kari Syreeni and Christopher Tuckett; NovTSup 103; Leiden: Brill, 2002), 457–85, esp. 469.

[23] William Wrede, *Das Messiasgeheimnis in den Evangelien* (Göttingen: Vandenhoeck & Ruprecht, 1901); Gaetan Minette de Tillesse, *Le secret messianique dans l'Évangile de Marc* (Paris: Cerf, 1968); Heikki Räisänen, *Das "Messiasgeheimnis" im Markusevangelium* (Helsinki: The Finnish Exegetical Society, 1976); Joel Marcus, *The Mystery of the Kingdom of God* (SBLDS 90; Atlanta, GA: Scholars Press, 1986).

Gos. Thom. 18 to his disciples' question about the end offers this characteristic paradox: "Have you found the beginning, then, that you are looking for the end? You see, the end will be where the beginning is. Blessed is the one who stands at the beginning: that one will know the end and will not taste death."

Another instance of Jesus' rejection of an apocalyptic construal of his message is found in *Gos. Thom.* 51: The disciples ask Jesus, "When will the rest for the dead take place, and when will the new world come?" Jesus replies to them, "What you are looking forward to has come, but you don't know it." Note again the theme of true 'life' and 'death.' A bit earlier, in *Gos. Thom.* 11, Jesus tells his audience, "This heaven will pass away. The dead are not alive, and the living will not die." Statements made by Jesus about the world elsewhere in *Thomas* help to explain this curious paradox: *Gos. Thom.* 27: "If you do not fast from the world, you will not find the Kingdom." *Gos. Thom.* 56: "Whoever has come to know the world has discovered a corpse, and whoever has discovered a corpse—the world is not worthy of such a person!" Very similar is *Gos. Thom.* 80: "Whoever has come to know the world has discovered the body, and whoever has discovered the body, the world is not worthy of that one!"[24] According to *Thomas*, the world is a corpse, a carcass, a place of death and darkness. *Corpse* and *body* and *flesh* are counterpoised with *spirit* and *singleness*—and especially with *light* and *life*—in a complex weave of images throughout the gospel. Yet the words are not mere pictures.

The force of *Thomas'* language derives in part from its use of words both as synonyms and as metaphors. Is the world 'really' a corpse, or is it merely being *compared* to a dead body? The complexity of the referents is closely analogous to the complicated semantics of the Gospel of John.[25] In both John and *Thomas*, 'life' *is* 'light' and yet also, and perhaps simultaneously, 'light' *symbolizes* or characterizes

---

[24] Jon Ma. Asgeirsson has explored the compositional implications and rhetorical effects of 'twinned words' in *Thomas* such as this doublet in 56 and 80: "Arguments and Audience(s) in the *Gospel of Thomas* (Part I)," *SBL SeminarPapers, 1997* (SBLSP 36; Atlanta, GA: Scholars Press, 1997), 47–85 and "Arguments and Audience(s) in the *Gospel of Thomas* (Part II)," *SBL Seminar Papers, 1998* (2 vols; SBLSP 37; Atlanta, GA: Scholars Press, 1998), 1:325–42.

[25] Norman R. Petersen has discussed John's paradoxical use of such terms in a significant if neglected study (*The Gospel of John and the Sociology of Light: Language and Characterization in the Fourth Gospel* [Valley Forge, PA: Trinity Press International, 1993]). The implications of his work for understanding *Thomas* are important, but will have to await another occasion.

'life.' John's 'word' *is* 'life' and yet also has a separable and definable existence ('the word became flesh'). In John 1:5 we read that "the light shines in the darkness," apparently a straightforward use of solar imagery,[26] but then in 1:9–11 we read that "the true light that enlightens every person was coming into the world; he was in the world . . . yet the world knew him not . . . and his own people received him not," where the light is now personified. So for John 'the word' (Jesus) is both 'like' the light (it shines) and yet also has become and 'is' the light, or the light 'is' it: the word/light travels, arrives, and is rejected. Jesus speaks in similar terms in the *Gospel of Thomas*: he both has the character of light and also claims to be that light itself (*Gos. Thom.* 24; 33; 77; 83), all the while challenging his listeners to recognize their own status as "children of the light" (11; 50).[27] The symbol has taken on personality and become a real 'being'—the word has, in a way, become flesh. Jesus' words are no longer mere metaphors. For the author of *Thomas*, I would claim, the world *really is* a corpse, and Jesus *really is* the light in that darkness; these are not literary conceits or mere explanatory comparisons.[28]

3. Thomas *and Creation*

Recent scholarship has emphasized the importance of the Genesis creation narratives in understanding *Thomas*' view of the world, and how the world came to have its character. In an important article published a decade ago, Stevan L. Davies drew attention to the 'protological' perspective that *Thomas* adopts and made some very helpful comparisons to similar aspects of the prologue to John's gospel.[29] In Davies' formulation, both *Thomas* and John have more of a protological than a truly eschatological view of the world and of salvation. He argues that for *Thomas* the world ought to be viewed from

---

[26] According to Davies, *Thomas* also uses solar imagery, though in his view "the image of the primordial light is our ordinary sunlight," "Christology and Protology," 669, referring to *Gos. Thom.* 50:1; 83; 87.

[27] For further discussion of these themes in *Thomas* and John see the excellent treatment of Dunderberg, "*Thomas*' I-Sayings and John," 46–60.

[28] Here I agree with Davies: "*Thomas*, like John, works from an allegorical logic foreign to our usual modes of thought" ("Christology and Protology," 666), yet I cannot see that *Thomas*' and John's shared term of 'light' for Jesus entails a shared perspective on matters of creation and worldview.

[29] Davies, "Christology and Protology."

the perspective of Gen 1:1–2:5, which means from the perspective
of God's first or original creation, in which the human being is made
in the divine image and likeness (1:26–27) before separation into the
gendered pair of Adam and Eve. "*Thomas* insists . . . accordingly that
people should restore themselves to the condition of the image of
God."[30] Elaine Pagels builds on Davies' insight, but points more helpfully to Gen 1:3, where the first reference is made to the division
of light from darkness through the shining of that primordial divine
light, which she argues forms the crucial link between the divine
image and humanity.[31]

To this point Davies and Pagels are surely correct: *Thomas* is clearly
influenced by the Genesis creation narrative, and the opening scene
of the divine light sent into the dark void is obviously of central
importance. Where Davies goes wrong, taking others with him, is
when he claims that *Thomas* portrays Jesus as the active agent in
creation, and consequently that *Thomas* must have a positive view of
the created world.[32] There is very little evidence that this is truly
the case, and much that contradicts it. Davies and Pagels are misled,
apparently, by two interpretive strategies, both of which are quite
reasonable in and of themselves. The first strategy is to compare
Thomas closely with the opening of the Gospel of John, which both
aids and confuses the picture; while *Thomas* shares the notion of Jesus
as the divine light sent into the cosmos, as was discussed above, the
cosmos itself is in no sense portrayed as a 'good' or 'divine' world.
Secondly, Davies and others have had the laudable goal of dissociating
Thomas from Gnosticism, and gnostic authors of course tend to reject
the created order as tragically flawed or utterly worthless. I agree
that *Thomas* is not best understood as a gnostic gospel, yet this should
not blind us to the severely critical view the text has toward creation
and the material world. As everyone knows, Paul, Plato, and many
other writers can also speak disapprovingly of the material world
without being labeled as 'gnostic' in any meaningful way.[33] Pagels

---

[30] Davies, "Christology and Protology," 664.

[31] Pagels, "Genesis 1 in Thomas and John." On this point at least, DeConick
would seemingly agree (*Seek to See Him*, 21–22).

[32] Cf. the balanced critique by Marjanen, "Is *Thomas* a Gnostic Gospel?," 121–24,
where the inherent contradictions of Davies' reading of *Thomas* on the world are
shown to lead to a forced or even incoherent reading of the text.

[33] Marjanen makes a useful comparison of *Thomas* with the Wisdom of Solomon,
the Gospel of John, the *Gospel of Philip*, and the *Apocryphon of John* ("Is *Thomas* a

correctly insists that the hermeneutical strategy visible in *Thomas* that scholars often call 'gnosticizing' in fact "articulates a conviction commonplace . . . in Jewish exegesis" and "follows an exegetical pattern articulated in a range of extant sources."[34]

Those scholars who assert that *Thomas* has a positive view of the world rely on one or two proof-texts and must ignore many contrary statements. To be sure, *Thomas* is filled with ambiguity, marked by sly juxtapositions and theological irony, as well as some outright contradiction; yet the overwhelming amount of evidence that *Thomas* disparages the world and life within it is impossible to ignore or explain away. Instead, the rare apparent indications of a positive view of creation should be analyzed more critically. Merely showing that *Thomas* reflects Genesis 1 in its use of the image of the divine light does not entail that the gospel evokes a 'biblical' view of the good found in creation: interpreters of the scriptural narrative frequently adopted some of its aspects while rejecting others, as even a quick review of the Nag Hammadi texts Pagels and others discuss in this connection will reveal.

More substantially, Davies, Pagels and others claim that when Jesus identifies himself with the "light that was before them all . . . from me all came forth, and to me all attained" (*Gos. Thom.* 77:1) he is asserting his own active participation in creation itself.[35] This interpretation is what seems to compel this otherwise odd reading of *Thomas*: if Jesus helped create the world, 'he' (and the gospel text) must have a positive view of that work. Without the influence of Johannine christological reflection on the Logos and its role in creation, however, it is hard to explain how this interpretation would apply to *Thomas* at all. Instead, in *Gos. Thom.* 77 Jesus is discussing his function as a divine messenger sent to illuminate and rescue a blind world and to recoup the lost particles of the divine light (the "all" means "all the light"). The "person of light" is not invisible in *Thomas'* world due to his awful brilliance, blinding the inhabitants of an already well-lit cosmos, as Davies would have it, though this notion would comport

---

Gnostic Gospel?," 130–38); see more generally the important study of Michael A. Williams, *Rethinking Gnosticism: An Argument for Dismantling a Dubious Category* (Princeton, NJ: Princeton University Press, 1996).

[34] Pagels, "Genesis 1 in Thomas and John," 479; cf. DeConick, *Seek to See Him*, 21–22.

[35] Davies, *Thomas and Wisdom*, 56; DeConick, *Seek to See Him*, 21; Pagels, "Genesis 1 in Thomas and John," 483–84.

with some pagan ideas about the overwhelming luminosity of the gods.[36]

Davies points further to the strange remark that Jesus makes in *Gos. Thom.* 77:2 (30:3–4 in *P.Oxy.* 1), that he can be found under a lifted stone or in a split piece of wood. Reading this trope as though it were a product of a Stoic pantheism of nature, Davies (and Pagels following him) believes that Jesus is somehow asserting his immanence throughout the physical world.[37] Davies' literalism as a reader is difficult to credit here. To begin with, the two examples are rather odd and even a little disgusting: what squalor and insects do we usually find when we lift a rock or split open a log? Instead of identifying himself with the least savory bits of nature, more likely Jesus is illustrating his power of illumination as the "person of light." What places are darker and less open to the light, under normal circumstances, than the inside of logs and what lies underneath stones? Yet when opened up to God's searchlight, even these dank realms experience some brightening as the divine light pours in. These are not symbols of God's immanence in our world but rather of its rank desolation instead.

April D. DeConick has framed her discussion of *Thomas'* view of creation as part of a persuasive refutation of a gnostic origin for the gospel (as opposed to its use by gnostic theologians).[38] DeConick shows how *Thomas* deploys exegetical traditions about the creation and fall of Adam in ways that are more consonant with encratite practice and with late antique Jewish mystical readings of Genesis than with the gnostic myth of a divided godhead whose tragic error results in our created world. Discussing such texts as *Gos. Thom.* 85 ("Adam came into being from a great power and a great wealth . . ."), DeConick argues that *Thomas* connects the creation of humanity with Jesus as divine hypostasis; human salvation requires a return to Adam's undivided state.[39] Because *Gos. Thom.* 85 refers to Adam's death due to his "unworthiness," she infers that the gospel blames the dark and deathly character of our world not on its inherent qualities but on

---

[36] Davies, "Christology and Protology," 669; Jean-Pierre Vernant, *Mortals and Immortals: Collected Essays* (Princeton, NJ: Princeton University Press, 1991), 44.

[37] Davies, "Christology and Protology," 664, followed by Pagels, "Genesis 1 in Thomas and John," 484.

[38] DeConick, *Seek to See Him*, 3–27.

[39] *Seek to See Him*, 16–21; she refers further to *Gos. Thom.* 11; 22; 37; 77; 114. It is not clear to me however that the "great power" of *Gos. Thom.* 85 need refer to Jesus as distinct from the God of Jesus; but I agree that for *Thomas* (elect) humanity originates with God.

Adam's or humanity's sinful fall.[40] But nowhere in *Thomas* do we read of the sin of Adam as such, as opposed to the deplorable character of fleshly humanity at large, though there is much discussion of return to humanity's (and thus Adam's) originally undivided state in Paradise (see *Gos. Thom.* 3; 4; 11; 15; 18; 19; 22; 37; 49). Adam's unworthiness is evident from his mortality, according to *Gos. Thom.* 85, but its causes are not spelled out.[41]

DeConick agrees with Davies (without citing him specifically on this point) in using *Gos. Thom.* 77:1 ("I am the light . . .") to argue that according to this gospel Jesus was involved in the creation of our world as a demiurgic agent. Unlike Davies, however, DeConick does not rely for this inference on the prologue of the Gospel of John, but points instead to a variety of Jewish mystical, apocalyptic, and Hermetic authors to show how Gen 1:3 could be employed in speculations about the divine light as demiurgic agent.[42] No doubt these traditions do offer important points of comparison; yet the mere presence of a demiurgic light (sometimes called "the son" of God) in such texts as the Wisdom of Solomon, *3 Enoch*, or the *Teachings of Silvanus* does little more than provide a valid hermeneutical context within which we can search out the particular interpretive strategy employed by *Thomas*. There is no clear rationale offered as to why we should believe that *Thomas* would agree with these other texts in their attitude toward creation of the cosmos as such, without recourse to DeConick's larger hypothesis situating the gospel or its sources alongside the heavenly ascent and vision texts of Jewish mysticism.[43] Although I agree with her that *Thomas* connects

---

[40] "*Thomas* presents the picture of a unified Godhead of Light from which creation comes. It is Adam's Sin that turns everything upside down, bringing about sex and lust, birth and ultimately death. The material world is a negative experience for these reasons, whereas in Gnosticism there is a depreciation of the world because of the cosmic Fall, the consequent division in the Godhead and creation through the will of the ignorant Demiurge" (*Seek to See Him*, 24; see also p. 117).

[41] The pair worthiness/unworthiness is a key motif in the text, especially in contrast with "the world"; see also *Gos. Thom.* 55; 56; 80; 111; 114 with n. 24 above. As for Adam in *Gos. Thom.* 85 in particular cf. Valantasis: "Adam contrasts negatively to the 'you' of the saying. The difference between the seekers ('you') and Adam revolves around the experience of death" (*Gospel of Thomas*, 165).

[42] *Seek to See Him*, 21–22.

[43] See especially DeConick's careful study of *Gos. Thom.* 50 in *Seek to See Him*, 43–96, where she mounts a compelling argument that the passage as it stands comments on an earlier text of ascent. Thus she proposes that *Gos. Thom.* 50 (far from being the gnostic 'smoking gun' so often cited by scholars) instead provides later

the origins of *elect humanity* with Jesus (or more likely with God),[44] this by itself leaves open Jesus' own role in the creation of the world at large, the dark "corpse" referred to so often by him in such disparaging terms.

In his careful discussion of these issues, Antti Marjanen finds that the imagery of *Gos. Thom.* 77 "does not provide any unambiguous evidence for examining *Thomas'* view of the world and of creation."[45] Part of the issue as explained so well in his article is the import of the term "the all" (ⲡⲧⲏⲣϥ) in several sayings in *Thomas* as either indicating the world (which would be an emphatically gnostic reading) or, better, the scattered particles of the divine light which will return with and to Jesus and thus on to God. Due to the ambiguity of this term "everything" or "the All," Marjanen must depend instead on the curious statement of Jesus about "James the Just" in *Gos. Thom.* 12 to conclude that the gospel has a positive view of creation and the world. Despite his recognition that almost everywhere else *Thomas* presents a strongly negative view of the world, Marjanen follows the conventional track in interpreting Jesus' remark that "heaven and earth came into being" for James' sake as non-ironic and unambiguous praise.[46] This is a highly implausible reading, in my opinion, for reasons that cannot delay us here; it must suffice to point out how the text denigrates Jewish ritual practices usually associated with James (*Gos. Thom.* 14; 53; 104); how prominently it

---

Christian gnostic readers with a source for their own further speculations. Though I agree with her analysis in that regard, I am less sure that *Gos. Thom.* 50 as it stands within the gospel must refer to a 'pre-mortem' ascent as opposed to an afterlife return of the divine spark to the heavenly light once the body and soul are separated at death (*Gos. Thom.* 11; 15; 18; 22). Even more likely would be the possibility that *Thomas* has redirected the earlier text of ascent.

[44] Cf. DeConick on this point: "In addition to this association with the traditions that the Light is responsible for the creation of the universe, the *Gospel of Thomas* is also aware of the motif that humanity comes from the Light. Thus in Logion 50, an elect portion of humanity is said to be generated from the Light through the image of the angels. These elect are known by the title, 'sons of light'" (*Seek to See Him*, 23). DeConick would agree that the elect originate specifically from God: elsewhere we read that the Thomasites "were God's elect because they were God's own children, born from his light, or as Logion 3 phrases it, they were 'sons of the living Father'" (88–89); with reference to the scenario of divine vision and worship in *Gos. Thom.* 15, we read that "it seems that the Father and the Light have been assimilated in *Thomas'* traditions" (100).

[45] Marjanen, "Is *Thomas* a Gnostic Gospel?," 123.

[46] Marjanen, "Is *Thomas* a Gnostic Gospel?," 118–20. Marjanen must then interpret such ambiguous statements as *Gos. Thom.* 77 (the light from the all) and 87 (the inside and the outside) as reflecting a similarly positive view of creation.

disparages leadership (3; 13); and how it stresses the confusion and misunderstanding of the disciples (6; 13; 18; 24; 34; 37; 43; 51; 52; 91; 99; 104; 113; 114). For modern readers to take Jesus' reply to his disciples' hapless request for a "leader when you are gone" (*Gos. Thom.* 12) at face value is quite surprising. Richard Valantasis is surely correct when he emphasizes that in *Thomas* "the question of leadership has always had an ironic component to it."[47] The immediate context is also illuminating: in the words preceding, Jesus warns that the heavens will "pass away" and that "the dead are not alive" (11), so James' "heaven and earth" seem none too lasting. In the next complex, other well-known candidates for apostolic authority, Peter and Matthew, fall short (13) while Thomas succeeds by his silence.[48]

4. Thomas' *Challenge to ordinary Notions of Light and Darkness*

This discussion of language, irony, and metaphor brings us back to the cultural setting of the *Gospel of Thomas* and the challenge it represents: a complete inversion of standard notions of Greco-Roman antiquity as to when we are truly alive, where we find and are bathed in the light, and how we will inevitably come to be trapped in a world of darkness, death, and gloom. The ordinary Mediterranean view of the eternal struggle between the darkness of night, overcome each morning by a newly triumphant sun, is based on straightforward observation and experience. The living get their time above ground, when they have a share in that immortal light, but then as death

---

[47] Valantasis, *Gospel of Thomas*, 73, and further: "Jesus' subsequent direction that they should 'go to' James the Just points them in a direction of a recognized authority in the world, an orientation also disavowed in other sayings (Saying 3, for example)."

[48] Marjanen recognizes that *Gos. Thom.* 13 has in some way "relativized" the "emphasis on a leader-centered organization among the disciples" ("Is *Thomas* a Gnostic Gospel?," 119), but interprets this (as is usually done) as "a reflection of a historical development" from leadership associated with the Apostle James to that of the Apostle Thomas. I agree instead with Uro that "a rather complicated network of meanings" in *Gos. Thom.* 12–13 cannot be "easily deciphered into a clear historical interpretation" ("'Who Will Be Our Leader?,'" 461). Marjanen's own important characterization of "the notion of a 'masterless' Christian identity associated with Thomas" (p. 120) should reveal that the apparent praise of James in *Gos. Thom.* 12 must be ironical. In the interest of space I must defer more detailed argument about James in *Gos. Thom.* 12 to another occasion (see my forthcoming article with the tentative title "James and the Rejection of Apostolic Authority in the *Gospel of Thomas*").

arrives, they quickly lose their contact with that brightness and are forever lost in the empty desolation below. "Between the shadows of death where they must finally lose themselves and the pure luminosity of the divine which remains inaccessible to them, human beings live in a middle world, divided between day and night."[49] *Thomas* makes the startling claim that this standard picture has it all backwards, or at least is badly confused: this our world, both above *and* below the barrier between what we mistakenly call 'life' and 'death,' is irredeemably dark, gloomy, and indeed dead, and what is worse, the apparent brightness of the earth by day is nothing but a prison and a trap.

Greek authors throughout antiquity, from the time of Homer down through the early Christian period, return time and again to the notion that our life on earth is but a moment in the sun, an all too temporary sojourn in the bright and well-lit world that is inhabited permanently by the immortal gods. "It is in the mutual reflection of gods and men that each understands not only the other but also itself. It is the existence of age and death which forms the great difference between the two."[50] In his eighth *Pythian Ode*, Pindar declares: "We are things of a day. What are we? What are we not? The dream of a shadow is man, no more; but when the brightness comes, and god gives it, there is a shining light on men, and their life is sweet."[51]

The Olympian deities (and most lesser divinities) freely traverse all the regions illuminated by the sun: the sky, the mountaintops, the flat plain of the earth. What is more, this bright-lit realm is and will be theirs—not ours—for countless ages both past and future.[52] "The association between light and the divine seems as old as the

---

[49] Vernant, *Mortals and Immortals*, 44.

[50] Jasper Griffin, *Homer on Life and Death* (Oxford: Clarendon, 1980), 187.

[51] Pindar, *Pythian Ode* 8.95–97: ἐπάμεροι· τί δέ τις; τί δ᾽ οὔ τις; σκιᾶς ὄναρ / ἄνθρωπος ἀλλ᾽ ὅταν αἴγλα διόσδοτος ἔλθῃ, / λαμπρὸν φέγγος ἔπεστιν ἀνδρῶν καὶ μείλιχος αἰών. Text quoted from Cecil Maurice Bowra, ed., *Pindari carmina cum fragmentis* (2nd ed.; Oxford: Clarendon, 1947); translation by Richmond Lattimore, *The Odes of Pindar* (2nd ed.; Chicago, IL: University of Chicago Press, 1976), 84.

[52] For especially informative treatments of this topic see further Emily Vermeule, *Aspects of Death in Early Greek Art and Poetry* (Berkeley, CA: University of California Press, 1979); Griffin, *Homer on Life and Death*; Vernant, *Mortals and Immortals*; Christiane Sourvinou-Inwood, *"Reading" Greek Death* (Oxford: Clarendon, 1995); Sarah Iles Johnston, *Restless Dead: Encounters between the Living and the Dead in Ancient Greece* (Berkeley, CA: University of California Press, 1999).

Greek pantheon itself. As an inextricable component of divine nature, brightness identifies, surrounds and reflects the presence of a god."[53] "Joy in the light . . . resounds everywhere in Greek poetry and literature. The attributes that characterize the light show that it is conceived not as something self-evident, but as a heavenly gift: it is the οὐράνιον φώς, the ἀγνὸν φώς, the ἱερὸν φώς."[54]

Conversely, and with only rare exceptions, the gods and goddesses are barred from transcending the boundary of the earth's surface to go below to the realm of Hades and the dead.[55] "Darkness and lack of sun consistently characterize Hades."[56] The permanence and impermeability of this boundary form a constituent part of "the articulation of the universe, the cosmic order which must not be violated."[57] The gods cannot enter a place where light and indeed the sun itself cannot go; if they did so they would risk turning our well-constructed cosmos into an anti-cosmos.[58]

We humans, in contrast, have only the most fleeting experience of this sunlit region in our pitifully short lives, before the inevitable moment comes when our bodies are consigned to the earth and our shadowy souls (*psychai*) begin down their endless journey to nothingness. As Gregory J. Riley so aptly says, for the Greeks "there is no cure for death."[59] The archaic poet Sappho threatens a rival:

---

[53] Eva Parisinou, *The Light of the Greek Gods: The Role of Light in Archaic and Classical Greek Cult* (London: Duckworth, 2000), 1.

[54] Translated from Rudolf Bultmann's "Zur Geschichte der Lichtsymbolik im Altertum," in *idem*, *Exegetica: Aufsätze zur Erforschung des Neuen Testaments* (ed. Erich Dinkler; Tübingen: Mohr, 1967), 323–55, esp. 325 (published originally in *Phil* 97 [1947]: 1–36). Bultmann cites dozens of examples from Archaic and Classical Greek poets on this theme in his article. The theme is truly pervasive, "so und ähnlich klingt es immer," says Bultmann (327). My independent survey of Greek poets produced only one citation in common with his, a lament offered by Iphigeneia (see n. 74 below).

[55] The key exceptions, thus themselves quite revealing on this point, are the transgressive Hermes among Olympian deities and Hekate and Persephone among chthonic divinities. Sourvinou-Inwood says that "the *Homeric Hymn to Demeter* shows that Hermes the god of passages is the only god of the upper world who can cross the infernal frontier . . . as seen in the stories of Herakles [*Od.* 11.625f] and Persephone" (*"Reading" Greek Death*, 105, citing J. Rudhardt, "À propos de l'hymne homérique à Déméter," *Museum Helveticum* 35 [1978]: 1–17).

[56] Sourvinou-Inwood, *"Reading" Greek Death*, 72.

[57] Sourvinou-Inwood, *"Reading" Greek Death*, 62.

[58] "Helios in Hades, instead of shining on mortals and immortal gods, is a threat, of a reversed, disordered world" (Sourvinou-Inwood, *"Reading" Greek Death*, 72 n. 180, comparing *Od.* 12.382–86.

[59] Riley, *Resurrection Reconsidered: Thomas and John in Controversy* (Minneapolis, MN: Fortress, 1995), 24, echoing the chorus in Sophocles' *Electra* 139.

> After death you will be forgotten,
> and there will never be any longing for you, because you have no share
> of the roses of Pieria. Unseen in the house of Hades,
> flown from our midst, you will wander amongst the shadowy dead.[60]

"The poets choose to emphasize the permanence and irreversibility of death. . . . Death is an emptiness, an absence of life."[61]

In an enduring Homeric metaphor, human beings are mere leaves, buffeted by the wind, quickly and inevitably replaced by the next year's growth. In the sixth book of the *Iliad*, the Lycian hero Glaucus, when queried about his lineage, remarks to Diomedes οἵη περ φύλλων γενεή, τοίη δὲ καὶ ἀνδρῶν:

> As is the generation of leaves, so too is the generation of men.
> As for leaves, some the wind pours on the ground, but others
> the burgeoning wood puts forth, and the season of spring returns;
> so of men the one generation comes forth and the other lets go.[62]

The elegiac poet Mimnermus (who flourished in seventh-century Ionia) developed Homer's comparison of human life to the ephemeral quality of leaves as a lament for lost youth. The poet explores this simile by equating our span of youth with one day's length of sunlight:

> And like leaves which the many-flowered season of spring
> brings forth, when they increase suddenly in the rays of the sun,
> we, resembling them, enjoy the flowers of youth for a measure's
> time, learning from the gods neither evil nor good;
> but black Fates of Death stand by, the one holding the end of
> grievous old age, the other of death; and brief is the fruit of youth,
> as lasting as the sun spreading light upon the earth.[63]

---

[60] Sappho frag. 55: κατθάνοισα δὲ κείσῃ/ οὐδέ ποτα μναμοσύνα σέθεν / ἔσσετ᾽ οὐδὲ πόθα εἰς ὕστερον· οὐ γὰρ πεδέχῃς / βρόδων / τὼν ἐκ Πιερίας, ἀλλ᾽ ἀφάνης κἀν Ἀΐδα δόμῳ / φοιτάσῃς πεδ᾽ ἀμαύρων νεκύων ἐκπεποταμένα. Text from David A. Campbell, *Greek Lyric Poetry: A Selection of Early Greek Lyric, Elegiac and Iambic Poetry* (London: Macmillan, 1967), 47, translation by Johnston, *Restless Dead*, 20.

[61] Johnston, *Restless Dead*, 20.

[62] *Iliad* 6.145–50, quoted from Eddie R. Lowry Jr., "Glaucus, the Leaves, and the Heroic Boast of *Iliad* 6.1246–211," in *The Ages of Homer: A Tribute to Emily T. Vermeule* (ed. Jane B. Carter and Sarah P. Morris; Austin, TX: University of Texas Press, 1995), 193–211 (here p. 193).

[63] Mimnermus 2.1–8 (ed. M. L. West, *Iambi et elegi graeci ante Alexandrum cantati* (2nd ed.; Oxford: Clarendon, 1989) 2. 85–86): ἡμεῖς δ᾽, οἷά τε φύλλα φύει πολυάνθερος ὥρη / ἔαρος, ὅτ᾽ αἶψ᾽ αὐγῆς αὔξεται ἠελίου, / τοῖς ἴκελοι πήχυιον ἐπὶ χρόνον ἄνθεσιν ἥβης / τερπόμεθα, πρὸς θεῶν εἰδότες οὔτε κακὸν / οὔτ᾽ ἀγαθέου· Κῆρες δὲ παρεστήκασι μέλαιναι,/ ἡ μὲν ἔχουσα τέλος γήραος ἀργαλέου, / ἡ δ᾽ ἑτέρη θανάτοιο· μίνυνθα δὲ γίνεται ἥβης / καρπός, ὅσον τ᾽ ἐπὶ γῆν κίδναται ἥλιος. I have followed the text and

The image recurs in the fifth-century poet Bacchylides of Ceos, whose *Fifth Ode* describes Heracles' descent to the underworld. There the hero sees "the souls of miserable mortals like the leaves the wind twirls" on the mountainsides. In answer to the sad tale told him by Meleager, Heracles exclaims: θνατοῖσι μὴ φῦναι φέριστον μηδ᾽ ἀελίου προσιδεῖν φέγγος ("for mortals it is best not to be born nor to look upon the light of the sun").[64] Sophocles the Attic tragedian has his chorus, when confronted by the tragic circumstance of Oedipus and Antigone, sing:

> μὴ φῦναι τὸν ἅπαντα νικᾷ λόγον· τὸ δ᾽ ἐπεὶ φανῇ
> βῆναι κεῖθεν ὅθεν περ ἥκει,
> πολὺ δεύτερον, ὡς τάχιστα.

> Not to be born is best of all; next best, by far,
> to look on the light and return with speed
> to the place whence one came.[65]

Coming into this world at birth gives us our first glimpse of that light; death provides our last. "Light marks the experience of the living, who exclusively enjoy the natural light of the sun, while darkness covers the eyes of the dead."[66]

Time and again, beyond the point of cliché, poets describe life here on earth, above the gloom and decay of the underworld, our ultimate and lasting destination, as one brief shining moment. While bathed in that divine light we too may glow.[67] Once sent below, our

---

translation of Lowry, "Glaucus," 193–94 (with πολυάνθερος in the first line for the MS reading πολυάνθεος instead of West's πολυάνθεμος). A slightly longer excerpt is translated in David G. Rice and John E. Stambaugh, *Sources for the Study of Greek Religion* (Missoula, MT: Scholars Press, 1979), 221. For a sensitive treatment of how Mimnermus has altered Homer's perspective see Mark Griffith, "Man and the Leaves: A Study of Mimnermus fr. 2," *California Studies in Classical Antiquity* 8 (1976): 73–88.

[64] Bacchylides, *Ode* 5.1260–62; text and translation Lowry, "Glaucus," 194.

[65] Sophocles, *Oedipus at Colonus* 1224–26; text and translation in Richmond Lattimore, *Themes in Greek and Latin Epitaphs* (Illinois Studies in Language and Literature 28:1–2; Urbana, IL: University of Illinois Press, 1942), 207.

[66] Parisinou, *Light of the Gods*, 166, who comments further: "This belief is repeatedly found in Homer and apparently forms the basis of several equally widespread concepts reflected in literature. These include the eternal brightness of the gods, who do not face the threat of death, and the firm association of the birth-goddess Eileithyia and other kourotrophic goddesses . . . with brightness, since they assist the newly-born in their first passage to the natural light of life." Parisinou provides extensive discussion of the theme of light in Greek cult as evidenced by visual and archaeological sources.

[67] Compare *Gos. Thom.* 24, where the divine light glows from within the "per-

connection with the sun's light is only a faint memory: εἰ δ᾽ οὖν τις ἀκτὶς ἡλίου νιν ἱστορεῖ, remarks the herald in the *Agamemnon* of Menelaus (shipwrecked and feared dead) ("If only some gleam of sun still searches him out").[68]

This perspective on human mortality permeated Mediterranean antiquity and is present in Roman authors much as in Greek sources. The only real exception is found among Platonist philosophers, who speculate about the possible immortality of the soul and its eventual return above to the Good. In the Roman period, philosophers like Seneca and Plutarch adopt something of a dualistic stance: "The true home of man's soul is the heavens and the Light to which he returns at death."[69] Thus these authors echo or anticipate the Gospel of John and *Thomas* in locating 'real life' in some sort of 'heaven'; but *Thomas*' denigration of the material world is much stronger than is the Platonists'.[70]

The common understanding that our 'afterlife' in whatever form was to be experienced below in the underworld is confirmed by the spread in popularity of mystery initiations or the rise of more personal 'salvation' religions of Classical and Hellenistic times. Mystery cults like that of the Great Gods on Samothrace or the better-known Demeter–Kore mysteries at Eleusis offered initiates a "bright and happy" afterlife *in a well-lit region of the underworld*, not in the divine realm of heaven. "Blessed is the mortal on earth who has seen these

---

son of light," with the Greek notion of divine luminosity: "The body of the gods shines with such an intense brilliance that no human being can bear it. Its splendor is blinding. Its radiance robs it of visibility through an excess of light in the way that darkness causes invisibility through a lack of light" (Vernant, *Mortals and Immortals*, 44).

[68] Aeschylus, *Agamemnon* 676, my translation (cf. Lattimore, *Epitaphs*, 161).

[69] Bultmann proposed an influence on Hellenistic philosophy from 'oriental' dualism ("Lichtsymbolik im Altertum," esp. 342–50), though some of these contrasts go back to Orphic teaching of undetermined date. The words quoted are from DeConick's helpful summary of Bultmann's discussion (*Seek to See Him*, 74), which in turn is what pointed me to his article.

[70] Riley offers a fine discussion of Greek views of the body and the soul, with special interest in Homer and the development of philosophical notions of the separability and immortality of the soul (*Resurrection Reconsidered*, 23–58). My colleague Amanda Wilcox points me to Cicero's remarks in his *Tusculan Disputations* 1.75: *Quo cum uenerimus, tum denique uiuemus; nam haec quidem uita mors est, quam lamentari possem, si liberet* ("When we will have come yonder, then finally we will live; for this life indeed is death, which if it were wished, I could bewail"). Based on the inscriptional and burial evidence to be discussed below, however, I do not consider the philosophers' views to have been broadly influential on pervasive pre-Christian (and many popular Christian) views of the afterlife.

rites," says the *Homeric Hymn to Demeter*, "but the uninitiated who has no share in them never has the same lot, *even when departed down to the moldy darkness*."[71] The value of Bacchic mystery initiations in the fifth century and later stemmed mostly from Dionysos' chthonic aspect as a deity associated with the vegetative cycle (parodied in Aristophanes' *Frogs*, where the hapless god of theater must have his ignorance of the underworld relieved). Isis promises her initiate Lucius:

> When you descend to those below, having measured out your lifetime, there also, in the vaulted subterranean world itself, inhabiting the Elysian fields, you will constantly worship me, whom you see, shining in the fields of Acheron and reigning over the inner Stygian reaches, and propitious to you.[72]

Even the Orphic mystagogues, who could offer potential divinization to their initiates, provided maps leading to a more blessed *region of the underworld* in the famous bronze and golden tablets found in Greek and Italian graves.[73]

And so Euripides' heroine Iphigeneia, when forced to contemplate her own tragic and imminent passage below, exclaims κοὐκέτι μοι φῶς οὐδ᾽ ἀηελίου τόδε φέγγος ("no longer for me the daylight, the bright sun"). This is her lament:

> τὸ φῶς τόδ᾽ ἀνθρώποισιν ἥδιστον βλέπειν,
> τὰ νέρθε δ᾽ οὐδέν. μαίνεται δ᾽ ὃς εὔχεται
> θανεῖν. κακῶς ζῆν κρεῖσσον ἢ καλῶς θανεῖν.

> The sweetest thing we humans can see is daylight.
> Below is nothing. Who prays for death is mad.
> Better to live a wretch than to die well![74]

---

[71] *H. Ceres* 480–82: ὄλβιος ὃς τάδ᾽ ὄπωπεν ἐπιχθονίων ἀνθρώπων· / ὃς δ᾽ ἀτελὴς ἱερῶν, ὅς τ᾽ ἄμμορος, οὔ ποθ᾽ ὁμοίων / αἶσαν ἔχει φθίμενός περ ὑπὸ ζόφῳ εὐρώεντι. Text and translation (slightly altered) from Helene P. Foley, ed., *The Homeric Hymn to Demeter: Translation, Commentary, and Interpretive Essays* (Princeton, NJ: Princeton University Press, 1994), 26–27; cf. Rice and Stambaugh, *Sources*, 183; Riley, *Resurrection Reconsidered*, 34–38.

[72] Apuleius, *Metamorphoses* 11.6, quoted from Riley, *Resurrection Reconsidered*, 36.

[73] Basic collection in Martin L. West, *The Orphic Poems* (Oxford: Clarendon, 1983); for analysis see Günther Zuntz, *Persephone: Three Essays on Religion and Thought in Magna Graecia* (Oxford: Clarendon, 1971); Fritz Graf, *Eleusis und die orphische Dichtung Athens in vorhellenistischer Zeit* (Religionsgeschictliche Versuche und Arbeiten 32; Berlin: de Gruyter, 1974); Robert Parker, *Miasma: Pollution and Purification in Early Greek Religion* (Oxford: Clarendon, 1983), 281–307; Walter Burkert, *Ancient Mystery Cults* (Cambridge, MA: Harvard University Press, 1987); Simon Price, *Religions of the Ancient Greeks* (Cambridge, MA: Cambridge University Press, 1999), 119–23.

[74] Euripides, *Iphigeneia at Aulis* 1281–82, 1250–52; text Lattimore, *Epitaphs*, 161, my translation; also cited by Bultmann, "Lichtsymbolik im Alterum," 328.

Thus the gods (and light) inhabit the heavens, the dead (and darkness) occupy the earth below, while the intermediate region is shared between immortals and humans in our short span of life. In a way, adopting the image of *Gos. Thom.* 86, we could say that the gods, who move freely between the upper world and the surface of the earth, play the part of birds with their nests; the dead are the foxes with their dens, dwelling below ground, yet when hungry able to range around the earth's surface in search of prey; while we children of humanity have no lasting place in this world.

Thomas seems to accept much of this picture: the sharp distinction between the divine world above and the gloomy world of death below, in particular, and the temporary nature of our own sojourn on this earth. But in *Thomas* the despair or resignation of the Greeks has been rendered more horrible: even our brief 'moment in the sun' is a cruel illusion. *Thomas* has reversed the scale of values, imparting not the bright light of heaven to our place on earth, in the sort of reflected glory of the Greek poetic imagination, but instead asserting, time and again, that our world is thoroughly, pervasively, and irredeemably infected by the death and decay of the dark underworld of ancient anxieties. As people walk about this world, and think they are alive, they are in reality walking corpses, they are zombies, the living dead. *Gos. Thom.* 11: "The dead are not alive, and the living will not die." The world of light has collapsed upon and within the darkness and indeed has become one and the same as the gloom below. Only by recognizing one's true character as bearers of the true light within, as "children of the Living Father" (*Gos. Thom.* 3), might one make it back home, as is explained in *Gos. Thom.* 50.

4. Thomas *and the Discourse of the Dead*

Those who travel around the Mediterranean and pass through the gates of ancient cities, whether in Greece, Italy, Turkey, or the Hellenized Near East, will have noticed a striking feature of the ancient Mediterranean landscape, quite different from our modern sensibilities: the placement of the dead. From the emergence of the Greek city-state in the eighth century BCE, the dead were no longer buried within city walls, but instead were set away from the civic center and the sacred precincts of the immortal gods. As the Archaic and Classical city developed its sense of place and character, the dead were banished save the numinous remains or at least gravesites of

founding heroes.[75] "Such extramural burial symbolically distanced
the dead from the living."[76] Among the worst acts of sacrilege for a
Greek or Roman was to kill or (worse) to die within a sanctuary.[77]
One of the strangest aspects of early Christianity from the Roman
perspective was the church's intense focus on and glorification of
death: the death of martyrs and of course the death of Jesus Christ.

For this reason, due to this central sacrality accorded to death,
we who live in Christian or post-Christian societies are accustomed
to encountering the graves and tombs of our dead not merely within
the city limits but even in churchyards, with some important people—bishops, patrons, and kings—buried right within the church
itself, with relics of the saints given place of honor underneath the
high altar.[78] From the Greek and Roman religious perspective this
practice is an abomination, a shocking breach of the fundamental
division of the place of the gods apart from our realm of mortal
existence and death. The dead must be disposed of not merely outside of town but out of view, down in the "moldy darkness," away
from the sight and consciousness of the shining gods above.

As the ancient traveler approached a city in the time and region
that the *Gospel of Thomas* was composed, however, he or she would
encounter countless monuments of the dead, thickly flanking the
roads in and out of the city.[79] The graves would be marked in some

[75] Donna C. Kurtz and John Boardman, *Greek Burial Customs* (Ithaca, NY: Cornell
University Press, 1971); Ian Morris, *Burial and Society: The Rise of the Greek City-State*
(Cambridge, MA: Cambridge University Press, 1987) and *idem, Death-Ritual and Social
Structure in Classical Antiquity* (Cambridge, MA: Cambridge University Press, 1992);
Sourvinou-Inwood, *"Reading" Greek Death*, 413–44; Richard Seaford, *Reciprocity and
Ritual: Homer and Tragedy in the Developing City-State* (Oxford: Clarendon, 1994), 74–143;
Johnston, *Restless Dead*, 3–81; Robert Garland, *The Greek Way of Death* (2nd ed.;
Ithaca, NY: Cornell University Press, 2001).

[76] Johnston, *Restless Dead*, 95–96.

[77] See especially Parker's chapter "Birth and Death" in *Miasma*, 32–73.

[78] The comments of Armando Petrucci are particularly eloquent in his book
Writing the Dead: Death and Writing Strategies in the Western Tradition (trans. M. Sullivan;
Stanford, CA: Stanford University Press, 1998); see his chapters "The Names and
the Crosses" (pp. 24–34) and "Writing the Great" (35–43) on Christian practices
in the transition from antiquity to the Middle Ages.

[79] Even literary "epitaphs mention explicitly that the grave is by the roadside, as
graves normally were. . . . and the more frequented the road, the better the site"
says Sally C. Humphreys, "Family Tombs and Tomb Cult in Ancient Athens:
Tradition or Traditionalism?," *JHS* 100 (1980): 96–126 (quote from p. 100). According
to I. Morris (*Death-Ritual and Social Structure*, 156) more than 180,000 sepulchral
inscriptions survive from the western Roman Empire, with about 10,000 from
Classical Attica alone (5th–4th centuries BCE). See further Lilian H. Jeffery, "The
Inscribed Gravestones of Archaic Attica," *ABSA* 57 (1962): 115–53.

way: by a simple slab, a stele, a pot, often ornamented further by grieving or ambitious relatives with sculpture or other art.[80] What is more, these roadside monuments did not simply face the roadway standing silent; the markers were painted or inscribed with words and pictures identifying the deceased and usually offering a memorial of his or her life, achievements, and family connections. "The erection of a tumulus crowned by an upright stone or by a planted wooden post marked the desire to inscribe the presence of the dead on the surface of the ground, too, and to mark it out to the living forever."[81]

Funerary or sepulchral epigrams reveal the widespread acceptance throughout the ancient Mediterranean of the stark division between the world of divine light and the gloomy place of death that we have seen expressed so powerfully in Greek poetry. The epigraphic evidence is ubiquitous throughout the Greek and Roman world for over a thousand years.[82] Here some consideration of the rhetorical strategies of funerary inscriptions will be helpful. Epitaphs are not meant as mute ornaments, but function more actively as attempts at communication. George B. Walsh has called this aspect of sepulchral speech educative: "An inscribed stone was meant not just to announce 'here lies so-and-so,' but also to disseminate this information as widely as possible. It had to incite an act of learning by way of its inscription. . . . Epitaph strives to motivate the reader, and to make him reach for knowledge in which he has no natural interest."[83]

Some of what the dead attempt to offer the living is the perspective of their own experience of the contrast between life and death. Many

---

[80] Some good examples in K. Friis Johansen, *The Attic Grave-Reliefs of the Classical Period: An Essay in Interpretation* (Copenhagen: Munksgaard, 1951); Christoph W. Clairmont, *Gravestone and Epigram: Greek Memorials from the Archaic and Classical Period* (Mainz: von Zabern, 1970); Joseph W. Day, "Rituals in Stone: Early Greek Grave Epigrams and Monuments," *JHS* 109 (1989): 16–28. On more general aspects see the works cited in nn. 52 and 75.

[81] Petrucci, *Writing the Dead*, 6, quoting Vernant.

[82] Lattimore's *Themes in Greek and Latin Epitaphs* is still a most useful collection and survey; for the Roman material see also the earlier studies of Bruno Lier, "Topica carminum sepulcralium latinorum," *Phil* 62 (1903): 445–77; Judson Allen Tolman, Jr. *A Study of the Sepulchral Inscriptions in Buecheler's "Carmina Epigraphica Latina"* (Chicago, IL: The University of Chicago Press, 1910); Édouard Galletier, *Étude sur la poésie funéraire romaine d'après les inscriptions* (Paris: Hachette, 1922). Morris' chapter "Famous Last Words: The Inscribed Tombstone" (*Death-Ritual and Social Structure*, 156–73) provides a useful archaeological and economic corrective to these largely literary treatments.

[83] George B. Walsh, "Callimachean Passages: The Rhetoric of Epitaph in Epigram," *Arethusa* 24 (1991): 77–105 (quote from p. 78).

epitaphs picture the deceased person as having left the realm of life
and light for that of death and darkness. For example, an epitaph
for a young woman of Thebes describes her in these terms:

ἥτις ἔλιπε φάος ἐννέα καὶ δέκ᾽ ἐτῶν

she who left the light at age nineteen.[84]

A girl from Roman-age Gazacene is described thus:

ἑπταέτην δὲ σεισμὸς καὶ μοῖρα γλυκεροῦ φάους ἐστέρεσεν.

She was seven years old when Fate and an earthquake
deprived her of sweet daylight.[85]

A gladiator struck down in his moment of victory left this epitaph
at Amisos:

ἀλλά με μοῖρ᾽ ὀλοὴ καὶ σουμμάρου δόλος αἰνὸς
ἔκτανον, ἐκ δὲ φάους ἤλυθον εἰς Ἀίδην.

Destructive Fate and the deadly treachery of a scorekeeper
killed me, and I left the daylight and went to Hades.[86]

The *Palatine Anthology* contains many literary epigrams composed in
imitation of sepulchral verse. This is what Philip of Thessaloniki
wrote upon encountering "a dismembered corpse cast up by the sea":

οὗτος ὁ πουλυμερὴς εἷς ἦν ποτε. φεῦ μακαριστοί,
ὅσσοι ἀπ᾽ ὠδίνων οὐκ ἴδον ἠέλιον.

These scattered fragments were once a man complete. Ah, how blessed are
those who never emerged from birth-pangs to see the light of the sun.[87]

---

[84] *IG* 7.254.1; text Lattimore, *Epitaphs*, 163, my translation.

[85] John G. Anderson, Franz Cumont and Henri Grégoire, eds., *Studia Pontica III:
Recueil des inscriptions grecques et latines du Pont et de l'Arménie* (Brussels: Lamertin, 1910)
no. 139 (dated 235/6 CE); text and translation Lattimore, *Epitaphs*, 147.

[86] *Studia Pontica* no. 7.3–4; text and translation Lattimore, *Epitaphs*, 145. I have
rendered the unattested word σουμμάρου as 'scorekeeper' on the analogy of the
late Latin use of the term *summarius* for an accountant. Liddell and Scott list an
inscription from Ancyra (SEG 6.60) using the term σουμμαρούδης, which they gloss
as Latin *summarudis*.

[87] *AP* 7.383.7–8; text and translation Lattimore, *Epitaphs*, 173, with many paral-
lels. The fascinating relationship between sepulchral and literary epigrams is one of
the themes explored in the valuable study of Jon S. Bruss, "Hidden Presences:
Monuments, Gravesites, and Corpses in Greek Funerary Epigram" (Ph.D. diss.,
University of Minnesota, 2000); see also Antony Erik Raubitschek, "Das Denkmal-
Epigramm," *L'Epigramme grecque: Fondation Hardt* 14 (1968): 3–36; reprinted in *idem,
The School of Hellas* (New York, NY: Oxford University Press, 1991), 245–65.

The span of human life continues to be compared to the shining of the sun, as in this elegiac couplet inscribed for a deceased couple at third-century BCE Arcesine:

ἡμᾶς καὶ ζῶντας κοινὸμ βίον ἥλιος ὥρα
 καὶ τάφος εἰς φθιμένους δέξατο γηραλείους.

When we lived, the sun looked down on our life together;
and now we are dead, in our old age we have a single tomb.[88]

An inscription now kept in the British Museum makes explicit the sharp contrast between our world and that 'other cosmos'—truly 'not-a-cosmos'—of dark disorder:

καταλίψας ταῦτα εἰς ἕτερον κόσμον ἄκοσμον ἀπελήλυθε,
 ὅπου οὐδὲν ὑπάρχει, εἰ μὴ μόνον σκοτίη.

Leaving these things he went to another and disorderly world,
where there is nothing save only darkness.[89]

These inscriptions help us see that this perspective is not the poetical conceit of a few privileged authors, or merely a literary cliché, but instead a widely shared understanding of ancient people: "much of the importance of epitaphs lies in the fact that they cut through the strata of society from top to bottom."[90]

Even more significant, when making connections with *Gos. Thom.* 42, we find that quite often the gravestones speak out directly to those walking past them.[91] From Panticapeum on the Bosporus, for example, we read this epitaph of the Roman period:

νῦν δ᾽ ἔτι κἂν νεκύεσσι χαίρειν δ᾽ ἔπος αὐδῶ.

And now even from among the dead I bid you hail.[92]

---

[88] *IG* 12.7.113, text and translation Lattimore, *Epitaphs*, 275.

[89] Edward L. Hicks et al., eds., *The Collection of Ancient Greek Inscriptions in the British Museum* (Oxford: Clarendon, 1874–1916; repr. Milan: Cisalpino, 1977–79) 4. no.1113 (provenance unknown); text and translation Lattimore, *Epitaphs*, 76.

[90] Lattimore, *Themes in Greek and Latin Epitaphs*, 16.

[91] For a basic collection of epitaphs in this style see Werner Peek, *Griechische Vers-Inschriften I: Grab-Epigramme* (Berlin: Akademie-Verlag, 1955) nos. 1209–1247 (pp. 357–68), with many other relevant examples elsewhere in his corpus.

[92] Basilius Latyshev, *Inscriptiones orae septentrionalis Ponti Euxini graecae et latinae* (St. Petersburg: Societas Archaeologica Imperii Russici, 1885–1916; repr. Hildesheim: Olms, 1965) vol. 4, no. 317.5; text and translation Lattimore, *Epitaphs*, 57.

These stones offer not some 'objective' third-person description of the
deceased by a bereaved survivor, but call out to the living in the
persona of the dead, often naming the wayfarer as—*passer-by*. "Epitaphs
take aim at a reader in motion, someone walking near a monument,
who must pause and read."[93] Addressing the unknown traveler becomes
a gambit for attention. "When the dead wish to touch us, they must
make us forget our business and pause a little longer."[94]

Dead people, in Greek and Roman sensibility, had only a marginal and shadowy existence. But to the extent that they did experience some sort of reality, this was nearly always focalized at the
spot of their burial, at their tomb.[95] The dead person trapped below,
sunk down into the earth, could hope at times to share a brief existence above the ground by mobilizing the voice and tongue of the
living passing by.[96] Interactions between the living and especially the
unhappy dead could be fearsome and needed to be controlled.
Though the unburied dead would typically be thought likely to haunt
and harass their killers or undutiful survivors, once buried, the
deceased was successfully and finally consigned to the underworld.[97]
The dead "liked to be greeted by the living who passed by."[98] Pausing
to read a dead person's words on his or her gravestone could itself
serve as a brief act of propitiation. "For a reader who walks among
the gravestones, simply pausing and uttering the name of the dead
constitutes a sufficient gesture of acknowledgment."[99]

One of the earliest and most studied examples (standing in the
place of honor in Kaibel's pioneering collection of epigrams) is this
elegy from sixth-century BCE Attica:

---

[93] Walsh, "Callimachean Passages," 79.
[94] Walsh, "Callimachean Passages," 80.
[95] On this point see the valuable study of Stephen E. Potthoff, "Refreshment and
Reunion in the Garden of Light" (Ph.D. diss., University of Minnesota, 2000),
10–41.
[96] Garland surveys Greek practices in visiting dead relatives in *The Greek Way of
Death*, 104–20. Riley discusses Greek and Roman family cult of the dead in *Resurrection
Reconsidered*, 43–47, stating that the dead "exhibited an effective spiritual presence
in the daily experience of the living," though, as his examples show, their presence
was effectively restricted to the gravesite itself, with uncanny powers of the dead
ascribed mostly to the special classes of heroes and the 'unhappy dead.' On the
latter category see Johnston, *Restless Dead*.
[97] Sourvinou-Inwood, *"Reading" Greek Death*, 109.
[98] Johnston, *Restless Dead*, 27.
[99] Walsh, "Callimachean Passages," 78–79.

εἶτ᾿ ἀστός τις ἀνὴρ εἴτε ξένος ἄλλοθεν ἐλθών,
  Τέττιχον οἰκτίρας ἄνδρ᾿ ἀγαθὸν <u>παρίτω</u>.

Whether you are a citizen or a stranger coming from elsewhere,
  take pity on Tettichos, a brave man, and then <u>pass on by</u>.[100]

Frequently the wayfarer is asked to pause and read, if only for a moment, as in this example from Cyprus:

κἂν τροχάδην βαίνῃς, φίλε ὦ <u>παροδεῖτα</u>, βαιὸν ἐπίσχου.

Even if you are going fast, pause for just a little, dear <u>passer-by</u>.[101]

Epitaphs dealt with the practical issue of having somehow to grab the attention and interest of busy and distracted travelers. Consider this case from Apamea:

Βαιὸν μεῖνον, ξεῖνε, καὶ ὕστερον ἔνθα <u>πορεύσῃ</u>,
  μὴ προλιπὼν στήλλην, ἀλλὰ μαθὼν τί λέγει.

Stop for a little, stranger, and then <u>go on your way</u>;
  do not leave the stele at once, but first see what it says.[102]

This couplet from Roman-period Paros uses *Thomas'* word παράγειν:

Σωχάρμου <u>παράγοντες</u> ἐμὸν τάφον εἴπατε χαίρειν,
  εἴ τι καὶ ἐς φθιμένους μοῖρα δέδωκε λαλεῖν.

You who <u>pass by</u> the tomb of Socharmus, bid me hail,
  if indeed Fate allows people to talk even with the dead.[103]

---

[100] *IG* 1.463 (= *IG* 1² 976; 560–550 BCE); full text in Georg Kaibel, *Epigrammata Graeca ex lapidibus conlecta* (Berlin, 1878; repr. Hildesheim: Olms, 1965) no. 1; Lier, "Topica carminum sepulcralium," 468; and Johannes Geffcken, *Griechische Epigramme* (Heidelberg: Winter, 1916) no. 47; text, translation, and discussion in Lattimore, *Epitaphs*, 231; Cecil Maurice Bowra, *Early Greek Elegists* (Cambridge, MA: Harvard University Press, 1938), 177; Peek, *Griechische Vers-Inschriften*, no. 1226; Jeffery, "Inscribed Gravestones of Attica," no. 34; Humphreys, "Family Tomb and Tomb Cult," 100; Peter Allan Hansen, *Carmina epigraphica graeca* (Berlin: de Gruyter, 1983) no. 13; Day, "Rituals in Stone," 17–22; Petrucci, *Writing the Dead*, 11; and most recently Bruss, "Hidden Presences," 118.

[101] Kaibel, *Epigrammata graeca*, no. 288; text and translation Lattimore, *Epitaphs*, 231.

[102] Kaibel, *Epigrammata graeca*, no. 388; text and translation Lattimore, *Epitaphs*, 232. Lattimore lists hundreds of additional examples of address to the passer-by in Greek and Latin sepulchral inscriptions in *Epitaphs*, 230–34.

[103] Kaibel, *Epigrammata graeca*, no. 217.1–2; text and translation (slightly altered) Lattimore, *Epitaphs*, 56 (with line endings largely restored). Note that Socharmus addresses his potential audience with the same word found in *Gos. Thom.* 42: παράγοντες.

The anxiety expressed in the last line about the reality of conversation between the living and the dead exposes the fundamental irony of first-person sepulchral inscriptions.

Other examples of direct address from the deceased to the passer-by can easily be multiplied. "The first person transforms a narrative into a dramatic text."[104] So this woman's tombstone from Sardis:

ἀλλ᾽ ὦ ξένε, τὸμ μ᾽ ὑπὸ τύμβωι
θέντα πόσιν μύθοις εὐλογέων <u>παρίοις</u>.

But stranger, speak in praise of my husband,
who laid me under the tomb, and so <u>pass on by</u>.[105]

The wayfarer who sounds out this text will in effect stage a brief enactment of a funerary eulogy on behalf of the deceased widow: "All praising epitaphs are in a sense mimetic; whoever reads one aloud plays the role of a praise poet."[106] Sepulchral speech can coyly seduce the traveler into performing this gesture of admiration, this momentary mimesis. From Athens:

ζηλωτὸν στέφανον τοῖς παριοῦσιν ὁδόν.

A garland admired by <u>those who pass along the road</u>.[107]

Perhaps the custom of first-person address began with attempts to allay the very real concern that one's tomb might not be ignored but rather tampered with or plundered. Better, it seems, for the dead to gain even a brief prayer from a wayfarer, a mere 'gesture of acknowledgment,' than sacrilege.[108] So this example from first-century CE Crete:

---

[104] Day, "Rituals in Stone," 26. David E. Aune says, "In epitaphs from both east and west the deceased speaks to posterity in the first person" (*The New Testament in Its Literary Environment* [Philadelphia, PA: Westminster, 1987], 28). Aune connects funerary epigraphy with the origins of the literary genre biography: "Obituaries were important in the development of ancient biography. In Greece and Rome dirges, eulogies, and epitaphs provided sketches of individual lives" (p. 27).

[105] SEG 4.633 (4th cent. BCE); text and translation Lattimore, *Epitaphs*, 231.

[106] Day, "Rituals in Stone," 26; Sourvinou-Inwood argues against Day for a more symbolic reading of these ritual factors: *"Reading" Greek Death*, 174–75 n. 277.

[107] Kaibel, *Epigrammata graeca*, no. 133; text and translation Lattimore, *Epitaphs*, 231.

[108] According to Lattimore, "by far the earliest case we have, a seventh-century epigram from Rhodes," was written by the dead man Idamaneus "while he was still living": σᾶμα τόζ᾽ Ἰδαμενεὺς ποίησα, ἵνα κλέος εἴη · Ζεὺ δέ νιν ὅστις πημαίνοι, λειόλη θείη. "I, Idameneus, built this tomb to (my own) glory. May Zeus utterly destroy anyone who disturbs it" (*Epitaphs*, 109, citing *IG* 12.1.737). Lattimore gives many examples of this sort of warning against harming tombs (*Epitaphs*, 108–25).

μή μου ἐνυβρίξῃς ἄγνον τάφον, ὦ παροδεῖτα,
   μή σοι μηνίσῃ πικρὸν ἐπ᾽ Ἀγεσίλας
Περσεφόνα τε κόρα Δαμάτερος· ἀλλὰ παρέρπων
   εἶπον Ἀρατίῳ· γαῖαν ἔχοις ἐλαφράν.

You who <u>pass by</u>, do not insult my sacred grave,
lest you incur the sharp anger of Agesilas and
Persephone, maiden daughter of Demeter.
But as you <u>go quietly by</u>, say to Aratius:
'May you have earth light upon you.'[109]

Still, as is illustrated by this third-century CE epitaph from the Piraeus, passers-by could also be warned with less direct reference to the deceased in the third person:

ἤν <u>παρίοις</u> εὔφημος ἀεί, ξένε, μηδ᾽ ἐπὶ λύμῃ
   χεῖρα βάλοις· φθιμένων ὠκυτάτη Νέμεσις.

Stranger, be ever respectful in speech to her whom <u>you pass by</u>, nor lay hands upon her in outrage. The vengeance of the dead is very swift.[110]

These nearly ubiquitous inscriptions, I submit, offer the most significant cultural context within which to hear Jesus' admonition in *Gos. Thom.* 42 to 'become passers-by'—the discourse of the dead.

Ancient readers of and listeners to the *Gospel of Thomas* would have made this connection easily and immediately. Their daily passage alongside the roadside graves had accustomed them to this particular significance, this specific association of the term 'passer-by' with the voice of the dead speaking from the tomb.[111] Through the clever device of direct address to the living wayfarer, grave markers momentarily implicate the living in an eerie sort of conversation with the dead. This dialogue can sometimes evoke the cultural traditions of funerary praise (eulogy) or lament (threnody). As Joseph Day has written, "passersby are asked to reiterate the ritual lament in the present,"

For a more recent discussion see J. H. M. Strubbe, "'Cursed Be He that Moves My Bones,'" in *Magika Hiera: Ancient Greek Magic and Religion* (ed. Christopher A. Faraone and Dirk Obbink; New York, NY: Oxford University Press, 1991), 33–59.

[109] Kaibel, *Epigrammata graeca*, no. 195; text and translation Lattimore, *Epitaphs*, 109. The last line is particularly favored in Latin inscriptions to the point of frequent abbreviation: *S.T.T.L.* (*sit tibi terra leuis*); see Lattimore, *Epitaphs*, 65–74.

[110] Kaibel, *Epigrammata graeca*, no. 119.3–4; text and translation Lattimore, *Epitaphs*, 109–10.

[111] The very same linguistic formula is employed as in the funerary epigrams: the prefix παρα-, meaning beside, along, or by, attached to a verb or noun of motion: ἄγω, εἶμι, or ὁδεύς, ὁδίτης.

an activity, says Walsh, that "itself propitiates the dead."[112] But the aspects of vivification and engagement with the dead seem paramount to me; and that is the context of warning in *Gos. Thom.* 42.

Often the deceased admit their dependence and their lack of the autonomous strength they exercised while alive. So this inscription from Athens in the Roman period:

> καὶ τὸ πρὶν ἐν πολέμοις τηρῶν πύργον, παροδῖτα,
>   καὶ νῦν τηρήσω, ὦ δύναμαι, νέκυς ὤν.

> Wayfarer, of old I guarded this tower in war, and now
>   also, though dead, I guard it as well as I can.[113]

Thus the dead could be re-vivified, at least for a moment, when a passer-by would pause and give voice to their script, by reading the inscription aloud. This scenario provides much of the wit and poignancy of the funerary epigrams I have selected here. In one rather alarming instance from the Troad, passers-by are caught up in a tale of adultery and murderous violence:

> My name, wayfarer (παροδεῖτα), is Aphrodisius: I am an Alexandrian, and my coffin is the middle one. I am dead by a most pitiful death, all through my wife, a vile, false mate, may Zeus destroy her utterly. Her secret lover, who was disgracing my name, dragged me to a cliff and threw me off like a discus, young as I was: for I was in my twentieth year when the spinning Fates made Hades a present of me. Farewell.[114]

For the brief moment that living travelers might pause and speak out loud the script of the dead, this murder victim could grasp for a share of their existence somehow, transcending the limits of the grave, be present however briefly in the zone the Greek poets so vividly describe as the realm of sunlight, escaping the molder of the dead below.

Sometimes inscriptions acknowledge the impossibility of true escape. From Rome, in the third century CE, another grave inscription in verse:

> Μή μου παρέλθῃς τὸ ἐπίγραμμα, ὁδοιπόρε,
>   ἀλλὰ σταθεὶς ἄκουε καὶ μαθὼν ἄπι·

---

[112] Day, "Rituals in Stone," 27–28; Walsh, "Callimachean Passages," 79. Day continues: "These are not factual reports of funerals or quotations of threnodies. Narrative and mimesis are processes, not of recreating something in detail, but of substituting for it a selection of typical features."

[113] Kaibel, *Epigrammata graeca*, no. 111; text Lattimore, *Epitaphs*, 58, my translation.

[114] Kaibel, *Epigrammata graeca*, no. 336; text and translation Lattimore, *Epitaphs*, 118.

οὐκ ἔστι ἐν Ἅδου πλοῖον, οὐ πορθμεὺς Χάρων,
οὐκ Αἴακος κλειδοῦχος, οὐχὶ Κέρβερος κύων.
ἡμεῖς δὲ πάντες οἱ κάτω τεθνηκότες
ὀστέα, τέφρα γεγόναμεν, ἄλλο δὲ οὐδὲ ἕν.
εἴρηκά σοι ὀρθῶς· ὕπαγε, ὁδοίπορε,
μὴ καὶ τεθνακώς ἀδόλεσχός σοι φανῶ.

Do not pass by my epitaph, o wayfarer,
but stand—listen—and when you have heard, then go on your way.
There is no boat in Hades, no ferryman Charon,
no Aiakos, keeper of the keys, no dog Cerberus.
All of us who have died and gone below
are bones and ashes, nothing else.
I have spoken with you truthfully. Go away, traveler!
lest I appear to you, though dead, to be speaking idle words.[115]

Walsh quotes another delightful example of the playful, even ventri-loquistic ambiguity that can at times emerge in these meta-conversations with the dead:

στῆθι φίλον παρὰ τύμβον, ὁδοιπόρε· τίς με κελεύει;
φρουρὸς ἐγώ σε λέων. αὐτὸς ὁ λαίνεος;
αὐτός. φωνήεις πόθεν ἔπλεο; δαίμονος αὐδῇ
ἀνδρὸς ὑποχθονίου . . .

"Stop by my tomb, wayfarer."—"Who says so?"
"I, the watching lion."—"The stone lion, no other?"
"No other."—"Where did you get your voice?"
"From a man's spirit below . . ."[116]

From Larisa, in northern Greece, my last example:

οὐδὲν γὰρ πλέον ἐστί θανόντα γὰρ οὐδὲν ἐγείρει
ἢ τείρειν ψυχὴν ἰώντων μόνον· ἄλλο γὰρ οὐδέν.

There is nothing more—nothing awakens to the dead—than to afflict the mind of passers-by. There is nothing else.[117]

Bringing our discussion back within the literary and theological context of the *Gospel of Thomas*, we can draw out some intriguing implications.

---

[115] Kaibel, *Epigrammata graeca*, no. 646 (3rd/4th cent.); text Lattimore, *Epitaphs*, 75, translation Rice and Stambaugh, 244–45.

[116] Peek, *Griechische Vers-Inschriften I*, 555, no. 1843 (text); translation Walsh, "Callimachean Passages," 85.

[117] *IG* 9.2, no. 640.8–9; text Lattimore, *Epitaphs*, 77, translation Rice & Stambaugh, *Sources*, 243.

6. *Conclusion*

As we have seen, for *Thomas* our world is a dark and forbidding and foreign place, not at all the happy and blessed arena of light and life pictured by Greek poetry. To use the language of the text, in short, the world is a *corpse*. Once again, *Gos. Thom.* 56: "Whoever has found the world has found a corpse—and the world is not worthy of such a person!" In this intellectual environment, Jesus' command in *Gos. Thom.* 42 to be or to become passers-by takes on a new and powerful significance.[118]

Jesus speaks in this gospel, we are told repeatedly, as the *living one* (incipit; 37; 52; 59), the one who *comes from the light* (50; 61; 83), indeed, the one who *is the light* (77). So when this Jesus addresses us using the vocabulary of funerary epigraphy, we need to stop for a moment and take notice. In a beautiful and moving paradox, Jesus speaks not *from* the grave, as though he were merely a dead and departed shade yearning for some momentary shadow-life by engaging the living traveler in conversation, however witty or jocular or pathetic; rather, Jesus speaks as one who has transcended death. His is the voice not *from* but instead *from beyond* the grave, from far outside the corpse or tomb that is our world. Jesus is not bound by the pious conventions of pagan myth that would forbid a god passage from the world of the light to that of death and back again.

When Jesus urges the readers of *Thomas* to become passers-by, he tells them not to linger in this world, not to be caught up in the trap of conversation, or better, relations with the "living dead" all around them. Just like the travelers that the buried dead attempt to ensnare through witty epitaph into conversation, acknowledgment, and thus shadowy vivification, the "children of the living Father" are objects of seduction from the "dead who are not alive" (*Gos. Thom.* 11). Instead of responding to the invitation to energize and validate the dead through mimetic performance, instead of engagement and entanglement with this world of corruption, the "living who will

---

[118] I made this suggestion in passing in my 1997 article "Death, the Body, and the World," 533, an observation that I now take the opportunity to spell out more fully. Kathleen E. Corley has adopted a similar interpretation in her book *Women and the Historical Jesus: Feminist Myths of Christian Origins* (Santa Rosa, CA: Polebridge Press, 2002), pp. 75, 175; my thanks to her for sharing the relevant section in pre-publication form.

not die" must recognize the world for the corpse it truly is and refuse to be caught up in its ways (*Gos. Thom.* 27; 50; 86). They must not pause on their journeys, they must pass by and through this life and this world, to escape the limits of material bodies, their true graves or tombs, to reach their heavenly home above in the realm of light. They must at all costs avoid being "drawn back to the world, without even noticing it."[119] Recognized as children of life and light, readers of this gospel can escape the world to return to the place of their beginning and their end, to have God's mysteries disclosed to them, as they gaze upon the divine itself.[120]

[119] So Haenchen, *Botschaft*, 50–61, as summarized by Marjanen, "Is *Thomas* a Gnostic Gospel?," 117.

[120] *Gos. Thom.* 50; 21; 28; 37; 18; 49; 23; 22; 62; 108; 15. An earlier form of this essay was delivered as a public lecture on "The World of the *Gospel of Thomas*" to a very engaging audience at Rhodes College in Memphis in March 2002. My thanks to Professors David H. Sick and Kenny Morrell of the Program in Greek and Roman Studies for arranging a most delightful and stimulating visit.

CHAPTER FOUR

THE TWENTY-FOUR PROPHETS OF ISRAEL ARE DEAD: *GOSPEL OF THOMAS* 52 AS A CRITIQUE OF EARLY CHRISTIAN HERMENEUTICS

MILTON MORELAND

Similar to what we find in the study of other early Christian groups who were responsible for our extant first- and second-century literary sources, the *Gospel of Thomas* gives us an insight into early Christian myth-making that occurs in the process of social formation. In the process of forming, differentiating, and legitimating their group, the authors of *Thomas* adopted, developed, and edited a set of sayings attributed to Jesus that contain the group's basic mythology.[1] In this mythology, the Thomasine community seems to have intentionally— and often strikingly—distinguished itself from other early Christian and Jewish communities. For example, unlike most other early Christian literature, *Thomas* shows a lack of interest in connecting Jesus to the motifs and epochs of the Hebrew epic, rejects common forms of Jewish ritual, and presents an idea about the presence of the "kingdom of God" that challenges the early Christian idea of a 'second coming.' In the present chapter, I examine the possible early Christian debate that is revealed in *Gos. Thom.* 52 between the Thomasine community, which had rejected the practice of linking Jesus to the Hebrew scriptures, and many other early Christian groups whose literature reveals that this practice was very common. Like several other *Thomas* sayings that were designed as scholastic dialogues between Jesus and his "disciples," *Gos. Thom.* 52 was formulated in order to illustrate the way that the Thomasine group distinguished

---

[1] I employ the terms "group" and "community" ("Thomasine community") in this essay in a broad sense, with no intention of suggesting the size and particular organizational features of the membership. The terms simply represent the common hypothesis that the sayings in the *Gospel of Thomas* derived from a group that was concerned with basic community functions, as is clear from the content of the sayings, such as group boundaries, ethics, rituals, myths, exclusion of non-members, etc.

itself from other early Christian communities, particularly with regard to their understanding of the use of the Hebrew scriptures.

While the distinction that the authors of *Thomas* made between their movement and characteristics of "common Judaism" has been a long-held interest of several scholars (with primary reference to *Gos. Thom.* 6, 14, 39, 43, 53, 102, 104),[2] more attention recently has been paid to the often polemical rhetoric of group boundaries that appears in the gospel. Many of the sayings have as their primary function the instruction to separate the Thomasine group from other forms of early Christianity. The most common form in *Thomas* for expressing opposition to other forms of early Christian practice and beliefs was the dialogue sayings between Jesus and his "disciples." The basis of the disagreements in these dialogue sayings can be categorized into four types: (A) the divergent ideas regarding the usefulness of the Jewish heritage and rituals (*Gos. Thom.* 6, 14, 53, 60, 104, and possibly 12, 99, and 114); (B) the corresponding divergence between *Thomas* and the opposing Christian groups that were beginning to systematically link Jesus to the Hebrew epic (*Gos. Thom.* 43 [?], 52); (C) the divergent views of the status of the "kingdom" as present reality verses future occurrence (*Gos Thom.* 3, 20, 22, 24, 37, 51, and 113); and (D) a basic conflict over the purpose of Jesus (*Gos. Thom.* 13 and 91). Although reference will be made in the present study to the logia that introduce types A, C, and D, my primary focus is on the way that the community used the dialogue format to counter Christians who, according to *Thomas*, linked themselves and their mythology too closely to Judaism and the Hebrew epic (disagreement type B). Since these oppositional sayings (like *Gos. Thom.* 52) are found in the form of dialogues that use the ancient literary motif of chreiai to express the disagreement between Thomasine and other Christian groups, I begin the essay with a brief overview of the use of chreiai in ancient literature in order to better understand the possible reasons why the community selected this type of rhetorical pattern to express their displeasure with competing ideology.

---

[2] See the review of scholarship and treatment of this issue by Antti Marjanen, "*Thomas* and Jewish Religious Practices," in *Thomas at the Crossroads: Essays on the Gospel of Thomas* (ed. R. Uro; Studies of the New Testament and Its World; Edinburgh: Clark, 1998), 163–82.

1. *The Use of Chreiai in Ancient Rhetoric and Early Christian Discourse*

It is quite clear that the mythology of *Thomas* did not develop in a vacuum. The sayings reveal the creative, intellectual labor of a group that found it necessary to clearly differentiate itself from other groups that claimed Jesus as their founder figure. In other words, many of the sayings appear to be argumentative, rhetorically charged sayings that directly contrast the mythology and practices of the Thomas group with that of other Christian movements. By using the rhetoric of scholastic dialogues, in the rhetorical format of abbreviated or unelaborated chreiai or anecdotes, the Thomasine community (cleverly) claimed that Jesus had condemned the very practices and mythology that were observed by and/or created in the competing Christian communities. By framing the teachings of Jesus as cryptic retorts to the disciples' questions, *Thomas* stressed the imperatival teaching of Jesus, presenting Jesus as the true authority figure who clearly initiated and supported *only* the Thomasine community.[3] For the true followers—the ones who could interpret the sayings (the Thomasine community)—the inquiring disciples' lack of understanding in the dialogues is directly proportionate to Jesus' knowledge (and thus the knowledge of those true followers who know "what is in front of their face" [*Gos. Thom.* 5]). But why did this group go to the trouble of creating these short dialogues? Why not simply state, "Jesus disagreed with the ideas and practices of our opponents!" and describe their negative characteristics, similar to the rhetorical style of Paul in several of his letters? A brief review of the use of chreiai in ancient literature should illustrate the possible function and benefits of this type of saying for the Thomas group.

A chreia was defined broadly by the ancient rhetorician Theon of Alexandria in his *Progymnasmata* (exercise books) as "a concise statement or action which is attributed with aptness to some specified character or to something analogous to a character."[4] Thus, a chreia

---

[3] Compare Burton L. Mack's description of similarly formatted Q sayings in his *Rhetoric and the New Testament* (GBS; Minneapolis, MN: Fortress, 1990), 33, 51.

[4] See the discussion of Theon and a translation of his chapter on chreiai from his *Progymnasmata*, by Ronald F. Hock and Edward N. O'Neil, eds., *The Progymnasmata* (vol. 1 of *The Chreia in Ancient Rhetoric*; SBLTT 27: Graeco-Roman Religion 9; Atlanta, GA: Scholars Press, 1986), 82–107.

is an anecdotal statement, usually in the form of a maxim that is attributed to a particular speaker, often revealing something about the occasion of the speech. The statement itself was intentionally puzzling or obscure: stated with wit, syllogism, enthymeme, or double entendre, or in a symbolic or figurative manner.[5] Burton L. Mack has suggested the following description: "that class of anecdotes that have as their chief characteristic a skillful and surprising rejoinder to a challenging encounter or situation."[6] In the Greco-Roman world, the process of producing and elaborating a chreia was a rhetorical skill taught in the schools. As Mack and Vernon K. Robbins have convincingly illustrated, the Thomasine community was not alone in their use of chreiai. This form of rhetorical argumentation is common in Q and Mark, and even more elaborate chreiai are frequent in Matthew and Luke. Using chreiai to present the teachings of Jesus was a mainstay of the rhetoric of many early Jesus movements.

The benefit of framing speech patterns in the form of chreiai is found in the concise and cryptic nature of the maxim. The reader/hearer of the chreia is able to quickly gain some insight into the temperament and ideology of the speaker, while the cryptic nature of the saying leads to a type of provocation or frustration. According to the principles of ancient rhetoric, a well-formed chreia could be attributed to a famous philosopher or wise man, as long as it fit the basic character traits of the designated speaker. However, the person creating the chreia was allowed to tease or provoke the audience into thinking about how the wise speaker might react to a wide variety of difficult situations or questions. Thus, in a school situation, a student might be assigned the task of creating a question or circumstance for a character like Socrates, to which he would develop a maxim that fits the basic character of Socrates, while teasing the audience to see the philosopher in a new light at the same time. As a rhetorical tool of biography, the chreia was a uniquely designed type of 'speech-in-character' that was used by ancient authors to develop and elaborate on a famous teacher's ideas by having them react to the relevant questions of the age.

The extant literary sources, from a variety of early Christian com-

---

[5] The terms are from Theon, "On the Chreia," lines 120–24, in Hock and O'Neil, *Progymnasmata*, 89.

[6] Burton L. Mack and Vernon K. Robbins, *Patterns of Persuasion in the Gospels* (FF: Literary Facets; Sonoma, CA: Polebridge Press, 1989), 47.

munities, suggest that this rhetorical logic was a key component of early Christian myth-making. Jesus, the wise speaker, could be imagined responding to all types of questions and situations that were relevant to the social contexts of his first- and second-century followers. By attributing maxims to Jesus, an early Christian group was able to legitimate and authorize its ethos and practices.[7] By developing chreiai that negatively characterized the group's opponents—as those who misunderstood or rejected Jesus—the group members were able to highlight their superiority and knowledge. Because of its intentionally concise and enigmatic qualities, the chreia was a perfectly suited rhetorical technique for the Thomasine community, whose members were undoubtedly interested in obscurity.

2. *The Negative Characterization of the "Disciples" in* Thomas

There are several logia that support the idea that the Thomasine community created chreiai for the purpose of undermining the teaching of competing Christian groups. In particular, this can be observed in the chreiai that use the term "disciples" (or "followers") as a reference to Jesus' followers who were actually not "true disciples." Scholars have often commented upon the fact that the term "disciples" is used negatively as a reference to the people who do not understand. The "disciples" were not simply well meaning followers who did not understand Jesus; the term can arguably be understood as a direct reference to Christian groups that were opposed by the authors of *Thomas*. There is reason to suspect that when reference was made to these misinformed and perplexed "disciples," the "true disciple" would be able to decipher the intended target of the critique.

Many of these chreiai were directed at actions that were being negated. They are generally polemical; Jesus was being incited to correct wrong actions and ideas, rather than being prompted to support agreeable or sympathetic ideas and actions. All the sayings that stem directly from the disciples, and even those whose speakers are simply "they" are characteristically oppositional. Jesus must counter or contradict those who ask the questions. The only positive, non-polemical teaching occurs in the context of dialogues with named

---

[7] See Burton L. Mack, *The Lost Gospel: The Book of Q and Christian Origins* (San Francisco, CA: HarperSanFrancisco, 1993), 197–202.

followers ("Thomas" in *Gos. Thom.* 13, "Mary" in *Gos. Thom.* 21, and
"Salome" in *Gos. Thom.* 61) where "true discipleship" is one of the
basic issues at hand. All three examples of positive dialogues occur
in logia that are elaborated chreiai, with a rather different style and
tone than is found in the usually cryptic, abbreviated chreiai that comprise the majority of the dialogue sayings. Even dialogues with unnamed
people ("a [person]" in *Gos. Thom.* 72, and a "woman" in *Gos. Thom.*
79) are intended to correct misinformed or misguided speakers.[8]

The dialogue in *Gos. Thom.* 43 is an interesting case in point. The
chreia presents the disciples challenging Jesus to prove he has the
authority to speak to them. In response, Jesus states a short maxim,
Gos. Thom. 43:

His disciples said to him,	[He responds,]
"Who are you	"You do not know who I am
to say these things to us?"	from what I say to you."

The maxim is a statement that directly responds to the disciples'
question with wit, and turns their critique on its head. The reply is
atypical since Jesus is not identified by the narrator.[9] Rather, the
speaker takes the two key components of the reproachful question
(knowing, and speaking) and accuses the disciples of being the problem. Thus, the issue is changed from a focus on the authority and
identity of Jesus to a concern with the lack of understanding among
the disciples.

The maxim is followed by what can be categorized—following the
terminology of Hermogenes[10]—as a brief elaboration (ἐργασία) in the

---

[8] Both dialogues are paralleled in Luke: compare *Gos. Thom.* 72 to Luke 12:13–14,
and *Gos. Thom.* 79 to Luke (Q?) 11:27–28.

[9] Richard Valantasis has suggested that since the saying does not explicitly state
that Jesus is the respondent, the disciples in this case might be directing their question at the "narrator of the sayings," rather than Jesus: "the question may actually
be put to the narrator of the sayings whose perspective on Jesus dominates the
entire collection." He continues, "The question could challenge the voice and the
authority of the narrator of the sayings or it could challenge Jesus" (*The Gospel of
Thomas* [New Testament Readings; London: Routledge, 1997], 119). I would suggest that it is not an either/or case. Jesus acts as the spokesperson for the community and narrator of the sayings. While the community placed the words into
the mouth of Jesus, thus making him the respondent on record, the act of inventing the speech-in-character always implies that the community is the 'actual' target of the questions; all the responses to the questions are both the words of Jesus
and the words of the community.

[10] For Hermogenes' description of the components of chreia elaboration, see

form of "a statement from the opposite" (κατὰ τὸ ἐναντίον): "Rather, you have become like the Jewish people, for they love the tree but hate its fruit, or they love the fruit but hate the tree." As a negative example or statement of the opposite, the elaboration negatively compares the disciples to the "Jewish people" who are characterized as being unable to love both the "tree" and the "fruit." Exactly what the tree and fruit represent has been a topic of some discussion. Without belaboring the technical aspects of the chreia elaboration or its possible meanings, it is interesting to note that the response focuses on the issue of "becoming like Jewish people." The elaboration takes up a common theme of the dialogue sayings: the disapproval of the relationship between the Thomasine community and Judaism or those like the Jewish people. The key here is that being "like the Jews" is detrimental. At this point it is sufficient to note in this saying the characteristically negative tone of the discourse with the "disciples" and the fact that being "like the Jewish people" is undesirable.

3. Gos. Thom. *52 in the Context of Early Christian Literature*

Gos. Thom. 52 is an important dialogue because it insinuates a particular action that the "disciples" positively affirm, but that is negatively evaluated by Jesus. Of the several examples of dialogue sayings in which Jesus corrects or criticizes the disciples, I have selected this saying for a more detailed examination since it appears to provide insight into the major concern that the Thomasine Christians had with other forms of early Christianity. The directive of Jesus that relates the twenty-four prophets of Israel to "the dead," thus effectively negating any attempts by early Christians to link Jesus to the Hebrew literary traditions, is a relatively clear statement of difference between the Thomasine community and almost all other forms of Christianity that are known from the first and early second centuries.

Gos. Thom. 52 is a specific type of chreia, a double chreia.[11] Both components of the saying can be understood as independent maxims.

Burton L. Mack and Edward N. O'Neil, "The Chreia Discussion of Hermogenes of Tarsus: Introduction, Translation and Comments," in Hock and O'Neil, *Progymnasmata*, 153–81.

[11] Mack and Robbins, *Patterns of Persuasion*, 162–63.

a. His disciples said to him,	b. He said to them,
"Twenty-four prophets	"You
have spoken	have disregarded the living one
	who is
in Israel,	in your presence,
and they	and you
all spoke	have spoken
of you."	of the dead."

In this case the statement of the disciples is not interrogative, like many of the other dialogue sayings. The disciples' statement appears as a short chreai formulation that succinctly expresses the idea that Jesus was foretold in the Hebrew scriptures. The disciples' chreia is quite similar to many of the sayings that were attributed to Jesus in *Thomas*, in that it captures a significant issue in a pithy maxim that involves some coded or ambiguous language. But in this case the maxim is misguided. Jesus' rejoinder takes up a familiar theme from the gospel more generally—an idea previously encountered in *Gos. Thom.* 51—and is intended to correct the disciples' error. The parallel nature of the two chreia in this saying illustrates the care that was taken in composing these sayings in an appropriate rhetorical style.

This saying provides an interesting insight into the basic myth-making process of the Thomasine group. As the members developed their ideas about the past, they intentionally moved away from linking Jesus and themselves to the stories of the Hebrew patriarchs, the idea of Israelite kingship, the traditions of the Prophets, and the rituals of early Judaism. While several scholars have recently argued that a key epoch for reflection, exegesis, and mythmaking was found in the Hebrew cosmological myths of Genesis 1–3,[12] it should be noted that even the appeal to the Hebrew myth of cosmic origins is very limited, and typically censorious. The type of mythmaking that occurred in the Thomasine community was disinterested in linking Jesus to the Hebrew epic. Among early Christian communities that we know of, Thomasine Christianity was unusual because of its

---

[12] For example, see Stevan L. Davies, "The Christology and Protology of the *Gospel of Thomas*," *JBL* 111 (1992): 663–82; April D. DeConick, *Seek to See Him: Ascent and Vision Mysticism in the Gospel of Thomas* (Supplements to Vigiliae Christianae 33; Leiden: Brill, 1996); and Elaine H. Pagels, "Exegesis of Genesis 1 in the *Gospels of Thomas* and John," *JBL* 118 (1999): 477–96. All three authors examine the similarities and/or dependence of *Thomas* on similar types of exegesis in various texts from Hellenistic Judaism and Platonism.

rejection and condemnation of using all other components of the Hebrew epic to explain the community's origins. A brief examination of the typical ways that early Christian literature links Jesus to the Hebrew "prophets" should help clarify the possible opponents that the authors of *Thomas* were targeting in this saying.

The abundance of literature from early Judaism and early Christianity that attempts to narrate the Hebrew epic, or the stories from the Hebrew heritage in diverse ways suggests that there were many communities competing for the right to claim the epic as their own.[13] In early Jewish and Christian communities, no dominant claim to the Hebrew epic existed, especially after the destruction of the Second Temple. Many communities in the late first and early second century were able to reorganize the symbolic world of this Hebrew mythology in order to depict their own epic account. In the development of first and second century Christianity, one can observe an increasingly complex connection between the reimagining of the Hebrew epic and christological interests (Q and Mark have less complex connections to the Hebrew epic, Luke and Matthew are much further developed).[14] Within early Christian communities, we see the classic examples of the Letters of Paul to the Galatians and Romans, the two-volume work attributed to "Luke," and the Gospel of Matthew, in which figures, epochs, and themes from the Hebrew epic were easily adapted in the new mythology of these authors and communities. Paul could claim the birthright of the Hebrew heritage for the Gentile Christians in Galatia by creatively re-imagining the stories of Abraham's family. The author of Luke-Acts carried this one step further by claiming that Jesus was a direct fulfillment of the Hebrew scriptures, and by crafting a story that accounted for the rise of his Christian community out of the Hebrew ancestry. The author claimed that the Christian movement was the logical and necessary result of the 'history' of Israel (Acts 7).

From very early in the origins of Christianity we can observe an interest in the Hebrew heritage. The credal formula of 1 Corinthians 15:3–4 suggests that when Paul was writing it was already common in some early Christian communities to scan the written texts of the

---

[13] See Erich S. Gruen, *Heritage and Hellenism: The Reinvention of Jewish Tradition* (Berkeley, CA: University of California Press, 1998).
[14] Burton L. Mack, *Who Wrote the New Testament: The Making of the Christian Myth* (San Francisco, CA: HarperSanFrancisco, 1995), 73.

Hebrew heritage in order to develop a lineage for the stories that were summarized in this early formula: "That Christ died for our sins in accordance with the scriptures, and that he was buried, and that he was raised on the third day in accordance with the scriptures." Thus, there was already a type of "prooftexting" or "proof from prophecy" hermeneutic established by the time of Paul. By the time the gospels of Matthew and Luke were written, the objective of linking the story of Jesus to the Hebrew heritage dominated much of the ideology of these early Christian authors. As Stendahl so convincingly illustrated a generation ago, in Matthew this enterprise was so advanced that it could rightly be called the work of a "school."[15]

Considering the specific language of *Gos. Thom.* 52, specifically the use of the term "prophets," an interesting example of linking Jesus to the Hebrew epic is found in Luke 24:27, where the author asserted that after his resurrection Jesus took time out while walking on the road to Emmaus to interpret "the things about himself in all the scriptures . . . beginning with Moses and all the prophets." And again at the end of Luke the author asserts that one of the final acts of Jesus with his gathered disciples was to teach them to interpret the scriptures: "Jesus said, 'These are my words that I spoke to you while I was still with you—that everything written about me in the law of Moses, the prophets, and the psalms must be fulfilled'" (Luke 24:44). Luke's Paul also confirms the need to link the figure of Jesus to the Hebrew heritage in Acts 26:22 and in 28:23. Luke closes the Acts of the Apostles with Paul in Rome receiving people at his "lodgings in great numbers" in order that he could testify to them about "the kingdom of God and try to convince them about Jesus both from the law of Moses and from the prophets." Thus, the author of Luke-Acts developed the use of the Hebrew heritage as a prooftext for the life and teachings of Jesus by ending both volumes of his narrative with his protagonists teaching their followers how to correctly read the scriptures.

The *Epistle of Barnabas* is also worth mentioning as a possible further development against the idea that is promoted in *Gos. Thom.* 52. *Barnabas* provides an argument that in many respects could be read as a response to Thomasine Christianity. In *Barnabas* there is an

---

[15] Krister Stendahl, *The School of St. Matthew and Its Use of the Old Testament* (2nd ed.; Philadelphia, PA: Fortress, 1968).

interesting relationship (or counter relationship) with *Gos. Thom.* 52, in view of the fact that chapter 6 references "Gnosis" as the speaker who directs the listener to hear the words of "the prophet" in order to "understand secret things" (*Barn.* 6.9–10). *Barnabas* employs several of the key terms that are found in *Thomas*, and arrives at the opposite conclusion: Gnosis says that only through the prophets can one understand the secret things! While there are several other noteworthy intersections between the texts of *Barnabas* and *Thomas*, this one clearly suggests that there was a lively tradition of early Christians who went to great lengths to prove that Jesus was announced by the Hebrew prophets. Considering that *Barnabas* also makes a lengthy argument for the importance of recognizing that Jesus came in the "flesh" (for example, *Barn.* 6.7, 9)—a notion that is downplayed or even opposed by *Thomas* (i.e., *Gos. Thom.* 112)—it could be suggested that the author of *Barnabas* was aware of the type of teachings that were popular in the Thomasine community, and wanted to provide a criticism of the group's ideology. While this remains speculative, further studies of the noticeable opposition between what is found in the sayings of *Thomas* and what is discussed in *Barnabas* may provide a more comprehensive picture of the ideological competition that occurred between these early Christian communities.

What is clear from this brief survey of early Christian literature is that for many first and second century authors the need to provide their group with a sense of history and to create a story that explained where they came from was a major objective. Even more than the letters of Paul, the synoptic gospels, or *Barnabas*, *Papyrus Egerton 2* (or Egerton Gospel) and the Gospel of John share this objective in a way that is especially interesting for the study of *Gos. Thom.* 52. In light of the fact that several scholars have observed the significant relationship (usually oppositional) between the ideology in *Thomas* and that found in John, it is interesting to see the possible connection between these texts.[16] In several sayings attributed to Jesus in John and *Papyrus Egerton 2*, Jesus is portrayed as having been

---

[16] See Ismo Dunderberg, "Thomas' I-sayings and the Gospel of John," in Uro, *Thomas at the Crossroads*, 33–64; and *idem*, "*Thomas* and the Beloved Disciple," in Uro, *Thomas at the Crossroads*, 65–88. Although less convinced of the relationship between John and *Thomas* than many of the scholars he surveys, Dunderberg's essays provide an excellent overview of the issues and the state of research on the relationship between John and *Thomas*.

spoken of by Moses. "The Jews" of John 5,[17] and the "rulers of the
people" in *Papyrus Egerton 2* verse 7, are told to "search the scriptures"
in order to understand who Jesus was.[18] After a more careful examination of both *Gos. Thom.* 52 and the texts from Egerton, and John,
it may be possible to begin to define more clearly the type of inter-
community conflict that is behind this dialogue saying.

Looking specifically at the wording of *Gos. Thom.* 52, one notes
that the chreia attributed to the disciples contains a few elements that
are rare in early Christian literature. The term "twenty-four prophets"
has generally been regarded as a generic reference to all the Israelite
Prophets. More specifically, the phrase here should be understood
as a reference to all the authors of the texts of the Hebrew Bible. The
earliest extant calculation of the number 24 for the books of the
Hebrew Bible canon is found in 4 Ezra 44–48, which dates to about
100 CE. The number 24 is also the traditional calculation found in
Rabbinic literature. Josephus (*Against Apion* 1.7ff) and the Greek translation of *Jubilees* give the number 22, which became the traditional
number of authors of the Hebrew Bible for the early Church Fathers.[19]

---

[17] John 5:39–40, 45–47: (39) "You search the scriptures because you think that
in them you have eternal life; and it is they that testify on my behalf. (40) Yet you
refuse to come to me to have life." ... (45) "Do not think that I will accuse you
before the Father; your accuser is Moses, on whom you have set your hope. (46)
If you believed Moses, you would believe me, for he wrote about me. (47) But if
you do not believe what he wrote, how will you believe what I say?" (NRSV).

[18] *Papyrus Egerton 2*, 7–20: (7) <And> having turn<ed> to <the> rulers of the
people he <sp>oke the following saying; "(Ye) search the scriptures in which ye
think that ye have life; these are they (10) which bear witness of me. Do not think
that I came to accuse <you> to my father! There is one <that ac>cuses <you>,
even Moses, on whom ye have set your hope." And when they sa(15)<id>: "We
know that God <hath> spok<en> to Moses, but as for thee, we know not <whence
thou art.>" Jesus answered and said unto them: "Now (already) accusation is raised
against <your> (20) unbelief in regard to the things testified by him. For if <you>
had <believed Moses>, you would have believed <me>; for <concerning> me he
<wrote> to your fathers." (translated by Joachim Jeremias and Wilhelm Schneemelcher
in *Gospels and Related Writings* [vol. 1 of *The New Testament Apocrypha*; ed. Wilhelm
Schneemelcher; English trans. ed. R. McL. Wilson; Louisville, KY: Westminster
John Knox, 1991]). *Papyrus Egerton 2*, 50–54 "... [com]ing to him they tested him
in [an exacting] way, s[aying,]" "Teacher Jesus, we know that you have come [from
God,] for what you do te[stifies] beyond all the prophets." (translated by Jon Daniels,
"The Egerton Gospel: Its place in Early Christianity" [Ph.D. diss., The Claremont
Graduate School, 1989]).

[19] The evidence that both numbers were widely recognized as early as the second century BCE is given by Roger Beckwith, *The Old Testament Canon of the New
Testament Church and its Background in Early Judaism* (Grand Rapids, MI: Eerdmans,
1985), 118–27.

The difference between 22 and 24 is explained by the various ways the texts could be combined. The number 22 is the tally when Jeremiah was combined with Lamentations, and Judges was combined with Ruth. Unfortunately, both numbers were recognized totals for the books in the Hebrew scriptures by the end of the first century CE, and thus the use of the number 24 in *Thomas* does not provide any clear evidence for defining the social context or date of the saying.

Like the number 24, the use of the term "prophet" as a reference to the authors of the Hebrew Bible is not unique or particularly informative about the historical context of the saying. The term has several parallels in the first century CE, most notably Josephus, who referred to those who wrote the 22 texts as "the prophets" (*Against Apion* 7ff). It is likely that when the phrase "24 prophets of Israel" was heard, the connection would have been made to the authors of the Hebrew Bible. Considering the mysterious or ambiguous nature of many of the sayings in *Thomas*, the use of this moderately "coded" term is not surprising.

As mentioned above, the statement of the disciples to Jesus in *Gos. Thom.* 52 was likely meant to imply that certain groups were using the texts written by "the 24 prophets of Israel" as an important source of knowledge about Jesus. This comment by the disciples is, of course, a rhetorical set-up to which Jesus must reply in order to correct the disciples and instruct them about how to regard his true nature. Similar dialogue patterns are found in *Gos. Thom.* 24; 37; 43; and 91. In response to this comment, Jesus stressed the idea that he was alive and that the 24 prophets who spoke in Israel were dead. The audience, those belonging to the Thomasine community, was instructed in Jesus' response not to listen to the dead, since the living one was with them. Thus, if we can define the "24 prophets" as representatives of the early formation of the Hebrew Bible canon, then the saying is a clear instruction for the community not to seek testimony about Jesus from within the textual tradition of the Hebrew heritage. Thomasine Christianity apparently rejected any attempt to link the community to the stories of the Hebrew past, excepting only the implicit references to the Hebrew myths of cosmic origins.

This interpretation of *Gos. Thom.* 52 corresponds to what we find in the *Gospel of Thomas* more generally. The only figure from the Hebrew epic tradition that even makes an appearance in the text of *Thomas* is Adam. He is characterized negatively in *Gos. Thom.* 85 because he "tasted death" and was shown to be unworthy. In *Gos. Thom.* 46 the entire epic past seems to be characterized in the sweeping phrase "from Adam to John the Baptist." Even though Adam and John the Baptist are worthy of mention—probably because they represent the most positive elements of the Hebrew heritage—in the end the Thomasine community could accept neither character into its own etiological account. In fact we learn that anyone who knows the "Kingdom" is better than John. Thus, there was a clear disregard for the Hebrew epic. The Thomasine community did not want to search the scriptures in order to link Jesus to the Hebrew past. Nor did it want to characterize any of the figures of this epic in a positive light. There seems to be a clear desire to link the community to a world before the time of Adam, a desire to link up with a time before the Hebrew epic.

4. Papyrus Egerton *2, John, and* Thomas:
Inter-community Debates

Within the context of most of the early Christian literature that we are aware of from the first two centuries of our era, the response of Jesus in *Gos. Thom.* 52 appears quite exceptional. The statement of the disciples in this logion implies that the Thomasine community was well aware of an early Christian hermeneutic that understood the Hebrew Bible to be a ready reference, or proof-text, for the traditions that were developing about the life of Jesus and the Christ story. *Thomas* rejected that hermeneutical practice without reservation. This logion appears to be directed against a common Christian practice. No doubt, a number of early Christian communities could be proposed as the one that was engaged in the practice that *Gos. Thom.* 52 was seeking to censure. As noted above, many communities were attempting to associate themselves with the Hebrew heritage in one way or another in order to provide themselves with a sense of history, and thus justify their existence. Yet there are two sources that contain similar themes to those found in *Gos. Thom.* 52 that may provide a clearer understanding of the social context for the origin of this logion.

There is no clear parallel to this saying in the synoptic gospels, and the most common reference listed in the secondary literature, John 5:39–40, is only analogous in its theme, not with regard to vocabulary or style. *Papyrus Egerton 2* also contains a close parallel to the saying, and thus should be considered in this discussion of the potential "opponents" of the Thomasine community in this saying. Even though there is no reason to think that there would have been

direct textual dependence of *Gos. Thom.* 52 on *Papyrus Egerton 2* or
John 5, the themes exhibited in Egerton and John are generally the
same as what we have seen in the *Gos. Thom.* 52. It could be argued
that there was at least some type of contact between the communities behind these three texts.

There are three themes that each gospel shares, though in opposing ways: the idea that one should or should not search the scriptures, the idea that the scriptures testify or do not testify about Jesus,
and the concept of "Life." *Thomas*, of course, understood the scriptures
negatively and Jesus' statement proclaims that Life is to be found
only in Jesus, not within the prophets of Israel. *Papyrus Egerton 2* and
John's statements also confirm that Life is not to be found in the
scriptures, yet they positively affirm the need to search the scriptures
in order to understand Jesus. Thus, there is agreement in the idea
that Jesus represents Life, but there is disagreement about the need
to search the scriptures.

The major topic of the debate within the Thomasine community
that generated *Gos. Thom.* 52 was the question of how to treat the
Hebrew epic and prophetic tradition. If John and *Papyrus Egerton 2*
could be seen as possible forerunners or competitors in the debate, then
we would be able to begin to clarify part of the social world in
which these sayings developed. A brief examination of the possible
contexts of *Papyrus Egerton 2* and the Gospel of John might help to
better clarify the context of *Gos. Thom.* 52.

The sayings collected in *Papyrus Egerton 2* are by far the most difficult to place within a social context. This difficulty stems mainly from
the fact that the text is rather uncertain at points and the scholarship
on this gospel is so divided with regard to the question of whether the
sayings are dependent on the canonical gospels. Particularly, scholarship is divided on the question of whether the story in Egerton of the
healing of the Leper is dependent on Luke, or whether the sayings
directed at the rulers of the people are dependent on John. This paper
certainly will not solve the question of dependency. Rather, accepting
the thesis that *Papyrus Egerton 2* was independent from the canonical
gospels—convincingly defended by the 1946 dissertation of G. Mayeda
and the 1989 dissertation of J. Daniels—it should be helpful to
explore the possible connection between *Papyrus Egerton 2* and John.[20]

---

[20] Goro Mayeda, *Das Leben-Jesu-Fragment Papyrus Egerton 2 und seine Stellung in der urchristlichen Literaturgeschichte* (Bern: Haupt, 1946); and Daniels, "The Egerton Gospel."

Mayeda and Daniels concluded that there is more evidence to suggest that the sayings found in *Papyrus Egerton 2* were principally derived from an oral tradition or shared milieu with the community of John, rather than a direct textual relationship. John Dominic Crossan, Helmut Koester, and Ron Cameron have all posited similar arguments, and Crossan and Koester have even suggested that the textual dependency may plausibly be reversed. Thus, Crossan has argued that in Mark 12:13–17 the author was dependent on *Papyrus Egerton 2* (a dialogue on the question of paying taxes).[21] Koester has argued with regard to the sayings in *Papyrus Egerton 2* that have parallels in John that it was John who expanded on *Papyrus Egerton 2*, rather than the opposite. He concluded that it was easier to posit that John drew on *Papyrus Egerton 2* at various places in his text, rather than think that the author of *Papyrus Egerton 2* "patched his text together from half a dozen passages in John . . . ."[22]

Similar to Koester, Cameron and Daniels have elaborated on the social situation that may have produced the collection of sayings in *Papyrus Egerton 2*, especially in relation to the Johannine community. I will briefly summarize their conclusions and move quickly to draw several inferences concerning how this might have affected the Thomasine community.

Papyrus Egerton 2 appears to derive from a period when there was an agitated debate between the so-called "Jewish-Christians" and several other Jewish groups.[23] The social context for the original desire to link Jesus to Moses, and even the claim that Moses wrote about Jesus and testified about Jesus (see *Papyrus Egerton 2*, 7–20), fits within a period of close contact between Jewish groups that believed Jesus to be the messiah, and Jewish groups that did not. One could suggest that *Papyrus Egerton 2* reflects an inter-Jewish controversy. This debate has often been regarded as one of the points of contention out of which the Gospel of John arose. John's gospel has been understood as deriving from a time when the sectarian distinctions between Jewish groups and Christian groups were more defined. John's gospel

---

[21] John Dominic Crossan, *Four Other Gospels: Shadows on the Contours of Canon* (Sonoma, CA: Polebridge Press, 1992).

[22] Helmut Koester, *History and Literature of Early Christianity* (Vol 2 of *Introduction to the New Testament*; Hermeneia: Foundations and Facets; Philadelphia, PA: Fortress, 1982), 182.

[23] See the comments of Helmut Koester, *Ancient Christian Gospels: Their History and Development* (Philadelphia, PA: Trinity Press International, 1990), 215–16.

was still involved in the debate, but at more of a distance than what is observed in *Papyrus Egerton 2*. By the time the Gospel of John was written, the lines were more clearly drawn between Jews and Christians.[24] The christological ideas were developed to a point where there was no longer a real argument about whether or not one could find testimony about Jesus in the Hebrew scriptures. John's community was actively involved in linking itself to the Hebrew epic, and claiming the story for itself, apart from Judaism. John's community was more distant from real Jewish opponents and competitors than the community responsible for *Papyrus Egerton 2*.

It may be in this context, or one similar, that *Gos. Thom.* 52 finds a setting. The Thomasine community was no longer involved in a debate with Jewish opponents. The debate was now with competing Christian communities, such as the Johannine group. The Thomasine community rejected the symbols of the Hebrew epic and replaced them with symbols from an "esoteric" ideology. The debate seen in *Gos. Thom.* 52 was with a Christian group like the Johannine community who found meaning in the ability to claim the Hebrew epic for itself. The *Gospel of Thomas* reveals a group that was familiar with how to claim the epic, but rejected this ideology and hermeneutic. For *Thomas*, the link to the past had to skip over the Hebrew heritage and connect the community to a mythological past that dates to a time before Adam. The epic is told in a way that see the community as deriving from the original androgynous state (*Gos. Thom.* 4; 11; 22; 61).

Thus, a potential reconstruction of the inter-community debates seen in these texts might appear as follows: in *Papyrus Egerton 2* we see a gradual drift from close, competitive contact with other Jewish groups, to a more distant relationship with Jewish opponents that is seen in the Gospel of John, and finally, with the Thomasine group we find a community that was not concerned specifically with "the Jews," but warned against acting "like the Jewish people" (*Gos. Thom.* 43). In *Thomas* the debate was with other early Christian communities who were linking themselves to the Hebrew epic. The *Gospel of Thomas* claimed that groups like those represented in *Papyrus Egerton 2* and the Gospel of John were linking up with "the dead" rather than with the living tradition of Jesus.

---

[24] Ron Cameron, *The Other Gospels: Non-Canonical Gospel Texts* (Philadelphia, PA: Westminster, 1982), 72–74.

CHAPTER FIVE

ON THE BRINK OF THE APOCALYPSE:
A PRELIMINARY EXAMINATION OF THE EARLIEST
SPEECHES IN THE *GOSPEL OF THOMAS*

APRIL D. DeCONICK

In a recent article on the compositional history of the *Gospel of Thomas*, I proposed from a traditio-historical perspective that *Thomas* is best understood as an aggregate text, an accumulation of traditions and their interpretations.[1] As such, it contains old core traditions to which additional material became aggregated over time. The newer materials were organized in relation to the old core sayings, serving to interpret, explain, and update the core. In other words, the text appears to have started as a small gospel of oracles of the prophet Jesus. Over time, this "Kernel" gospel was modified with the addition of later materials as the community experienced crises and shifts in ideology and group constituency.

I set forth in that article a set of historical-critical principles by which the later accretions might be separated from the earlier, offered a brief analysis of the gospel according to these principles, and presented a tentative list of sayings belonging to the Kernel.[2] What I

---

[1] April D. DeConick, "The Original *Gospel of Thomas*," *VC* 56 (2002): 167–99.

[2] See now also, A. D. DeConick *Recovering the Original Gospel of Thomas: A History of the Gospel and Its Growth* (JSNTSup 286; London: T & T Clark International, 2005). The present article provides a summary of the ideas developed in chapter 4 of the monograph. In this monograph, I continue to develop my methodology, particularly drawing on studies of oral and rhetorical cultures and more literary theory. The tentative list of Kernel sayings in my preliminary article has remained very stable with the exception of *Gos. Thom.* 69:1 which I now understand as belonging to a later rhetorical unit. Some earlier form of *Gos. Thom.* 60:1, perhaps a parable, may be behind the present dialogue, but, if this is so, it has been so reworked as to be unrecoverable. In this revised list, I have bracketed the two sayings where I think earlier versions were present in the Kernel and can be recovered with some certainty. Kernel sayings: 2; 4:2–3; 5; 6:2–3; 8; 9; 10; 11:1; 14:4; 15; 16:1–3; 17; 20:2–4; 21:5; 10–11; 23:1; 24:2–3; 25; 26; ((30)); 31; 32; 33; 34; 35; 36; 38:1; 39; 40; 41; 42; ((44)); 45; 46; 47; 48; 54; 55; 57; 58; 61:1; 62; 63; 64:1–11; 65; 66; 68:1; 69:2; 71; 72; 73; 74; 76; 78; 79; 81; 82; 86; 89; 90; 91; 92; 93; 94; 95; 96; 97; 98; 99; 100:1–3; 102; 103; 104; 107; 109; 111:1.

think I have recovered are the bones of a very old version of the *Gospel of Thomas*, a version which was modified significantly after the fall of the Jerusalem Temple when the Syrian Christians were faced with the pressure of Gentile conversion as they began to disassociate from the synagogue and come to terms with the unfulfilled promise of an "imminent" Eschaton.

A preliminary analysis of this Kernel gospel will offer us an opportunity to explore the origins of the Thomasine tradition in ways that previous analyses have not done. Most prior studies have been based on the assumption that the sayings in the text represent a form of Christianity that is considered by scholars to be either early or late.[3] When the *Gospel of Thomas* has been regarded "early," scholars have generally reconstructed a non-apocalyptic Christianity from it since they can point to many logia that seem more proverbial than apocalyptic.[4] The error in this approach has been a relative naivete regarding the age of the various logia and the accretive nature of this gospel: the later sayings have not been adequately distinguished from the earlier, if at all. When the *Gospel of Thomas* has been regarded "late," scholars have generally created a pre-gnostic or gnostic Christianity from it since they can point to many logia that seem to be more esoteric than the synoptic tradition.[5] The problem with this

---

[3] For an overview of various positions, refer to DeConick, "The Original *Gospel of Thomas*," 168–79.

[4] Proponents of this view rely heavily on the work of James M. Robinson and Helmut Koester in their pioneering volume, *Trajectories through Early Christianity* (Philadelphia, PA: Fortress, 1971). This view is most dominant in American scholarship, particularly among those scholars who belong to the Jesus Seminar, and has even been the basis for the reconstruction of a non-apocalyptic Historical Jesus by some contemporary scholars. For examples of this position, see Stevan L. Davies, *The Gospel of Thomas and Christian Wisdom* (New York, NY: Seabury, 1983), 13–17; John Dominic Crossan, *The Historical Jesus: The Life of a Mediterranean Jewish Peasant* (New York, NY: HarperSanFrancisco, 1991), 227–302; Ron Cameron, "The *Gospel of Thomas* and Christian Origins," in *The Future of Early Christianity: Essays in Honor of Helmut Koester* (ed. Birger A. Pearson et al.; Minneapolis, MN: Fortress, 1991), 381–92; Stephen J. Patterson, *The Gospel of Thomas and Jesus* (FF: Reference Series; Sonoma, CA: Polebridge Press, 1993), 94–112; Robert W. Funk, *Honest to Jesus* (New York, NY: HarperCollins, 1996), 121–39.

[5] This view seems to have been most popular in early analyses of *Thomas*. Cf. Lucien Cerfaux and Gérard Garitte, "Les paraboles du Royaume dans L'Évangile de Thomas," *Muséon* 70 (1957): 307–27; Robert McL. Wilson, "The Coptic '*Gospel of Thomas*'," *NTS* 5 (1958–1959): 273–76; Robert M. Grant, "Notes on the *Gospel of Thomas*," *VC* 13 (1959): 170–80; Robert McL. Wilson, "'Thomas' and the Growth of the Gospels," *HTR* 53 (1960): 231–50; Robert McL. Wilson, *Studies in the Gospel of Thomas* (London: Mowbray, 1960); Robert M. Grant and David Noel Freedman, *The Secret Sayings of Jesus* (with an English translation of the *Gospel of Thomas* by

approach is twofold. First, it has assumed an undiscriminating and easy use of the category "Gnosticism" and its corollaries,[6] categories which have been confused with early Jewish esotericism and Hermetism. Second, it has tainted its historical reconstruction with theological assumptions, particularly the assumption that the canonical version of Christianity is more historical or authentic than the non-canonical.

Thus, an analysis of the earliest layer of sayings in the *Gospel of Thomas*, the Kernel gospel, is extremely important to our understanding of the origin and nature of the Thomasine tradition. Was it sapiential, gnostic, or something else? In fact, since a study of the themes and structures of this old gospel will provide us with Christian traditions that possibly pre-date Q and Paul, an examination of the Kernel sayings may provide us with material with which to reexamine the assumptions we have made about the origins of Christianity itself and the continued quest for the Historical Jesus. For now, this latter suggestion will have to remain a question since its investigation is unfortunately beyond the scope of this preliminary examination of the Kernel gospel.

William R. Schoedel; London: Collins, 1960); J. Bauer, "Das Thomas-Evangelium in der neuesten Forschung," in *Geheime Worte Jesu: Das Thomas-Evangelium* (ed. R. Grant and D. Freedman; Frankfurt: Scheffler, 1960), 182–205; René Roques, "Gnosticisme et Christianisme: L'Évangile selon Thomas," *Irénikon* 33 (1960): 29–40; René Roques, " 'L'Évangile selon Thomas': Son édition critique et son identification," *RHR* 157 (1960): 187–218; William R. Schoedel, "Naassene Themes in the Coptic *Gospel of Thomas*," *VC* 14 (1960): 225–34; K. Smyth, "Gnosticism in 'The Gospel according to Thomas'," *HeyJ* 1 (1960): 189–98; E. Cornélis, "Quelques éléments pour une comparison entre l'Évangile de Thomas et la notice d'Hippolyte sur les Naassènes," *VC* 15 (1961): 83–104; Bertil Gärtner, *The Theology of the Gospel of Thomas* (trans. E. Sharpe; London: Collins, 1961); Ernst Haenchen, *Die Botschaft des Thomas-Evangeliums* (Theologische Bibliothek Töpelmann 6; Berlin: Töpelmann, 1961); H. E. W. Turner and Hugh Montefiore, *Thomas and the Evangelists* (SBT 35; London: SCM, 1962); J. Bauer, "The Synoptic Tradition in the *Gospel of Thomas*," (*SE* 3/TU 88; Berlin: Akademie Verlag, 1964), 314–17; Wolfgang Schrage, *Das Verhältnis des Thomas-Evangeliums zur synoptischen Tradition und zu den koptischen Evangelienübersetzungen: Zugleich ein Beitrag zur gnostischen Synopitkerdeutung* (BZNW 29; Berlin: Töpelmann, 1964); Torgny Säve-Söderbergh, "Gnostic and Canonical Gospel Traditions (with special reference to the *Gospel of Thomas*)," in *Le origini dello gnosticismo, colloquio di Messina, 13–18 aprile, 1966: Testi e discussioni* (ed. U. Bianchi; SHR 12; Leiden: Brill, 1967), 552–62; Jacques-É. Ménard, *L'Évangile selon Thomas* (NHS 5; Leiden: Brill, 1975); the most recent attempt is that of Michael Fieger, *Das Thomasevangelium: Einleitung, Kommentar, und Systematik* (NtAbh, n.F. 22; Münster: Aschendorff, 1991).

[6] Cf. Michael A. Williams, *Rethinking "Gnosticism": An Argument for Dismantling a Dubious Category* (Princeton, NJ: Princeton University Press, 1996).

1. *Distinguishing the Kernel from* Thomas' *Sources*

The Kernel gospel is to be distinguished from the gospel "sources" that previous scholars have suggested for *Thomas* when they have attempted to deduce the origins of this gospel from its content or the form of its sayings. Even though it is *possible* that the Kernel gospel may be related to an old Jewish Christian gospel or ancient written collections of sayings, the Kernel gospel itself is neither Gilles Quispel's Jewish Christian gospel, nor Helmut Koester's ancient written collections of Q-like sayings. Because some of the assumptions that these theories are based upon seem problematic to me for various reasons, my approach to the problem of *Thomas'* origins, in fact, is quite different from either Quispel's source-critical approach or Koester's form-critical one.

Quispel has attempted to identify the earliest source for the *Gospel of Thomas* with a Jewish Christian gospel in which were integrated very early sayings "perhaps reflecting a development in the oral tradition of the Aramaic material underlying the Greek Q."[7] He concludes this on the basis that many of the sayings are "positively Jewish Christian,"[8] and reflect versions of sayings that are also found in our fragments of the Jewish Christian gospels, particularly the *Gospel of the Nazorees*.[9] Based on their "Jewish Christian elements," he identifies particular sayings to have been among those drawn from this early Jewish Christian gospel.[10] His attempt to recover the earliest source for *Thomas* raises some methodological concerns for me not because I find the theory to be implausible or even improbable, but because the theory seems to develop out of more circular reasoning than I prefer. That is, once the sayings that contain Jewish Christian elements are identified, the source is determined to be a Jewish Christian gospel because some of the identified sayings reflect versions of the sayings in our Jewish Christian gospel fragments.

---

[7] Gilles Quispel, "Gnosis and the New Sayings of Jesus," in *Gnostic Studies II* (Uitgaven van het Nederlands Historisch–Archaeologisch Instituut te Istanbul 34:2; Istanbul: Nederlands Historisch-Archaeologisch Instituut te Istanbul, 1975), 194.

[8] Gilles Quispel, "The Discussion of Judaic Christianity," in *Gnostic Studies II*, 150.

[9] Quispel, "Gnosis," 193.

[10] Gilles Quispel, "The *Gospel of Thomas* Revisited," in *Colloque International sur Les Textes de Nag Hammadi, Québec, 22–25 août 1978* (ed. B. Barc; BCNH 1; Louvain: Peeters, 1981), 245–54.

I also have reservations about Koester's theory regarding the source of *Thomas'* sayings which he develops by comparing this gospel with Q. He suggests that *Thomas* did not use Q directly but represents "the eastern branch of the gattung, *logoi*, the western branch being represented by the synoptic *logoi* of Q."[11] The sayings they share in common come from earlier and smaller collections of logia like those used in *1 Clement* 13 and *Didache* 1, collections which were independently incorporated into the *Gospel of Thomas* and Q.[12]

This hypothesis is certainly conceivable, but it is not without its own problems. Even if we set aside the messy problem of Q's reconstruction as a minimal document and the assumptions that we have made about its genre, content, and development, another problem persists. Is the presence of variants of some of the sayings enough evidence to suggest that Q and *Thomas* drew from the same sources? I think that this question is especially important for us to consider since many of *Thomas'* variants are so different from the parallel Q versions. In fact, many scholars have argued on this basis that the sayings tradition in *Thomas* is independent of and, in some cases, earlier than the synoptic tradition.

I have even more concerns when I am faced with the further implications that Koester builds upon his hypothesis. Since *Thomas* did not "reproduce" the apocalyptic Son of Man sayings so prevalent in Q, Koester maintains that *Thomas* must presuppose a stage when the sayings tradition did not yet include the apocalyptic expectation of the Son of Man.[13] Because of this, the earliest form of Q must have been similar to *Thomas*, the apocalyptic Son of Man sayings entering the text at a later date.[14] This means to Koester that the oldest stage of sayings were "wisdom" sayings rather than apocalyptic in which Jesus is the "teacher" and "presence" of heavenly Wisdom whose words revealed some kind of existential "eschatology," some decisive moment of encounter with the power of God's Kingdom.[15]

---

[11] Helmut Koester, "GNOMAI DIAPHOROI: The Origin and Nature of Diversification in the History of Early Christianity," in James M. Robinson and Helmut Koester, *Trajectories through Early Christianity* (Philadelphia, PA: Fortress, 1971), 136.

[12] Koester, "GNOMAI," 135.

[13] Koester, "One Jesus and Four Primitive Gospels," in James M. Robinson and Helmut Koester, *Trajectories*, 171.

[14] Koester, "Apocryphal and Canonical Gospels," *HTR* 73 (1980): 113.

[15] Koester, "Apocryphal and Canonical Gospels," 113.

The evidence, however, does not seem to me to support this conclusion. The absence of apocalyptic Son of Man sayings in *Thomas* should not necessarily indicate to us that *Thomas* or other early sayings collections were non-apocalyptic. The Christian apocalyptic tradition was much more complex than this as was the Son of Man Christology itself which developed over several decades. For instance, what are we to make of the identification of Jesus in *Thomas'* Kernel sayings with some sort of apocalyptic Judge, sayings that associate Jesus with a figure who will cast God's judgment on the world, select those who will be saved, and cast out those who are to perish (*Gos. Thom.* 8; 10; 16:1–3; 23:1; 40; 57; 61:1; 82; 107)? Might this represent an early stage in the development of the Son of Man Christology?

Frustrated by the inadequacies of earlier explanations of *Thomas'* origins and nature, my own analysis of the *Gospel of Thomas* has stayed away from trying to reconstruct a genealogy of written sources for the gospel. Although I admit there must have been some, I am reluctant to try to identify them. So my approach in the past has been that of a tradition critic, to examine *the various religious traditions* that we find in the *Gospel of Thomas*: a Christian Jewish tradition from Jerusalem, an encratic tradition from Alexandria, a Hermetic tradition from Alexandria, and Jewish apocalyptic-mystical traditions from Palestine and Alexandria.[16] I have attempted, even in my discussions about possible relationships between the gospels of John and *Thomas*, to analyze the relationship on the level of *the dialogue of shared traditions*, not

---

[16] April D. DeConick, *Seek to See Him: Ascent and Vision Mysticism in the Gospel of Thomas* (Supplements to Vigiliae Christianae 33; Leiden: Brill, 1996).
    I have begun to use the term "Christian Judaism" instead of "Jewish Christian" because scholars have meant various things when using the latter phrase. Some have applied the term to any Christian text that uses Jewish ideas. Others have understood it ethnically: Christians with Jewish parents. Most recently, it has come to delineate Christians who observed the Mosaic Law. I now have discarded this term in favor of "Christian Judaism" which I believe to be more historically descriptive in this period. It is only in the second century that we find groups which can be properly labeled "Jewish Christian." These groups (i.e., Ebionites, Nazoreans, and the Elkesaites) clearly identify themselves as Christians who have maintained their connections with the Mosaic Law. By making "Christian" the adjective and "Jews" the noun, I hope to emphasize that the first Christian Jewish communities were expressions of pre-Rabbinic Judaism. Like other forms of first-century Judaism, Christian Judaism was discussing the major themes of Judaism and its history: monotheism, the interpretation and observation of the Mosaic Law, the Temple cultus, and apocalypticism including mystical as well as eschatological subjects. The conservative faction was centered in Jerusalem and initially was led by James and the disciples of Jesus. The liberal faction was based in Antioch and heralded Paul as its great missionary and theologian at least in its early years.

direct literary dependence.[17] Further, I have subjected the *Gospel of Thomas* to a stringent method, the "new" *traditionsgeschichtliche* approach,[18] in order to identify the later accretions and recover *the oldest version of Thomas* rather than the ancient sources upon which the gospel might have been based.[19] This old version I call the Kernel gospel.

2. *Uncovering the Bones of the Kernel Gospel*

Because it is impossible for us to know the extent to which various Kernel sayings may have been moved around or deleted entirely at the levels of revision and manuscript transmission, any attempt to discuss the original structure or sequence of sayings in Kernel *Thomas* must, to some extent, be speculative. Therefore, the reconstruction of the "original" gospel must be understood to be a minimal and tentative reconstruction. My analysis should not be mistaken to suggest that I understand the Kernel sayings I have isolated to be a complete coherent document.

Having said this, however, it is intriguing that once the later sayings have been removed, upon examination of the remaining sayings in their present order, a striking structure for the Kernel gospel and rhetorical arrangement of sayings emerges. Buried beneath layers of later interpretation there emerges an early gospel that, even in its minimal form, seems to have consisted of five speeches of Jesus, speeches which appear to have been intended to "reperform" and "compose anew" selections of Jesus' sayings.

Each of the five speeches begins with admonitions calling the person to seek the truth or promises offering the hearer revelation of the truth (*Gos. Thom.* 2, 17, 38:1, 62:1, 92). The sayings that follow each of these opening "calls" seem to have been strung together mnemonically in order to elaborate the meanings and meaning-effects of a particular theme, a theme which is more often than not left unexpressed with the presumption that it will be obvious from the

---

[17] April D. DeConick, *Voices of the Mystics: Early Christian Discourse in the Gospels of John and Thomas and Other Ancient Christian Literature* (JSNTSup 157; Sheffield: Sheffield Academic Press, 2001).

[18] This approach is detailed in my monograph, *The Original Gospel of Thomas.*

[19] DeConick, "The Original *Gospel of Thomas*," 187–94.

overall content of the sayings within each discourse. The speech is centered around certain admonitions and promises which are then elaborated upon in order to convince the reader to consent to the admonition or believe the promise. These speeches appear to have concluded with a saying about the Eschaton or its demands, serving to underscore the gravity of the discourse and urgency of the message, thus bringing each speech to a close (*Gos. Thom.* 16:1–3, 36, 61:1, 91, 111:1). So it appears that the speech themes were developed by a rhetorical process of elaboration consisting of a compilation of rhetorical questions, maxims, examples, analogies, promises and even warnings.

(a) *Rhetorical Composition*

Is this type of rhetorical composition and gospel speech-structure a salient plausibility in early Christianity especially since we have understood the compositional process of the ancient Jewish and Christian texts to be very scribal?[20] Traditionally, we have thought of an ancient "author" as someone who collects materials from oral and written sources and edits them together, preserving much of the original source material. Modifications are perceived to be minimal, for editorial or specific theological purposes. Most of these modifications are to be located in the editorial bridges that link together the source materials or characteristic clauses appended to the source materials.

Within the last decade, rhetorical critics have challenged this understanding of the ancient compositional process, arguing that the scribal culture that began to dominate the transmission of ancient Christian literature in the late second century has been imposed upon the earlier compositional period.[21] This earlier period, it is argued, is better understood as a "rhetorical culture" enlivened by a creative interaction between oral and written composition. It is a culture that uses both oral and written language interactively *and* rhetorically in the compositional process.[22]

---

[20] Vernon K. Robbins, "Progymnastic Rhetorical Composition and Pre-Gospel Traditions: A New Approach," in *The Synoptic Gospels: Source Criticism and the New Literary Criticism* (ed. C. Focant; BETL 110; Leuven: Peeters & Leuven University Press, 1993), 116–21.

[21] Robbins, "Progymnastic Rhetorical Composition," 111–47; cf. Helmut Koester, *Ancient Christian Gospels: Their History and Development* (Philadelphia, PA: Trinity Press International, 1990), 31–43.

[22] Tony M. Lentz, *Orality and Literacy in Hellenic Greece* (Carbondale, IL: Southern Illinois University Press, 1989).

Evidence of this culture is preserved in the rhetorical handbooks from the ancient world.[23] For instance, Aelius Theon of Alexandria reveals in the earliest manuscript of *Progymnasmata*, that a composition, whether verbal or written, will have its own inner rhetorical nature even when the topic of the composition is focused on the chreia, the speech or action of a specific personage. This inner rhetorical nature was argumentative, the composition was meant to persuade the hearer or reader to a particular action or point of view. The chreia could be presented as a maxim, an explanation, a witty remark, a syllogism, an enthymene, an example, a wish, a symbol, an ambiguous statement, a change of subject, or a combination of these. In fact, Theon tells us that a chreia could be elaborated into a fuller speech or essay in order to create a more complete argument by adding rationales, statements from the opposite, examples, amplifications, and more. This type of elaboration will often develop an argument that would give a meaning to the chreia that a hearer or reader might not be able to gain for him or herself.[24]

Part of this compositional process, Theon reveals, is that it involved an oral dimension. Theon's first exercise with the chreia is "the recitation." The teacher would present a speech or action gleaned from oral or written sources, and his students would write it down "clearly in the same words or in others as well."[25] The students were encouraged to write down as much or as little verbatim from the speech as they saw fit. The point of the exercise was for the students to develop clarity of argument, not verbatim repetition. Certainly their arguments would contain a significant repetition of the teacher's speech, but this would appear in varied contexts in order to make the old traditions meet the needs of a new day or persuade a different

[23] Ronald F. Hock and Edward N. O'Neil, eds., *The Progymnasmata* (vol. 1 of *The Chreia in Ancient Rhetoric*; SBLTT 27: Graeco-Roman Religion Series 9; Atlanta, GA: Scholars Press, 1986); James Butts, "The 'Progymnasmata' of Theon: A New Text with Translation and Commentary" (Ph.D. diss., The Claremont Graduate School; 1987); George A. Kennedy, *New Testament Interpretation through Rhetorical Criticism* (Chapel Hill: University of North Carolina Press, 1984); Burton L. Mack, *A Myth of Innocence: Mark and Christian Origins* (Philadelphia, PA: Fortress, 1988), 161–65, 186–92, 198–204; Burton L. Mack and Vernon K. Robbins, *Patterns of Persuasion in the Gospels* (FF: Literary Facets; Sonoma, CA: Polebridge Press, 1989); Burton L. Mack, *Rhetoric and the New Testament* (GBS; Minneapolis: Fortress, 1990).

[24] I am indebted to Vernon Robbins for this understanding of the compositional process which he lays out so eloquently in "Progymnastic Rhetorical Composition," 119–21.

[25] Hock and O'Neil, *The Progymnasmata*, 95.

audience. Examples from the *Progynmasmata* show that the students' compositions featured different inflections, expansions, and abbreviations. The beginnings and endings of the recitations were frequently modified to link subjects, provide commentary, or extend the argument. The body of the recitations could be abbreviated as well as lengthened by adding questions, responses, acts, and much more.[26]

I agree with the rhetorical critics that this understanding of ancient composition certainly explains well what we have long observed in early Christian texts: the extensive variation of words in the gospels alongside extensive verbatim repetition.[27] In fact, I would go even farther to argue that it gives us insight into the accrual of older traditions and newer traditions in our gospels as well. Our early Christian gospel texts are about the "reperformance" of Jesus' words and deeds. In the process of the reperformance, the old oral and written traditions are given new life by juxtaposing them with newer oral and written traditions, interpretations and contexts. In this way, the relevance of the older material is maintained in the face of changing times and situations.

The repercussions of this are far-reaching. We already knew from literary-critical and historical-critical analyses of the gospels that the early sayings traditions were unstable. Now it is clearer how and why this was the case. The first Christians did not just preserve traditions of Jesus in haphazard collections or lists that were later organized and used as "sources" for the gospel authors. Rather when they first began to write down the sayings of Jesus, they apparently did so rhetorically in speeches with the knowledge or intent that these speeches would be reperformed and developed in the process.

The reperformance, of course, would have varied depending upon the audience, the purpose of the speaker or author, and the occasion. This alone gives new insight into the passing remarks made by Papias when he writes that Peter used to "adapt his teachings to the occasion" and that Mark, "his interpreter, wrote down carefully, but not in order" the traditions of the Lord. Papias sees his own work, *The Sayings*

---

[26] Vernon Robbins, "The Chreia," in *Greco-Roman Literature and the New Testament: Selected Forms and Genres* (ed. David E. Aune; SBLSBS 21; Atlanta, GA: Scholars Press, 1988), 13–16; Robbins, "Progymnastic Rhetorical Composition," 119–21.

[27] Vernon Robbins, "Writing as a Rhetorical Act in Plutarch and the Gospels," in *Persuasive Artistry: Studies in New Testament Rhetoric in Honor of George A. Kennedy* (ed. D. F. Watson; JSNTSSup 50; Sheffield: Sheffield Academic Press, 1991), 142–68.

of the Lord Explained, in much the same manner: he is furnishing his reader with the traditions he has heard from the presbyters "along with the interpretations" of the traditions (Eusebius, *Hist. eccl.* 39).

This type of transmission is very clearly described by Clement in the *Pseudo-Clementine* corpus. The process of composition is characterized here in very interactive terms, having both oral and written dimensions of remembrance and interpretation, beginning with a teacher delivering a speech to his pupils. The pupils were commissioned to transmit these teachings and their interpretations in both verbal and written formats. Thus, in the *Recognitions*, Peter tells us that the charge to Jesus' disciples was an oral one, to go out and "expound the sayings and affirm the judgments" of the Prophet Jesus. "We are not commissioned to say anything of our own, but to unfold the truth of his words" (*Rec.* 2.34). After Clement is instructed about the teachings of the True Prophet by Peter, he makes some fascinating comments about the sequencing of Peter's speeches:

> I shall now call to mind the things which were spoken, in which the order of your discussion greatly helps me; for the way in which the things that you said followed by consequence upon one another, and were arranged in a balanced manner, makes them easily recalled to memory by the lines of their order. For the order of sayings is useful for remembering them: for when you begin to follow them point by point in succession, when anything is wanting, immediately the sense seeks for it; and when it has found it, retains it, or at all events, if it cannot discover it, there will be no reluctance to ask it of the master (*Rec.* 1.23).

The *Pseudo-Clementines* seem to be preserving a very old memory from the early movement about the process of transmission of the traditions associated with Jesus. It appears that the sayings of Jesus first began to be collected into speeches in which the sayings were arranged rhetorically to provide a memorable interpretation or present an argument to the audience. If the sense of the rhetoric was unclear, it was expected that the pupil would inquire after it by asking the teacher. The teacher would expound or justify the sayings accordingly.

Clement goes on to tell us that he himself has been commissioned to write down the words and instructions of the True Prophet which had been spoken by his own teacher, Peter. This record was to be sent to James for use in proselytizing (*Rec.* 1.17; *Hom. Epistle of Peter to James* 2). When the pupil wrote down the speech of his teacher, it appears that another layer of interpretation was imposed upon the sayings since Clement says that after he heard the teachings of the True Prophet from Peter, he *"reduced into order what he had spoken to me* and compiled a book concerning the True Prophet" (*Rec.* 1.17). This seems to have further complicated the matter since Peter tells us that the words which Jesus himself said were "plainly spoken" by him but "not plainly written" afterwards. This meant that "when they were read" to proselytes, they could not be understood "without an expounder" (*Rec.* 1.21).

Thus the process seems to have begun with the collection and arrangement of sayings of Jesus into speeches which were used by the first Christians to convert others. These speeches were explained by the preacher whenever the need arose. The speeches were sometimes written down. The sayings were rearranged and reinterpreted in the scribal process. When these written speeches were then read to audiences, they too had to be expounded in order to continue to make sense of them or perhaps to provide alternative interpretations for them. So it appears that the "pre-gospel" sayings traditions were subjected to subsequent updating and interpretation when they were reperformed, something that occurred whenever the sayings were recited or rewritten. The "final" form of the traditions preserved in our gospels is thus the result of their reperformance over a lengthy period of time.

(b) *A Rhetorical Reading of the Kernel Speeches*

The *Gospel of Thomas* is a fine example of this process of reperformance, a gospel which I understand to be an aggregate collection of sayings that accumulated over time. It began as a gospel of speech-acts of Jesus in which select themes were elaborated through a mnemonic and rhetorical arrangement of sayings of the Lord. This elaboration reflects the *progymnastic* patterns of recitation and composition such as those referred to by Aelius Theon of Alexandria in his *Progymnasmata* and other pre-gospel sources like Luke's Sermon on the Plain.[28] What were the themes of these five speeches? How might the rhetoric have flowed? I offer here a possible reading of the speeches based on my understanding of their *progymnastic* rhetorical patterns.

---

[28] Vernon Robbins, "Progymnastic Rhetorical Composition," 111–47; see also, Richard A. Horsley with Jonathan A. Draper, *Whoever Hears You Hears Me: Prophets, Performance, and Tradition in Q* (Harrisburg, PA: Trinity Press International, 1999), 123–94.

First Speech: ESCHATOLOGICAL URGENCY

Jesus introduces the collected speeches by leading off his first speech with two admonitions that the hearer seek the truth (*Gos. Thom.* 2:1, 5:1 opening admonitions). The person who seeks the truth is promised an amazing journey that will ultimately lead to "rest" (*Gos. Thom.* 2 Gr., rationale). Counter the wisdom of the world, those hearers who think they already know the truth are told that they do not, while those who think themselves to be ignorant will be the ones to gain knowledge. Thus "many who are first will become last, and the last will be first" (*Gos. Thom.* 4:2–3: contrawisdom rule). Jesus promises to reveal what has previously been hidden because "there is nothing hidden which will not become manifest" (*Gos. Thom.* 5:2: rationale).

The subsequent sayings in this first speech, through rhetorical elaboration, stress the critical nature of the times. Jesus tells his followers that they must behave correctly: they must not lie or do to others what they hate to have done to themselves (*Gos. Thom.* 6:2–3: admonitions). They should be exclusively committed to the truth which is about to be revealed to them just like the fisherman who casts his net into the sea keeping only the one fine large fish and casting all others back (*Gos. Thom.* 8: analogy). They should be like the seed that fell on good soil and produced good fruit rather than the seed that the birds gathered, or fell on rock or among thorns and did not survive (*Gos. Thom.* 9: analogy). Their decision is critical since Jesus is already casting God's Judgment upon the world (*Gos. Thom.* 10: rationale). The universe is quickly passing away (*Gos. Thom.* 11:1: rationale). They should take this message to others, eating what is set before them and healing (*Gos. Thom.* 14:4). So imminent is the end, that they, even now, have direct access to God's throne where they can bow down before God in worship (*Gos. Thom.* 15: admonition). Unfortunately, people have not understood Jesus or this time of distress. Although people think that Jesus came to cast peace on the earth, the truth is that he came to cast God's Judgment: fire, sword and war (*Gos. Thom.* 16:1–3: contrawisdom rule).

Second Speech: ESCHATOLOGICAL CHALLENGES

This type of *progymnastic* rhetorical discourse is visible in the second speech as well which elaborates the theme of true discipleship in an eschatological time. In this speech the truth about discipleship is revealed to the hearer, truth that Jesus claims has been hidden until now (*Gos. Thom.* 17: promise). The time is ripe for this revelation

since the Kingdom of God has already broken into the world and
soon will be fully manifested; like a small mustard seed which has been
sown in tilled soil, the Kingdom will quickly mature into "a great
plant" (*Gos. Thom.* 20: rationale). Jesus tells the hearer that his disciple must be ready for the coming of God's Kingdom and the practical difficulties that are expected to come along with it (*Gos. Thom.*
21:5: analogy), to understand that the Judgment is as near as the
sickle which is in hand ready to reap the ripened grain (*Gos. Thom.*
21:9–10: analogy). Jesus promises that he himself will be the judge,
choosing "you, one out of a thousand, and two out of ten thousand"
(*Gos. Thom.* 23:1: promise).

Jesus says that he expects the hearer will follow him as "a man
of light," lighting up "the whole world" (*Gos. Thom.* 24:3: maxim).
He admonishes the hearer to "love" and "guard" his brother like
his own "soul" and to remove the "mote" from his own eye before
trying to do the same to his brother's (*Gos. Thom.* 25 and 26: admonitions). Jesus both promises his hearer that he will be with him (*Gos.
Thom.* 30:2: promise) and warns him that his followers will be persecuted like he was. Like all prophets, they can expect to be rejected,
like a physician, they can not heal people they know (*Gos. Thom.* 31:
examples). Even so, they must be like a city built on a high mountain
(*Gos. Thom.* 32: analogy), preaching from the housetops (*Gos. Thom.*
33:1: admonition). They must be like a lamp set out on a lampstand
rather than hiding themselves under a bushel basket (*Gos. Thom.* 33:2:
analogy). They are not to be like blind men leading blind men (*Gos.
Thom.* 34: statement from the opposite). When faced with an opponent,
they should bind him first and then take him on (*Gos. Thom.* 35:
example). The situation that the disciples face is so urgent that they
can not be concerned about even the most essential daily matters
like clothing or food. They must rely on God for all of their needs
(*Gos. Thom.* 36: admonition).

Third Speech: EXCLUSIVE COMMITMENT TO JESUS
The focus of this speech is on the theme that only Jesus reveals the
truth so the hearer must listen to him and serve him exclusively (Gos.
Thom. 38:1: maxim). Particularly important to this section is Jesus'
insistence that the Pharisees, even though they possess the keys of
the Kingdom, should not be heeded by the hearer because they have
hidden the truth from themselves and others (Gos. Thom. 39:1–2:
example). Readers are admonished to be as "wise as serpents and as

innocent as doves" when it comes to listening to the Pharisees (Gos. Thom. 39:3: admonition). The rationale for this is twofold: the Pharisees are compared to a grapevine that has been planted outside the Father and that will be yanked out by its roots (Gos. Thom. 40: rationale); the Pharisees have nothing and will be deprived even of that (Gos. Thom. 41: rationale). In this context, Jesus commands the hearer to "pass by" the teaching of the Pharisees and others (Gos. Thom. 42: admonitions). The Pharisees are blasphemers who will not be forgiven (Gos. Thom. 44: maxim). The truth can not be harvested from the Pharisees because they have evil in their hearts (Gos. Thom. 45: analogy). Even John the Baptist who is so highly regarded does not have the truth. In fact, the person to whom Jesus has revealed the truth is greater than John (Gos. Thom. 46: example).

Because of this, the hearer must choose to serve Jesus alone. Rationale is provided: it is "impossible for a man to mount two horses or to stretch two bows" or "to serve two masters" (*Gos. Thom.* 47:1–2: rationale). Analogies are made to wine drinking, wine manufacturing, and mending a garment (47:3–5: analogies) and promises are given: serving Jesus means that the disciple is a peacemaker whose words will have tremendous power, even moving mountains (*Gos. Thom.* 48). By blessing the poor, Jesus is telling the hearer that serving him alone means that the disciple must have not divide his interests between Jesus and wealth (*Gos. Thom.* 54: example). Serving Jesus alone means that the disciple must even hate his own family (*Gos. Thom.* 55: example). The hearer is reminded that his decision to exclusively follow Jesus is critical because he will be held accountable for it. There will be a harvest. The hearer does not want to make the wrong decision and, like a weed, be pulled up on that day and burned (*Gos. Thom.* 57: rationale). Rather those disciples who suffer by serving Jesus now are blessed (*Gos. Thom.* 58: rule). At the End, only the few who make the right choice will receive the final reward (*Gos. Thom.* 61:1: promise): "Two will rest on a bed: the one will die, the other will live."

Fourth Speech: THE SELECTION OF THE WORTHY FEW
In the fourth speech, this type of *progymnasmatic* elaboration continues, emphasizing that only a select number of people are worthy to know the truth that Jesus reveals about himself (*Gos. Thom.* 62:1: promise). The rationale that Jesus provides for this seems to come from some ancient adage that a person generally does not let his left hand know

what his right hand is doing (*Gos. Thom.* 62:2: rationale). Jesus then discusses the characteristics of those who are not worthy to receive his teaching: the person who does things for personal gain (*Gos. Thom.* 63: statement of the opposite) and the person who has other obligations, obligations that keep him from the Messianic banquet table (*Gos. Thom.* 64:1: analogy). In fact, most of the people that Jesus met were so unworthy that they were even responsible for his death (*Gos. Thom.* 65: example), a fact that is given authoritative testimony as support (*Gos. Thom.* 66: authoritative testimony).

The speech then appears to turn to elaborate on the characteristics of those who are worthy of his teaching. Those people who are hated and persecuted are the worthy ones (*Gos. Thom.* 68:1: contrawisdom rule) as well as those who are hungry (*Gos. Thom.* 69:2: contrawisdom rule). Counter to the wisdom of the majority, Jesus denies that the Temple provides the way to achieve worthiness by warning that the Temple will be destroyed and will not be rebuilt (*Gos. Thom.* 71: contrawisdom rule). Those who are worthy of Jesus' teaching are not to be like the silly man who came to Jesus concerned about his inheritance (*Gos. Thom.* 72: example from the opposite). Rather they are to be like a few hardworking field hands bringing in a large harvest (*Gos. Thom.* 73: analogy). The worthy are not to be counted among the many who are standing around an empty drinking trough (*Gos. Thom.* 74: analogy from the opposite). Rather they are to be like the shrewd merchant who sold everything for a single pearl (*Gos. Thom.* 76: analogy).

This speech seems to have used a set of rhetorical questions to shift the discussion so that the sayings progressively begin to reveal to the worthy the truth about Jesus. The worthy disciple is unlike those people who journey to the desert to see great men because Jesus is not like a king or other men (*Gos. Thom.* 78: rhetorical questions). Jesus is not like these kings and great men because he alone is blessed from the womb and speaks God's word (*Gos. Thom.* 79: rationale). In fact, Jesus admonishes people other than himself to be kings (*Gos. Thom.* 81: admonition). In contrast, Jesus dwells in a heavenly Kingdom of fire and it is there that he will reveal himself to the worthy (*Gos. Thom.* 82: maxim) because the earth is not the permanent residence of the human being and "rest" cannot be found here (*Gos. Thom.* 86: rationale). The hearer is asked in the two rhetorical questions that follow, why he is concerned with observing Jewish rituals in the way that some Pharisees have demanded (*Gos. Thom.* 89: rhetorical questions). The hearer is admonished to choose Jesus' leadership instead because his yoke is "easy" and his lordship is "mild" and his future promise is "rest" (*Gos. Thom.* 90: admonition). The speech concludes on the note that there are some who are not worthy since they have examined "the face of heaven and earth" but do not understand who Jesus is or the urgency of this time (*Gos. Thom.* 91: contrawisdom rule).

Fifth Speech: THE IMMINENT KINGDOM OF GOD
In the last speech, the truth about God's Kingdom is revealed. Hearers are admonished to seek the truth because Jesus wants to reveal it now even though Jesus has not always done so (*Gos. Thom.* 92: admonition). Jesus has not revealed the truth previously because a person must be careful not to give "what is holy to the dogs" or throw "the pearls to swine" (*Gos. Thom.* 93: rationale). But now if the hearer seeks the truth, Jesus will give it to him; if the hearer knocks on the door, Jesus will let him in (*Gos. Thom.* 94: promise). Jesus implies that because the hearer has received the truth freely, he must now freely give it to others by presenting an analogous situation in which a person is told to lend money at no interest to the person who can not pay it back (*Gos. Thom.* 95: admonition).

What follows is a series of parables and examples that reveal the truth of God's Kingdom. The inauguration of the Kingdom is like the amazing surprise of a pinch of leaven growing large loaves of bread (*Gos. Thom.* 96: analogy); although its beginnings look small and impossible now, the rule of God will soon be fully established. Its coming is astonishing like the reaction of a woman who returns home with a jar of meal, only to find it empty because the handle had broken off on the way (*Gos. Thom.* 97: analogy). It requires preparation like the man who prepared himself before murdering another man (*Gos. Thom.* 98: analogy). Those people who do the will of God will enter the Kingdom and they will form a family that will replace their human families (*Gos. Thom.* 99: example). Unlike earthly rulers such as Caesar and his earthly kingdom Rome, God does not demand money and taxes (*Gos. Thom.* 100:1–2: example). The Pharisees do not have the answers about God's Kingdom because they are like a dog sleeping in the manger of oxen, "neither does he eat nor does he let the oxen eat" (*Gos. Thom.* 102: woe). The hearer is warned that he must be ready for God's Kingdom and any distress associated with its coming (*Gos. Thom.* 103: maxim): "Fortunate is the man who knows where the brigands will enter, so that he may get up, muster his domain, and arm himself before they invade." The time of God's Kingdom is compared to a wedding, a time of celebration rather than a time of fasting (*Gos. Thom.* 104: analogy). It is compared to the joyous story about recovering a sheep that had strayed from the flock (*Gos. Thom.* 107: analogy). The surprise and elation that the disciple experiences as the Kingdom is established is like finding a hidden treasure in a field and being able to loan money to other people (*Gos. Thom.* 109). The imminence of God's Kingdom is underscored with what appears to have been the closing to the last speech in the collection: "The heavens and the earth will be rolled up in your presence" (*Gos. Thom.* 111:1: promise).

3. *Hearing the Voice of the Prophet*

Jesus appears to have a very specific role in the sayings found in the old Kernel gospel. The sayings are oracles collected into instructional speeches pronounced by the Prophet Jesus. His words are to be heeded because he alone is able to reveal the truth about God's Kingdom and instruct people how to prepare for the imminent Judgment. Like the faithful remnant that heeded the voices of the previous prophets of Israel, only a few people are worthy enough to hear and understand Jesus' message, a message that *only* Jesus can give. Because this message has been previously hidden and is only known to God, the person who wants to know the truth must receive it from Jesus who alone reveals God's word. So, as we saw, Jesus introduces the collected speeches with two admonitions that the hearer seek the truth (*Gos. Thom.* 2:1; 5:1). The person who seeks the truth is promised an amazing journey that will ultimately lead to "rest" (*Gos. Thom.* 2). Jesus promises to reveal what has previously been hidden because "there is nothing hidden which will not become manifest" (*Gos. Thom.* 5:2). Hearers are admonished repeatedly to seek the truth because Jesus wants to reveal it now even though Jesus has not always done so (*Gos. Thom.* 92). Jesus has not revealed the truth previously because a person must be careful not to give "what is holy to the dogs" or throw "the pearls to swine" (*Gos. Thom.* 93). But now if the hearer seeks the truth, Jesus will give it to him; if the hearer knocks on the door, Jesus will let him in (*Gos. Thom.* 94).

Like previous Jewish prophets, Jesus is portrayed in the Kernel sayings as the prophet who is rejected even in his own village (*Gos. Thom.* 31). In fact, he is characterized as a prophet in the long line of prophets who have been killed over the course of Jewish history. Comparable to the tenant farmers who seized and murdered the landlord's servants and son, the Israelites have killed all of God's prophets including Jesus (*Gos. Thom.* 65). This was understood to be the fulfillment of the prophecy in Psalm 118:22: "Show me the stone which the builders have rejected. That one is the cornerstone" (*Gos. Thom.* 66). Jesus is a prophet whose message is superior even to the message of the revered John the Baptist (*Gos. Thom.* 46).

This depiction of Jesus in the Kernel gospel as a great Jewish "prophet" is similar to the depiction of Jesus in the traditions of the early Christianity from Jerusalem, a tradition I call conservative Christian Judaism.[29] The Jerusalem tradition presented Jesus' earthly role in connection with a line of Jewish prophets who came as models of righteousness and interpreters of the Law. He was the Prophet-like-Moses promised in Deuteronomy (Acts 3:18–26; 7:37). But he was greater than Moses or any other prophet, even his predecessor, John the Baptist (Acts 3:17–26; 7:37). Ultimately though, he was rejected, starting with his own village (Acts 2:23; 3:17–18; 7:51–53; cf. Mark 6:4–5; Matthew 13:57–58; Luke 4:23–24; John 4:44): he was the rejected cornerstone mentioned in the ancient prophecies (Acts 4:11; Mark 12:10–11; Matthew 21:42; Luke 20:17; 1 Peter 2:4–8).

The earliest Christian Jews, the itinerant prophets from Jerusalem, were missionaries with a message, an eschatological message to be sure. They took seriously the continuation of Jesus' own preaching that "the time is fulfilled, the Kingdom of God has drawn near!" (Mark 1:15), insisting that people need to "repent and believe in the gospel" (Mark 1:15). This stanza is taken up in Matthew's discourse on discipleship in chapter 10 of his gospel. Jesus commissions the disciples to "Go nowhere among the Gentiles, and enter no town of the Samaritans, but go rather to the lost sheep of the house of Israel. And preach as you go, saying, 'The Kingdom of Heaven has drawn near!'" (Matt 10:5–7; cf. Luke 10:9, 11). So immediate was the coming of the Kingdom and the Judgment that they believed that Jesus would return as the great Judge, the Son of Man, even before they

[29] See n. 16 above.

had finished preaching in all of the towns of Israel (Matt 10:23).[30]
So their message of repentance and piety was of the utmost urgency.

This understanding of Jesus was not replaced in all forms of later
Christianity. It survived and was further developed in communities
of Ebiontite Christians in eastern Syria, Christians responsible for
the traditions recorded in the *Pseudo-Clementine* corpus. Although the
Ebionite traditions display some later second-century christological
developments, the core elements from the Jerusalem tradition remain
embedded in the later Ebionite materials. These elements are remarkably similar to those features that characterize the Prophet Jesus so
prominently in the Kernel *Thomas*. The Ebionites state over and over
again that Jesus is the only one who reveals the truth. He is the
only one who could "enlighten the soul" (*Hom.* 1.19) because "it is
impossible for a person to know anything, unless he learn from the
True Prophet" (*Rec.* 9.1). Truth can be found nowhere but from him
(*Hom.* 3.11). Jesus' revelation of the truth is so exclusive that it is
even compared to the natural process of gaining knowledge through
our human senses: "no one can see without eyes, nor hear without
ears, nor smell without nostrils, nor taste without a tongue, nor handle anything without hands, so it is impossible without the True
Prophet to know what is pleasing to God" (*Rec.* 1.44). This knowledge
is the truth about the Kingdom of God (*Rec.* 5.10), righteous living,
and promised Judgment (cf. *Rec.* 1.33; 2.20; 3.20).

The "knowledge of truth" given to us by Jesus the Prophet must
be "eagerly sought after" because "no one can confer it except the
True Prophet" himself (*Rec.* 4.5). If anyone desires to learn "all things,
let him seek after the True Prophet" (*Rec.* 8.60; cf. 8.62). In one
passage, people are admonished to "seek the True Prophet" because

> it is he alone who knows all things and who knows what and how
> every man is seeking . . . he works in those who seek after that which
> is profitable to their souls, and kindles in them the light of knowledge.
> Wherefore, seek him first of all; and if you do not find him, expect
> not that you shall learn anything from any other. But he is soon found
> by those who diligently seek him through love of truth . . . (*Rec.* 8.59).

Thus readers are admonished consistently to seek the truth from Jesus
solely because "from none but himself alone can it be known what
is true" (*Rec.* 1.16; cf. *Hom.* 1.19; 2.4; 2.5; 2.6; 2.7; 3.54).

---

[30] For more discussion of the eschatological nature of the itinerants message and
their connection to Jesus' proclamation, see D. Georgi, *The Opponents of Paul in Second
Corinthians* (Philadelphia, PA: Fortress, 1986), 164–67.

There is also a very developed rhetoric in this corpus against the Pharisees who are said to possess the truth because they are the receivers of the tradition of Moses, the keeper of the keys of knowledge. It has already been recognized by Gilles Quispel that the *Pseudo-Clementines* preserve a variant of logion 39 that shows more affinity with the *Thomas* variant than its synoptic counterparts (Mt. 23:13; Luke 11:52). It has been suggested that the reason for this is a common Jewish-Christian source.[31] But the similarities may indicate something even more remarkable than this since it appears that several *Pseudo-Clementine* passages show knowledge of sayings that appear in clusters in the Kernel gospel and apply them hermeneutically in comparable ways. Are we possibly witnessing in the Kernel gospel a particular interpretation of some of Jesus' sayings that became standard in some forms of later eastern Christianity? Or is it possible that at least one of the sources of the *Pseudo-Clementine* corpus was some version of the Kernel gospel?

In the case of logion 39, many of the same rhetorical clusters that we find in the beginning of the third speech of the Kernel gospel, are also applied to the Pharisees in the *Clementine* literature. The focus of the third speech is on the theme that Jesus exclusively reveals the truth so the hearer must listen to him and serve him alone (*Gos. Thom.* 38:1). Just as Jesus insists in the Kernel speech that the Pharisees have the keys of knowledge, they have "hidden" them, not allowing themselves or others to enter (*Gos. Thom.* 39) so the *Pseudo-Clementines* state that the Pharisees have "hidden" the key of the Kingdom of Heaven" (*Rec.* 1.54; cf. *Rec.* 2.46; *Hom.* 3.18).[32] In the Kernel the Pharisees are immediately compared to a grapevine that is "unsound" (*Gos. Thom.* 40) who bring forth "evil" things from their hearts (*Gos. Thom.* 45). They are to be associated with John the Baptist who is great, but not greater than the followers of Jesus (*Gos. Thom.* 46). This understanding of the Pharisees is very similar to the description of them in *Clementines* as men with "unsound doctrine" and "evil deeds" who have hidden the key of knowledge (*Rec.* 2.30). The Pharisees

---

[31] Gilles Quispel, "The *Gospel of Thomas* and the New Testament," in *Gnostic Studies II* (Uitgaven van het Nederlands Historisch-Arachaeologisch Instituut te Istanbul 34:2; Istanbul: Nederlands Historisch-Arachaeologisch Instituut te Istanbul, 1975), 13–14; G. Quispel, "L'Evangile selon Thomas et les Clementines," in *Gnostic Studies II* (Uitgaven van het Nederlands Historisch-Arachaeologisch Instituut te Istanbul 34:2; Istanbul: Nederlands Historisch-Arachaeologisch Instituut te Istanbul, 1975), 24–25.

[32] The synoptics state that they have "taken away" the key (Luke 11:52) or they have "shut the kingdom" (Matthew 23:13).

elevate John the Baptist to the level of Moses and do not understand that Jesus, because he is the Christ, is greater than both; they
have received the truth from Moses as "the key of the Kingdom of
Heaven" but have hid it from the people (*Rec.* 1.54, 59–60).

Furthermore, in the Kernel, the worthy disciple is supposed to
"pass by (ⲣ̄ⲡⲁⲣⲁⲅⲉ)" the teachings of the Pharisees and all others
(*Gos. Thom.* 42).[33] So also, according to the *Pseudo-Clementines*, a person ought to "pass by (παρέρχεσθαι)" all teachings other than those
of Jesus and "commit himself to the Prophet of the truth alone (*Hom.*
2.9).[34] We should note that the Coptic translation ⲣ̄ⲡⲁⲣⲁⲅⲉ probably was rendering the Greek phrase, ἔστε παρερχόμενοι.[35] This reconstruction is collaborated by this passage from the Greek *Homilies*. It
is quite possible that this expression translated the Hebrew עבר as
several scholars have suggested.[36] But it did not originally evoke the
image of a traveller or wanderer, but the notion to pass by or turn
away from someone or something such as we find in Psalm 119:37:
"Turn my eyes away from looking at vanities: and give me life in
your ways" (cf. 2 Sam 12:13; 1 Kg 15:12; Eccl 11:10). In this particular case, Jesus was instructing them to pass by the teachings of
the Pharisees and other teachers, to listen exclusively to his words.

In the Kernel speech, another saying belonging to this rhetorical
cluster implies that the Pharisees possess nothing to give, so they will

---

[33] Bentley Layton, ed., *Gospel According to Thomas, Gospel According to Philip, Hypostasis of the Archons, and Indexes* (vol. 1 of *Nag Hammadi Codex II,2–7 together with XIII, 2*, Brit. Lib. Or. 4926(1), and P.Oxy. 1, 654, 655*; NHS 20; Leiden: Brill, 1989), 70.

[34] Bernhard Rehm, *Homilien* (vol. 1 of *Die Pseudoklementinen;* ed. B. Rehm; GCS 42; Berlin: Akademie–Verlag, 1953), 39.

[35] The first to propose this was Rodolphe Kasser, *L' Évangile selon Thomas: Présentation et commentaire théologique* (Bibliotèque théologique; Neuchâtel: Delachaux & Niestlé, 1961), 71. In fact, we find similar translations of παρέρχομαι in Matt 5:18, 24:35; Mark 6:48, 13:13, and Luke 16:17. For further use of this verb in texts, refer to Erik Peterson, *Frühkirche, Judentum und Gnosis: Studien und Untersuchungen* (Freiburg: Herder, 1959), 297, 301 and n. 64. For other translation suggestions, see Tjitze Baarda, "Jesus said: Be Passers-By: On the meaning and origin of logion 42 of the *Gospel of Thomas,*" in *idem, Early Transmission of Words of Jesus: Thomas, Tatian and the Text of the New Testament* (ed. J. Helderman and S. J. Noorda; Amsterdam: VU Boekhandel/Uitgeverij, 1983), 179–205.

[36] Joachim Jeremias, *Unbekannte Jesusworte* (3rd ed.; Gütersloh: Mohn, 1963), 107–10, esp. notes 240 and 251; Gilles Quispel, *Makarius, Das Thomasevangelium, und das Lied von der Perle* (NovTSup 15; Leiden: Brill, 1967), 20–22; Gilles Quispel, "Gnosticism and the New Testament," in *Gnostic Studies I* (Nederlands Historisch–Archaeologisch Instituut te Istanbul 34; Istanbul: Nederlands Historisch-Archaeologisch Instituut, 1974), 197.

be deprived even of that (*Gos. Thom.* 41). In *Homily* 18.16, also in the context of a discussion of the Pharisees' possession of the key of the Kingdom of Heaven, the point is made that the Pharisees will not be allowed to keep the key indefinitely: "but from him who is not worthy, even should he seem to have anything, it is taken away, even if he be wise in other matters." It is striking that the rhetorical use of this saying in the *Homilies* mirrors its use in the Kernel gospel which is so different from its Lukan context (Luke 8:19).

Like logion 5, in the Ebionite tradition we are told that the truth which people should seek is hidden and that Jesus alone can reveal it. As we have seen already, in the Kernel it is argued that the truth has not always been revealed to everyone who seeks for it (*Gos. Thom.* 92) because Jesus does not give "what is holy to the dogs" or toss "the pearls to swine" (*Gos. Thom.* 93). Only if the worthy person seeks the truth, will Jesus give it to him (*Gos. Thom.* 94). Again we find that the *Pseudo-Clementine* literature seems to be familiar with this interpretative cluster of sayings, applying the "Dogs and Swine" saying to this precise situation, something that the synoptic variant does not do (Matt 7:6). In one passage we learn that "we ought to be careful, yea, extremely careful, that we cast not our pearls before swine" when we preach the words of truth to an audience filled with worthy and unworthy people alike (*Rec. 2.3*). The teacher of the truth must be very cautious when setting forth the truth in a mixed crowd because "if he set forth pure truth to those who do not desire to obtain salvation, he does injury to him by whom he has been sent, and from whom he received the commandment not to throw the pearls of his words before swine and dogs" (*Rec. 3.1*).

According to the *Pseudo-Clementines*, Jesus "knows hidden things" (*Hom.* 3.13), and reveals "that which lies secretly veiled in all human hearts" (*Hom.* 18.6). He "enables some to find easily what they seek, while to others he renders even that obscure which is before their eyes." This preserves the truth for the righteous, the worthy people whose minds "will fill up secretly" with understanding (*Rec.* 2.25; cf. *Hom.* 18.8). Jesus explains the "mysteries" to the disciples because the truth has had to be hidden from the impious (*Hom.* 19.20). In the Kernel gospel, Jesus similarly states that only a select number of people are worthy to know the truth that Jesus reveals (*Gos. Thom.* 62:1). The reason? Because a person does not normally let his left hand know what his right hand is doing (*Gos. Thom.* 62:2). We discover a comparable application of this saying in *Homily* 18:7–10, an application that is not made by its synoptic variant (Matt 6:3). Embedded in a discussion about preaching to an audience that potentially contains both worthy and unworthy company is the explanatory note: "Since God, who is just, judges the mind of each one, he would not have wished this [truth] to be given through the left hand to those on the right hand." Thus, those present and listening must all be known to the Son and worthy of the revelation. The Son is "alone appointed to give the revelation to those to whom he wishes to give it" (*Hom.* 18.13).

According to the Ebionites, part of the revelation that Jesus is responsible to deliver is the teaching that "God desires mercy and not sacrifice." People were to learn from Jesus that the "place" that God chooses for purification is baptism when one's sins are forgiven through "his wisdom." They are to hear from the Prophet Jesus that the Temple, although instrumental for a time, is the "place" that has often been harassed by "hostile invasions and plunderings" and "at last" will be "wholly destroyed" (*Rec.* 1.37–38; cf. 1.64). Similarly, the Kernel *Gos. Thom.* 71 implies that the Temple will be utterly destroyed. But an even more interesting parallel is the fact that the Kernel saying is embedded in a cluster of logia which are addressing the question, "What makes a person worthy or blessed?" We are told that the hated, persecuted, and hunger are the blessed ones (*Gos. Thom.* 68:1, 69:2). The Temple will be destroyed. The worthy are not to be like the fool who came to Jesus seeking his portion of his father's inheritance (*Gos. Thom.* 72). The blessed are the hard workers laboring in the fields (*Gos. Thom.* 73). They are unlike the majority who are standing around an empty drinking trough (*Gos. Thom.* 74). They are compared to the shrewd merchant who sold everything he had to buy a single pearl (*Gos. Thom.* 76). It appears that, in this rhetorical context, *Gos. Thom.* 71 was understood to imply what the *Pseudo-Clementines* make explicit: worship at the Temple does not make a person worthy before God or blessed by him as many mistakenly think.

In the *Recognitions* it is stated that although the seeker will find a difficult journey to the Kingdom, the "labor" should not be considered "hard" because "at the end of it there shall be rest" (*Rec.* 2.22), a teaching not unlike that of logia 2 and 90. Why is it so essential for the person to seek the truth from Jesus? What "rest" is being promised? As was implied by the sayings in the Kernel gospel, the *Clementine* literature states consistently that the reason for this journey is because it will result in Judgment: "Humans must inquire whether they have it in their power by seeking to find what is good, and to do it when they have found it; for this is that which they are to be judged" (*Rec.* 3.37). The looming Judgment means that people must make the immediate choice to seek the truth or perish (*Hom.* 9.19; 15.6; 20.3). "At the time of harvest," the *Recognitions* say, "the crops are gathered into the barn, but the chaff or the tares are burned in the fire." This is the Day of Judgment, "when the righteous shall be introduced into the Kingdom of Heaven, and the unrighteous shall be cast out, then the justice of God shall be known" (*Rec.* 3.38). At the Judgment, the worthy person will be the one whose mind has received "the best seed" and has brought forth "joyful fruits by good deeds." If a person refuses to receive this seed, "he shall have the cause of his perishing, not from us, but from himself" (*Rec.* 4.6–8; 5.8). "Ignorance" will make a person "the enemy of God," and he can be certain that he will perish (*Rec.* 5.18, 28).

4. *The Origins of the* Gospel of Thomas

The apocalyptic expectations and christological ideas in the Kernel *Thomas* appear to be most similar to the traditions associated with conservative Christian Judaism from Jerusalem and those developed later by the Ebionites. It seems very likely that this collection of speeches was used by the Jerusalem mission between 30–50 CE as it labored to convert people to the faith especially in Palestine and its environments (cf. Acts 10–11:18; 15:1, 22, 27, 32).[37] It should not go unnoticed that the *Pseudo-Clementine* corpus claims to have knowledge of the teachings of the True Prophet, teachings that had been collected into books of speeches in order to be used by Christian missionaries in their proselytizing efforts in and around Palestine. I think it is quite conceivable that the Kernel gospel is a representative example of one of these old speech books from Jerusalem. This association of the original Thomasine Christians with the conservative Christian Jewish tradition certainly indicates that Gilles Quispel's intuition about the origin of the oldest source for the *Gospel of Thomas* was correct. But, based on the speech-structure of the Kernel that

---

[37] For a detailed discussion of missionary activities among Jews and the first Christian-Jews, see Georgi, *The Opponents of Paul*, 83–228.

has emerged in my research, I am not convinced that such a source was an Aramaic narrative gospel.

It appears that the vogue hypothesis that the *Gospel of Thomas* is a collection of "wisdom" sayings warrants substantial modification. In its earliest form at least, it was not a collection of sayings of Jesus the Sage as some scholars have previously proposed. In fact, this early gospel of Jesus' sayings was not independent of the apocalyptic tradition. It did not represent the message of a non-eschatological proverbial Jesus. Rather it was a collection of oracles of the Prophet Jesus, the Prophet who taught the worthy how to live righteously in preparation for God's imminent Judgment. As God's Prophet, he embodied God's wisdom and passed on this wisdom to those who sought it.

Jesus' message at this early stage of interpretation had an apocalyptic character, featuring eschatological dimensions as well as mystical ones. He was the chosen one from birth, the one whose prophetic voice prepared the faithful for their glorious future and warned the unworthy of their future demise. He was God's Judge who was in the process of selecting the few from the many to receive fully the joys of God's Kingdom when its glorious establishment was complete. Jesus, according to the Kernel, taught that God's power and judgment would soon bring this world to an end, that, in fact, this process was already underway. God's presence was directly accessible to the faithful now that the world was coming to an end and the boundary between heaven and earth was becoming more and more permeable. Members of the community believed that they were already participating in the Kingdom as it was gradually being inaugurated. They were already worshiping before God's throne. Jesus, in fact, instructs the faithful in the Kernel *Thomas* about the proper way to worship before God's throne in heaven, patterning the response after those of the heroes in apocalyptic lore (*Gos. Thom.* 15). He tells them to expect to experience a fiery theophany of him as they enter the Kingdom (*Gos. Thom.* 82).

These mystical ideas, however, took on a life of their own once, after the fall of the Jerusalem Temple, when the Thomasine Christians felt the impact of the "delayed" Eschaton. With the collapse of their teleology came a reformation of their apocalyptic thought. This reformation resulted in a shift that served to isolate the mystical dimension from the temporal, making the mystical an end unto itself.

CHAPTER SIX

"LET HIM WHO SEEKS, CONTINUE SEEKING": THE RELATIONSHIP BETWEEN THE JEWISH-CHRISTIAN GOSPELS AND THE *GOSPEL OF THOMAS*

Petri Luomanen

Soon after the *Gospel of Thomas* was available for scholars, Gilles Quispel presented a hypothesis that a significant amount of *Thomas'* logia would be based on a Jewish-Christian gospel.[1] As such, the hypothesis has not found many supporters but it is acknowledged that Quispel's studies include important observations about similarities between the *Gospel of Thomas* and the Jewish-Christian gospel tradition.[2] At least the following similarities are obvious: (1) Some of the logia of the *Gospel of Thomas* are paralleled in Jewish-Christian gospel fragments. (2) Both the *Gospel of Thomas* and the Jewish-Christian gospel fragments

---

[1] Quispel attributed about 60% of *Thomas'* logia to a Jewish-Christian gospel. See, Gilles Quispel, *Makarius, das Thomasevangelium und das Leid von der Perle* (NovTSup 15; Leiden: Brill, 1967), 75. First (see, *Makarius*, 75–111, esp. 106) Quispel assumed that the author of the *Gospel of Thomas* had used two sources: a Jewish-Christian gospel of the Nazoreans/Hebrews and an encritite gospel of the Egyptians. Later on, a third, Hermetic source was added. For the summary of Quispel's hypothesis, see Francis T. Fallon and Ron Cameron, "The *Gospel of Thomas*: A Forschungsbericht and Analysis," *ANRW* 25.6: 4195–251, esp. 4216–19.

[2] Recently, April D. DeConick has presented the hypothesis that *Thomas* was a "rolling corpus" and suggested that its earliest kernel could be related to the Jewish-Christian gospel postulated by Quispel. See, April D. DeConick, "The Original *Gospel of Thomas*," *VC* 56 (2002): 167–99, esp. 197. Some scholars also assume a Jewish-Christian *collection of sayings* behind the *Gospel of Thomas*. Thus, Oscar Cullmann, "Das Thomasevangelium und die Frage nach dem Alter in ihm enthaltenen Tradition," *TLZ* 85 (1960): 321–34. W. H. C. Frend, "The *Gospel of Thomas*: Is Rehabilitation Possible," *JTS* 18 (1967): 13–26; Kendrick Grobel, "How Gnostic is the *Gospel of Thomas*?" *NTS* 8 (1961–62): 367–73, esp. 370, 373. Grobel supports his view with Semiticisms he finds in some of the logia of the *Gospel of Thomas*, and locates the *Gospel of Thomas* in Egypt. Several scholars also assume a connection between *Thomas* and Q's earliest layers. Helmut Koester, in particular, has emphasized the independence of the traditions of the *Gospel of Thomas* and its connection to the earliest layer of Q's wisdom sayings, prophetic sayings, proverbs and community rules. See Helmut Koester, *Ancient Christian Gospels: Their History and Development* (Philadelphia, PA: Trinity Press International, 1990), 86–89.

include readings paralleled in the Western and Syrian textual traditions as well as in Diatessaronic witnesses. (3) Some of the logia in the *Gospel of Thomas* are thought to be based on Semitic originals, and if we are to believe Jerome, the gospel that was used by the Nazoreans was written in a Semitic language. (4) James the Just has a central role in both *Gos. Thom* 12 and in Jewish Christianity. (5) Both criticize riches and business. (6) Jewish religious practices are explicitly discussed in the *Gospel of Thomas*, which suggests a connection—at least a polemical one—between the Thomasine Christians and a Jewish/Jewish-Christian community.

In addition to Quispel's hypothesis, it is possible to discern four other scholarly stances on the relation between *Thomas* and Jewish-Christian gospels: 1) *Agnosticism*. Because so little is known about Jewish-Christian gospels, it is impossible to draw definite conclusions.[3] 2) *Pure coincidence*. A "free-floating" saying may have ended up in several gospels that do not necessarily have any genetic connection with each other.[4] 3) *Common independent tradition*. H. Koester has defended the independence of *Thomas'* traditions from the canonical gospels. If this is correct and Jewish-Christian gospel fragments also partly draw on the same independent gospel/sayings tradition, this may explain some of the similarities.[5] 4) *Common post-Diatessaronic tradition*. H. J. W.

---

[3] See, for instance, Tjitze Baarda, *Early Transmission of Words of Jesus: Thomas, Tatian and the Text of the New Testament* (ed. J. Helderman and S. J. Noorda; Amsterdam: VU Boekhandel/Uitgeverij, 1983), 137.

[4] Thus, Ron Cameron, "The Gospel of the Hebrews," in *The Other Bible* (ed. W. Barnstone; San Francisco, CA: HarperCollins, 1984), 333–35, esp. 334 and Michael Fieger, *Das Thomasevangelium: Einleitung, Kommentar und Systematik*. (NTAbh, n.F. 22; Münster: Aschendorff, 1991), 22. In fact, this explanation partly overlaps with the third one. Sometimes it is difficult to discern whether scholars are thinking about independent sayings collections to which Thomas would have a genetic connection or only referring to traditions that were freely floating around. Cameron and Fieger offer clear examples of the latter, coincidental explanation. See also Philipp Vielhauer and Gerhard Strecker, "Jewish-Christian Gospels," in *Gospels and Related Writings* (vol. 1 of *New Testament Apocrypha*; revised edition ed. W. Schneemelcher; English transl. R. McL. Wilson; Cambridge: Clarke, 1991), 136, and A. F. J. Klijn, *Jewish-Christian Gospel Tradition* (Supplements to Vigiliae Christianae 17; Leiden: Brill, 1992), 36–37, who emphasizes that the traditions in the "Gospel of the Hebrews" (including the parallel to *Gos. Thom*. 2) must have been "circulating in the Christian community."

[5] See Helmut Koester, "Introduction" [to the *Gospel according to Thomas*], in *Gospel according to Thomas, Gospel according to Philip, Hypostasis of the Archons, and Indexes* (vol. 1 of *Nag Hammadi Codex II, 2–7 together with XIII, 2*, Brit. Lib. Or. 4926(1), and P.Oxy 1, 654, 655*; ed. B. Layton; NHS 20; Leiden: Brill, 1989), 38–49, esp. 38–39. Stephen J. Patterson, *The Gospel of Thomas and Jesus* (FF: Reference Series; Sonoma, CA: Polebridge Press, 1993), 68.

Drijvers, for instance, has argued that both the *Gospel of Thomas* and the "Gospel of the Ebionites" must depend on Tatian's *Diatessaron*.[6]

Instead of grand scale hypothesizing, this article focuses on discussing the logia and fragments which are similar enough to suggest a literary dependence. The passages to be discussed are: (1) *Gos. Thom.* 2 (*P.Oxy.* 654.5–9) / Clement, *Strom.* 2.9.45.5; 5.14.96.3, (2) *Gos. Thom.* 99 / Epiphanius, *Pan.* 30.14.5, (3) *Gos. Thom.* 39 (*P.Oxy.* 655) / A "Jewish" marginal reading in Matt. 10:16 ("To Ioudaikon;" Codex Novi Testamenti 1424, ad Matth. 10:16), (4) *Gos. Thom.* 72 / Origen, *Comm. Matt.* 15.14.

Because there is only a handful of points of contact and even among these there are some cases where we have only indirect evidence of agreement, it is clear that all explanations will remain hypothetical. However, although the observations are few and inconclusive as single cases, when they are viewed together a remarkably coherent picture emerges which justifies the following hypothesis: the *Gospel of Thomas* and Jewish-Christian gospel fragments are partly drawing on the same harmonizing pre-Diatessaronic gospel tradition but interpreting it freely in their own theological frameworks.

1. *The Provenance of the Jewish-Christian Gospels and the* Gospel of Thomas

Before the actual analysis of the points of contact, it is necessary to discuss briefly the current commonly accepted views about the provenance of the *Gospel of Thomas* and the number and provenance of the Jewish-Christian gospels. The assumptions about the geographical locations of these gospels have their effect on what kinds of contacts between them are deemed possible and probable.

The provenance of the *Gospel of Thomas* is generally located in Syria because the apostle Thomas and especially the name Didymos

---

[6] H. J. W. Drijvers and G. J. Reinink, "Taufe und Licht: Tatian, Ebionäerevangelium und Thomasakten" in *Text and Testimony: Essays in Honour of A. F. J. Klijn* (ed. T. Baarda, A. Hilhorst, G. P. Luttikhuizen, and A. S. van der Wonde; Kampen: Kok, 1988), 91–110, esp. 92, 104; repr. in Han J. W. Drijvers, *History and Religion in Late Antique Syria* (Aldershot: Variorum, 1994), IV. Recently, this hypothesis has been defended by Nicholas Perrin, *Thomas and Tatian: The Relationship between the Gospel of Thomas and the Diatessaron* (Academia Biblica 5; Atlanta, GA: Society of Biblical Literature, 2002).

Judas Thomas (*Gos. Thom.* Prol.) are closely connected to Christianity in Syria and because there are similarities between the *Gospel of Thomas* and Syrian literature, in particular the *Acts of Thomas*.[7]

According to a widely accepted theory, there were three Jewish-Christian gospels: (1) "The Gospel of the Hebrews" written in Greek, used only by Christians in Egypt and originally quoted by Origen, Clement of Alexandria and Didymus the Blind. In addition, the supporters of this theory ascribe some passages quoted by Jerome to this gospel, assuming that Jerome must have found the passages in the writings of Origen. (2) "The Gospel of the Ebionites," a Greek harmonistic gospel quoted only by Epiphanius in his *Panarion*, (3) "The Gospel of the Nazoreans," used by Aramaic-speaking Nazoreans near Beroia in Syria, and quoted several times by Jerome.[8] In the following, this theory will be called the Three Gospel Hypothesis.

For purposes of comparison with the *Gospel of Thomas*, it is noteworthy that the "Gospel of the Hebrews," which is regarded as the most "gnostic" of these Jewish-Christian gospels, is located in Egypt. It is precisely this hypothesized gospel which has clear connections to Thomasine traditions. It is supposed to include a saying that is similar to *Gos. Thom.* 2 and *P. Oxy.* 654. 5–9 (Clement, *Strom.* 2.9.45.5; 5.14.96.3) and a saying that talks about the Holy Spirit as Jesus'

---

[7] See Fallon and Cameron, "The *Gospel of Thomas*," 4227; Koester, "Introduction," 38–40; Fieger, *Das Thomasevangelium*, 4–5.

[8] See, Klijn, *Jewish-Christian Gospel Tradition*, 27–32, 38. With minor differences, Klijn's reconstruction is the same as the one presented in Vielhauer and Strecker, "Jewish-Christian Gospels," 160–65, 169–71; Robert W. Funk, *John and the Other Gospels* (vol. 2 of *New Gospel Parallels*; ed. Robert W. Funk; Philadelphia, PA: Fortress, 1985), 365–70, 372–89. The Three Gospel Hypothesis has a prominent position because it is presented in widely used handbooks. Nevertheless, there are scholars who do not want to make a distinction between the "Gospel of the Hebrews" and the "Gospel of the Nazoreans." See, for instance, Simon Mimouni, *Le judéo-christianisme ancien: Essais historiques* (Paris: Cerf, 1998), 209–11, 215–16; Ray A. Pritz, *Nazarene Jewish Christianity: From the End of the New Testament Period until Its Disappearance in the Fourth Century* (Leiden: Brill, 1988), 85. Furthermore, from the viewpoint of Diatessaronic studies, William L. Petersen has raised the question whether the fragments usually thought to derive from two (or three) different gospels could as well be rooted in one and the same gospel related to Diatessaronic tradition because there are Diatessaronic readings in both the reconstructed "Gospel of the Nazoreans" and in the "Gospel of the Ebionities." See, William L. Petersen, *Tatian's Diatessaron: Its Creation, Dissemination, Significance and History in Scholarship* (Supplements to Vigiliae Christianae 25; Leiden: Brill, 1994), 29–31, 39–41. For the earliest history of research, see Rudolf Handmann, *Hebräer-Evangelium: Ein Beitrag zur Geschichte und Kritik des Hebräischen Matthäus* (Leipzig: Hinrichs, 1888), 1–25.

mother (Origen, *Comm. Jo.* 2.12)—a theme characteristic of Syrian Christianity and the *Acts of Thomas* (cc. 7, 27, 39, 50). In addition, a couple of Jerome's quotations that deal with the Spirit (Jerome, *Comm. Isa.* 11.1–3; Jerome, *Comm. Ezech.* 18.5–9) and James the Just (Jerome, *Vir. ill.* 2) are also attributed to this gospel. Consequently, according to Vielhauer and Strecker, the Jewish Christianity of the "Gospel of the Hebrews" "contains syncretistic-gnostic elements," and its Christology of the baptism pericopae belongs "to the circle of such gnostic speculations" as can be found in the "Jewish-Christan-gnostic *Kerygmata Petrou*" (see *Ps.-Clem. Hom.* 3.20.2).[9] Notably, Klijn, a well-known supporter of the Three Gospel Hypothesis, emphasizes that the "Gospel of the Hebrews" was composed in the first half of the second century and "known in Egypt only."[10] In his view, the "Gospel of the Hebrews" "reflects material that was current during a pre-canonical period" and the "Gospel was composed without the help of canonical traditions." Thus, the Three Gospel Hypothesis postulates an independent, pre-canonical gospel tradition and locates it in Egypt although it represents the same kind of Wisdom and Spirit traditions that appear in the Thomasine writings composed in Syria.

The discrepancy between the present majority views on the provenance of the *Gospel of Thomas* and the "Gospel of the Hebrews" justifies the question whether present scholarship has correctly located these gospels. In this case, it is the reconstruction of the "Gospel of the Hebrews" and its Egyptian origin that are most prone to criticism.

A closer look at the criteria on which the reconstruction of the three separate Jewish-Christian gospels is based reveals the circular character of the argumentation. Because Epiphanius' "Gospel of the Ebionites" is clearly an entity of its own, the touchstone of the reconstruction is the distinction made between the "Gospel of the Hebrews"

---

[9] Vielhauer and Strecker, "The Jewish-Christian Gospels," 173–74.

[10] Klijn, *Jewish-Christian Gospel Tradition*, 33. However, a few pages earlier (p. 12, 30) Klijn notes that the "Gospel of the Hebrews" was said to be known to the Palestinian Christian Hegesippus (Eusebius, *Hist. eccl.* 4.25.1). Elsewhere Klijn has also argued that the "Gospel of the Hebrews" was a product of one of the Egyptian wisdom schools. See, *Jewish-Christian Gospel Tradition*, 40; A. F. J. Klijn, "Jewish-Christianity in Egypt," in *The Roots of Egyptian Jewish Christianity* (ed. B. A. Pearson and J. E. Goehring; SAC; Philadelphia, PA: Fortress, 1986), 161–75. Also Vielhauer and Strecker emphasize that the "Gospel of the Hebrews" differs "considerably from the canonical Gospels" and that "Its stories and sayings scarcely permit of their being understood as developments of synoptic or Johannine texts" ("The Jewish-Christian Gospels," 172).

and the "Gospel of the Nazoreans." Vielhauer and Strecker describe the criteria as follows:[11]

> Criteria for derivation from the Aramaic GN [the Gospel of the Nazoreans] must be: (a) indications that the text has a Semitic basis and (b) the Synoptic character of the text or its affinity in particular with Mt., since the GH [the Gospel of the Hebrews], according to all that we know of it, diverged very much from the synoptic type.

Vielhauer and Strecker back up the latter criterion by pointing out that "according to all that we know" the Gospel of the Hebrews "diverged very much from the synoptic type." But how much do we know about the contents of an Egyptian "Gospel of the Hebrews?" Only three authors cited that gospel in Egypt and of these, Didymus the Blind's quotation (*Comm. Ps.*) deals only with the problem of a disciple's double name (Matthew = Levi or Matthias = Levi). Therefore, we are left with only two pertinent sayings: Clement's saying about finding rest (*Strom.* 2.9.45.5 and 5.14.96.3),[12] and Origen's saying about the Spirit as Jesus' mother (*Comm. Jo.* 2.12). However, precisely these sayings are most clearly paralleled in the *Gospel of Thomas* and the *Acts of Thomas*.[13] Moreover, synoptic and non-synoptic types of sayings

---

[11] Vielhauer and Strecker, "Jewish-Christian Gospels," 148. In his earlier publication with Reinink, Klijn refers approvingly to Vielhauer's criteria. See, A. F. J. Klijn and. G. J. Reinink, *Patristic Evidence for Jewish-Christian Sects* (NovTSup 36; Leiden: Brill, 1973), 49, n. 3. In Klijn's monograph on the Jewish-Christian gospels, the discussion of the criteria to be used emphasizes Jerome's chronology and singles out the year 392 as a turning point in Jerome's knowledge about Nazoreans (see, Klijn, *Jewish-Christian Gospel Tradition*, 16–19, 31). Although the discussion occasionally may—inadvertently—give the impression that chronology settles the question (see, esp. 31), in practice the reconstruction seems to follow Vielhauer's criteria.

[12] *Strom.* 2.9.45.5: "He who has become astonished will become king and he who has become king will rest." *Strom.* 5.14.96.3: "He who seeks will not cease until he finds and having found he will marvel and having marvelled he will become king and having become king, he will rest." Origen, *Comm. Jo.* 2.12: "A moment ago my Mother the Holy Spirit, took me by one of my hairs and brought me to the great hill, the Tabor."

[13] In the *Acts of Thomas*, the Holy Spirit is often called "Mother:" *Acts Thom.* 7, 27, 39, 50. Vielhauer and Strecker ("Jewish-Christian Gospels," 174) contend that in Egypt the *Apocryphon of James* (6.19–20) also refers to Jesus as the Son of the Holy Ghost. However, the translation of the passage is difficult. Francis E. Willams translates: "Become better than I; make yourselves like the Son of the Holy Spirit." See, Francis E. Williams, "The Apocryphon of James," in *Introductions, Texts, Translations, Indices* (vol. 1 of *Nag Hammadi Codex I*; ed. H. W. Attridge; NHS 22; Leiden: Brill, 1985), 13–53. According to Klijn (*Jewish-Christian Gospel Tradition*, 55), the idea about the Spirit as mother "may go back to pre-Christian Syriac of Mesopotamian sources." Nevertheless, Klijn also refers to Philo (*Ebr.* 30) and to the idea about the sons of

stand together in the *Gospel of Thomas*. Thus, the existing evidence we do have from an entire gospel (*Thomas*) does not give any support for the assumption that the saying quoted by Clement should be from a gospel that did not include synoptic-type material. The fact that Eusebius lists the "Gospel of the Hebrews" as one of the "disputed" writings but not among those that were used by the heretics (like the *Gospel of Thomas*) also suggests that the "Gospel of the Hebrews" did not deviate too much from the canonical gospels.[14] We may also note that the other "hard evidence" about the character of the Egyptian "Gospel of the Hebrews," namely Origen's saying about the Holy Spirit as Jesus' mother, meets Vielhauer's criterion of Semitic background because the Spirit is feminine in Semitic languages.[15] This, in fact, suggests that the passage should be ascribed to the "Gospel of the Nazoreans."

Three out-of-context sayings quoted by writers in Egypt hardly make a gospel but the Three Gospel Hypothesis is able to collect more sayings from the writings of Jerome. The logic of the hypothesis is as follows: Jerome quoted several times the same saying about the Holy Spirit as Origen had quoted in Egypt but claimed that he himself had found the saying in the "Gospel of the Nazoreans" recently translated by him (Jerome, *Comm. Mich.* 7.5–7; *Comm. Isa.* 40.9–11; *Comm. Ezech.* 16.13). Therefore, it is probable that there are also other places where Jerome says that he had received a saying directly from the Nazoreans although he in fact found it in Origen's

---

Wisdom in Sir. 4.11 and Luke 7:35, concluding that the fragment must be understood "against the background of Jewish Hellenistic traditions." This hypothesis makes it possible for him to locate the "Gospel of the Hebrews" in Egypt.

[14] Eusebius (*Hist. eccl.* 3.25.3) has three main categories: (1) Generally accepted books (ὁμολογούμενα) that are true, genuine, and accepted in the tradition of the church, (2) Disputed (ἀντιλεγόμενα) writings that are not canonical but familiar to most church writers. (3) The writings used by the heretics. The "Gospel of the Hebrews" is placed in the second category but as a kind of addition: "Among those some have placed also the Gospel according to the Hebrews with which those of the Hebrews that have accepted Christ are especially pleased." Of course, the value of Eusebius' statement depends on the question of how well Eusebius' himself, or the "some" he is referring to, really knew the "Gospel of the Hebrews." Usually it is assumed that Eusebius himself had not seen the gospel. Nevertheless, he seems to have received information about it from several sources since he states elsewhere that it was used by the Ebionites (*Hist. eccl.* 3.27.4), Papias knew a story from it (*Hist. eccl.* 3.39.17), and finally he relates that it was used by Hegesippus (*Hist. eccl.* 4.2.28).

[15] As a matter of fact, the "untrustworthy" Jerome (cf. below) refers to this in one of the instances where he cites the Spirit saying (*Comm. Isa.* 40.9–11).

writings. Consequently, it is up to modern scholars to decide which fragments Jerome "stole" from Origen (= the "Gospel of the Hebrews") and which he really received from the Nazoreans (= the "Gospel of the Nazoreans").

Certainly Jerome was not the most trustworthy of witnesses. For instance, it is unlikely he ever completed a translation of the "Gospel according to the Hebrews" although he boasted about it in his *On Illustrious Men* (*Vir. ill.* 2, 3, 16).[16] The Three Gospel Hypothesis' reconstruction is not problematic because it is suspicious of Jerome's information but because it ascribes the fragments to the "Gospel of the Hebrews" and the "Gospel of the Nazoreans" on the basis of a questionable assumption about a "gnostic" Egyptian Jewish-Christian gospel, thereby ignoring discussion about the historical setting where Jerome presented his quotations and his reasons for doing what he did. It follows that sometimes Jerome is accused of "cheating" although all the evidence about Jerome's historical setting would suggest that his information is trustworthy.

One such case is the fragment about Jesus' baptism which Jerome presented in his *Commentary on Isaiah* (Jerome, *Comm. Isa.* 11.1–3).

> But according to the Gospel that was written in Hebrew language and read by the Nazoreans: "The whole fountain of the Holy Spirit came upon him." . . . Further in the gospel . . .: "It happened then when the Lord ascended from the water, that the whole fountain of the Holy Spirit descended and rested upon him and said to him: My son, I expected you among all the prophets that you should come and that I should rest upon you. For you are my rest, you are my first-born son, who shall reign in eternity.

Jerome wrote the commentary between 408 and 410[17] and it is generally acknowledged that by that time he did possess information

---

[16] Last but not least in Jerome's list of the "illustrious men" is Jerome himself (*Vir. ill.* 135). Thus the whole work culminates in Jerome's own list of publications, which includes translations of the New and the Old Testament, although he never completed the translation of the New Testament and the Old Testament was published a decade later. Something similar must have happened with the "Gospel of the Nazoreans." Jerome had collected material, presumably fragments, for the translation and because the translation was in his plans, he already talked about it as a finished work in *On Illustrious Men* (and in his *Commentary on Micha* which was published a bit earlier). Thus, already Alfred Schmidtke, *Neue Fragmente und Unterschungen zu den Judenchristlichen Evangelien: Ein Beitrag zur Literatur und Geschichte der Judenchristen* (TU 37:1; Leipzig: Hinrichs, 1911), 255, followed by Pritz (*Nazarene Jewish Christianity*, 52). For the factual timetable of Jerome's translations, see Stefan Rebenich, "Jerome: The 'Vir Trilinguis' and the 'Hebraica Veritas,'" *VC* 47 (1993): 50–77, esp. 51–53.

[17] See, Klijn and Reinink, *Patristic Evidence*, 218.

about the Nazoreans, their gospel and their Isaiah exegesis which
he cites in the commentary (*Comm. Isa.* 8.11–15, 19–22; 9.1; 11.1–3;
29.17–21; 31.6–9). The only reason why the description of Jesus'
baptism should be assigned to the Egyptian "Gospel of the Hebrews"
is because it accords so well with Clement's quotation paralleled in
Gos. Thom. 2.[18] But as the *Gospel of Thomas*—which was probably
written in Syria—indicates, the roots of Clement's quotation can be
traced back to Syria as well.

The assumed origin of the baptism fragment is connected to the
question about the provenance of the Wisdom and Spirit traditions
shared by the Jewish-Christian gospels and the *Gospel of Thomas*. If
Jerome gave correct information and the fragment about Jesus' baptism was in the gospel that the Nazorean Jewish-Christians used in
Beroia in Syria, this is one more indicator of where to look for the
origins of these traditions. Would it not be easier to assume that the
Thomasine and Jewish-Christian writings entertained similar speculations about Wisdom and Spirit in the Syro-Palestinian area and that
these writings or fragments of them ended up in Egypt only secondarily?

If the Egyptian "gnostic" Jewish-Christian gospel is a mistaken
hypothesis, then the origin of all the fragments is to be sought in a
Syro-Palestinian context. Because Epiphanius uses a Greek gospel
and Jerome knows about a Semitic one and there are also two
different descriptions of Jesus' baptism, it is clear that there were at
least two different "editions" of a Jewish-Christian gospel if not two
distinctly different gospels.[19] In this scenario, the Jewish-Christian gospel
traditions in the Syro-Palestinian area were influenced by Jewish
Wisdom speculation. Probably these speculations were to be found
in the "Gospel of the Nazoreans/Hebrews" because many of the
fragments are from Jerome's writings. There is no reason why Clement's
fragment (parelleled in *Gos. Thom.* 2) could not have been in this same
gospel. As we have seen, the idea that the "Gospel of the Nazoreans"
must closely resemble the Gospel of Matthew goes with the hypothesis about the Egyptian "gnostic" Jewish-Christian gospel. The fragments themselves do not support this assumption. A more detailed
discussion about the reconstruction of the Jewish-Christian gospels

---

[18] See, Vielhauer and Strecker, "Jewish-Christian Gospels," 149.
[19] Of course, the borderline between a "new edition" and a "new gospel" is not
always clear. Even gospels that are usually regarded as distinct entities may have
much in common, as the synoptic gospels do.

would go beyond the scope of this article. What was said above should be enough to justify a working hypothesis for the present discussion: All the fragments are rooted in the Syro-Palestinian area and they were derived from at least two different Jewish-Christian gospel editions, the "Gospel of the Ebionites" and the "Gospel of the Nazoreans/Hebrews," the latter tinted by Jewish Wisdom traditions.

2. *Comparison of Parallel Passages*

"Let Him Who Seeks Continue Seeking"[20]

Gos. Thom. 2	Clement, *Strom.* 2.9.45.5 (TGH: "The Gospel of the Hebrews")[21]
Jesus said, "Let him who seeks continue seeking until he finds. When he finds, he will become troubled. When he becomes troubled, he will be astonished, and he will rule over the all."	"He who has become astonished will become king and he who has become king will rest."
P. Oxy. 654.5–9	*Strom.* 5.14.96.3
[Jesus said], "Let him who seeks continue seeking until he finds. When he finds, he will be amazed. And when he becomes amazed, he will rule. And [once he has ruled], he will [attain rest]."	"He who seeks will not cease until he finds and having found he will marvel and having marvelled he will become king and having become king, he will rest."

---

[20] If not otherwise indicated, the translations of the *Gospel of Thomas* are from Bentley Layton, ed., *Gospel according to Thomas, Gospel according to Philip, Hypostasis of the Archons, and Indexes* (vol. 1 of *Nag Hammadi Codex II, 2–7 together with XIII, 2*, Brit. Lib. Or. 4926(1), and P. Oxy. 1, 654, 655*; NHS 20; Leiden: Brill, 1989). Translations from the Coptic are by Thomas Lambdin (pp. 53–93) and from the Greek (*P.Oxy.*) by Harold W. Attridge (pp. 126–28). The translations of the Jewish-Christian fragments are—if not otherwise indicated—from Klijn, *Jewish-Christian Gospel Tradition*, 47–48, 74, 109–10. A remote synoptic parallel for the admonition "to seek" is to be found in Matt 7:8/Luke 11:9 (Q) but there are so many differences between *Gos. Thom.* 2 and the synoptic passage that there is no need to assume any literary dependence. *Gos. Thom.* 38, 92 and 94 are much closer parallels for the Q-saying, but their analysis would go beyond the scope of this discussion.

[21] For the convenience of the reader, the attributions presented in connection with the translations are according to the Three Gospel Hypothesis (TGH). Thus, they do not necessarily reflect my own opinion.

The Jewish-Christian version of the saying has to be reconstructed from two quotations presented by Clement in his *Stromata* (2.9.45.5; 5.14.96.3). Clement's first quotation seems to be an abbreviated version which is presented as a parallel to Plato's thought according to which the beginning of all knowledge is wondering (*Theaetetus* 155d).[22]

It is often noted that the second, more complete, quotation agrees better with the Greek *P. Oxy.* version of the saying than with the Coptic Nag Hammadi version. The sequence in the Coptic version is: seeking, finding, being troubled, being astonished, ruling over the all, while the Greek Jewish-Christian/*P. Oxy.* version has: seeking, finding, being astonished, ruling, resting. Thus, the Coptic version has one more step in the middle of the sequence: being troubled[23] and at the end, it refers to "ruling over the all" while the Greek version refers to rest. Rest and reigning often appear as parallel expressions in Wisdom traditions describing the last stage(s) in the process of "salvation" (*Acts Thom.* c. 136; *Thom. Cont.* 145.8–15; *2 Apoc. Jas.* 56.2–5).[24]

---

[22] Connection to Plato's wondering (θαυμάζω) also explains why the first quotation uses the verb θαυμάζω while the second one has ταμβέω. The second quotation is to be regarded as original. The first quotation also uses the verb ἀναπαύω while the second one has ἐπαναπαύομαι. Because there is no difference in meaning between these words, there is no need to try to decide which one was in the Jewish-Christian gospel.

[23] The addition is correctly noted by Fieger, *Thomasevangelium*, 20–21. However, Harold W. Attridge, "The Greek Fragments," in Layton, *Nag Hammadi Codex II,2–7*, 1:95–128, esp. 100 followed by Fallon and Cameron ("*Gospel of Thomas*," 4203) and Klijn ("Jewish-Christian Gospel Tradition," 49)—note that in contrast to the Coptic text, the Greek *P. Oxy.* version of *Gos. Thom.* 2 does not have the expression "he will be astonished, and" (ϥⲛⲁⲣ̄ϣⲡⲏⲣⲉ ⲁⲩⲱ).This remark implies that the verb θαμβέω in the Greek fragment would correspond to ϣⲧⲟⲣⲧⲣ̄ of the Coptic text. If this is correct, then the Coptic text did not add the expression "being troubled" but "being astonished." However, although θαμβέω may sometimes include an element of being "astounded" or "shocked" in amazement, it is not so clearly connected to the idea of being "disturbed," "upset" or "troubled" as the Coptic ϣⲧⲟⲣⲧⲣ̄, and if one has to choose which one of the Coptic expressions (ϣⲧⲟⲣⲧⲣ̄ or ⲣ̄ ϣⲡⲏⲣⲉ) is the one that stands for θαμβέω, ⲣ̄ ϣⲡϩⲣⲉ would seem to be a more natural choice. See H. G. Liddell and R. Scott, *Greek-English Lexicon* (London: Clarendon, 1973), θαμβέω and Walter E. Crum, *A Coptic Dictionary* (Oxford: Oxford University Press, 1939), ϣⲡⲏⲣⲉ, ϣⲧⲟⲣⲧⲣ̄ (pp. 581, 597–98). Notably, Attridge also translates the Greek θαμβέω in *Gos. Thom.* 2 "being amazed," and in the same edition, Thomas O. Lambdin translates the Coptic ϣⲧⲟⲣⲧⲣ̄ "become troubled." For the use of ⲣ̄ ϣⲡⲏⲣⲉ elsewhere in the gospel, see *Gos. Thom.* 29. Unfortunately, due to a misprint in Klijn's book (there is the same translation for *Thomas* and *P. Oxy.* version; Klijn, *Jewish-Christian Gospel Tradition*, 47–48) it is impossible to say for sure which translation he follows.

[24] For instance, Fieger, *Thomasevangelium*, 21, thinks that the *P. Oxy.* version, which contains both "rest and reigning," corresponds better with gnostic theology and

Although the theme of resting is prominent in the Coptic *Gospel of Thomas* elsewhere (50; 51; 60), it is omitted in *Gos. Thom.* 2. These changes are obviously linked together: "rest" has been removed, "trouble" added and at the end it is emphasized that the persistent seeker will "rule over the all." The changes suggest that the Coptic version of the saying—or a Greek "second edition" preceding it—was written in a more polemical context than the Greek Jewish-Christian/*P.Oxy.* version. The troubles the author has in mind could be connected to the fight against one's "corpse" (56, 60), i.e., "persecution within oneself" (69) or even to the actual persecution of Thomasine Christians. As a matter of fact, both these themes are paralleled in the *Book of Thomas the Contender* (142.24–32; 145.8–15). If the *Book of Thomas the Contender* is a later product of the same sphere of tradition as the *Gospel of Thomas*, it is logical to link the editing of the Nag Hammadi version of *Gos. Thom.* 2 to the time when the *Book of Thomas the Contender* was composed or attached to the same Nag Hammadi codex as the *Gospel of Thomas*. In any case, the Coptic version of the saying seems to have re-selected and re-arranged traditional wisdom topics for the service of a persecuted or more ascetically oriented community. The Coptic version evidently represents a later stage in the development of the tradition than the Jewish-Christian/*P.Oxy.* version.[25]

"Your Brothers and Mother Are Standing Outside"

Gos. Thom. 99	Epiphanius, *Pan. 30.14.5.* (TGH: "The Gospel of the Ebionites")
The disciples said to him, "Your brothers and your mother are standing outside."	"Further they deny that he is a man, apparently from the word that the Savior spoke when he was told: See thy Mother and brothers stand outside, viz. Who is my mother and who are my

---

must therefore be original. In Fieger's view, the Coptic translator may have misread ἀνὰ πάντα in the place of ἀναπαήσεται. This conjecture is unlikely to be correct because in that case the translator should also have skipped καὶ βασιλεύσας. Below, it will be argued that the differences between the Coptic and Greek versions probably resulted from conscious re-editing.

[25] Scholars usually ascribe the differences between the *P. Oxy.* version and the Coptic version to the (Coptic) editor of the *Gospel of Thomas*. See Klijn, *Jewish-Christian Gospel Tradition*, 51; Joseph A. Fitzmyer, "The Oxyrhynchus Logoi of Jesus and the Coptic *Gospel according to Thomas*," in idem, *Essays on the Semitic Background of the New Testament* (London: Chapman, 1971), 355–433, esp. 416; Fieger, *Thomasevangelium*, 20–23.

He said to them, "Those here who do the will of my father are my brothers and my mother. It is they who will enter the kingdom of my father."

brothers? And he stretched his hand over the disciples and said: Those are my brothers and my mother and my sisters who do the will of my father."

2 Clem. 9:11: For the Lord also said: "My brothers are those who do the will of my Father."[26]

The Jewish-Christian Fragment

Epiphanius quotes the "Gospel of the Ebionites" in order to show that the Ebionites deny Jesus' being a man. The synoptic parallels for the quotation are in Matt 12:46–50/Mark 3:31–35/Luke 8:19–21. "The Gospel of the Ebionites" is generally known as a harmonizing gospel which contains readings from all synoptic gospels. The phenomenon is also observable here.

SYNOPSIS

Matthew	Mark	Luke
12.47		
[εἶπεν δέ τις αὐτῷ· ἰδοὺ ἡ μήτηρ σου καὶ οἱ ἀδελφοί σου ἔξω ἑστήκασιν ζητοῦντές σοι λαλῆσαι.] 12.48 ὁ δὲ ἀποκριθεὶς εἶπεν τῷ λέγοντι αὐτῷ· τίς ἐστιν ἡ μήτηρ μου καὶ τίνες εἰσὶν οἱ ἀδελφοί μου; 12.49 καὶ ἐκτείνας τὴν χεῖρα αὐτοῦ ἐπὶ τοὺς μαθητὰς αὐτοῦ εἶπεν· ἰδοὺ ἡ μήτηρ μου καὶ οἱ ἀδελφοί μου. 12.50 ὅστις γὰρ ἂν ποιήσῃ τὸ θέλημα τοῦ πατρός μου τοῦ ἐν οὐρανοῖς αὐτός μου ἀδελφὸς καὶ ἀδελφὴ καὶ μήτηρ ἐστίν.	3.32 καὶ ἐκάθητο περὶ αὐτὸν ὄχλος, καὶ λέγουσιν αὐτῷ, ἰδοὺ ἡ μήτηρ σου καὶ οἱ ἀδελφοί σου καὶ αἱ ἀδελφαί σου ἔξω ζητοῦσίν σε. 3.33 καὶ ἀποκριθεὶς αὐτοῖς λέγει· τίς ἐστιν ἡ μήτηρ μου καὶ οἱ ἀδελφοί μου; 3.34 καὶ περιβλεψάμενος τοὺς περὶ αὐτὸν κύκλῳ καθημένους λέγει· ἴδε ἡ μήτηρ μου καὶ οἱ ἀδελφοί μου. 3.35 ὃς γὰρ ἂν ποιήσῃ τὸ θέλημα τοῦ θεοῦ, οὗτος ἀδελφός μου καὶ ἀδελφὴ καὶ μήτηρ ἐστίν.	8.20 ἀπηγγέλη δὲ αὐτῷ· ἡ μήτηρ σου καὶ οἱ ἀδελφοί σου ἑστήκασιν ἔξω ἰδεῖν θέλοντές σε. 8.21 ὁ δὲ ἀποκριθεὶς εἶπεν πρὸς αὐτούς· μήτηρ μου καὶ ἀδελφοί μου οὗτοί εἰσιν οἱ τὸν λόγον τοῦ θεοῦ ἀκούοντες καὶ ποιοῦντες.

---

[26] The translation is from Michael W. Holmes, ed., *The Apostolic Fathers: Greek Texts and English Translations* (Grand Rapids, MI: Baker, 1999), 115.

The "Gospel of the Ebionites"	The Gospel of Thomas
Πάλιν δὲ ἀρνοῦνται εἶναι αὐτὸν ἄνθρωπον, δῆθεν ἀπὸ τοῦ λόγου οὗ εἴρηκεν ὁ σωτὴρ ἐν τῷ ἀναγγελῆναι αὐτῷ ὅτι <u>ἰδοὺ ἡ μήτηρ σου καὶ οἱ ἀδελφοί σου ἔξω ἑστήκασιν</u>, ὅτι τίς μού ἐστι μήτηρ καὶ ἀδελφοί; <u>καὶ ἐκτείνας τὴν χεῖρα ἐπὶ τοὺς μαθητὰς</u> ἔφη· <u>οὗτοί εἰσιν</u>	ΠΕϪΕ ⲙⲙⲁⲑⲏⲧⲏⲥ ⲛⲁϥ Ϫⲉ <u>ⲛⲉⲕⲥⲛⲏⲩ ⲙⲛ ⲧⲉⲕⲙⲁⲁⲩ ⲥⲉⲁϩⲉⲣⲁⲧⲟⲩ ϩⲓⲡⲥⲁ ⲛⲃⲟⲗ</u>
<u>οἱ ἀδελφοί μου καὶ</u> ἡ μήτηρ μου καὶ ἀδελφαὶ <u>οἱ ποιοῦντες τὰ θελήματα τοῦ πατρός μου</u>.	ΠΕϪⲁϥⲛⲁⲩ Ϫⲉ <u>ⲛⲉⲧⲛ ⲛⲉⲉⲓⲙⲁ</u> ⲉ†ⲣⲉ <u>ⲙⲡⲟⲩⲱϣ ⲙⲡⲉⲓⲱⲧ</u> ⲛⲁⲉⲓⲛⲉ ⲛⲁⲥⲛⲏⲩ ⲙⲛ ⲧⲁⲙⲁⲁⲩ
	ⲛⲧⲟⲟⲩ ⲡⲉ ⲉⲧⲛⲁⲃⲱⲕ ⲉϩⲟⲩⲛ ⲉⲧⲙⲛⲧⲉⲣⲟ ⲙⲡⲁⲉⲓⲱⲧ

2 Clem. 9:11 καὶ γὰρ εἶπεν ὁ κύριος· ἀδελφοί μου **οὗτοί** εἰσιν <u>οἱ ποιοῦντες</u> <u>τὸ θέλημα τοῦ πατρός</u> μου.

The exact extent of Epiphanius' direct quotation is not perfectly clear because he seems to fill in the setting of the saying with his own words. The verb ἀναγγελῆναι is likely to be a reminiscence from Luke 8:20 (ἀπηγγέλη). The "Gospel of the Ebionites" also shares with Luke the expression οὗτοί εἰσιν οἱ . . . ποιοῦντες in contrast to ὅστις/ὅς γὰρ ἂν ποιήσῃ of Matthew and Mark. Epiphanius himself may have added the verb ἀναγγελῆναι but less likely the expression οὗτοί εἰσιν. Most of the other synoptic expressions in the quotation are paralleled in the Gospel of Matthew. ἰδοὺ ἡ μήτηρ σου καὶ οἱ ἀδελφοί σου ἔξω ἑστήκασιν is directly from Matt 12:47.[27] The word order of Jesus' rhetorical question τίς μού ἐστι μήτηρ καὶ ἀδελφοί differs from both Matthew and Mark (Luke omitted the question), but the wording is a bit closer to Mark because Matthew has filled in the plural subject and predicate (τίνες εἰσίν). Nevertheless, καὶ ἐκτείνας τὴν χεῖρα ἐπὶ τοὺς μαθητάς follows Matthew again and at the end of the quotation, the "Gospel of the Ebionites" refers to the will of "my father" (τὰ θελήματα / τὸ θέλημα τοῦ πατρός μου), which is paralleled only in Matthew. Thus, Epiphanius' quotation has connections to all the synoptic gospels, most clearly to Matthew. It also repeats words that are without doubt editorial in Matthew's gospel: καὶ ἐκτείνας τὴν χεῖρα ἐπὶ τοὺς μαθητὰς, τὸ θέλημα τοῦ πατρός μου (τοῦ ἐν οὐρανοῖς).

---

[27] The verse is in the majority of Greek manuscripts but is omitted in: ℵ*, B, L, Γ, *pc*, ff[1], *k*, sy[s.c], sa. Obviously, the verse was in the copy on which the "Gospel of the Ebionites" is based although it may not have been in Matthew's "original" manuscript.

The Gospel of Thomas

In *Gos. Thom.* 99, the disciples address Jesus as they do in several other logia. Thus, the introduction of the logion is typical of the *Gospel of Thomas* in general.[28] The *Gospel of Thomas* agrees with the synoptic version of the story by saying that Jesus' relatives are "standing outside" (ϲⲉⲁϩⲉⲣⲁⲧⲟⲩ ϩⲓⲡⲓⲥⲁ ⲛⲃⲟⲗ). The expression is most natural in the synoptic narrative context but it comes out of the blue in the introduction of *Gos. Thom.* 99. It is not a precise "brief situational introduction" as in *Gos. Thom.* 22 and 100.[29] Rather, it *presupposes* a situation which is not described in the actual saying. This suggests that the saying is based on a tradition that was at some point transmitted within a wider narrative framework.

In contrast to Mark, Matthew and the "Gospel of the Ebionites," the *Gospel of Thomas* skips Jesus' rhetorical question and gives only his answer. In this respect *Thomas* resembles Luke who also omits Jesus' rhetorical question. However, the wording of Jesus' answer goes its own way in Luke—for which there are no parallels in Matthew, Mark, the "Gospel of the Ebionites" or *Thomas*—when it refers to the "word" of God which one has to hear in order to be regarded as Jesus' true relative.

In the *Gospel of Thomas*, there is an additional remark which cannot be found in the parallel passages: "It is they who will enter the kingdom of my father." However, the same idea is expressed in Matt 7:21: "Not everyone who says to me, 'Lord, Lord' will enter the kingdom of heaven but the one who does the will of my father in heaven." According to Schrage, this clearly shows that *Thomas* must depend on the Gospel of Matthew.[30] Even if this is the case here, it could be a sign of a secondary development within *Thomas*' own tradition history.[31]

---

[28] However, it can be noted that some manuscripts of Matthew's gospel (according to Nestle–Aland, ℵ¹, (892), *pc*, (bo)) explicate that it was "someone of the disciples" who notified Jesus about his relatives who were "standing outside."

[29] Patterson, *Gospel of Thomas*, 67–68, contends that both *Thomas* and Mark have "a brief situational introduction (*Gos. Thom.* 99a; Mk 3:31f.)." Similarly Koester, *Ancient Christian Gospels*, 110. In contrast to *Gos. Thom.* 22 ("Jesus saw infants being sucked.") and 100 ("They showed Jesus a gold coin.") saying 99 *presupposes* a situation—which if described—would read: "Jesus was teaching in a house." In Mark the situation is already described in 3:20–21.

[30] W. Schrage, *Das Verhältnis des Thomas-evangeliums zur synoptischen Tradition und zu den koptischen Evangelienübersetzungen: Zugleich ein Beitrag zur gnostischen Synoptikerdeutung* (BZNW 29; Berlin: Töpelmann, 1964), 187.

[31] Even Patterson, *Gospel of Thomas*, 68 and Koester, *Ancient Christian Gospels*, 110, who argue for the independence of *Thomas*' traditions, take the final clause as sign of the secondary influence of the synoptic gospels on *Thomas*.

Since there is no parallel for the clause in the "Gospel of the Ebionites," the question will be left open here.

Agreement Between Thomas and the Jewish-Christian Fragment
It is more important that there are three points where the *Gospel of Thomas* and the "Gospel of the Ebionites" agree against synoptic parallels. Two of these common phrases are also paralleled in *2 Clem.* 9:11:[32] (1) Matthew and Mark open Jesus' answer with an exclamation: "See, my mother and my brothers" which is followed by a generalizing statement "Whoever does . . ." In the *Gospel of Thomas* and in the "Gospel of the Ebionites" Jesus' answer is directed only to the people around him and is *opened* with the Lukan "These/those here (οὗτοι/ΝΕΤℲΝΕΕΙΜΔ. . .). Originally Luke had placed this phrase after "mother and brother." Lukan οὗτοί εἰσιν οἱ ποιοῦντες can also be found in *2 Clem.* 9:11. (2) "The Gospel of the Ebionites," *Thomas* and *2 Clem.* refer to the "will of the Father." Notably, the "Gospel of the Ebionites," which in this passage mostly follows Matthew, has shortened the Matthean "my Father in heaven" and refers only to "my Father." (3) Only *Thomas* and the "Gospel of the Ebionites" have the sequence "brothers and mother" (followed by sisters in the "Gospel of the Ebionites") in the final clause. In the synoptic gospels, the order is "brothers, sisters, mother" (Mark and Matthew)[33] or "mother and brothers" (Luke).

These similarities show that the *Gospel of Thomas* and the "Gospel of the Ebionites" are drawing on a non-canonical tradition. As regards the character of this tradition, two hypotheses have been presented:

---

[32] Also Clement of Alexandria seems to have known one version of the same saying. *Ecl.* 20.3: ἀδελφοὶ γάρ, φησὶν ὁ κύριος, καὶ συγκληρονόμοι οἱ ποιοῦντες τὸ θέλημα τοῦ πατρός μου. Although Clement's version comes quite close to *2 Clem.* 9:11, it does not have οὗτοί εἰσιν. Therefore its parallelism with *Thomas* and the "Gospel of the Ebionites" is less significant.

[33] However, the majority of Greek manuscripts read in Mark 3:31 "brothers and mother" (Nestle–Aland: (A al), 074, 0134, f^{13}, M, sy[(s).h]). In addition, the Old Latin manuscript *b* has the same reading in Luke 8:21. Notably Mark 3:31 forms the beginning of the present synoptic passage but it is not explicitly quoted in the "Gospel of the Ebionites" or in the *Gospel of Thomas*. Therefore, if one wishes to see the influence of Mark's variant in the "Gospel of the Ebionites" and *Thomas*, one must also assume that their passages were originally part of a larger narrative. Even so, the dependence of *Thomas* and the "Gospel of the Ebionites" on the common harmonizing tradition is indicated by the combination of this secondary Markan reading with the elements paralleled in Luke and Matthew, which characterizes only *Gos. Thom* and the "Gospel of the Ebionites," (with the exception of Old Latin *b* that is also probably influenced by Mark's secondary reading).

(1) The *Gospel of Thomas* and the "Gospel of the Ebionies" both draw on an independent sayings tradition.[34] (2) The *Gospel of Thomas* and the "Gospel of the Ebionites" depend on a gospel harmony.[35]

Patterson, who has argued for the first option, ascribes to the independent, "less embellished," tradition the phrases πατρός μου and οὗτοί εἰσιν, which are common to *2 Clem.* 9:11, the "Gospel of the Ebionites" and *Thomas*, as well as the absence of Jesus' rhetorical question and gesture (Mark 3:33–34/Matt 12:48–49), omitted by *Thomas* and Luke. In practice, Patterson's hypothesis means that the independent tradition would have had a multiple impact on the formation of the passage in the "Gospel of the Ebionites." In the first stage, it would have been available to the editor of Luke's gospel (omission of the question and the gesture, οὗτοί εἰσιν) and to the editor of Matthew's gospel (πατρός μου). In addition, the same independent tradition should have been still available to the editor of the "Gospel of the Ebionites," who at least used canonical Matthew for this passage but took from the independent tradition the form of the final clause (οὗτοί εἰσιν), the sequence "brothers and mother,"[36] and on the basis of the "original," decided to drop Matthew's "in heaven" after the "Father." The *Gospel of Thomas*, for its part, would have stuck quite close to the original form of the tradition. Although a process like this is not totally impossible, it has to be asked if it is really believable that, in the synoptic/Jewish-Christian trajectory, the independent tradition would have been "hanging around" and conveniently available for so many editors who used only parts of it whereas in *Thomas*' trajectory, the tradition would have remained almost intact from pre-synoptic times until the composition of the Coptic edition of the *Gospel of Thomas*.

The gospel harmony hypothesis provides an easier explanation. The final clause in the "Gospel of the Ebionites is understandable as a combination of Lukan οὗτοί εἰσιν . . . οἱ ποιοῦντες with Matthean τὸ θέλημα τοῦ πατρός μου. These two phrases are also conflated in *2 Clem* 9:11 (see above). Although *2 Clem* 9:11 is sometimes taken as an

---

[34] Patterson, *Gospel of Thomas*, 68. John H. Sieber, "A Redactional Analysis of the Synoptic Gospels with regard to the Question of the Sources of the Gospel according to Thomas" (Ph.D. diss., The Claremont Graduate School, 1965), 152.

[35] Schrage, *Verhältnis*, 187; Fieger, *Thomasevangelium*, 252.

[36] Patterson himself has not noted the same order of "brothers and mother" in the "Gospel of the Ebionites" and *Thomas*.

indication of the independent character of the tradition,[37] it speaks more
for the gospel harmony theory. As Koester has shown, several citations in *2 Clem.* are harmonizations of Matthew and Luke. According
to him, the above conflation of the "Matthean and Lukan redactional changes of Mark's text" in *2 Clem.* 9:11 are one example of this
secondary harmonization.[38] Consequently, the combination of "those
here who do" with "the will of my Father" in the *Gospel of Thomas*
should also suggest the existence of the same harmonizing tradition
in the *Gospel of Thomas.*[39] Because *Thomas* and the "Gospel of the
Ebionites" also share the same order "brothers and mother," it is
difficult to explain the similarities between *Thomas* and the "Gospel
of the Ebionites" as a result of two independent harmonizations that
would agree only incidentally. Thus, the dependence of these gospels
on the same harmonized tradition is the easiest solution. Notably, there
are no parallels for the above harmonized readings that *Thomas* and
the "Gospel of the Ebionites" share in the Old Latin, Old Syriac or
other Diatessaronic witnesses.[40] This shows that, at least in this case,
the common denominator of *Thomas* and the "Gospel of the Ebionites"
does not depend on Diatessaronic traditions. Instead, it probably is
pre-Diatessaronic because it agrees with *2 Clement.*

   This assumption is confirmed by the fact that the connections
between *2 Clement, Thomas* and the Jewish-Christian gospel(s) are not
restricted to this passage. It is well known that *Gos. Thom.* 22 ("When
you make the two one . . .") is paralleled in *2 Clem.* 12.2,6.[41] On the
other hand, *2 Clem.* 4.5a ("If you were . . . in my bosom . . .") finds a
parallel in a "Jewish gospel," i.e., in the marginal reading of the
minuscle 1424 ("To Ioudaikon"; Codex Novi Testamenti 1424, ad.

---

[37] Patterson, *Gospel of Thomas*, 68.
[38] See, Helmut Koester, *Synoptische Überlieferung bei den apostolischen Vätern* (TU 65;
Berlin: Akademie–Verlag, 1957), 77–78, 109–111; Koester, *Ancient Christian Gospels*,
351, 360.
[39] However, Koester does not draw this conclusion. In *Synoptische Überlieferung*,
77–79, (when *Thomas* was not yet available to him?) he argues that *2 Clem* 9:11
and the parallel in the "Gospel of the Ebionites" combine Matthean and Lukan
editorial elements. In *Ancient Christian Gospels*, 351, he summarizes his earlier arguments referring to his "more detailed documentation" in *Synoptische Überlieferung*.
Nevertheless, when in the *Ancient Christian Gospels* he discusses *Gos. Thom.* 99 (p. 110),
he does not deal with the existence of the "Matthean" and "Lukan" elements in
Gos. Thom. 99 or with its connections to *2 Clem* and "the Gospel of the Ebionites."
[40] See, Baarda, *Early Transmission*, 46.
[41] See, for instance, Koester, *Ancient Christian Gospels*, 358.

Matth. 7:5).[42] Because *2 Clem.* 12.2,6 / *Gos. Thom.* 22 is a non-canon-ical saying, it does not reveal anything about possible harmonization. However, *2 Clem.* 4.5a—although a non-canonical saying itself—is in the middle of a collection of sayings which otherwise harmonize with canonical Matthew and Luke.[43] This confirms that the author of *2 Clement* had access to pre-Diatessaronic harmonizing traditions that also ended up in the *Gospel of Thomas* and in the Jewish-Christian gospel fragments.[44]

"Wise as Serpents"

According to a marginal note in manuscript 1424, a "Jewish Gospel" ("To Ioudaikon") reads for Matthew 10:16: "more than serpents" (ὑπερ ὄφεις).[45] Thus the whole verse must have read: "See, I am sending you like sheep into the midst of wolves; so be *wiser than serpents* and innocent as doves."

The saying is paralleled at the end of *Gos. Thom.* 39/*P. Oxy.* 655. The reconstructed Greek version of the saying in *P. Oxy.* 655 is different from the "Jewish" reading. In practice, it is the same as verse 10:16b in the canonical Matthew.

> The pharisees and the scribes have taken the keys of knowledge (gno-sis) and hidden them. They themselves have not entered, nor have they allowed to enter those who wish to. You, however, be as wise as serpents and as innocent as doves (*Gos. Thom.* 39 [Coptic]).

---

[42] The Three Gospel Hypothesis ascribes this fragment to the "Gospel of the Nazoreans."

[43] See, Koester, *Ancient Christian Gospels*, 355–57. Koester argues that the saying in *2 Clement* 4:5a cannot be from the "Gospel of the Nazoreans" because there are no traces of Matthean language. It is true that the Matthean "will of my father in heaven" is missing in *2 Clem.* 4:5a and that this shows that *2 Clem.* 4:5a cannot be directly dependant on the "Jewish Gospel" ("To Ioudaikon;" Cod. NT 1424, ad. Matth. 7:5). Nevertheless, it does not prove that the saying quoted in *2 Clem.* 4:5. must have been in a "free tradition." Moreover, *2 Clem.* 4:5 uses the verb ἀποβάλλω which coheres well with the (ἐκ)βάλλω repeated several times in verses Matt 7:4–6.

[44] It is to be noted that *Thomas* and the "Gospel of the Ebionites" did not get their common readings directly from *2 Clement* or from a collection that would have included only the "Sayings of Lord" (cf. *2 Clem.* 9:11) because they have one addi-tional expression in common and they also both presuppose a larger narrative frame-work when they refer to Jesus' relatives that are "standing outside."

[45] The Three Gospel Hypothesis ascribes all "To Ioudaikon" variants to the "Gospel of the Nazoreans." See, Klijn, *Jewish-Christian Gospel Tradition*, 25, 31–32.

The beginning of *Gos. Thom.* 39 is paralleled in the Q-woe against Jewish authorities (lawyers/scribes and Pharisees in Luke 11:52/Matt 23:13). Although there is no parallel for the first part of *Thomas'* saying in the Jewish-Christian gospel fragments, it is relevant for the present theme because there are Jewish-Christian parallels in *Pseudo-Clementine Recognitiones* and *Homilies.*

> Both the scribes and the Pharisees are drawn away into another schism. They were baptized by John, and holding on to the word of truth received from Moses' tradition as being the key to the kingdom of heaven, they hid it from the ears of the people (*Ps.-Clem. Rec.* 1.54.6–7 [Latin]).[46]
>
> The scribes and the Pharisees sit in Moses' seat; all things whatsoever they say to you, hear them. Hear *them*, He said, as entrusted with the key of the kingdom, which is knowledge, which alone can open the gate of life, through which alone is the entrance to eternal life. But truly, He says, they possess the key, but those wishing to enter they do not suffer to do so (*Ps.-Clem. Hom.* 3.18.2–3).

SYNOPSIS

Matt 23:13	Luke 11:52
Οὐαὶ δὲ ὑμῖν, γραμματεῖς καὶ <u>Φαρισαῖοι</u> ὑποκριταί, ὅτι κλείετε τὴν βασιλείαν τῶν οὐρανῶν ἔμπροσθεν τῶν ἀνθρώπων· ὑμεῖς γὰρ οὐκ εἰσέρχεσθε <u>οὐδὲ τοὺς εἰσερχομένους ἀφίετε εἰσελθεῖν.</u>	οὐαὶ ὑμῖν τοῖς νομικοῖς, <u>ὅτι ἤρατε τὴν κλεῖδα τῆς γνώσεως·</u> αὐτοὶ οὐκ εἰσήλθατε καὶ <u>τοὺς εἰσερχομένους</u> ἐκωλύσατε.

Matt 10:16b
<u>γίνεσθε οὖν φρόνιμοι ὡς οἱ ὄφεις καὶ ἀκέραιοι ὡς αἱ περιστεραί.</u>

"To Ioudaikon" in Matt 10:16b
(reconstruction)
γίνεσθε οὖν φρόνιμοι ὑπὲρ ὄφεις καὶ ἀκέραιοι ὡς αἱ περιστεραί.

---

[46] Translation is from F. Stanley Jones, *An Ancient Jewish Christian Source on the History of Christianity: Pseudo-Clementine Recognitions 1.27–71* (SBLTT 37; Atlanta, GA: Scholars Press, 1995), 88. Jones provides a useful translation of Syriac and Latin *Rec.* in parallel columns.

P. Oxy. 655
λέγει Ἰησοῦς· οἱ φαρισαῖοι καὶ οἱ γραμματεῖς ἔλαβον τὰς κλεῖδας τῆς
γνώσεως. αὐτοὶ ἔκρυψαν αὐτάς. οὔτε εἰσῆλθον, οὔτε τοὺς εἰσερχομένους
ἀφῆκαν εἰσελθεῖν. ὑμεῖς δὲ γείνεσθε φρόνιμοι ὡς ὄφεις καὶ ἀκέραιοι ὡς
περιστεραί.[47]

Gos. Thom. 39
ⲡⲉϫⲉ ⲓ̅ⲥ̅ ϫⲉ ⲙ̅ⲫⲁⲣⲓⲥⲁⲓⲟⲥ ⲙ̅ⲛ̅ ⲛ̅ⲅⲣⲁⲙⲙⲁⲧⲉⲩⲥ ⲁⲩϫⲓ ⲛ̅ϣⲁϣⲧ
ⲛ̅ⲧⲅⲛⲱⲥⲓⲥ ⲁⲩϩⲟⲡⲟⲩ ⲟⲩⲧⲉ ⲙ̅ⲡⲟⲩⲃⲱⲕ ⲉϩⲟⲩⲛ ⲁⲩⲱ ⲛⲉⲧⲟⲩⲱϣ
ⲉⲃⲱⲕ ⲉϩⲟⲩⲛ ⲙ̅ⲡⲟⲩⲕⲁⲁⲩ ⲛ̅ⲧⲱⲧⲛ̅ ⲇⲉ
ϣⲱⲡⲉ ⲙ̅ⲫⲣⲟⲛⲓⲙⲟⲥ ⲛ̅ⲑⲉ ⲛ̅ⲛ̅ϩⲟϥ ⲁⲩⲱ ⲛ̅ⲁⲕⲉⲣⲁⲓⲟⲥ ⲛ̅ⲑⲉ
ⲛ̅ⲛ̅ϭⲣⲟⲙⲡⲉ.

Ps.-Clem. Rec. 1.54.6–7
Scribae quoque et Pharisaei in aliud schisma deducuntur. sed hi
baptizati ab Iohanne, et velut **clavem** regni caelorum verbum ver-
itatis tenentes ex Moysei traditione **susceptum, occultarunt** ab
auribus populi.

Ps.-Clem. Hom. 3.18.3. αὐτῶν δὲ εἶπεν ὡς τὴν **κλεῖδα** τῆς βασιλείας πεπισ-
τευμένων, ἥτιξ ἐστὶν γνῶσις, ἣ μόνη τὴν πύλην τῆς ζωῆς ἀνοῖξαι δύναται,
δι᾽ ἧς μόνης εἰς τὴν αἰωνίαν ζωὴν εἰσελθεῖν ἔστιν. ἀλλὰ ναί (φησίν),
κρατοῦσι μὲν τὴν κλεῖν, τοῖς δε **βουλομένοις εἰσελθεῖν** οὐ παρέχουσιν.

Thomas' Relation to the Synoptic Gospels
The original wording of Q in Luke 11:52/Matt 23:13 is not easy
to reconstruct but no matter how it is done, it is clear that in this
case *Thomas* follows at least the canonical Matthew and Luke/Q. First
of all, *Thomas* agrees with Matthew's "scribes and Pharisees," and it
is generally accepted that this is Matthew's editorial formulation.[48] It
is possible to argue that, in other parts of the saying, *Thomas* is following the original Q although there is no consensus about this: *Thomas*

---

[47] The Greek is translated: [Jesus said: "The pharisees and the scribes have taken
the keys] of [knowledge (gnosis)] and hidden [them. They themselves have not]
entered, [nor have they allowed to enter those who were about to] come in. [You],
however, [be as wise as serpents and as] innocent [as doves]."
[48] See Ulrich Luz, *Das Evangelium nach Matthäus, Mt 18–25* (EKKNT I/3; Zürich:
Benziger Verlag, 1997), 318–19. Patterson (*Gospel of Thomas*, 36), who argues for
the independence of *Thomas*, also acknowledges the connection to Matthew but
characterizes it as a relatively late harmonization, a text critical problem.

agrees with Luke's "key(s) of knowledge" against Matthew's "locking people out of the kingdom of heaven," and here Luke may have followed the original wording of Q.[49] Furthermore, *Thomas* and Matthew use the verb ἀφίημι while Luke has κωλύω, which is often used in Lukan writings (occurs in the New Testament 23 times; in Luke-Acts 12 times). Thus, *Thomas'* and Matthew's ἀφίημι may also be closer to the Q-wording. Nevertheless, it is clear that *Thomas'* saying combines at least Matthean and Lukan/Q elements with each other and connects the unit with a saying to be found elsewhere in Matthew's gospel. The same phenomenon was observed in *Gos. Thom.* 99.

It is likely that the author/editor of the *Gospel of Thomas* was responsible for the combination of the Keys of Knowledge saying with the Wise as Serpents saying. Concerning the Wise as Serpents saying, we may note that the first part of the verse Matt 10:16 is from Q (Luke 10:3/Matt 10:16a) but the second half (Matt 10:16b) is regarded as a Matthean addition.[50] If this is correct, then also the latter part of *Thomas'* saying shows knowledge of Matthew's redaction.

Thomas' Relation to the Diatessaron and Pseudo-Clementine Recognitiones
No Jewish-Christian gospel parallel has survived for the first part of *Thomas'* saying but as was noted above, Quispel has pointed out a Jewish-Christian parallel in the *Pseudo-Clementine Recognitiones*.[51] The parallel shares with *Thomas* the expressions "scribes and Pharisees," "receiving," "keys" and "hiding." A closer look at *Thomas'* relation to Luke also reveals that *Thomas'* readings agree especially with the variants in Old Latin, Old Syriac and Diatessaronic textual tradition. Thus, we are dealing here with a classic example of *Thomas'* relationship to Tatian's *Diatessaron*.[52] Quispel has explained the similarities by

---

[49] See, for instance, Luz, *Das Evangelium nach Matthäus*, 320.
[50] See James M. Robinson, Paul Hoffmann, and John S. Kloppenborg, eds., *The Critical Edition of Q. Synopsis including the Gospels of Matthew and Luke, Mark and Thomas* (Hermeneia Supplement; Minneapolis, MN: Fortress, 2000), 162–63; Risto Uro, *Sheep among the Wolves: A Study on the Mission Instructions of Q* (AASF: Dissertationes humanarum litterarum 47; Helsinki: Academia Scientiarum Fennica, 1987), 75–76. Ulrich Luz, *Das Evangelium nach Matthäus, Mt 8–17* (EKKNT 1/2; Zürich: Benziger Verlag, 1990), 105 assumes an addition in Q^Mt.
[51] Gilles Quispel, "L 'Evangile selon Thomas et les Clementines" in G. Quispel, *Gnostic Studies II* (Nederlands Historisch–Arachaeologisch Instituut te Istanbul 34. Istanbul: Nederland's Historisch-Archaeological Instituut te Istanbul, 1975), 17–29, esp. 24–25. For the summary and assessment of Quispel's arguments, see Petersen, *Tatian's Diatessaron*, 273–300.
[52] See, Baarda, *Early Transmission*, 41.

assuming that both *Thomas* and the *Diatessaron* depend on a Jewish-Christian gospel.

Thomas and *Ps.-Clem. Hom.* (3.18.3) refer to the "those who wish to"[53] enter in contrast to "those who were entering" (τοὺς εἰσερχομένους) of Matthew and Luke.[54] The reading is also to be found in some Diatessaronic witnesses (Persian, Tuscan and Venetian harmonies). *Thomas'* plural "keys" is also attested in Diatessaronic witnesses (Persian harmony, Ephraem and Aphrahat). However, the plural is used by Justin as well (*Dial.* 17.4).

The reading "have hidden" instead of Luke's canonical "have taken away" is attested in D and several Old Latin (*a b c d e q r²*) and Old Syriac (Sy^{s.c}) manuscripts as well as in Ephrem's commentary on the *Diatessaron* and in the Arabic version of the *Diatessaron*.[55] As such, the agreement of these Eastern and Western witnesses to the *Diatessaron* does indicate that Tatian's original used the verb "hide."[56] But where did the authors of the *Recognitiones* and *Thomas* get the same verb? Do they depend on the *Diatessaron* or are they perhaps both using a pre-Diatessaronic Jewish-Christian gospel?

The wording of the Arabic *Diatessaron* suggests (but does not prove) that Tatian did not conflate Matthew 23:13 with Luke 11:52, as *Thomas* and *Recognitiones* did, but presented them separately and successively.

> 43 Woe unto you, scribes and Pharisees, hypocrites! because ye have shut the kingdom of God before men. 44 Woe unto you that know the law! for ye concealed the keys of knowledge: ye enter not, and those that are entering ye suffer not to enter (*Diatessaron* XL 42–44 [Arabic]).

This shows that harmonization in *Thomas* and *Rec.* goes further than in the (Arabic) *Diatessaron*. Moreover, both *Thomas* and *Recognitiones* refer to the "receiving"[57] of the keys which is not present in synoptic parallels or in Diatessaronic witnesses.

---

[53] For an overview of the connections of *Gos. Thom.* 39 to *Homilies* and *Recognitiones*, see Baarda, *Early Transmission*, 41. The connections were already pointed out by Quispel, "L'Evangile selon Thomas," 24.

[54] The Greek reconstruction of *Gos. Thom.* 39 here follows the wording of Matthew and Luke but because the fragment is so badly damaged, the reconstruction remains hypothetical.

[55] See Petersen, *Tatian's Diatessaron*, 275.

[56] For the criteria to be used in the reconstruction of the *Diatessaron's* readings, see Petersen, *Tatian's Diatessaron*, 373–377, 490.

[57] Notably, both the Coptic ϫı as well as the Greek λαμβάνω in *Gos. Thom.* 39 can be translated 'to take' or 'to receive.' In Layton's edition (*Nag Hammadi Codex*

All the above similarities show that both *Thomas* and *Pseudo-Clementines* used the same harmonizing gospel tradition that has some connections to Diatessaronic traditions. However, the tradition was not identical with the *Diatessaron*. Is it possible that we are dealing here with the same tradition that surfaced in *Gos. Thom.* 99 and is paralleled in the "Gospel of the Ebionites"? The existence of the same tradition in Epiphanius' "Gospel of the Ebionies" and in *Pseudo-Clementines* would not be surprising because it is often assumed that Epiphanius was creating his picture of the Ebionites on the basis of Pseudo-Clementine writings (or their sources). Moreover, F. Stanley Jones, in his monograph on *Rec.* 1.27–71, concludes that the source of *Rec.* 1 was using the "Gospel of the Ebionites." According to Jones: "The most remarkable common element is the explicit statement that the Pharisees were baptized by John (*Pan.* 30.13.4; *Rec.* 1.54.6–7)."[58] In *Recognitiones* this is stated in the same verses that we are now dealing with. Because it is never stated in the canonical gospels that the Pharisees really were baptized by John,[59] it is highly probable that the writer of *Rec.* 1 derived the information from the "Gospel of the Ebionites" or its source. Consequently, the harmonizing source from which *Thomas* received the expressions that it shares with *Recognitiones* (and perhaps also *Hom.*) was presumably the "Gospel of the Ebionites" itself—or its source, as was the case with *Gos. Thom.* 99/*Pan.* 30.14.5.

"O Man" and "he turned to"

One of the arguments which Quispel has presented to support his view that *Thomas* must have used the "Gospel of the Hebrews" is a stylistic affinity between *Gos. Thom.* 72 and a fragment that is quoted in Origen's *Commentary on Matthew* (*Comm. Matt.* 15.14).[60] Both these passages include the expressions "man" and "he turned to."

II,2–7), Lambdin (Coptic) and Attridge (Greek) have translated "have taken the keys." However, "have received the keys" would also be an acceptable translation. The Greek especially might even read better if the meaning is 'to receive' because the lacuna in the manuscript seems to presuppose a full stop after the "keys of knowledge." For the reconstruction, see Attridge, "The Greek Fragments," 123.

[58] Jones, *Ancient Jewish Christian Source*, 148–49.

[59] In Matt 3:7 they have just come to John in order to be baptized when John starts to reprimand them.

[60] Gilles Quispel, " 'The *Gospel of Thomas*' and the 'Gospel of the Hebrews,' " *NTS* 12 (1965–66): 378–79. Another instance where some scholars have seen stylistic

[A man said] to him, "Tell my brothers to divide my father's posses-
sions with me." He said to him, "*O man*, who has made me a divider?"
He turned to his *disciples* and said to them, "I am not a divider, am I?"
(*Gos. Thom.* 72).

It is written in a certain gospel which is called according to the Hebrews
(if, however, it pleases somebody to accept it, not as authority but in
order to bring to light the question that has been put): Another rich
man, it says, said to him: "Master what good must I do in order to
live?" He said to him: "*Man*, do the Law and the Prophets." He
answered him: "I have done." He said to him: "Go, sell all that you
possess and divide it among the poor and come, follow me." But the
rich man begun to scratch his head and it did not please him. The Lord
said to him: "How can you say: I have done the Law and the Prophets?
For it is written in the Law: love your neighbor as yourself. See, many
of your brothers, sons of Abraham, are covered with dung, dying from
hunger and your house is full of many good things, and nothing at
all comes out of it for them." *He turned* and said *to* Simon, *his disciple*
that was sitting by him: "Simon, Son of Jonah, it is easier for a camel
to go through the eye of a needle than for a rich man to enter the
kingdom of heaven." (Origen, *Comm in Matth* 15.14[61] [TGH: "The
Gospel of the Nazoreans"]).

Stylistic Similarity

Quispel notes that the expression στραφεὶς πρὸς τοὺς μαθητάς is found
in the NT only in Luke 10:23 but he thinks that "Thomas and H.
Ev., however, show that this stylistic device is not exclusively Lukan."[62]
For Quispel, the rarity of the expression seems to indicate that there
must be a connection between the fragment in Origen's passage and
the *Gospel of Thomas*, but in his view, the connection is not related
to Luke.

Quispel's stylistic argument has not received much attention.
However, he may have been on the right track although the hypothesis about the independence of the *Gospel of Thomas* and the "Gospel
of the Ebionites" from Luke is difficult to prove. First of all, the

---

affinity is the expression "what sin have I committed" that is found in *Gos. Thom.*
104 and Jerome, *Pel.* 3.2. However, although both passages discuss practices that
the synoptic gospels connect to John the Baptist, there seems to no other points of
contact between these passages, making it impossible to draw any conclusions about
their literary relationship.

[61] The translation draws on Klijn and Reinink, *Patristic Evidence*, 128–29, and
P. Vielhauer and G. Strecker, "Jewish-Christian Gospels," 161.

[62] Quispel, " 'The *Gospel of Thomas*' and the 'Gospel of the Hebrews,' " 371–82,
esp. 378–79.

only unique feature in the expression στραφεὶς πρὸς τοὺς μαθητάς is an explicit use of the noun μαθητής. Second, both ἄνθρωπε and στραφεὶς πρὸς τοὺς. . . . are clearly compatible with Luke's style and are used several times in his gospel. Luke is the only synoptic writer that uses the address "man" (ἄνθρωπε) and it is also typical of Luke to describe Jesus' "turning to" people.[63] Thus it seems clear that the phrases were originally created by Luke. Nevertheless, there is evidence which indicates that both *Thomas* and the "Gospel of the Hebrews" did not get these expressions directly from the Gospel of Luke but from a harmonistic gospel that is somehow related to the *Diatessaron*.

Three Rich Men in the Diatessaron
The synoptic parallel for *Gos. Thom.* 72 is in Luke 12:13–15. Because these verses are only found in Luke, the discussion about the tradition history of *Gos. Thom.* 72 has usually focused on the question of whether or not it is possible to see traces of Luke's editorial work in *Thomas'* saying, and it has often escaped the notice of scholars that the same verses were also in the *Diatessaron*. It is known that, in the *Diatessaron*, Luke 12:13–15 functioned as an introduction to the Parable of the Rich Fool (Luke 12:16–21) which was the first story in the sequence of three stories about rich men. The second one in the series was the Parable of the Rich Man (Mark 10:17–22; Matthew 19:16–22; Luke 18:18–23). That is precisely the same story of which a Jewish-Christian version is quoted in Origen's *Commentary on Matthew*. The third story in the *Diatessaron* was the Parable of the Rich Man and Lazarus (Luke 16:14–15, 19–31).[64] Thus, when Quispel pointed out a stylistic similarity between *Gos. Thom.* 72 and the fragment in Origen's *Commentary*, he was in fact referring to two passages that followed each other in the *Diatessaron*. Because these passages are not linked together in the synoptic gospels, the observation that they followed each other in the *Diatessaron* increases the probability that their stylistic similarities are not coincidental. Yet the *Diatessaron's* sequence of pas-

---

[63] ἄνθρωπε occurs three times in Luke: in 5:20 it replaces Mark's τέκνον, 12:14 is in Luke's own tradition, and in 22:58 Luke probably rewrites Mark 14:70. Mark does not use στρέφω at all, and, in Matthew, Jesus "turns to" his disciples (Peter) or supplicants twice: Matt 9:22 and 16:23. In Luke this happens seven times: 7:9, 44; 9:55; 10:23; 14:25; 22:61; 23:28.

[64] The first one to notice this Diatessaronic sequence of passages was C. A. Phillips in 1931. For the summary of Phillips' observations, see Petersen, *Tatian's Diatessaron*, 257–59.

sages cannot prove anything unless there is further evidence which shows that the writers of *Gos. Thom.* 72 and the Jewish-Christian fragment knew the same sequence. Because I have dealt with Origen's passage in detail elsewhere,[65] I will only summarize the points that explain how the expressions ἄνθρωπε and στραφεὶς πρὸς ended up in both Origen's fragment and the *Gospel of Thomas.*

Three Rich Men in Origen's fragment
In the case of Origen's fragment, the knowledge of the Diatessaronic sequence is generally acknowledged. One indicator of the sequence is the expression "another rich man" which shows that the passage presupposes a sequence of at least two stories about rich men. In addition, several readings common to the fragment and Diatessaronic witnesses have been discovered.[66] However, what is not usually noticed is the infusion of ideas and phrases from the two surrounding sto-ries into the fragment preserved in Origen's commentary. As in the Parable of the Rich Fool (Luke 12:16–21; the first story), the rich man in Origen's fragment is a man whose house is "full of many good things" (domus tua plena est multis bonis; cf. Luke 12:19 (ψυχή, ἔχεις πολλὰ ἀγαθά). Furthermore, he is addressed as "man" (*homo*) like in Luke 12:14 (ἄνθρωπε). The third story, for its part, is reflected in the idea that the rich man should know, on the basis of the *law and the prophets*, to take care of his *brothers, the sons of Abraham*, just like the rich man and his *brothers, the "sons of Abraham"* (the rich man addresses Abraham as "father") should know merely on the basis of *Moses and the prophets* how to take care of poor people like Lazarus.

---

[65] "Where Did Another Rich Man Come From? The Jewish-Christian Profile of the Story about the Rich Man in the 'Gospel of the Hebrews' (Origen, *Comm. in Matth.* 15.14)," *VC* 57 (2003): 243–75. The article argues that the version recorded in the Latin translation of Origen's commentary must be post-Diatessaronic because— almost without exception—all the features that can be compared with synoptic mate-rial are attested in Diatessaronic witnesses. This coheres with the conventional dating of the fragment which is usually regarded a later addition to Origen's commentary, done by the Latin translator between the 5th and 9th centuries. Nevertheless, there are some features, for instance an agreement with the Old Latin manuscript *k* (i.e. *divide* in Luke 18:22), that are not attested among Diatessaronic witnesses. Drawing on William L. Petersen's observations about Justin's pre-Diatessaronic harmony and its connections to the Old Latin versions (see, Petersen, *Tatian's Diatessaron*, 420–424), the article concludes that Origen's story probably has roots in the pre-Diatessaronic harmonistic tradition. The Diatessaronic language dominates the passage because it was translated from Greek into Syriac (and later on into Latin) after Tatian's *Diatessaron* was composed.

[66] See, for instance, Klijn, *Jewish-Christian Gospel Tradition*, 56–60.

The above observations about the impact of the surrounding stories make clear the route along which the Lukan address ἄνθρωπε
traveled to end up in the "Gospel of the Hebrews:" It was adopted from
the "first" story about the rich man (Luke 12:13–15), from verses that
are also paralleled in *Gos. Thom.* 72. But where did the expression
"he turned to" come from?

In Luke's gospel, the Lawyer's Question is in many respects a
twin to the story about the Rich Man. Both stories open with a similar question "(Good) teacher, what must I do to inherit eternal life,"
and both deal with obeying the Jewish Law. Eusebius's canon tables,
for instance, give both Luke 10:25–28 and 18:18–21 as parallels for
the story about the Rich Man.[67] The Lawyer's Question shares several features with the passage in Origen's commentary.[68] All these
similarities show that the framer of the second story about a rich man
in the "Gospel of Hebrews" consulted both the story about the Rich
Man and the Lawyer's Question. When he consulted the Lawyer's
Question in Luke 10:25–28, he probably also found the expression
"he turned to" in Luke 10:23. This is the same verse where Quispel
saw the "unique" stylistic similarity for *Gos. Thom.* 72 and the "Gospel
of the Hebrews."

Notably, all the above observations indicate that the fragment in
Origen's commentary is not pre-synoptic and it is clearly from a
harmonizing gospel. If the fragment is really from the "Gospel of
the Nazoreans"—as the Three Gospel Hypothesis assumes—it is clear
that the "Gospel of the Nazoreans" was not connected only with
the Gospel of Matthew.

Three Rich Men in Thomas' Source?
There is no conclusive evidence which would make it absolutely clear
that the people who passed on *Thomas'* traditions must have known

---

[67] For Eusebius' canon tables, see Nestle–Aland, *Novum Testamentum Graece* (27.
ed.; Stuttgart: Deutsche Bibelgesellschaft, 1993), 84–89.
[68] In addition to the participle *faciens*, which Luke 18:18 and 20:25 share with
Origen's passage in contrast to Matthew and Mark, the phrasing of Jesus' rhetorical question is similar. Origen's passage reads: "**dixit ad eum** *dominus:* **quomodo
dicis . . . quoniam scriptum est in lege**." Luke 10:26 reads in the Vulgate: "**dixit
ad eum in lege** *quid* **scriptum est quomodo** *legis*." Interestingly, the parallel passages in Matthew and Mark do not mention at all "what is written in the Law."
Furthermore, Origen's passage and the Lawyer's Question do not discuss individual commandments as do all the synoptic gospels in the story about the Rich Man.
Instead, they concentrate only on the (double) Commandment of Love.

the same collection of passages as the "Gospel of the Hebrews" but there are several observations which speak for this hypothesis. First, the parallel to the story about the Rich Fool is to be found in *Gos. Thom.* 63. Thus, in the *Gos. Thom.* 72 and 63, there is parallel material for the whole Diatessaronic story about the "first" rich man. Second, both these logia include Diatessaronic readings. Especially *Gos. Thom.* 63 (Rich Fool) is a classic example of the case where *Thomas'* readings crop up in several Old Latin and Old Syriac translations and Diatessaronic witnesses.[69] Third, in the *Gospel of Thomas* the Rich Fool also opens a cluster of logia where rich people, "businessmen and merchants" are criticized. We might note in passing that "marked animosity against business" was one of the features that indicated to Quispel a close connection between the *Gospel of Thomas* and the "Gospel of the Hebrews."[70] Fourth, the other two Diatessaronic stories—the Rich Man and the Rich Man and Lazarus—are so clearly connected to Jewish tradition and observance of the Jewish Law that their absence in the *Gospel of Thomas* is no surprise (cf. *Gos. Thom.* 6, 14, 27, 53, 89, 104).[71] Finally, Origen's version of the story about the Rich Man made clear the infusion of expressions from the surrounding Diatessaronic stories and from the Lawyer's Question into the second story about a rich man. Therefore, the appearance of the same phenomenon in the first story of the same cluster would be natural. In this case, the emergence of the Lukan "he turned to" in *Gos. Thom.* 72 would reveal the hand of the same editor who, at some point, implanted the same expression in the second story.

We may also consider that all the above similarities are purely coincidental: It is only a coincidence that both the *Gospel of Thomas* and the fragment in Origen's commentary have independently—in contrast to known synoptic parallels—added the (Lukan) "he turned to" to a story where one can also find another Lukan expression, the address "(O) man." It is only a coincidence that, in these passages, both these gospels have Diatessaronic readings. And it is only a

---

[69] See, Baarda, *Early Transmission*, 44.

[70] Quispel, "*Gospel of Thomas*' and the 'Gospel of Hebrews,'" 379.

[71] For *Thomas'* relation to Jewish religious practices, see Antti Marjanen, "*Thomas* and Jewish Religious Practices," in *Thomas at the Crossroads: Essays on the Gospel of Thomas* (ed. Risto Uro; Studies of the New Testament and Its World; Edinburgh: Clark, 1998), 163–82. Marjanen convincingly argues that *Thomas'* negative attitude towards Jewish practices reflects the position of the author in an ongoing debate about Thomasine Christians' relation to Judaism (pp. 180–82).

coincidence that these stories happened to follow each other in the *Diatessaron*, and so on. Of course, all this is possible, but as the list of coincidences grows, the probability of a more simple explanation also grows: the *Gospel of Thomas* and Origen's fragment have made use of the same harmonizing gospel tradition that is related to the *Diatessaron*. The exact character of the relation to the *Diatessaron* cannot be determined in this connection, but on the basis of my earlier analysis of Origen's passage, it seems probable that the cluster of three stories about rich men already existed in the pre-Diatessaronic tradition. The Latin passage in Origen's commentary is most likely based on an earlier Syriac version which is clearly later than the *Diatessaron* but there are some features in Origen's story which speak for the assumption that there was an even earlier Greek version of the story that may have been connected to Justin's harmony.[72] Thus, the above connections to the Diatessaronic composition do not necessarily mean that *Thomas* must depend on the *Diatessaron* itself.

To summarize, the *Gospel of Thomas* and the Jewish-Christian gospel fragments have one non-canonical saying in common. The wording of the Jewish-Christian version of this saying is closer to *Thomas'* Greek logion. The paleographical dating of the Greek fragments (between 200 and 250 CE)[73] and the date of Clement's quotation (202/215 CE) cohere, showing that the similarities already existed in the beginning of the third century.

Gos. Thom. 99 and a quotation from the "Gospel of the Ebionites" share three variant readings and two of them can also be found in *2 Clement* (9:11). Notably, the author of *2 Clement* has received the variants as part of a tradition that had harmonized canonical Matthew and Luke. Assuming that *2 Clem.* was written between 100–150 CE, it is evident that, at least in this case, the common denominator of the *Gospel of Thomas* and the "Gospel of the Ebionites" is independent of the *Diatessaron*. No Diatessaronic witnesses for the variants have been found.

Gos. Thom. 39 and the manuscript 1424 (in Matt 10:16) indicate that both the *Gospel of Thomas* and a Jewish-Christian gospel had a parallel to Matt 10:16. Their wording is different but the beginning of the Thomasine logion harmonizes canonical Matthew and Luke/Q.

---

[72] See above footnote 65.
[73] Attridge, "Greek Fragments," 96–98.

Gos. Thom. 39 also agrees with some expressions in *Ps-Clem. Rec.* 1.54.6–7 that are not attested in the synoptic gospels or in the Diatessaronic tradition. It is highly likely these were derived from the "Gospel of the Ebionites" or its source. In addition, there are some connections to Diatessaronic traditions. The analysis of the mechanism of how they are connected to the harmonizing traditions in *Thomas* and the "Gospel of the Ebionies" cannot be accomplished here.

Gos. Thom. 72 (with 63) shares two stylistic features with the story about the Rich Man in Origen's *Commentary on Matthew*. This stylistic similarity is easiest to explain by assuming that both depend on the same harmonistic tradition which is somehow related to the *Diatessaron*. Probably the cluster of three stories about rich men already existed in the pre-Diatessaronic tradition.

Some more general conclusions can be drawn. First, the three cases for which there is synoptic parallel material available show a close connection of both *Thomas* and Jewish-Christian fragments to a harmonizing gospel tradition. Second, although *Thomas* and the Jewish-Christian fragments are generally known for their connections to Diatessaronic readings, the harmonizing features that they share in the analyzed passages have only indirect connections to the *Diatessaron*. Their connections to *2 Clement* and Justin also indicate that the common readings are probably pre-Diatessaronic. Therefore, Drijvers' suggestion, that the *Gospel of Thomas* and the "Gospel of the Ebionites" would depend on the *Diatessaron* is problematic.[74] It is also clear that Quispel's hypothesis concerning a *pre-synoptic Jewish-Christian gospel* behind the *Gospel of Thomas* and the *Diatessaron* does not find any support in the above observations.

---

[74] The same applies to Nicholas Perrin's recent thesis. According to Perrin, the catchword connections he finds in his Syriac retroversion of the *Gospel of Thomas* indicate that the *Gospel of Thomas* must have been written in Syriac. Because the *Diatessaron* was the first gospel record in Syriac it must have been among *Thomas'* sources. Perrin also finds support for his thesis in the fact that at some points *Thomas'* logia follow the order of Diatessaronic tradition (See *Thomas and Tatian*, 183–88). Although the study includes several valuable observations about *Thomas'* connections to Syriac (or Semitic) gospel traditions, I do not find convincing Perrin's arguments for Syriac as the original language of *Thomas*, mainly because the definition of the catchword connection is too broad—Perrin accepts semantical, phonological and even etymological (!) associations as catchword connections (p. 50). The observations about the Diatessaronic order of some of the logia of *Thomas* are more promising but in the light of the present analysis I would suggest that the same order is derived from a common pre-Diatessaronic tradition.

However, it cannot be ruled out that the harmonizing features shared by *Thomas* and the Jewish-Christian fragments were in fact derived from a *harmonizing Jewish-Christian gospel*. As a matter of fact, if one is to draw conclusions only on the basis of the analyzed material, Ockham's razor would cut through all the hypotheses which speculate about an unknown harmony behind *Thomas* and the Jewish-Christian fragments because it is quite possible that *Gos. Thom.* 39, 99 and 72 derived their harmonizing readings from the same gospel(s) from which the Jewish-Christian fragments come. Nevertheless, the number of passages common to the *Gospel of Thomas* and the Jewish-Christian fragments is too small to allow any firm conclusions. It is also possible to hypothesize about "floating" harmonistic collections available to Thomasine Christians and Jewish Christians. It is to be noted that this explanation also works better if *Thomas* and the Jewish-Christian fragments are placed in the same cultural and geographical setting.

3. *Concluding Remarks*

Overall, the observations about the literary connections between *Thomas* and the Jewish-Christian fragments are compatible with the hypothesis that *Thomas* and the Jewish-Christian fragments were composed in the same Syro-Palestinian milieu but, due to the writers' different ideological orientation, they cultivated different parts of their common scriptural tradition. If the reconstruction of the "Diatessaronic" sequence of three rich men, of which *Thomas* used the first one and the "Gospel of the Hebrews" the second one, is on the right track then it is a prime example of the "pick and choose" that was going on: *Thomas* developed further the discussion about the "divider" that was closely connected to its ideology and used the Rich Fool as one example in its own criticism of the "businessmen." The framers of the *Gospel of Thomas* had no interest in the Jewish story about the Rich Man but that story inspired the editors of a Jewish-Christian gospel who used it in their own inner-Jewish polemics against the rich who did not show mercy to their Jewish compatriots, "sons of Abraham."

The material analyzed in this article is too restricted to allow any firm conclusions about *Thomas'* relation to the *Diatessaron*, but it suggests that it might be profitable to look for the answer in harmonizing traditions that preceded the *Diatessaron* rather than trying to show that *Thomas* depended directly on the *Diatessaron* or vice versa. Perhaps a hypothesis that suggests pre-Diatessaronic harmonizing gospel traditions to be the source of sayings that were further developed in a context where "scribal and oral cultures were intertwined"[75] could provide a fruitful starting point for future discussion about *Thomas'* origins.

Although it is often presented in defense of *Thomas'* independence that there is no editorial coherence in the way in which snippets of synoptic expressions from different gospels and from different parts of the same gospel are found together in *Thomas*,[76] the same phenomenon is observable in harmonizing collections of Jesus' sayings. This is clearly demonstrated in several studies on the harmonizing collections.[77] Harmonizing collections focused on certain topics rather than on following the narrative setting of the synoptic gospels or on coherent repeating of the style and favorite expressions of individual synoptic editors. Therefore, their impact on gospel traditions cannot be traced with conventional redaction-critical tools. For the study of the *Gospel of Thomas* this means that if the hypothesis of the influence of harmonistic tradition on *Thomas* is taken seriously—and many observations suggest that this is what should be done—then the discussion about *Thomas'* dependence should make more room for comparison with harmonizing collections and less room for assessing *Thomas* merely on the basis of what is known about the work of the editors of the synoptic gospels.

---

[75] Thus Uro, who provides a useful summary and assessment of the discussion about the role of oral tradition in the formation of the *Gospel of Thomas*. See Uro, *Thomas: Seeking the Historical Context of the Gospel of Thomas* (London: Clark, 2003), 106–33, esp. 132–33.

[76] In the case of *Gos. Thom.* 36 Patterson (*The Gospel of Thomas*, 36) argues that "if Thomas were intentionally borrowing this topos ["scribes and pharisees"] from Matthew one would expect to see it incorporated into *Thomas'* text more frequently."

[77] See A. J. Bellinzoni, *The Sayings of Jesus in the Writings of Justin Martyr* (NovTSup 17; Leiden: Brill, 1967), 140–42; Koester, *Synoptische Überlieferung*, 109–11; Leslie L. Kline, *The Sayings of Jesus in the Pseudo-Clementine Homilies* (SBLDS 14; Missoula, MT: Scholars Press, 1975), 81–84. Kline makes a helpful distinction (p. 13) between "harmonized readings" (from different gospels) and "conflated readings" (from different parts of the same gospel).

Parallel Sayings and Common Harmonizing Readings in the Jewish-Christian Gospel Fragments and the Gospel of Thomas

Symbols: C.Rd = common reading, Diat. = Diatessaron(ic), Lk = typical of Luke, Mt/Lk = combination of Matthean and Lukan elements, Syn. = the synoptic gospels.

Lines connect the parrallel passages, dotted lines the passages that freely use the same tradition

Circles list the common readings in the passages to which the arrows point.

Example: Pan. 30.14.5. and *Gos.Thom* 99 are parallels that have 1 C.Rd.,≠Syn = one common reading, different from the synoptic gospels ("my brothers and mother").

1. *Let Him Who Seeks Continue Seeking*

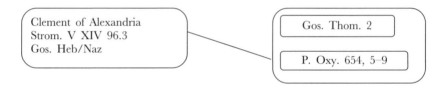

2. *Your Brothers and Mother Are Standing Outside*

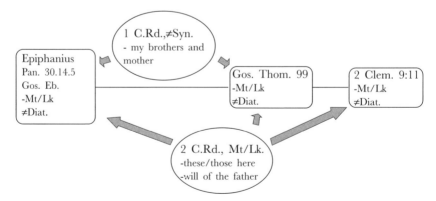

3. *The Scribes and the Pharisees Hid the Keys, Be Wise as Serpents*

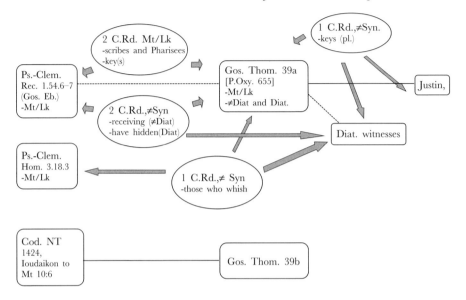

4. *"O Man" and "He Turned To"*

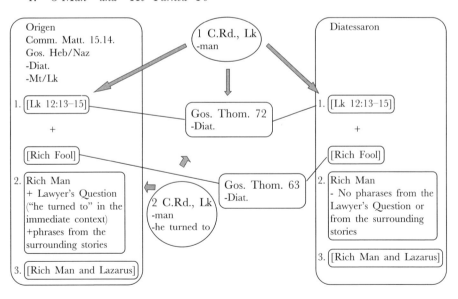

CHAPTER SEVEN

CONFLICTING EPIC WORLDS

Jon Ma. Asgeirsson

1. *Introduction*

The *Gospel of Thomas* is in many respects a piece of literature reminiscent of Hellenistic philosophical texts in the tradition of wisdom literature and chriae collections.[1] The same or closely related literary genre is attested in biblical and Old Testament Apocrypha texts as well as in other New Testament Apocrypha literature for several centuries around the turn of the calendar. In content the same texts express for the most part an amazing combination of Jewish, Greek or Hellenistic, and Christian thought divided, of course, along the emerging line of Christianity. The extent of Greek and Hellenistic influence on Jewish culture has long been debated among Jewish scholars. Within the field of New Testament studies scholars have been inclined to see the development of the narrative gospels as an attestation of a more refined literary production, albeit not close to the classical Greek or Roman tradition, in comparison to the alleged crude literary format of the earliest sayings of Jesus. At the same time Moses and not Plato has been seen to constitute the epic background of early and late Christian texts. The Gospel of Matthew, generally acknowledged for its reverence for Jewish legal practice and Mosaic typology, however, unfolds as an example of Hellenistic *encomia*[2] once viewed from Hellenistic rhetorical practice. The *Gospel of Thomas*, to the contrary, unfolds as a text generally accustomed with Platonic philosophy in a dialogue far removed from that of Socrates, once viewed not as an interpretation of Jewish epic but Greek philosophical

---

[1] See, e.g., Jon Ma. Asgeirsson, "Doublets and Strata: Towards a Rhetorical Approach to the *Gospel of Thomas*" (Ph.D. diss., Claremont Graduate University, 1998), 23–54.

[2] See, e.g., Jerome H. Neyrey, *Honor and Shame in the Gospel of Matthew* (Louisville, KY: Westminster John Knox Press, 1998).

tradition. The genre *encomium* already elevates the Gospel of Matthew over the more or less undefined definition of a gospel genre (when considered a new invention). In a similar manner the presence of Greek classical philosophical tradition in the *Gospel of Thomas* elevates this gospel above prejudiced conclusions about its contents (when viewed as a simple form of Gnosticism or ascetic commonality). This study compares and discusses the origins of different creation accounts in the *Gospel of Thomas* and the Gospel of Matthew in order to demonstrate the Greek classical roots of the former over against the Jewish background of the latter.

While the Gospel of Matthew literally constitutes a bridge between the epic world of the Old Testament and the canon of the New Testament in view of its very location, its author makes no doubt about the role played by a scribe when stating in the words of Jesus: "Therefore every scribe who has been trained for the kingdom of heaven is like a householder who brings out of his treasure what is new and what is old" (13:52b).[3]

In the *Gospel of Thomas* the mixture of old and new is made suspicious (cf. 47:3–5) while in a different context it is obvious that one shade of "old" is labeled "dead" against "the living one":

> His disciples said to him, "Twenty-four prophets spoke in Israel, and all of them spoke in you."
> He said to them, "You have omitted the one living in your presence and have spoken (only) of the dead" (52).[4]

In these many words the epic tradition of Israel is, indeed, rejected in the *Gospel of Thomas*. Jewish cultic practices as well as observance of the law are further rejected throughout the gospel[5] which comes as no surprise when it is noted right at the outset that a non-circumcised child is more knowledgeable about the place of life than the people of the covenant, Israel (cf. *Gos. Thom.* 4).

---

[3] For biblical citations, see Herbert G. May and Bruce M. Metzger, eds., *The New Oxford Annotated Bible with the Apocrypha: Revised Standard Version* (Containing the Second Edition of the New Testament and an Expanded Edition of the Apocrypha; An Ecumenical Study Bible; New York, NY: Oxford University Press, 1977).

[4] For citations to the *Gospel of Thomas* see, Thomas Lambdin's transl. in *Gospel according to Thomas, Gospel according to Philip, Hypostasis of the Archons, and Indexes* (vol. 1 of *Nag Hammadi Codex II,2–7: Together with XIII,2*, Brit. Lib. Or. 4926(1), and P. Oxy. 1, 654, 655*; ed. Bentley Layton; NHS 20; Leiden: Brill, 1989).

[5] See, e.g., the discussion by Antti Marjanen, "*Thomas* and Jewish Religious Practices," in *Thomas at the Crossroads: Essay on the Gospel of Thomas* (ed. Risto Uro; Studies of the New Testament and Its World; Edinburgh: Clark, 1998), 163–82.

It has long been noted that the *Gospel of Thomas* and the Synoptic Sayings Source (Q) share a considerable amount of materials. They seem, indeed, to have the closest parallels in what is considered some of the most original and most authentic materials in the Jesus tradition.[6] Within each of these documents a later development may be traced in different if not contradicting directions: The *Gospel of Thomas* takes a turn into a philosophical direction[7] whereas the Synoptic Sayings Source turns into the direction of the prophetic tradition[8] of Israel. A still later development within the *Gospel of Thomas* is a redactional addition towards the end of the gospel in which the original message is reemphasized[9] whereas in the Synoptic Sayings Source a last addition seems to move in the direction of Jewish piety and practice.[10]

Furthermore, the *Gospel of Thomas* shares a curious phenomenon with the Gospel of Mark. Thus, in Mark like in *Thomas* the words and parables of Jesus are as if framed with a sense of secrecy that the readers (the disciples) must decode in order to understand their meaning. In Mark, as James M. Robinson has pointed out,[11] the persona of Jesus himself becomes the hermeneutical key for the disciples' ability to understand the parables of Jesus (cf. Mark 4:33–34) whereas in *Thomas* seeking and finding the hermeneutics of the words of Jesus becomes the key to their understanding of Jesus and eternal life (cf. *Gos. Thom.* 1 and 2). In the context of his Markan source Matthew adds the parable of the weeds (tares) to which he later adds an explanation (cf. Matt 13:24–30 & 36–43). The commentary

---

[6] See, e.g., Helmut Koester, *Ancient Christian Gospels: Their History and Development* (Philadelphia, PA: Trinity Press International, 1990), 87–99; *idem*, "Q and Its Relatives," in *Gospel Origins and Christian Beginnings: In Honor of James M. Robinson* (ed. James E. Goehring, Charles W. Hedrick, Jack T. Sanders with Hans Dieter Betz; ForFasc 1; Sonoma, CA: Polebridge Press, 1990), 49–63; cf. James M. Robinson and Helmut Koester, *Trajectories through Early Christianity* (Philadelphia, PA: Fortress, 1971); Stephen J. Patterson, *The Gospel of Thomas and Jesus* (FF: Reference Series; Sonoma, CA: Polebridge Press, 1993).

[7] See, e.g., William E. Arnal, "The Rhetoric of Marginality: Apocalypticism, Gnosticism, and Sayings Gospels," *HTR* 88 (1995), esp. 474–80.

[8] See John S. Kloppenborg, *The Formation of Q: Trajectories in Ancient Wisdom Collections* (SAC; Philadelphia, PA: Fortress, 1987), 102–170.

[9] See Asgeirsson, "Doublets and Strata," esp. 177–97.

[10] See Kloppenborg, *Formation of Q*, 246–262; *idem*, "Nomos and Ethos in Q," in *Gospel Origins and Christian Beginnings: In Honor of James M. Robinson* (ed. James E. Goehring, Charles W. Hedrick Jack T. Sanders with Hans Dieter Betz; ForFasc 1; Sonoma, CA: Polebridge Press, 1990), 35–48.

[11] "Gnosticism and the New Testament," in *Gnosis: Festschrift für Hans Jonas* (ed. Barbara Aland; Göttingen: Vandenhoeck & Ruprecht, 1978), 125–43.

emphasizes the salvific role of the son of man (Matt 13:37) becoming at the same time what separates the just from the unjust. Thus,
the motif of salvation is most prominent as only through it does the
future judgment materialize.[12] In the Gospel of Luke the Christ resurrected becomes the hermeneutical key to the disciples' understanding
(cf. Luke 24:13–35, esp. 28–32). This motif of the resurrection does
not exist in either the *Gospel of Thomas* or the Synoptic Sayings
Source.[13] Such dialogues with the resurrected become a favorite in
Gnostic writings of the second century and later which, indeed, make
the canonical gospels a closer relative to Gnostic circles in this sense
rather than the *Gospel of Thomas*.

The relationship of the *Gospel of Thomas* with the Synoptic Sayings
Source in terms of the early Jesus tradition and the Gospel of Mark
as regards the esoteric nature of his discourse are far removed from
the larger framework of the canonical gospels. While Matthew has
his hands in two worlds: the old world of Judaism and the world of
the new Moses, "old" for *Thomas* surely has a very different reference.
It will be argued below that "old" for *Thomas* has a basic reference
to Greek classical tradition whereas "new" implies motifs from the
Jewish epic held in no high regard in *Thomas*.

2. *Exemplum Socratis*

The early form critics came to an inconsistent conclusion when they
claimed that Semitic literature was crude in comparison to Greek
literary forms and that the New Testament writings were inferior

---

[12] *Pace* Daniel J. Harrington, S.J., *The Gospel of Matthew* (Sacra Pagina 1; Collegeville,
MN: The Liturgical Press, 1991). He says: "If it is correct to attribute the explanations of those parables (13:36–43, 49–50) to Matthew himself, then it seems that
his special interest was the future judgment," 209.

[13] Cf. the discussion by John S. Kloppenborg Verbin about the Synoptic Sayings
Source as a "theological problem," where he identifies this fact about the absence
of the resurrection or "salvific interpretation of Jesus' death" in the context of the
different Jesus tradition found in the pre-canonical sources over against the canonical ones. A second problem is characterized as that of "Q's immanent *Tendenz*"
expressly found in the sapiential materials. A third problem has to do with the
question about the "historical Jesus" whereas the fourth one is identified as the
"social-historical denomination of Q and the people it represents," "A Dog among
the Pigeons," in *From Quest to Q: Festschrift James M. Robinson* (ed. Jon Ma. Asgeirsson,
Kristine De Troyer and Marvin Meyer; BETL 146; Leuven: Peeters & Leuven
University Press, 2000), 73–80.

composition (*Kleinliteratur*) in comparison to the classical tradition even though they were written in Greek.[14] The earliest Jesus tradition was further considered exemplary of Semitic genre while the gospels were believed to demonstrate a far higher sense of Greek composition albeit not anything in the direction of classical Greek literature. It is not least through the application of insights from rhetorical criticism that biblical scholars have more recently come to acknowledge the careful construction of biblical texts—whether Greek or Semitic—in accordance with Greek or Hellenistic rhetorical and compositional practice.[15] This development may, indeed, be seen as a precursor to viewing the New Testament and New Testament Apocrypha literature from the perspective of classical Greek literature (*Hochliteratur*) and, thus, the possible influence of the classical tradition on not only the literary style of biblical writings but also its very contents.[16]

When viewing literary, philosophical or religious sources from around the turn of the calendar it is important, however, to keep

---

[14] See, e.g., Martin Dibelius, *Die Formgeschichte des Evangeliums* (4th ed.; with a Foreword by G. Bornkamm; Tübingen: Mohr, 1961 [1919]). Dibelius claims that the gospels be mere collections of sources in which the hand of the authors are to be characterized as those of editors and not of creative thinkers, 2; cf. Richard A. Burridge, *What Are the Gospels? A Comparison with Graeco-Roman Biography* (SNTSMS 70; Cambridge, MA: Cambridge University Press, 1992).

[15] See, e.g., Burton L. Mack and Vernon K. Robbins, *Patterns of Persuasion in the Gospels* (FF: Literary Facets; Sonoma, CA: Polebridge Press, 1989); H. A. Fischel, "Prolegomenon," in *Essays in Graeco-Roman and Related Talmudic Literature* (Selected by H. A. Fischel; ed. H. M. Orlinsky; New York, NY: KTAV, 1977), xii–xxiv.

[16] See in particular in this regard the contributions by Günter Glockmann, *Homer in der frühchristlichen Literatur bis Justinus* (TUGAL 105; Berlin: Akademie-Verlag, 1968); F. Gerald Downing, "Ethical Pagan Theism and the Speeches in Acts," *NTS* 27 (1981): 544–63; *idem*, "Common Ground with Paganism in Luke and in Josephus," *NTS* 28 (1982): 546–59; Dennis R. MacDonald, ed., *Christianizing Homer: The Odyssey, Plato and the Acts of Andrew* (New York, NY: Oxford University Press, 1994); *idem*, *The Homeric Epics and the Gospel of Mark* (New Haven, CT: Yale University Press, 2000); Ronald F. Hock, "Homer in Greco-Roman Education," in *Mimesis and Intertextuality in Antiquity and Christianity* (ed. Dennis R. MacDonald; SAC; Harrisburg, PA: Trinity Press International, 2001), 56–77; Gregory J. Riley, "Mimesis of Classical Ideals in the Second Christian Century," in *Mimesis and Intertextuality*, 91–103. For the influence of a Jewish motif on the Graeco-Roman world cf. John G. Gager, *Moses in Greco-Roman Paganism* (SBLMS 16; Nashville, TN: Abingdon, 1972). Far more studies have appeared on Hellenistic philosophy and its possible influence on New Testament writers, e.g., Abraham J. Malherbe, *Paul and the Popular Philosophers* (Minneapolis, MN: Fortress, 1989); F. Gerald Downing, *Cynics and Christian Origins* (Edinburgh: Clark, 1992); Troels Engberg-Pedersen, *Paul and the Stoics* (Louisville, KY: Westminster John Knox, 2000); Bruce W. Winter, *Philo and Paul among the Sophists: Alexandrian and Corinthian Responses to a Julio-Claudain Movement* (2nd ed.; foreword by G. W. Bowersock; Grand Rapids, MI: Eerdmans, 2002 [1997]).

in mind the extent to which the classical tradition is present in its more original form or through the many intertextual and changeable channels in its later Hellenistic context. In other words, how was the classical tradition known in the last century before the common era or after it? Is it for instance possible to talk about direct Platonic influence on the *Gospel of Thomas*? Are philosophical motifs in the *Gospel of Thomas* known except through the windows of Hellenistic philosophers? Furthermore, it must be asked in what sense the author of the gospel is him-/herself an independent thinker and/or interpreter of philosophy.

The close affinity of the literary genre of the *Gospel of Thomas* to the Hellenistic chriae collections immediately links the gospel to traditions of Cynic and Stoic origin. Thus the Cynics, for instance, use this very format to express their own philosophical thinking as well as to interpret or criticize the thinking of their *magistri* or classical forerunners. Attributing the chriae to Socrates was a commonality among Cynic philosophers and thus many of the collections may be labeled *Exempla Socratis* such as *Epistles of Socrates and the Socratics* among the corpus of Cynic traditions collected under the name of the *Cynic Epistles.*[17]

The reception of the Socratic tradition proves to have been both positive and negative all the way back to the very contemporaries of Socrates himself. Socrates is, thus, a victim of sarcasm in the writings of many of the ancient comedians whereas among his own pupils he is either praised beyond criticism or considered esoteric and hard to understand as Klaus Döring has exemplified.[18] The different if not contradicting perception of Socrates goes even further back into the very writings of Plato himself. In the early dialogues Socrates appears more or less as a complicated man of irony (*Ironiker*) whereas in the later ones the theory of ideas is attributed to Socrates and he may be labeled a political analyst and an expert on metaphysics. In the treatment of Aristotle, Döring continues, Socrates has already been assigned a place in the history of philosophy and there as a philosopher of ethics first and foremost. Among the first pupils of Aristotle, Socrates is still a revered individual but before long his character becomes of less interest to the Peripatetic school and he

---

[17] See Abraham J. Malherbe, *The Cynic Epistles* (A Study Edition; SBLSBS 12; Atlanta, GA: Scholars Press, 1977), 217–307.

[18] *Exemplum Socratis: Studien zur Sokratesnachwirkung in der kynisch-stoischen Popularphilosophie der frühen Kaiserzeit und im frühen Christentum* (Hermes 42, Wiesbaden: Steiner, 1979), 1.

is of disinterest to the Epicureans as well. It is within the circles of the Stoics that Socrates gains attention again due to their common interest in human virtues. Furthermore, within the New Academy (Arkesilaos) Socrates becomes important due to their emphasis on the idea of being conscious about one's own lack of understanding. Finally, in Middle-Platonic and Neo-Platonic circles, Döring contends, Socrates becomes of interest due to his idea of the spirit or the soul. However, it is among the Cynics, that Socrates becomes the paradigm of authority (*exempla Socratis*). For the purpose of adding force and importance to an idea or a statement, the Cynics frequently attribute a motif or a thought to Socrates.[19]

In a sense, this idea of the *Exempla Socratis* culminates in the early Jesus tradition. Here, Jesus, not Socrates, becomes the ultimate authority behind the chriae collections in the *Gospel of Thomas*, the Synoptic Sayings Source and the Gospel of Mark as Burton L. Mack has argued. Jesus is his own authority and the sayings, the chriae, are attributed to him as well. Thus, argumentative presuppositions, argumentative elaborations, as well as any supportive attestation or data are all attributed to Jesus himself. Jesus may even elaborate on his own words and arguments while at the same time making his very own statements the ultimate issue of life and death.[20] Thus, also Jesus takes the place Socrates has among the Cynics and other Hellenistic philosophers.

Behind the literary genre of the *Gospel of Thomas*, thus, emerges a tradition reflected throughout the Hellenistic world despite the fact that the authority of Socrates has been replaced with that of Jesus. But what about motifs and ideas that would clearly seem to reflect Greek philosophical tradition? In this regard scholars have, on the one hand, been more inclined to argue for their understanding in the context of Hellenistic philosophy contemporaneous with that of *Thomas*. Thus, for instance, Stevan L. Davies makes an attempt to understand several passages in the *Gospel of Thomas* on the basis of how Philo of Alexandria treats the same or related motifs in his writings.[21] But is Philo the most obvious parallel to philosophical motifs

---

[19] Cf. *Ibid.*, 3–12. Döring considers the continuation of this Socratic influence later exemplified in Christian martyrological literature and apologetic writings (143–61).

[20] See the further discussion in his book, *A Myth of Innocence: Mark and Christian Origins* (Philadelphia, PA: Fortress, 1988), 199.

[21] *The Gospel of Thomas and Christian Wisdom* (New York, NY: Seabury, 1983), 62–80.

in the *Gospel of Thomas* not least in view of the fact that Philo is pre-occupied with interpreting the Hebrew epic within the conceptual world of Hellenistic philosophy—the epic background otherwise challenged or totally rejected by *Thomas*? On the other hand, scholars have time and again attempted to read *Thomas* in the context of second century Gnosticism—far removed from its original context.[22]

What if the author(s) of the *Gospel of Thomas* was/were themselves reading Plato and/or applying popular assumptions of the Platonic tradition in the gospel? That much is certain that during the fourth century C.E. individuals or groups producing and/or using the Nag Hammadi corpus were reading Plato in Greek and Coptic translation. In the sixth book of the collection (NHC VI,5) is a Coptic translation from Plato's *Republic* (588A–589B) on Socrates' explanation of the nature of the soul.[23] Thus, it would seem only reasonable to assume that also the author(s) of the *Gospel of Thomas* may have had direct knowledge of classical philosophy from the first century on.[24]

3. Conflicting Epic Accounts of the Creation

Once observed that the genre of the *Gospel of Thomas* is closely related to literary forms applied by Hellenistic philosophers it might seem only reasonable to seek an ideological identity between the *Gospel of Thomas* and Hellenistic philosophic traditions. However, just like Philo is of uncertain character for comparison, so are many oblique references

---

[22] For a recent discussion on the issue of *Thomas* and Gnosticism see, e.g., James M. Robinson, "On Bridging the Gulf from Q to the *Gospel of Thomas* (or Vice Versa)," in *Nag Hammadi, Gnosticism, and Early Christianity* (ed. Charles W. Hedrick and Robert Hodgson, Jr.; Peabody, MA: Hendrickson, 1986), 127–75; Antti Marjanen, "Is Thomas a Gnostic Gospel?," in *Thomas at the Crossroads. Essays on the Gospel of Thomas* (ed. Risto Uro; Studies of the New Testament and Its World; Edinburgh: Clark, 1998), 107–39.

[23] Cf. James M. Robinson ed., *The Nag Hammadi Library* (rev. ed.; The Definitive New Translation of the Gnostic Scriptures, Complete in One Volume; San Francisco, CA: Harper & Row, 1988), 318–20.

[24] Howard M. Jackson maintains that such a knowledge is present in the *Gospel of Thomas* in the context of *Gos. Thom.* 7, *The Lion Becomes Man: The Gnostic Leontomorphic Creator and the Platonic Tradition* (SBLDS 81; Atlanta, GA: Scholars Press, 1983), esp. 175–211. Jackson notes in particular the Platonic understanding of the composition of the human soul in this context. His linking of the Platonic understanding perception of the soul with Gnostic mythology is, on the other hand problematic, for a critique see, e.g., Risto Uro, *Thomas: Seeking the Historical Context of the Gospel of Thomas* (London: Clark, 2003), 40–42.

to what could have affinities with other and different trends of Hellenistic philosophical thought. It would not be difficult to point to a sense of irony in the logia of the *Gospel of Thomas*, for instance in Jesus' comparison of the Pharisees to a dog: "Jesus said: "Woe to the Pharisees, for they are like a dog sleeping in the manger of oxen, for neither does he eat nor does he [let] the oxen eat" (*Gos. Thom.* 102).

But such a common characteristic of Cynic argumentation will not be traced to a specific school or individual among the Cynics any more than would a motif on itinerancy (cf. *Gos. Thom.* 14:4 and 42) as such motifs are common to the entire tradition from the fifth century BCE and on.[25] Attempts at reading Stoic influence in the *Gospel of Thomas* would seem even more far fetched even though an echo of Stoic thought may be traced in individual logia—something that may be due to a pure coincidence.[26] Indeed, in the absence of a central idea such as of the logos, typical of Stoicism, in the *Gospel of Thomas*, it would seem doubtful at best to maintain the presence of Stoic ideology for the gospel.[27]

The emphasis of the *Gospel of Thomas* on acquiring knowledge through proper understanding is revealing about just how difficult is each of these endeavors. This abstruse nature of knowledge would seem to have much in common with Skepticism usually attributed to Pyrrho of Elis (360–270 BCE).[28] Yet, in the *Gospel of Thomas*, the disciples and, indeed, the reader (any reader) is encouraged to seek the meaning (knowledge) of the words of Jesus; the result of which will lead to eternal life. Through this very encouragement the motif

[25] On Cynicism in general see, e.g., Donald R. Dudley, *A History of Cynicism: From Diogenes to the 6th Century AD* (repr.; Chicago, IL: Ares, 1980 [1937]); Downing, *Cynics and Christian Origins*.

[26] Uro discusses the possibility of understanding the parable of children in the field (*Gos. Thom.* 21) from a Stoic perspective in which the distinction between the field, not belonging to the children, and the children in it would be readily recognized as a distinction between things being mastered by an individual (namely moral issues) and ones not under an individual's discipline (practically everything else), *Thomas*, 67–70.

[27] On Stoicism see, e.g., Max Pohlenx, *Die Stoa: Geschichte einer geistigen Bewegung* (2 vols.; Göttingen: Vandenhoeck & Ruprecht, 1948–1949); Andrew Erskine, *The Hellenistic Stoa: Political Thought and Action* (Ithaca, NY: Cornell University Press, 1990). James M. Robinson notes that the Synoptic Sayings Source would at times show better signs of Stoicism than the *Gospel of Thomas*—referring to Q 12:22–31 and *Gos. Thom.* 36 but the appeal to nature is absent in the Thomasine parallel, *The Jesus of the Sayings Gospel Q* (Occasional Papers of the Institute for Antiquity and Christianity; Claremont, CA: Institute for Antiquity and Christianity, 1993),14–15.

[28] On Pyrrhonism see, e.g., Sextus Empiricus (3rd century), *Outlines of Pyrrhonism* (transl. G. R. Bury; Great Books in Philosophy; Buffalo, NY: Prometheus, 1990).

of guidance (*paideia*)[29] emerges in its typical application in Middle-Platonist thought.[30]

While the *Gospel of Thomas* may show sporadic affinities with any or all of these different schools of thought of Late Antiquity, it is perhaps closest to the one last mentioned if only because it combines a certain procedure (*paideia*) and the very application of Platonic (epic) motifs comparable to religious (mythological) texts of the same period. The application of Platonic motifs in the *Gospel of Thomas* may be arranged in several categories: (a) motifs relating to human nature as such (components of the soul in particular); (b) motifs having to do with human destiny (a state of singleness over against division); (c) motifs on the origin of the world and the relation of the disciples to that very origin; and (d) motifs on the creation of the world and the relation of human beings to that very creation.[31] The first two categories deal in particular with the reality of human beings (the anthropology of human nature and condition) whereas the last two categories deal with cosmogony (the ultimate origin of the world or the universe) and cosmology (the creation of the physical world as such).

In what follows but one example from the *Gospel of Thomas* will be discussed belonging to the last category mentioned. It is revealing of the very conflicting epic accounts present in the *Gospel of Thomas* in contrast to the one exemplified in the Gospel of Matthew. While the author(s) of the *Gospel of Thomas* amply demonstrate knowledge of the Genesis creation accounts, the knowledge of a different creation account in the gospel, namely that of Plato's *Timaeus*, has been surprisingly overlooked in many studies of *Thomas*.[32]

In the Coptic *Gospel of Thomas* the Greek loan-word ⲈⲒⲔⲰⲚ (image) appears in four logia (22, 50, 83, and 84) whereas the word for idea (*eidos*) does not. The word image is used four times in *Gos. Thom.* 83–84 but in the latter saying 84 another word for image or likeness

---

[29] On the *paideia* see, e.g., Werner Jaeger, *Early Christianity and Greek Paideia* (Cambridge, MA: Harvard University Press, 1962).

[30] On Middle-Platonism see, e.g., Robert M. Berchman, *From Philo to Origen: Middle Platonism in Transition* (BJS 69; Chico, CA: Scholars Press, 1984).

[31] On this classification see, Jon Ma. Asgeirsson, "The *Gospel of Thomas*: The Original Scent of Christianity," *Gangleri* 76 (2002): 17–20 [in Icelandic].

[32] This despite the fact that Bentley Layton emphasizes the cosmological framework as found in *Timaeus* as a model for understanding this aspect of the literature (scriptures) collected in his volume, *The Gnostic Scriptures: A New Translation with Annotations and Introductions* (Garden City, NY: Doubleday, 1987), 15–16.

is also used (ϵΙΝϵ). The conceptual context in which these words occur does on the other hand imply a presumed knowledge and application of Plato's theory of ideas.

> Jesus said, "The images are manifest to man, but the light in them remains concealed in the image or the light of the father. He will become manifest, but his image will remain concealed by his light" (83).

> Jesus said, "When you see your likeness, you rejoice. But when you see your images which came into being before you, and which neither die nor become manifest, how much you will have to bear!" (84).

In *Gos. Thom.* 83 the image-concept (ϵΙΚⲰΝ) is used to describe the perceivable and tangible (physical) reality. Its opposite is expressed in this same context by the concept of light (Coptic: ⲞⲨⲞϵΙΝ)—a concept the author of the *Gospel of Thomas* would seem to treat in the same sense as Plato's concept of idea (*eidos*) (cf. *Republic* 595–596).[33] Needless to say, the theory of ideas is generally considered to have developed over a considerable period of time with its most original roots possibly predating Plato himself. The theory changes as well in Plato's own writings and to be exact the theory would best be explained as it appears in different ways in several of his works like *Euthyphro, Phaedo,* and the *Republic.* However, regardless of the theoretical presentation of the theory or theories it becomes in its core identified with Plato in the development and history of the Greek epic or the idea of the real world against the unreal one.[34] The different application of this idea in the *Gospel of Thomas* may, indeed, attest to the author's(') familiarity with different versions of the theory and/or his own version(s) of it.

The rejection of the Hebrew epic at large (*Gos. Thom.* 52), the breaking of the seal of the covenant (and, thus, the covenant itself) (*Gos. Thom.* 4) and the disclaim of observance to the law (cf. among others 14a, 53, and 99–112)[35] would all seem to call for a caution in the

---

[33] For English citations to the works of Plato see, Edith Hamilton and Huntington Cairns eds., *Plato: The Collected Dialogues including the Letters* (With Introduction and Prefaratory Notes; Bollingen Series 71; Princeton, NJ: Princeton University Press, 1961).

[34] Cf., e.g., the discussion by R. E. Allen, *Plato's Euthyphro and the Earlier Theory of Forms* (New York, NY: Oxford University Press, 1970); William David Ross, *Plato's Theory of Ideas* (Oxford: Oxford University Press, 1976); Abraham P. Bos, "'Aristotelian' and 'Platonic' Dualism in Hellenistic and Early Christian Philosophy and in Gnosticism," *VC* 56 (2002): 273–91.

[35] Cf. Asgeirsson, "Doublets and Strata," 168–206.

interpretation of the reference to the creation accounts and Adam in Genesis 1–2 in *Gos. Thom.* 83–85—a trilogy of sayings as they seem to be arranged.

That the author(s) has/have in mind the creation of the world or the universe should be obvious by the reference to the real world and the physical world as well as to the (polemical) reference to Adam. Could it be that the author(s) has/have in mind the epic account of the creation of the world according to *Timaeus*, the most famous narration of the creation of the world in the classical world, rather than Genesis 1:26–27 and 2:7? The former Genesis account talks, indeed, about the formation of human beings in the "image" and "likeness" of God but is lacks entirely the most important reference in *Gos. Thom.* 84, which compares the earthly human form with its eternal twin "that came into being before you"! It would seem that the Genesis account is being outright challenged by reference to the creation account in *Timaeus*. From the perspective of intertextuality, the reference to *Timaeus* is far closer than to Genesis in *Gos. Thom.* 83–84 even though the logical presuppositions are expressed with different categories:

> When the father and creator saw the creature which he had made moving and living, the created image of the eternal gods, he rejoiced, and in his joy determined to make the copy still more like the original, and as this was an eternal living being, he sought to make the universe eternal, so far as it might be. Now the nature of the ideal being was everlasting, but to bestow this attribute in its fullness upon a creature was impossible (37d).

Against this background the words of *Gos. Thom.* 83 would seem to be a clear echo of this citation from Plato's *Timaeus* or when it says in the logion that "the light in them [i.e., the images manifest to man] remains concealed in the image of the light of the father." This echo continues towards the end of *Timaeus*. The discussion moves away from the objects of creation to the maker and just like in *Gos. Thom.* 83 the image of the Father remains concealed due to his different nature while his presence is made known:

> The world has received animals, mortal and immortal, and is fulfilled with them, and has become a visible animal containing the visible— the sensible God who is the image of the intellectual, the greatest, best, fairest, most perfect—the only begotten heaven (*Tim.* 92c).

The purpose of *Gos. Thom.* 85 in the context of logia 83–84 would seem in this very context only to further contrast the creation myth revered by the *Thomas* people over against those who they apparently are in disagreement with or people building their understanding of the creation on the basis of Genesis 1–2. Thus, in *Gos. Thom.* 85 the second creation myth of human beings in Genesis (2:7) is rejected. The author(s) of the *Gospel of Thomas* make(s) no hesitation in giving this creation its due recognition: It is great in its own way! The generous comment about the coming into being of Adam can, however, only be understood as pure sarcasm as it is obvious that the creation of Adam out of physical elements is far inferior to that of the coming into being of the true self of the *Thomas* believers. The creation of human beings without their true counterpart in heaven (or the world of the ideas) is nothing short of death it self: "Jesus said, "Adam came into being from a great power and a great wealth, but he did not become worthy of you. For had he been worthy, (he would) not (have experienced) death" (*Gos. Thom.* 85).

Thus here, yet again, the *Gospel of Thomas* proclaims death over the expectations and traditions of the Hebrew epic! Following the trilogy of *Gos. Thom.* 83–85 are three sayings: the one on the son of man who has no place in the world, the one reminding against trusting the flesh and, finally, the one promising the gift of angels consisting of what "you (already) have" (*Gos. Thom.* 86–88). Following this conclusion to the creation discussion is a cluster of admonitions and parables (89–98) which may very well have constituted an early ending to the *Gospel of Thomas* or before the redactional addition of the Doublet Stratum (99–112).[36]

To maintain, as Davies does, that the trilogy of *Gos. Thom.* 83–85 be basically an allegorical interpretation of the creation of Adam (*Gos. Thom.* 85) as one in the "image" and "likeness" of God (83–84) with partial aid from Philo of Alexandria (concerning the use of image for "the things of the world" as well as for things of the invisible world)[37] simply does not hold against the contrast in what has been demonstrated to be a rejection of the creation accounts in Genesis 1–2. Jewish apocalypticism, wisdom traditions and Philo—all of which Davies evokes to his aid in interpreting the trilogy—do not add to the comprehensive picture he attempts at constructing of the *Gospel of Thomas* as "a collection of metaphors for a single underlying set of ideas."[38] And what unites the metaphors (such as "light,

---

[36] *Ibid.*, esp. 177–97.
[37] Davies, *Gospel of Thomas*, 63–65.
[38] *Ibid.*, 68.

kingdom, image"), according to Davies, is a return to the human condition prior to the expelling of Adam from Paradise. In other words Adam's original status in Paradise is identical with the kingdom, the true image of human beings, sought by the *Thomas* adherents in the understanding of Davies.[39]

If the *Gospel of Thomas* is under the influence of Hellenistic philosophy such as Middle-Platonism the author(s) must have had a reasonable first hand knowledge of some of the main writings of Plato himself as has already been pointed out. At the same time, the author's (or authors') own innovative interpretation of the basic concept behind the theory of ideas should not be minimized. Applying the same concept of image (ЄІΚШΝ) in order to express the central issue of unity over against duality (schism) in a cumulative list of opposites that culminates in overcoming the very opposite of the concept applied, image, in *Gos. Thom.* 22, may, indeed, demonstrate the author's (or authors') innovative ways of thinking. It would seem far fetched to see in this logion a reference to the primordial state of Paradise lost according to the Genesis account (3). The logion reads:

> They said to him, "Shall we then, as children, enter the kingdom?" Jesus said to them, "When you make the two one, and when you make the inside like the outside and the outside like the inside, and the above like the below, and when you make the male and the female one and the same, so that the male not be male nor the female female; and you fashion eyes in place of an eye, and a hand in place of a hand, and a foot in place of a foot, and a likeness in place of a likeness; then will you enter (the kingdom)" (22:3–7).

Within the larger context of the *Gospel of Thomas* the idea of twinship, already expressed right at the outset of the text (cf. the Incipit and *Gos. Thom.* 1 and 13), would by all counts seem to refer to the Greek epic of a single source of every form—a source back to which its faint or sick image strives to return to. Away from its source, the

---

[39] *Ibid.*, 68–69. Davies says further: "The sequence 83–85 indicates that attainment of the unitive state is equivalent to 'seeing' the original Image (lost by Adam) which is hidden in light. Indeed, if we follow Thomas' line of thought, this Image of God can be recaptured temporally . . ., or discerned cognitively . . ., and possibly even apprehended spatially, although it is not clear how one might spatially apprehend such an Image," 69; cf. Roberto Radice, "Observations on the Theory of the Ideas as the Thoughts of God in Philo of Alexandria," in *Heirs of the Septuagint: Philo, Hellenistic Judaism and Early Christianity: Festschrift for Earle Hilgert* (ed. David T. Runia; SPhilo 3; Atlanta, GA: Scholars Press, 1991), 127–34.

image is but a shadow on a wall—most unreal! In view of this core principle in the *Gospel of Thomas* it is probably no wonder that the author would use the one and same concept to express two aspects of one reality! The shadow is caused by lack of knowledge and understanding (cf. *Gos. Thom.* 18) of its true origin! In the Genesis account innocence and not knowledge is lost. Could the contrast be any sharper? Again, in *Gos. Thom.* 89 the reader is reminded about the tarnish of the cup: It is no less the work of the creator than the alleged pureness of its inside. The Thomas followers will not be left out from the kingdom because the true source is only one!

This perception of reality builds on one form or the other of the theory of ideas as attributed to Plato in the world of the Greek epic regardless of how far or close it actually comes to his own treatment of the theory. Close to the center of the *Gospel of Thomas* the issue of the disciples' origins comes to the fore:

> Jesus said, "If they say to you, 'Where did you come from?' say to them, 'We came from the light, the place where the light came into being on its own accord and established (itself) and became manifest through their image.' If they say to you, 'Is it you?' say, 'We are its children, and we are the elect of the living father.' If they ask you, 'What is the sign of your father in you?' say to them, 'It is movement and repose'" (50).

Again, in this logion of the *Gospel of Thomas* the reader is reminded of Plato's words in *Timaeus* where he is discussing the difference of created beings over against eternal ones. The Father, faced with the impossibility of assigning eternal faculties onto creatures, comes up with the following solution: "Wherefore he resolved to have a moving image of eternity, and when he set in order the heaven, he made this image eternal but moving according to number, while eternity itself rests in unity, and this image we call time" (*Tim.* 37d).

So prominent are the parallels between *Timaeus* and *the Gospel of Thomas* in the context of the question about origins and creation as exemplified in *Gos. Thom.* 50, and 83–85 that it practically takes an effort to overlook them or ignore them. How can the Genesis account call for a closer parallel in comparison to what is present in the creation details of *Timaeus*? Could it be that the judgment rendered by the early form critics, about the literary nature of New Testament texts and Apocrypha or all the more the lack there of, still lingers in New Testament scholarship? If far removed from the literary genre then presumably also from the classical contents or motifs! The *Gospel of*

Thomas does, indeed, share many features with philosophical texts of the Hellenistic age as has been demonstrated in various studies over the past few decades.[40] Why not also the Greek and Hellenistic epic traditions? Once the rhetorical elements in the *Gospel of Thomas* are recognized, a more coherent structure may be detected all throughout the gospel. Acknowledging the presence of classical philosophical motifs still strengthens the coherency of the text as a comprehensive construction and not merely an arbitrary collection of the sayings of Jesus.

In the Gospel of Matthew a very different perspective on the creation is to be found in the curious debate between the Pharisees and Jesus over the issue of divorce (19:3–12). In this context Jesus refers directly to the Genesis account about the creation of male and female (1:27) as well as to the admonition to the same male to leave his parent's home and marry a woman in order to establish a new home as one flesh (cf. Gen 2:24). To the words of Genesis Jesus adds the comment, "What therefore God has joined together, let not man put asunder" (Matt 19:6). When challenged on the issue that divorce had, indeed, been allowed, Jesus attributes the exception to Moses— a derogation from the original purpose of marriage and union of male and female.

The Matthean account, thus, assumes a totally different scenario of the creation in comparison to the *Gospel of Thomas*. The emphasis is on the gender differentiation established by the very creative act of God. The unity created by marriage is, however, one unrelated to the concept of the kingdom of God in view of the fact that there are some "eunuchs who have made themselves eunuchs for the sake of the kingdom of heaven" (19:12a). Thus, the very idea of duality (gender) is understood completely differently in the Gospel of Matthew and the *Gospel of Thomas*. In the latter the idea of twinship—between the real and the unreal—is crucial for understanding the origins and fate of human beings. In the former the union of two different sexes does not constitute the road to heaven but merely allegiance to the law of God.

Thus, whenever the understanding of the creation account in the book of Genesis is invoked it must be first understood in its very

---

[40] Cf. Kloppenborg, *Formation of Q,* 263–316; Asgeirsson, "Doublets and Strata," 6–54.

own context and subsequently in the context of any author or authority using the accounts. The *Gospel of Thomas* would seem in view of what has been argued above only refer to the motif of Adam in order to sharpen the contrast between the creation myth important to the Thomas people, namely as found in *Timaeus*, whereas Matthew directly cites the Genesis stories in order to interpret the accounts in his own historical context. And in a Midrashic fashion Matthew has words put on the lips of Jesus adding to the apparent meaning of the words as found in Genesis. *Thomas* too, is able to do just that, that is to add to the epic motifs at his disposal or in his case those found in *Timaeus*. But he is fighting a different battle and the polemic is utterly against the very epic background Matthew uses in his own exposition of the Genesis stories.

What is "old" for the scribe in Matthew has a completely different reference than what is "old" garment in the *Gospel of Thomas*: two separate and distinct epic worlds. Is merging them together but an allegorical invention of modern scholarship?

4. *From the Core to the Frame*

It would be fair to state that within the western theological university education at large, students have been trained in paying due attention to the close cultural environment of any religious (mythological) text under discussion. This, indeed, has been an emphasis warning students and scholars to by-step various filters separating earlier (in this case classical) traditions from the text being analyzed at any time. Yet, the intertextual reality echoed in any given text is not a chronological or a linear development. The compositional process reveals itself in most cases, for sure, to be far more complicated than any such simple idea of a taxonomy. Authors move freely across any chronologically datable sources under which they may be influenced or actually imitating or reworking into their present composition. It is being suggested here that the author(s) (the plural implying the redactional process) of the *Gospel of Thomas* are influenced both by contemporary method of applying data and the use of a classical source. It is in the reworking of the author(s) of the *Gospel of Thomas* that these different intertextual sources come to build a new text (itself a metatext) in which the genius of the author(s) is reflected. The difficulty in tracing the sources and traditions used in a text like the *Gospel of*

Thomas consists not only of constituting its sources and traditions but exactly how they must be dismantled in the text in order to approach the constructive processes involved (the compositional history).

Principles of guidance (*paideia*) for coming to proper understanding in the *Gospel of Thomas* are expressed in the very nature of discipleship (*discipulus* over against *magister*) throughout the gospel as well as in the introductory saying on seeking and finding (*Gos. Thom.* 2). It is being maintained here that this saying is part of a redactional framework of the gospel, the motif of which fits perfectly the general agenda of the disciples' effort to decipher the words of Jesus.[41] It is a motif most prominent in the emergeing tradition of Middle-Platonic thought at the same time. Yet, a more recent redaction consists of the Introductory Saying and *Gos. Thom.* 1. This is the framework of the twinship tradition characterized in the persona of Didymus Judas Thomas. It is a framework that becomes applied to all three texts attributed to the name of Thomas in Late Antiquity and known as the *Gospel*, the *Book*, and the *Acts of Thomas*.[42]

In what has been labeled the "religion of the heavenly twin,"[43] a motif has been applied to the *Gospel of Thomas* in which an even older epic tradition is being manipulated for framing the entire text of the gospel and, indeed, the other literary works attributed to Thomas. This tradition may at least be traced back to Homer and the idea of the two sons of Zeus and Leda (the wife of Tyndareus king of Sparta), Castor and Pollux. While in popular legend Castor was considered the son of Tyndareus and Pollux the son of Zeus, traditionally the two were always considered the sons of Zeus (Dioscuri). In the development of their epic history they certainly undergo various transformations. In the Homeric tradition they stand for sportsmanship and brotherly affection whereas in the tradition of dedicating specific

---

[41] The main bulk of the contents of the *Gospel of Thomas* consists in the analysis of the present author of *Gos. Thom.* 4–98. The main redactional stratum consists of *Gos. Thom.* 99–112. These two main bulks of the contents is framed in with two logia on the kingdom of God (*Gos. Thom.* 3 and 113). A later redaction adds the motif on *Gos. Thom.* 2 and a still later redaction the motif of the heavenly twins (Incipit and *Gos. Thom.* 1)—logion 114 is considered to be a still later addition, cf. Asgeirsson, "Doublets and Strata," 88–131, 168–206.

[42] On the idea of Thomas(ine) Christianity see, e.g., Gregory J. Riley,"Thomas Traditions and the *Acts of Thomas*" in *SBL Seminar Papers, 1993* (SBLSP 30; Atlanta, GA: Scholars Press, 1993), 533–42.

[43] See Gregory J. Riley, "Thomas Christianity" (SBL Annual Meeting; Washington, DC, 1993).

crafts or occupations to members of the pantheon they become the protectors of sailors.[44] Yet, the popularity of the Dioscuri may have been mostly indebted to the fact that the Homeric Hymns (of the sixth century BCE),[45] that enjoyed enormous popularity, were dedicated to the brothers.[46]

It is as if the *paideia* motif of seeking and finding (cf. *Gos. Thom.* 2), reflected throughout the *Gospel of Thomas* in the questions of the disciples (for instance 12, 18, 20, 21, 22:3, 24, 37, 43, 51–53, 61:2, 79, 91, 99–100, 113–114) and even comments by the author(s) (cf. 111b), needed a final boosting provided be means of the motif of the heavenly twins. The motif, which may even predate the Homeric tradition,[47] places the search for eternal life in the *Gospel of Thomas* along an age old idea about the individual's better self residing away from the very individual in the world of heavens. It is, thus, reminiscent of imitating the hero in the Greek tradition: to become like the ideal of all ideals or Jesus in the context of the *Gospel of Thomas*.[48]

As with the motif of secrecy, here, again, the motif of the divine twins in the *Gospel of Thomas* has a curious link with the Gospel of Mark. In Mark the brothers James and John, sons of Zebedee, are characterized in exactly this same manner of the Dioscuri. It has been noted that Matthew, Luke and John seem to pay less attention to these brothers if not deliberately avoiding references to them in their sources.[49] The identification in Mark with the Dioscuri tradition cannot be overlooked for the very fact that in Mark Jesus

---

[44] See, e.g., Walter Burkert, *Greek Religion* (trans. John Raffan; Cambridge, MA: Harvard Universtity Press, 1985 [1977]), esp. 212–213; J. V. Muir, "Religion and the New Education: The Challenge of the Sophists," in *Greek Religion and Society* (ed. P. E. Easterling and J. V. Muir; with a foreword by Sir Moses Finley; London: Cambridge University Press, 1985), 195.

[45] On the Homeric Hymns see, e.g., Albin Lesky, *Geschichte der griechischen Literatur* (3rd ed.; Bern & Munich: Francke Verlag, 1971 [1957–1958]), 106–111.

[46] See MacDonald, *Homeric Epics*, 26.

[47] Burkert, *Greek Religion*, 212; cf. MacDonald, *Homeric Epics*, 25.

[48] On the idea of alter ego in ancient literature see, e.g., Thomas van Nortwick, *Somewhere I Have Never Travelled: The Second Self and the Hero's Journey in Ancient Epic* (New York, NY: Oxford University Press, 1992); on the motif of the hero in Homer, e.g., Jasper Griffin, *Homer on Life and Death* (Oxford: Clarendon, 1980); on the motif of the hero in Christianity, e.g., David E. Aune, "Heracles and Christ: Heracles Imagery in the Christology of Early Christianity," in *Greeks, Romans, and Christians: Essays in Honor of Abraham J. Malherbe* (ed. David L. Balch, Everett Ferguson and Wayne A. Meeks; Minneapolis, MN: Fortress, 1990), 3–19.

[49] So MacDonald, *Homeric Epics*, 24.

gives them the epithet "Sons of Thunder" ("Boanerges") (Mark 3:17).[50]
Thus, like in the *Gospel of Thomas*, an ancient Greek epic tradition
emerges in a gospel (Mark) contemporaneous with *Thomas*. The
Gospels of Matthew Luke and John seem all to avoid it at the expense
of other epic motifs more important for their very own context.

Despite its late redaction in the *Gospel of Thomas*, the application
of the Dioscuri motif is yet another indication of how the author(s)
of the gospel obviously knew and applied classical epic motifs whether
from the world of myth (Homer) or logic (Plato). The *paideia* motif
linked with the search for knowledge, finally, implies the application
of a more recent philosophical development in the cultural environment of *Thomas*. Thus, while the *Gospel of Thomas* certainly shows
knowledge of the Hebrew epic and, indeed, argues against it, it uses
Greek epical motifs for its very own presentation.

[50] MacDonald suggests the original readers of these gospels (*Thomas* and Mark)
would immediately have understood these references in terms of a "Christian
Dioscurism," *Homeric Epics*, 25; cf. J. Rendel Harris, *Boanerges* (Cambridge, MA:
Cambridge University Press, 1913).

CHAPTER EIGHT

ENTHYMEME AND PICTURE IN THE
GOSPEL OF THOMAS

Vernon K. Robbins

In many sections of early Christian writings, assertions do not simply
stand alongside other assertions. Either rationales support them or
conclusions follow them. In rhetorical terms, this can appropriately
be called rhetology, namely, expressible (*rhētos*)[1] reasoning (*logos*). The
presence of rationales and conclusions indicates that the speaker/author
is engaged in some kind of reasoning about the world and the things
and processes in it. Aristotle used the term "enthymeme" for this
kind of reasoning, giving the example: "There is no man who is
really free, for he is the slave of either wealth or fortune" (*Rhet.*
2.21.6 [1394B]).

A special challenge for interpretation of enthymemes is to interpret
the function of pictures in them. Pictorial narration on its own can
appropriately be called rhetography, expressible graphic images.[2] In
rhetography, rationales regularly function as "explanations" rather
than "arguments." An instance of this is present in *Gos. Thom.* 57:1–4:

> Jesus said, "The kingdom of the Father is like a person who had [good]
> seed. [2]His enemy came at night and sowed weeds among the good
> seed. [3]The person did not let the workers pull up the weeds, but said
> to them, 'No, lest you go to pull up the weeds and pull up the wheat
> along with them.' [4]For on the day of the harvest the weeds will be
> conspicuous, and will be pulled up and burned."

The assertion in v. 1 creates two pictures: (1) a picture waiting to be
clarified (the kingdom of the Father) and (2) a well-known picture
(a person with good seed). The well-known picture continues with a

---

[1] See the "*rhēt-*" words in Polybius, *Hist.* 32.6.7 (to give a stated [*rhētēn*] answer);
Plato, *Theaet.* 205d, 205e (syllables are expressible [*rhētai*]); *Epistles* 341c (subject matter that admits of verbal expression [*rhēton*]), 341d (things which can be stated [*rhēta*]).
[2] Cf. the term "theography" in Jack Miles, *God: A Biography* (New York, NY:
Vintage Books, 1996), 12.

pictorial sequence that makes it a narrative: after the person sows good seed, an enemy comes and sows weeds, etc. The rationale in v. 4 of this logion explains an action in the narrative sequence: "why" the person did not let the workers pull up the weeds. The rationale, then, is an "explanation" in the context of a description, rather than a major or minor premise in a syllogistic argument. In other words, the rhetology is explanatory rather than argumentative. "The day of the harvest" in the explanation, however, is a topos.[3] This means that it is a social, cultural, and/or ideological "location of thought." As a social, cultural, and/or ideological phenomenon, it is intertwined with multiple networks of meanings. In early Christianity, this topos exists interactively with concepts of the "end of time."

An assertion and a rationale present argumentative rhetology only if the rationale attempts to prove "that" something is the case.[4] The rationale in *Gos. Thom.* 57:4 does not attempt to prove that the person did not let the workers pull up the weeds; it only explains why. When a rationale is an explanation,[5] it regularly is a constituent in the presentation of conventional wisdom. The explanatory rationale provides a context or location of thought that may contribute to an argument that tries to convince someone to draw a specific conclusion.

In contrast to *Gos. Thom.* 57, the parable in *Gos. Thom.* 20:2–4 is a description without an explanation:

> The disciples said to Jesus, "Tell us what the kingdom of heaven is like." [2]He said to them, "It is like a mustard seed. [3]<It> is the tiniest of all seeds, [4]but when it falls on prepared soil, it produces a large plant and becomes a shelter for birds of heaven."

"A description consists of one or more statements that, taken together, cause a certain picture to appear in the mind of a reader or listener."[6] While a description is neither an explanation nor an argument, it may also present well-known information that can function as grounds

---

[3] For basic insights into a sociorhetorical approach to topoi (plural of topos), see Vernon K. Robbins, "The Intertexture of Apocalyptic Discourse in the Gospel of Mark," in *The Intertexture of Apocalyptic Discourse in the New Testament* (ed. Duane F. Watson; SBLSymS 14; Atlanta, GA: Society of Biblical Literature, 2002), 11–15.

[4] Patrick J. Hurley, *A Concise Introduction to Logic* (2d ed.; Belmont: Wadsworth, 1985), 17.

[5] An explanation contains two distinct components: the explanandum and the explanans. "The explanandum is the statement that describes the event or phenomenon to be explained, and the explanans is the statement or group of statements that purport to do the explaining" (Hurley, *Logic,* 17).

[6] Hurley, *Logic,* 12.

(a case/minor premise) for drawing a particular conclusion. As in *Gos. Thom.* 57:1–4, so in 20:1–4, the argument lies in the assertion of rhetographical similarity between the kingdom of heaven and the narrative description.

Much early Christian discourse moves beyond a presentation of descriptions and explanations into a presentation of arguments. *Gos. Thom.* 54 is an instance of an assertion with a rationale that presents an argument: "Jesus said, 'Blessed are the poor, for yours is the kingdom of heaven.'"

In this instance the rationale presents grounds for believing the claim that the poor are blessed. In other words, the saying contains argumentative rhetology. At the same time, the rhetography is general rather than specific. The kingdom of heaven, a generalized picture, belongs to the generalized picture of the poor. The assertion and the rationale use generalized pictures to argue for a conviction that most people would not usually hold (that the poor possess a special benefit in the form of the kingdom of heaven).[7] An interpreter may begin to wonder, then, if argumentative rationales that occur in the context of general pictures and explanatory rationales more naturally occur with specific pictures.

When argumentative rationales occur in discourse, they can be displayed as syllogisms and are regularly called "enthymemes." The Greek noun "enthymeme" has a substantive relation to "thinking," "reasoning," "pondering," "imagining," and "holding a conviction."[8] The dynamic function of enthymemes recently has been explained by Jeffrey Walker:

> An "enthymeme" is, on the one hand, a complex, quasi-syllogistic structure of inference and affect that constitutes the substance and persuasive force of an argument *as perceived by an audience*. On the other hand, an "enthymeme" will typically and perhaps most forcefully appear in *discourse* as an emphatic, structural/stylistic turn that caps an exetasis,[9]

---

[7] Vernon K. Robbins, "Pragmatic Relations as a Criterion for Authentic Sayings," *Forum* 1:3 (1985): 35–63.

[8] Cf. Matt 1:20; 9:4; 12:25; Acts 10:19; 17:29; Heb 4:12; see Anders Eriksson, *Traditions as Rhetorical Proof: Pauline Argumentation in 1 Corinthians* (ConBNT 29; Stockholm: Almquist & Wiksell, 1998), 41–43.

[9] Jeffrey Walker, *Rhetoric and Poetics in Antiquity* (New York, NY: Oxford University Press, 2000), 134 (cf. 176–77), defines *exetasis* as "the skeptical 'examination' of fissures, contradictions, and inconsistencies in any discourse, in order to refute it, argue its opposite, or to open an alternative position."

gives the inferential/affective substance of a particular realization with
a particular salience within a particular discursive moment, and thereby
shapes its audience's perception of (and responses to) just what "the
argument" is. Ultimately, the enthymeme is both these things at once
and as such is the "body of persuasion."[10]

It is important to notice the repetition of the term "particular" in this
definition: "an 'enthymeme' . . . gives the inferential/affective substance
of a particular realization with a particular salience within a particular
discursive moment." Enthymemes, it would appear, interrelate the
general, the specific, the argumentative, and the explanatory in very
particular ways for very particular purposes. In the present essay, sayings in early Christian gospels that contain assertions accompanied
by argumentative rationales are called "enthymematic logia." These
logia exhibit social, cultural, ideological, eschatological, christological, and theological argumentation by early Christians.[11]

The *Gospel of Thomas* contains an inner network of enthymematic
logia built upon conventional Mediterranean wisdom. This means
that some enthymematic logia in *Thomas* contain descriptions and/or
explanations as cases or grounds for arguments. Many logia that
contain descriptions or explanations are part of the "bedrock of tradition" in the variant forms of Q, synoptic, and Thomasine tradition.[12]
One of the characteristics of this tradition is to present pictorial
explanations and descriptions in a negative form, either as negative
assertions or as questions expecting a negative answer. In other words,
instead of presenting Jesus as saying "Whoever lights a lamp puts it
on a lampstand," the tradition presents Jesus as saying either "No one
after lighting a lamp puts it in a cellar or under a bushel, but on
a stand, that those who enter may see the light" (Luke 11:33 par.)

---

[10] Walker, *Rhetoric*, 184.
[11] Burton L. Mack and Vernon K. Robbins, *Patterns of Persuasion in the Gospels*
(FF: Literary Facets; Sonoma, CA: Polebridge Press, 1989); Robbins, "Pragmatic
Relations"; *idem*, *The Tapestry of Early Christian Discourse: Rhetoric, Society and Ideology*
(London: Routledge, 1996); *idem*, *Exploring the Texture of Texts: A Guide to Socio-Rhetorical
Interpretation* (Valley Forge, PA: Trinity Press International, 1996); *idem*, "From
Enthymeme to Theology in Luke 11:1–13," in *Literary Studies in Luke-Acts: A Collection
of Essays in Honor of Joseph B. Tyson* (ed. R. P. Thompson and T. E. Phillips; Macon:
Mercer University Press, 1998), 191–214; *idem*, "Argumentative Textures in Socio-
Rhetorical Interpretation," in *Rhetorical Argumentation in Biblical Texts* (ed. A. Eriksson,
T. H. Olbricht, and W. Übelacker; Emory Studies in Early Christianity; Harrisburg,
PA: Trinity Press International, 2002), 27–65.
[12] Stephen J. Patterson, *The Gospel of Thomas and Jesus* (FF: Reference Series;
Sonoma, CA: Polebridge Press, 1993), 225.

or "Is a lamp brought in to be put under a bushel, or under a bed, and not on a stand?" (Mark 4:21). One of the goals of these specific pictorial descriptions or explanations is to introduce either a positive or negative "implication." In the realm of logic, an implication is a conclusion implied from premises.[13] In rhetorical terms, an implication regularly takes the form of exhortation toward a certain kind of action or an appeal not to engage in a certain kind of action. A positive implication, then, takes the form of persuasion to do something (protrepsis) and a negative implication takes the form of dissuasion from doing something (apotrepsis).[14] *Gos. Thom.* 33 uses two specific pictures to present a positive implication (protrepsis) in its presentation about the lamp:

> Jesus said, [Implication] "What you will hear in your ear, in the other ear proclaim from your rooftops. [Explanation (Case/Grounds)] ²For no one lights a lamp and puts it under a basket, nor does one put it in a hidden place. ³Rather, one puts it on a stand so that all who come and go will see its light."

Jesus' statement to his disciples that they should proclaim from their rooftops what they will hear in their ear is an initial positive picture that contains an implication grounded in the explanation about the lamp. The reasoning here is inductive, from case to implication and from specific picture to specific picture. The explanation presents conventional wisdom in a negative form that gives it rhetorical force. There is nothing counter to conventional wisdom in the saying. Its formulation in a negative manner provides an opportunity to introduce various negative alternatives[15] in a manner that invites elaboration of the concepts it articulates.[16]

---

[13] Hurley, *Logic*, 306.

[14] Aristotle, *Rhet.* 1.3.5; George A. Kennedy, *Aristotle On Rhetoric: A Theory of Civic Discourse* (New York, NY: Oxford University Press, 1991), 49.

[15] E.g., not under a jar (Luke 8:16) or bed (Mark 4:21/Luke 8:16) or in a cellar (Luke 11:33). For a discussion of negative alternatives, see Vernon K. Robbins, "A Comparison of Mishnah Gittin 1:1–2:2 and James 2:1–13 from a Perspective of Greco-Roman Rhetorical Elaboration," in *Mishnah and the Social Formation of the Early Rabbinic Guild: A Socio-Rhetorical Approach* (ed. Jack N. Lightstone; Studies in Christianity and Judaism/Études sur le christianisme et le judaïsme 11; Waterloo: Wilfrid Laurier University Press for the Canadian Corporation for Studies in Religion/Corporation Canadienne des Sciences Religieuses, 2002), 201–16.

[16] Vernon K. Robbins, "Rhetorical Argument about Lamps and Light in Early Christian Gospels," in *Context: Festskrift til Peder Johan Borgen* (ed. P. W. Böckman and R. E. Kristiansen; Relief: Publikasjoner Utgitt av Religionsvitenskapelig Institutt, Universitetet i Trondheim 24; Trondheim: Tapir, 1987), 177–95.

In the midst of negative formulations that present conventional wisdom, Q, synoptic tradition, and the *Gospel of Thomas* contain generalized assertions that invert and divert conventional wisdom. An example is the assertion that "nothing is covered up that will not be revealed, or hidden that will not be known" (Q 12:2). Here the pictures are general, rather than specific. Conventional wisdom asserts that some things that are hidden will be lost and never found. This saying inverts conventional wisdom, perhaps through analogy with a person's inability to hide his or her deceptions or evildoing, which has given rise to sayings like, "Your sins will find you out." The things hidden, therefore, may not be specific, concrete objects like money or pearls, but intentions or desires. In this essay, wisdom that inverts conventional wisdom is called "contrawisdom." With certain topics, Q, synoptic tradition, and *Thomas* move away from conventional wisdom into contrawisdom. At these points an interpreter sees aspects of the ideological texture of this tradition that set it in opposition to conventional Mediterranean wisdom.

For all the gospels, whether their enthymematic formulations are presented in positive terms, negative terms, or in terms of contrawisdom, they become productive by means of interaction among deductive, inductive, and abductive social, cultural, and ideological reasoning.[17] Most people are familiar with deductive reasoning. Deductive reasoning proceeds according to a standard that "an argument is good only if the conclusion follows *necessarily* from the premises."[18] Contrary to Aristotle, who argued that deductive arguments only proceed from the general to the particular, "there are deductive arguments that proceed from the general to the general, from the particular to the particular, and from the particular to the general, as well as from the general to the particular."[19] The key is that in deductive arguments "the conclusion follows necessarily and with complete certainty from the premises."[20] This means that the general premise ("rule" or "warrant") in a deductive argument contains, implicitly or explicitly, the assertions made both in the minor premise ("case" or "grounds") and

---

[17] Richard L. Lanigan, "From Enthymeme to Abduction: The Classical Law of Logic and the Postmodern Rule of Rhetoric," in *Recovering Pragmatism's Voice: The Classical Tradition, Rorty, and the Philosophy of Communication* (eds. L. Langsdorf and A. R. Smith; Albany, NY: SUNY, 1995), 49–70; Robbins, "Enthymeme."

[18] Hurley, *Logic*, 25.

[19] Hurley, *Logic*, 30.

[20] Hurley, *Logic*, 29.

the conclusion ("result" or "claim").[21] Thus, deduction does not generate any new information; it simply clarifies or helps one to find information accurately.

In contrast to deductive reasoning, inductive reasoning is a means by which we get new knowledge. Inductive reasoning moves to new knowledge by following a standard of probability rather than certainty; therefore, the inductive standard is that "an argument is good only if the conclusion follows *probably* from the premises."[22] An initial way to think about induction is reasoning from specific pictures to a general statement. An inductive argument presents claims (results) that enlarge upon and go beyond the evidence. Nancey Murphy presents the following example:

> Fox number 1 is red; fox number 2 is red; fox number 3 is red. . . . Therefore all foxes are red. This is induction at its simplest. . . . Inductive reasoning is essential for expanding our knowledge. Its drawback is that it does so at the expense of the comforting certitude of deductive reasoning—we can never be sure that the next fox will not be grey.[23]

While Hurley discusses only four kinds of deductive syllogisms (see n. 18), he discusses six kinds of inductive syllogisms: (1) prediction; (2) argument from analogy; (3) inductive generalization; (4) argument from authority; (5) argument based on signs; and (6) causal inference.[24] In each instance, the standard is "probability": the conclusion in some way moves beyond the premises, which are somehow specific, to something that is less familiar or that little is known about. In induction, the reasoning has specific warrants and grounds that make it reasonable to think that the conclusion is probable.

Still another means of moving toward new knowledge is through abductive reasoning, "that form of reasoning in which a recognizable similarity between A and B proposes the possibility of further similarity."[25] Abductive reasoning draws an insight in the context of

---

[21] Nancey C. Murphy, *Reasoning & Rhetoric in Religion* (Valley Forge, PA: Trinity Press International, 1994), 35; Hurley, *Logic*, 26–27, presents four kinds of deductive syllogisms: (1) argument from definition; (2) categorical syllogisms (all . . . no . . .); (3) hypothetical syllogisms (if . . . then . . .); and (4) disjunctive syllogisms (either . . . or . . .).

[22] Hurley, *Logic*, 25.

[23] Murphy, *Reasoning*, 35.

[24] Hurley, *Logic*, 28–29.

[25] Gregory Bateson and Mary C. Bateson, *Angels Fear: Towards an Epistemology of the Sacred* (New York, NY: Macmillan, 1987), 206; cf. Lanigan, "Enthymeme," 60.

similarity a person observes among phenomena in different fields. There is disagreement among interpreters whether the rhetor or inquirer "invents" or "discovers" similarity. Richard L. Lanigan proposes that "by shock, question, puzzlement, surprise, and the like, the rhetor or inquirer *discovers similarity*" in a context of deductive and inductive reasoning.[26] In the words of C. S. Peirce:

> The abductive suggestion comes to us like a flash. It is an act of insight, although of extremely fallible insight. It is true that the different elements of the hypothesis were in our minds before; but it is the idea of putting together [metonymy] what we had never before dreamed of putting together which flashes the new suggestion [metaphor] before our contemplation.[27]

"Putting together what we had never before dreamed of putting together" is in many ways a key to understanding abductive reasoning. When the context of reasoning is a deductive-inductive cycle of argumentation, abduction regularly is a matter of putting the case (grounds or minor premise) together with the result (claim or conclusion) in a way that discovers a new insight. This new combination of case and result becomes a case (grounds or minor premise) that creates a new result (claim or conclusion).[28] We will see instances of this in the enthymematic logia that stand among the first nineteen logia in

---

[26] Lanigan, "Enthymeme," 59. For an alternative approach to abduction, see L. Gregory Bloomquist, "A Possible Direction for Providing Programmatic Correlation of Textures in Socio-Rhetorical Analysis," in *Rhetorical Criticism and the Bible* (ed. S. E. Porter and D. L. Stamps; JSNTSup 195; Sheffield: Sheffield Academic Press), 74–95.

[27] C. S. Peirce in Lanigan, "Enthymeme," 66 [Lanigan's insertions].

[28] See Lanigan, "Enthymeme," 61: "On Sabre's account . . ., the abduction creates as its conclusion (1: claim) a hypothesis [All S are M], which supplies [→] the *minor premise* (2: data) in a rhetor's deduction. This judgment is based upon the *major premise* (3: warrant) of the rhetor's deduction supplied [←] by the conclusion [All M are P] of an induction (4: backing). The deductive *conclusion* [All S are P] is susceptible to material error (5: reservation) since (a) it has already functioned as the all important minor premise in the abduction—a premise [All S are P!] intuitively (non-logically) generated in shock, question, puzzlement or assertion (6: qualifier), and (b) since the major premise of the deduction and the abduction are *identical* [All M are P]. Note that the deduction relies on the claim that M and P are *identical*, hence the hypothesis that P *either* explains the meaning of S *or* not. By contrast, the abduction relies on the claim that M and P are *similar*, hence the hypothesis that M explains the meaning of *both S and P*, as Sabre correctly notes for the wrong reasons. The right reasons involve a contemporary understanding of *tropic logic* as it emerges in rhetoric, not science" (referring to Ru Michael Sabre, "Peirce's Abductive Argument and the Enthymeme," *Transactions of the Charles S. Peirce Society* 36 [1990]: 365–69).

the *Gospel of Thomas*. Since the abductive process is perhaps the most difficult aspect of this essay to grasp, we will postpone trying to explain it further until we have explored some other logia that present deductive-inductive reasoning. When we analyze abductive reasoning, we will see that it does not simply follow an inductive-deductive cycle of argumentation but "leaps" imaginatively to distinctive insights by perceiving or inventing similarity among data in a number of fields. In the context of reasoning from conventional wisdom about hosts and guests, friends, fathers and sons, patrons and clients, plants, animals, and good people and bad people, abductive reasoning discovers and invents special insights that create a rich system of transcendent understanding about the nature of God, God's son, God's world, and the joys and responsibilities of being a child of God in the world.[29]

Interwoven into the conventional social and cultural wisdom in the *Gospel of Thomas* is a thick network of enthymematic logia that exhibit not only abductive reasoning but contrawisdom. Using pictorial images from conventional Mediterranean society and culture, these enthymematic logia invert and divert conventional wisdom in ways that are mysterious, unusual, or even bizarre to the ordinary reader. This is not accidental. The purpose of the sayings is to create an environment that takes people on a search for meanings that lie beyond conventional understanding into a realm that produces wonder and inducts people into a special kingdom of knowledge that makes them royalty among other people of understanding. *Gos. Thom.* 2:1–4 straightforwardly presents the program for this activity:

> Jesus said, "Let one who seeks not stop seeking until one finds. [2]When one finds, one will be disturbed. [3]When one is disturbed, one will marvel, [4]and will reign over all."

This logion refers directly to the shock, question, puzzlement, and surprise referred to in the discussion of abductive reasoning. In fact, the *Gospel of Thomas* introduces a sequence of pictures: (1) finding, (2) being disturbed, (3) marveling, (4) reigning over all. Seeking to understand leads one not simply to conventional wisdom based on deductive-inductive reasoning but to a special narrative sequence that leads to secret, hidden knowledge and power. The narrative sequence

---

[29] Robbins, "Enthymeme"; *idem*, "Argumentative Textures."

presupposes abductive reasoning, namely leaps of insight that dis-
turb conventional wisdom and introduce unusual knowledge known
only by certain people—those who are members of a "royal" circle
who, because of their special understanding, rule over all other people.

The procedure of this essay is first to examine two enthymematic
logia in the *Gospel of Thomas* that build upon conventional social and
cultural wisdom in the Mediterranean world. These logia are variants
of Q and synoptic tradition. After the analysis of logia containing
conventional enthymematic reasoning, the essay displays eight enthymematic logia that occur in the context of the first nineteen logia
in *Thomas*. These logia in the opening progressive texture of *Thomas*
exhibit in an especially dramatic manner how Thomasine tradition
builds its point of view on contrawisdom. Many of them use abductive reasoning in addition to deductive and inductive reasoning.

1. *Enthymematic Logia Exhibiting Conventional Wisdom*

This section contains an analysis of two enthymematic logia in *Thomas*
oriented theoretically, at least, toward all people in the world. The
purpose of this section is to introduce a procedure for analyzing and
interpreting enthymematic logia that contain negative formulations.
In the overall text of the *Gospel of Thomas*, universal enthymemes
establish primary polarities within the Thomasine view of the world:
good plant/bad plant, good person/bad person, good seed/bad seed,
one/two. The term "universal" is used here in the sense of reasoning
that purports to apply to every person everywhere. In other words,
these logia do not contain "you" or some other formulation that
directs the reasoning toward a limited group of people. In addition,
these logia are pictorial in a manner that allows almost any person
to envision them.

Universal enthymemes in the *Gospel of Thomas* are part of the
enthymematic network of wisdom that *Thomas* shares with Q and
synoptic material. These enthymemes do not contain startling information or inverted modes of reasoning. Rather, they contain negative formulations that use conventional Mediterranean wisdom forcefully
toward their rhetorical goals.

Gospel of Thomas 45:1–4

This logion argues that grapes and figs are analogous to good people, and thorn trees and thistles are analogous to bad people. Here the pictures of the vegetation are specific enough to be powerful and clear, but general enough to be effectively universal. Any region in the world with viticulture as part of its food source is ready for the pictorial reasoning in this logion. The reasoning moves from plants with some particular specificity to more generalized people. Bad people are like thorn trees and thistles. They do not produce nourishing fruit but evil actions and speech. Good people are like grapes and figs; they produce nourishing actions and speech. There is no attempt to present reasoning about more specific people, like slaves, rulers, householders, or the like. Rather, the logion moves from generally specific vegetation to people in two generalized categories (bad/good):

> Jesus said, "Grapes are not harvested from thorn trees, nor are figs gathered from thistles, for they yield no fruit. [2]A good person brings forth good from the storehouse; [3]a bad person brings forth evil things from the corrupt storehouse in the heart, and says evil things. [4]For from the abundance of the heart this person brings forth evil things."

The reasoning in this logion works inductively from the pictorial case that thorn trees and thistles yield no fruit (but grapevines and fig trees do), and this inductive reasoning is applied by analogy to people who bring good or bad things from a storehouse (where food, twigs, etc. can be kept until they are used). An inductive display of the reasoning in the logion looks as follows:

> *Explanation (Case/Ground/Minor Premise)*: Grapes are not harvested from thorn trees, nor are figs gathered from thistles, for they yield no fruit.

> *Analogy (Result/Claim):* A good person brings forth good from the storehouse; a bad person brings forth evil things from the corrupt storehouse in the heart, and says evil things. For from the abundance of the heart the evil person brings forth evil things.

> [*Major Premise (Rule/Warrant):* (Unexpressed)]

> [*Protrepsis/Apotrepsis (Implication)*: (Unexpressed)]

The reasoning from analogy in this logion is inductive,[30] since it requires reasoning beyond viticulture to human culture in a manner

---

[30] Hurley, *Logic*, 28.

that is probable but not certain. Since nourishing fruit is gathered from plants like grapevines and fig trees, rather than thorns and thistles which yield no fruit, by analogy (induction) good people are like grapevines and fig trees and bad people are like thorn trees and thistles. Bad people produce evil rather than good things from the abundance of their hearts, much like thorn trees and thistles produce thorns and thistles rather than fruit. The *Thomas* logion does not express either a warrant (major premise or rule) or an implication (protrepsis or apotrepsis). Rather, it expresses two explanations in support of the reasoning: (1) for they yield no fruit; (2) for from the abundance of the heart the evil person brings forth evil things.

The reasoning about grapes and figs in *Gos. Thom.* 45 comes directly out of the environment of Q sayings. The variation between *Gos. Thom.* 45:1, Luke 6:44b and Matt 7:16b displays well the oral variation that exists among Q/*Thomas* sayings that express this conventional wisdom in some kind of negative formulation:[31]

Gos. Thom. 45:1	Luke 6:44b	Matthew 7:16b
Grapes are not harvested from thorn trees, nor are figs gathered from thistles.	Figs are not gathered from thorns, nor are grapes picked from a bramble bush.	Are grapes gathered from thorns, or figs from thistles?

Gos. Thom. 45:1 arranges the relation of grapes, thorns, figs, and thistles like the saying in Matt 7:16b, but its form is not interrogative but declarative, like Luke 6:44b. This is a natural relationship of sayings to one another in a context of oral transmission. It is noticeable that none of them simply contains a straightforward assertion that grapes are harvested from grapevines and figs from fig trees. Rather, the sayings gain their rhetorical force and their potential for expansion and elaboration through their use of the negative topic of thorns and thistles. A display of the full versions of the *Thomas*/Luke/Matthew reasoning looks as follows, and here we see an interactive oral/written environment of relationships:

[31] Risto Uro, " 'Secondary Orality' in the *Gospel of Thomas?* Logion 14 as a Test Case," *Forum* 9:3–4 (1993): 305–29 (reprinted in *Thomas at the Crossroads: Essays on the Gospel of Thomas* [ed. Risto Uro; Studies of the New Testament and Its World; Edinburgh: Clark, 1998], 8–32); Vernon K. Robbins, "Rhetorical Composition and Sources in the *Gospel of Thomas*," *SBL Seminar Papers, 1997* (SBLSP 36; Atlanta, GA: Scholars Press, 1997), 86–114.

Gos. Thom. 45:1–4	Luke 6:43–45	Matthew 7:16–20	Matthew 12:33–35
	Explanation (Rule): [43] No good tree bears bad fruit, nor again does a bad tree bear good fruit, [44a] for each tree is known by its own fruit.	*Warning (Implication):* [15] Beware of false prophets, who come to you in sheep's clothing but inwardly are ravenous wolves. [16a] You will know them by their fruit. [20] Thus you will know them by their fruits.	*Explanation (Implication):* [33] Either make the tree good, and its fruit good; or make the tree bad, and its fruit bad; for the tree is known by its fruit.
Explanation (Case): [1] Grapes are not harvested from thorn trees, nor are figs gathered from thistles, for they yield no fruit.	*Description (Case):* [44b] Figs are not gathered from thorns, nor are grapes picked from a bramble bush.	*Analogy (Case):* [16b] Are grapes gathered from thorns, or figs from thistles? [17] In the same way, every good tree bears good fruit, but the bad tree bears bad fruit. [18] A good tree cannot bear bad fruit, nor can a bad tree bear good fruit.	*Analogous Explanation (Case):* [34] You brood of vipers! How can you speak good things, when you are evil? For out of the abundance of the heart the mouth speaks. [35] The good person brings good things out of a good treasure, and the evil person brings evil things out of an evil treasure.
Analogous Explanation (Result): [2] A good person brings forth good from the storehouse; [3] a bad person brings forth evil things from the corrupt storehouse in the heart, and says evil things. [4] For from the abundance of the heart a bad person brings forth evil things.	*Analogous Explanation (Result):* [45] The good person out of the good treasure of the heart produces good, and the evil person out of evil treasure produces evil; for it is out of the abundance of the heart that the mouth speaks.	*Description (Result):* [19] Every tree that does not bear good fruit is cut down and thrown into the fire.	*Explanation (Result):* [36] I tell you, on the day of judgment you will have to give an account for every careless word you utter; for by your words you will be justified, and by your words you will be condemned.

Gos. Thom. 45:1–4	Luke 6:43–45	Matthew 7:16–20	Matthew 12:33–35
	Illustration (Implication): [46] Why do you call me 'Lord, Lord,' ad do not do what I tell you? [47] I will show you what someone is like who comes to me, hears my words, and acts on them. [48] That one is like a man building a house, who dug deeply and laid the foundation on rock; when a flood arose, the river burst against that house but could not shake it, because it had been well built. [49] But the one who hears and does not act is like a man who built a house on the ground without a foundation. When the river burst against it, immediately it fell, and great was the ruin of that house.		

First, this display shows how a variety of rules and implications may be generated from or attracted to a negative inductive case. Luke 6:43, Matt 7:15–16, 20, 46–49, and Matt 12:33 display rules and implications. The generation or attraction of variant positive and negative rules and implications leads naturally to different emphases within the elaboration of the reasoning. Second, the Matthew 7 version contains aspects of both the Lukan and Thomasine version. Matt 7:16b, 18 combines a variant version of _Gos. Thom._ 45:1a with a variant version of Luke 6:43. This must have occurred through use by Luke, *Thomas*, and Matthew of Q material in an interactive oral/written environment. Third, each gospel develops the reasoning in a variant manner. Luke develops the reasoning in a christological manner: in Luke 6:46–47, 49 Jesus speaks as the authoritative Lord whose words must be obeyed or else calamity will come. Matthew develops the reasoning agonistically in an environment of the end-time: on the one hand in relation to false prophets (7:15–20) and on the other hand through challenge-riposte (12:24, 34, 36–37) that uses the day of judgment as a special means of shaming Pharisees (12:36). *Thomas*, in contrast, places the logion in a section that begins with the disciples asking Jesus, "Who are you to say these things to us?" (43:1) and ends with Jesus telling them, "If they ask you, 'What is the evidence of your Father in you?' say to them, 'It is motion and rest.'" (49:3). In other words, Jesus answers their question by diverting the discussion from himself to them and people they are like (Jews [43:3], people who blaspheme [44], bad people [45], people from Adam to John the Baptist [46], people who try to serve two masters [47], people who make peace with each other [48], people who are alone and chosen [49], and people who ask them where they come from [50]). The entire section in *Thomas*, then, engages the reader in a series of comparisons of various people with disciples who wonder who Jesus is to say these things to them. In the midst of the comparisons, reasoning about grapes, figs, thorns, and thistles is part of an argument from analogy that explains the nature not only of good and bad people but of disciples who do and do not understand who Jesus is. But this understanding of Jesus is not so much christological or eschatological as it is cosmological and epistemological. As we will see below, in *Thomas* Jesus knows he is from the place of light. The disciples also are from the place of light, but they do not understand this. Jesus' coming from the place of light, then, is not exceptional. Only his knowledge of it is.

Gospel of Thomas 47:1–5

The second logion after *Gos. Thom.* 45 contains a series of six instances of pictorial, conventional wisdom:

> Jesus said, "A person cannot mount two horses or bend two bows. ²And a servant cannot serve two masters, or that servant will honor

the one and offend the other. [3] No person drinks aged wine and immediately desires to drink new wine. [4] New wine is not poured into aged
wineskins, lest they break, and aged wine is not poured into a new
wineskin, lest it spoil. [5] An old patch is not sewn onto a new garment,
for there would be a tear."

The reasoning in this logion is based on unsuccessful experiences in
the world. Again, the pictures are specific enough to be powerful,
but general enough to be effectively universal. The pictures present
descriptions and explanations in a negative mode. Like *Gos. Thom.*
45, the reasoning presents negative statements, some of which are
supported by rationales and some of which are not. In the inductive reasoning in *Gos. Thom.* 47, some negative cases are descriptions
with no supportive statement, and some are explanations with rationales.
Four of the six instances in *Gos. Thom.* 47 are explanations: (2) serving
two masters; (4) putting new wine in old wineskins; (5) putting old
wine in new wineskins; and (6) putting an old patch on a new garment. The instances of the two horses and bows (1) and the person
not desiring new wine (3) are simply descriptions. A noticeable feature
of the progression is the absence of argumentation that evokes implications. We noticed in the analysis of *Gos. Thom.* 45 and its parallels
that negative cases regularly generate or attract rules and implications.
In fact, in all instances parallel to *Gos. Thom.* 45 rules and implications play an important role in the amplification or elaboration of
the unit. In *Gos. Thom.* 47 the initial negative description about two
horses and two bows provides the context for four negative explanations and one more negative description. It is noticeable that the
descriptions and explanations in *Gos. Thom.* 47 do not generate
amplification or elaboration of the topics. The reason may be that
the topic of new and old does not have special importance for
Thomasine tradition. That which is new and that which is old is
important to redemptive wisdom only if people consider the sequence
of history to be run by redemptive forces. Within a context of redemptive history, either that which is old is better because it was not yet
corrupted by certain events, or that which is new is better because
it replaces certain imperfect things in the past. If redemptive wisdom is more interested in cosmological and epistemological issues
than the sequence of history, the categories of new and old simply
are ways of talking about two different kinds of things. This seems
to be the case in *Gos. Thom.* 47. The new and the old do not hold
the potential for special insights into the process of redemption; thus
the logion progresses through the entire series without generating

any rules (warrants) or implications that give rise to amplification and elaboration of the new and the old.

As the topic of two incompatible things unfolds in *Gos. Thom.* 47 beyond the first instance, which is distinctive to *Thomas*, the reasoning about serving two masters exists in variant form in Q tradition:

Gos. Thom. 47:2	Luke 16:13	Matthew 6:24
		Rule (Warrant): No one can serve two masters;
1st Explanation (Negative Case): A servant cannot serve two masters, or that servant will honor the one and offend the other.	*Explanation (Negative Case):* No slave can serve two masters, for a slave will either hate one and love the other, or be devoted to the one and despise the other.	*Description (Case):* for a slave will either hate one and love the other, or be devoted to the one and despise the other.
	Analogy (Result): You cannot serve God and wealth.	*Analogy (Result)*: You cannot serve God and wealth.

In Q, the tradition either in the form of an explanation or a rule and description about slaves and masters becomes the basis for an inductive argument from analogy about serving God and wealth (mammon). The Thomasine logion appears to be an oral variant of the Q tradition without the argument from analogy. Since *Gos. Thom.* 47 also is part of *Gos. Thom.* 43–50 discussed above, the context is a comparison of the disciples with a series of people and things in an attempt to get them to focus on who they themselves are and what they must do to enter the kingdom, rather than questioning who Jesus is to say what he does say to them. In this context, wealth does not come into the discussion, as a result of its absence from this saying. For *Thomas*, it appears that wealth would be only one minor symptom of a much larger challenge—understanding the nature of the world itself, the nature of people in the world, and the nature of the search that can lead to redemption.

The four remaining cases about wine and cloth present a variation in sequence in a context of overall agreement concerning the polarities. It is noticeable that all three synoptic gospels contain positive cases or results, which *Thomas* does not. The positive formulations in the synoptic gospels show an interest in the new and the old that simply is not shared by the *Gospel of Thomas*:

Gos. Thom. 47:3–5	Mark 2:21–22	Matthew 9:16–17	Luke 5:36–39
2nd Description (Negative Case): ³ No person drinks aged wine and immediately desires to drink new wine.			*3rd Explanation (Negative Case):* ³⁹ And no one after drinking old wine desires new wine, but says, "The old is good."
2nd Explanation (Negative Case): ^{4a} New wine is not poured into aged wineskins, lest they break.	*2nd Explanation (Negative Case):* ^{22a–b} And no one puts new wine into old wineskins. Otherwise, the wine will burst the skins, and the wine is lost, and so are the skins.	*2nd Explanation (Negative Case):* ^{17a–b} Neither is new wine put into old wineskins. Otherwise, the skins burst, and the wine is spilled, and the skins are destroyed.	*2nd Explanation (Negative Case):* ³⁷ And no one puts new wine into old wineskins. Otherwise the new wine will burst the skins and will be spilled, and the skins will be destroyed.
3rd Explanation (Negative Case): ^{4b} And aged wine is not poured into a new wineskin, lest it spoil.	*Description (Positive Case):* ^{22c} But one puts new wine into fresh wineskins.	*3rd Explanation (Positive Case):* ^{17c–d} New wine is put into fresh wineskins, and so both are preserved.	*Belief (Positive Case):* ³⁸ But new wine must be put into fresh wineskins.
4th Explanation (Negative Case): ⁵ An old patch is not sewn onto a new garment, for there would be a tear.	*1st Explanation (Negative Case):* ²¹ No one sews a piece of unshrunk cloth on an old cloak. Otherwise, the patch pulls away from it, the new from the old, and a worse tear is made.	*1st Explanation (Negative Case):* ¹⁶ No one sews a piece of unshrunk cloth on an old cloak, for the patch pulls away from the cloak, and a worse tear is made.	*1st Explanation (Negative Case):* ³⁶ No one tears a piece from a new garment and sews it on an old garment. Otherwise the new will be torn, and the piece from the new will not match the old.

Instead of beginning with the case of sewing a new, unshrunk piece of cloth on an old garment, *Gos. Thom.* 47:3 begins with a focus on the manner in which people desire the old rather than the new. The emphasis is on the nature of people rather than on the nature of that which is old and that which is new. In contrast to the synoptic tradition, *Gos. Thom.* 47 does not say either that the old wine is good (Luke 5:39) or that new wine is put into fresh wineskins so that both the new wine and the new wineskins are preserved (Matt 9:17). Rather, *Gos. Thom.* 47 emphasizes that desire for the old creates a conflict with desire for the new, and there is no preference indicated for the new or the old as the logion progresses. Richard Valantasis surely is right that the topic is the redemptive subjectivity and identity available to the person who chooses the interpretation of these sayings as the avenue to a spiritual life that stores up good things in one's heart. It is not clear, however, that "[t]he aged wine presumably refers to the richness of the spiritual life presented to those who interpret these sayings, while the young wine refers to the lesser things of the world."[32] As noted above, the *Gospel of Thomas* neither has Jesus say that the old wine is good nor that having everything new preserves that which is new. In contrast to the synoptic gospels where historical events create patterns in which the new and the old vie with one another for superiority, the *Gospel of Thomas* simply distinguishes between a mode of life that seeks understanding and a mode of life that proceeds without knowledge of the kingdom. In *Thomas*, the new and old garments, wine, and wineskins simply are ways of talking about things that are incompatible with one another.[33] The issue is whether a person lives in a bifurcated state that spoils one's life and tears it apart or in a unified state that seeks and finds understanding. In other words, specific pictorial images of spoiling, spilling, or tearing apart are used to create a generalized, or even abstract, opposite image of a person as buoyant wine or a newly restored garment. It is noticeable that the logion in *Thomas* generates no positive rule, case, or implication. The force of the logion is to create pictures that demonstrate that people cannot have things two ways at once. Either people will seek to understand the redemptive wisdom offered by these sayings or they will not.

2. *The First Eight Enthymematic Logia*

Among the first nineteen logia in the *Gospel of Thomas*, a section that forms an extended introduction to the work, eight (forty-two percent) contain explicit rationales. While some of these rationales simply

---

[32] Richard Valantasis, *The Gospel of Thomas* (New Testament Readings; London: Routledge, 1997), 124.

[33] Cf. John Dominic Crossan, *In Fragments: The Aphorisms of Jesus* (San Francisco, CA: Harper & Row, 1983), 124–27.

function as explanations, others are premises (rules/warrants/major premises or cases/grounds/minor premises) in arguments. In contrast to the logia analyzed above, the enthymematic logia in the introduction feature contrawisdom and abductive reasoning. These logia invert and divert conventional wisdom to direct a person toward important inner reasonings and presuppositions in Thomasine culture. Some of these logia have a close relation to logia in the canonical gospels; others do not.

(a) *Gospel of Thomas 4:1–3*

A person who reads the *Gospel of Thomas* in sequence from the beginning encounters three enthymematic logia in a row in *Gos. Thom.* 4–6. In contrast to *Gos. Thom.* 45 and 47, these logia present contrawisdom. *Gos. Thom.* 4–5 are enthymematic logia addressed to anyone who reads the *Gospel of Thomas*. They set the stage for the discussion Jesus has with his disciples in logion 6. *Gos. Thom.* 4 reads as follows:

> Jesus said, "The person old in days will not hesitate to ask a little child seven days old about the place of life, and that person will live. ²For many of the first will be last, ³and will become a single one."

This logion contains a potential case where the person who acts on the basis of a particular kind of contrawisdom will attain life. Inspiration for the contrawisdom appears to have come from the tradition in Q 10:21 about hidden things being revealed to infants. A well-known saying in gospel tradition about first and last provides a rule or warrant for the contrawisdom:

Gos. Thom. 4:1–3	Luke 10:21–22	Matt 11:25–27
Contrawisdom Belief (Rule): ⁴˸² For many of the first will be last.	*Explanation (Rule):* ²¹ I thank you, Father, Lord of heaven and earth, that you have hidden these things from the wise and the intelligent and have revealed them to infants; yes, Father, for such was your gracious will.	*Explanation (Rule):* ²⁵ I thank you, Father, Lord of heaven and earth, that you have hidden these things from the wise and the intelligent and have revealed them to infants; ²⁶ yes, Father, for such was your gracious will.

Gos. Thom. 4:1–3	Luke 10:21–22	Matt 11:25–27
Contrawisdom Description (Case): [4:1a] The person old in days will not hesitate to ask a little child seven days old about the place of life,	*Description (Case):* [22] All things have been handed over to me by my Father;	*Description (Case):* [27] All things have been handed over to me by my Father;
Description (Result): [4:1b] and that person will live. [4:3] And will become a single one.	*Description (Result):* and no one knows who the Son is except the Father, or who the Father is except the Son and anyone to whom the Son chooses to reveal him.	*Description (Result):* and no one knows the Son except the Father, and no one knows the Father except the Son and anyone to whom the Son chooses to reveal him.

Q material (Luke 10:21–22/Matt 11:25–27) christologizes the tradition by making Jesus the son who receives the knowledge of all hidden things from God the father. This approach develops the tradition according to conventional, pictorial wisdom about fathers teaching their sons. The Thomasine logion, in contrast, neither builds on the conventional wisdom that fathers teach sons nor christologizes the tradition. Rather, it inverts conventional reasoning about the necessity for old people to teach infants. The age of seven days old appears to be related to the day of circumcision on the eighth day. Prior to the eighth day, a child was not considered a viable living being on earth. If the child made it to the eighth day, it had become a viable earthly being. If an old person asks a seven day old child about the place of life, that person is asking a full-term pre-earthly being who has, from the perspective of Thomasine culture, recently come from the place of life. *Gos. Thom.* 4:2 provides a warrant for the inversion between the role of the young with the dictum that "many of the first will be last." *Gos. Thom.* 4:3 is an additional result that is appended to the warrant. The result of the old man's asking the seven day old child is that the old person will live and will become a single one. This again is part of Thomasine belief. While on earth a person becomes two (male and female is one of these forms of two). When people return to the place of life, once again they become one. In contrast to enthymematic reasoning that grounds its assertions in conventional reasoning, every step of this reasoning is contrawisdom: (a) many of the first will be last; (b) the old person will become wise through instruction by a seven day old child; and (c) people who know this contrawisdom will live and overcome their duality to become a single one. While *Gos. Thom.* 5 has the form of inductive-deductive argumentation, its reasoning will persuade only those who are willing to enter its contrawisdom and reason on its basis.

Gospel of Thomas 5:1–2; 6:1–6

The next two logia present a sequence concerning hidden things being revealed:

> *Gos. Thom. 5:1–2*: Jesus said, "Know what is before your face, and what is hidden from you will be disclosed to you. [2] For there is nothing hidden that will not be revealed."

> *Gos. Thom. 6:1–6*: His disciples asked him and said to him, "Do you want us to fast? How shall we pray? Shall we give alms? What diet shall we observe?" [2] Jesus said, "Do not lie, [3] and do not do what you hate, [4] because all things are disclosed before heaven. [5] For there is nothing hidden that will not be revealed, [6] and there is nothing covered that will remain without being disclosed."

Gos. Thom. 5 presents a deductive line of reasoning that provides a basis for abductive reasoning in the next logion. *Gos. Thom.* 5 contains the following argumentation:

> *Contrawisdom Belief (Rule/Major Premise)*: (5:2) There is nothing hidden that will not be revealed.

> *Case/Minor Premise*: (5:1a) (If you) know what is before your face,
> Result: (5:1b) (then) what is hidden from you will be disclosed to you.

The statement that nothing is hidden that will not be revealed functions as a major premise, rule, or warrant for deductive reasoning. The conditional assertion about knowing what is before your face functions as a case that produces the result that what is hidden will be disclosed to you. The reasoning in the major premise is contrawisdom, so most people probably would not consider the reasoning in this logion to meet the standard either of deductive or inductive reasoning. If a person grants the truth of the warrant, however, the logic is straightforward: If everything has an inclination to reveal rather than hide itself, then if people know what is before their face, what is hidden from them will be disclosed to them. The reasoning is contrawisdom, but its logic could be persuasive to people who believe the major premise or rule.

The next logion, *Gos. Thom.* 6, applies the reasoning about hiddenness in *Gos. Thom.* 5 to an inquiry by the disciples concerning what diet they should observe and if they should fast, pray, and give alms. Jesus' response is that they should not lie and do what they hate, because all things are disclosed before heaven. Conventional religious wisdom in the Mediterranean world probably would say that fasting, praying, giving alms, and observing a special diet would disclose a special religious person who will receive the benefits of heaven. Thus, if people would grant the initial premise, they probably would construct the reasoning as follows:

> *Contrawisdom Explanation (Rule)*: (6:5) There is nothing hidden that will not be revealed, (6:6) and there is nothing covered that will remain without being disclosed, (6:4) because all things are disclosed before heaven.
>
> [*Case*: Fasting, praying, giving alms, and observing a special diet discloses a devoted religious person.]
>
> [*Result*: A person who fasts, prays, gives alms, and follows a special diet will receive the benefits of heaven.]

Instead of this reasoning, the logion contains abductive reasoning:

> *Contrawisdom Explanation (Rule)*: (6:5) There is nothing hidden that will not be revealed, (6:6) and there is nothing covered that will remain without being disclosed, (6:4) because all things are disclosed before heaven.
>
> *Case put together with Result from previous logion*: Do you want us to fast? How shall we pray? Shall we give alms? What diet shall we observe? What is hidden from you will be disclosed to you [as unimportant]!
>
> [*Abductive Result*: Fasting, praying, giving alms, and following a special diet hides from people what they must do to live and become a single one.]
>
> *Apotrepsis (Implication)*: (6:2–3) Do not lie, and do not do what you hate.

Building on the major premise in the reasoning, the logion joins the minor premise (the case of fasting, praying, giving alms, and observing a special diet) with the result (what is hidden from you will be disclosed to you). When this happens, there is a "discovery" that fasting, praying, giving alms, and observing a special diet are disclosed as "unimportant" (activities that hide), and this discovery uncovers the activities people actually should be engaging in to seek life (seeking the understanding of these logia). One suddenly becomes aware, then, that the phenomenal world, the world we see, regularly deceives us. It hides what we should truly see until we look at it long enough that it reveals itself as secondary and unimportant. This produces the result that fasting, praying, giving alms, and following a special diet hide rather than reveal the important things a person should do. In enthymematic fashion, this logion does not state this result. Rather, it states the implication of the unstated result: one should not lie to oneself about the things that matter and one should not do the things one hates to do. In other words, one should not deceive oneself by thinking that religious rites and dietary practices can truly achieve life. What they seem to achieve is really a lie; they are a matter of doing what one hates. Rather, one must devote oneself to seeking understanding that lies in and through the things in the phenomenal world that hide. Regular rituals that seek to understand Jesus' sayings are the practices that really matter, for they are the means for bringing that which is hidden forth into understanding.

In Mark 4:21–22 and Luke 8:16–17, conventional wisdom about lamps is interwoven with the conviction that all things hidden will be revealed. There is no such link in *Thomas*. In *Gos. Thom.* 5–6, the insight about hiddenness being revealed is treated like a true statement that should be convincing in and of itself. The problem, as mentioned above, is that conventional wisdom suggests that some things that are hidden remain hidden and lost forever. Contrawisdom in *Thomas* holds an opposite view as a conviction that functions as a proposition (major premise/warrant/rule) both for deductive and abductive reasoning. The underlying contrawisdom is present in Q and synoptic tradition. The *Gospel of Thomas* accepts the contrawisdom of this environment of reasoning and makes the abductive "discovery" that the entire phenomenal world hides true understanding from us until we look it in the face and invite it to reveal itself to us. When we do this, the logion states, fasting, praying, giving alms, and following a special diet reveal themselves as ways of telling lies about the religious practices that really matter. Rather than being activities that enact love, they are activities, the logion says, that enact hate both for oneself and for others.

Gospel of Thomas 14:1–5

We observed that, in characteristic enthymematic manner, the result was unexpressed in *Gos. Thom.* 6. The logion expresses the implication without stating the result. *Gos. Thom.* 14:1–4 contains the result of the reasoning in a series of statements to the disciples:

> Jesus said to them, "If you fast, you will bring sin upon yourselves, [2] and if you pray, you will be condemned, [3] and if you give alms, you will harm your spirits. [4] When you go into any country and walk from place to place, when the people receive you, eat what they serve you and heal the sick among them. [5] For what goes into your mouth will not defile you; rather, it is what comes out of your mouth that will defile you."

This logion, *Gos. Thom.*14, presents the result of the reasoning in *Gos. Thom.* 6 in the form of three descriptions and an explanation that answer the four questions the disciples asked:

Description (Result):	Description (Result):	Description (Result):	Explanation (Result):
If you fast, you will bring sin upon yourselves.	[2] if you pray, you will be condemned.	[3] if you give alms, you will harm your spirits.	[4] When you go into any country and walk from place to place, when the people receive you, eat what they serve you and heal the sick among them. [5] For what goes into your mouth will not defile you; rather, it is what comes out of your mouth that will defile you.

If regular religious rituals deceive people into thinking they are really what matters, people will bring sin upon themselves, be condemned, and harm their spirits. These descriptions quickly answer the first three questions about fasting, praying, and giving alms. The question about observing a diet calls forth two pictorial traditions well-known from the synoptic gospels: eating what is set before you when people receive you in their house and it is what comes out of your mouth that defiles you. The interesting thing is that no synoptic gospel brings these two traditions together. As we know from the discussion above, a key to abductive reasoning is putting together things that we had never before dreamed of putting together. *Gos. Thom.* 14:4–5 displays precisely this process. In a context where deductive reasoning has produced a result that one should not fast, pray, or give alms lest they bring about a harmful result, the result lies ready at hand that one should eat whatever one is given to eat, rather than observing a diet. In the context of this result, the rhetor "discovers" a further insight that provides the reason why: it is what comes out of the mouth rather than what goes in that defiles a person. But what is the importance of this conclusion to *Gos. Thom.* 14? In order to see this, we must turn to *Gos. Thom.* 13, which occurs just before it.

Gospel of Thomas 13:1–8

In addition to leaving premises and results unexpressed in logia, it is characteristic of the *Gospel of Thomas* either to delay answers to questions the disciples ask or never to give direct answers to the questions. As we have just seen, the answers to the disciples' questions in *Gos. Thom.* 6 are delayed until *Gos. Thom.* 14. Readers engaged in linear reading of the sayings, therefore, hold enthymematic, abductive reasoning in their minds as they read through *Gos. Thom.* 7–13 until they find the results expressed in *Gos. Thom.* 14. The question, then, is what the reader encounters in the intervening span of text.

   Just prior to the logion where Jesus presents the answers to the disciples' questions, Jesus asks the disciples to compare him to something and to tell him what he is like:

> Jesus said to his disciples, "Compare me to something and tell me what I am like." [2] Simon Peter said to him, "You are like a just angel." [3] Matthew said to him, "You are like a wise philosopher." [4] Thomas said to him, "Teacher, my mouth is utterly unable to say what you are like." [5] Jesus said, "I am not your teacher. Because you have drunk, you have become intoxicated from the bubbling spring that I have tended." [6] And he took him, and withdrew, and spoke three sayings to him. [7] When Thomas came back to his friends, they asked him, "What did Jesus say to you?" [8] Thomas said to them, "If I tell you one of the sayings he spoke to me, you will pick up rocks and stone me, and fire will come from the rocks and devour you."

The enthymematic reasoning in this logion works abductively from contrawisdom that functions as a rule/warrant/major premise for the reasoning that follows. Conventional wisdom suggests that Jesus teaches his disciples throughout the *Gospel of Thomas*. Jesus, however, introduces as a rule/warrant/major premise the contrawisdom that he is not their teacher. This contrawisdom establishes an environment for abductive reasoning in Jesus' reply. Conventional reasoning could fill out the sequence as follows:

> *Contrawisdom Belief (Rule)*: I am not your teacher.
>
> *Case*: [Thomas's] mouth is unable to say what Jesus is like.
>
> [*Result*: Thomas has had some other teacher not wise enough to teach him what Jesus is like.]

Instead of this reasoning, the process has worked abductively. Working from the major premise, which has arisen because Thomas has unwittingly called Jesus "teacher" when he replied to him, the reasoning joins the case and the result in a manner that produces a discovery about Thomas' inability to say who Jesus is like. Thomas is not simply without knowledge; he has drunk from a source of wisdom that tells him that Jesus is not simply like an angel (Simon Peter) or a wise philosopher (Matthew). This produces a different result as follows:

> *Contrawisdom Belief (Rule)*: I am not your teacher.
>
> *Case put together with Result producing a Discovery*: [Thomas's] mouth is unable to say what Jesus is like, because he has drunk (from some other source of wisdom)!
>
> *Result*: You [Thomas] have become intoxicated from the bubbling spring that I have tended.

Thomas's inability to say what Jesus is like comes from his drinking deeply from the well of wisdom Jesus has made available to those who will listen and seek. Thomas's statement "that language cannot articulate the experience"[34] is better than Simon Peter's answer that Jesus is a just angel and Matthew's answer that Jesus is a wise philosopher. Again, this is not grounded in conventional wisdom. It may well be that the reasoning here is grounded in the point of view articulated in the Discourse on the Eighth and Ninth in the Nag Hammadi Library:

> I have found the beginning of the power that is above all powers, the one that has no beginning. I see a fountain bubbling with life. I have said, my son, that I am Mind. I have seen! Language is not able to reveal this.[35]

---

[34] Valantasis, *Thomas*, 76.

[35] James M. Robinson, *Nag Hammadi Library in English* (3rd completely revised ed.; San Francisco, CA: Harper & Row, 1988), 324–25; quoted from Valantasis, *Thomas*, 76.

Thomas has said that he has no language to describe what Jesus is like. Jesus' response suggests that Thomas, through Jesus' words, has seen and drunk deeply from a fountain bubbling with life. Jesus' response suggests that Thomas's drinking of a deep draft from the bubbling spring has left him unable to speak. It is noticeable that the logion does not relate the speaking to the presence of spirit. Here, instead of the spirit providing what one will say (Mark 13:11), intoxication leaves Thomas without utterable words that can describe who Jesus is. Now we get a hint of the significance of the conclusion of the logion that immediately follows this one: what goes into your mouth will not defile you; rather, it is what comes out of your mouth that will defile you. One can answer far too quickly with one's mouth, and this answer will wed a person to ignorance. Drinking deeply from the fountain of wisdom Jesus makes available may produce an inability to state with certainty what something is like. This uncertainty is not ignorance. Rather, it is an initial kind of wisdom that creates within a person the possibility of receiving amazing wisdom from Jesus that most people (even other disciples) cannot even begin to fathom.

Gospel of Thomas 16:1–4

This logion also contains a statement by Jesus concerning who he is not. It also contains an argument about who he is:

> Jesus said, "Perhaps people think that I have come to cast peace upon the world. [2] They do not know that I have come to cast conflicts upon the earth: fire, sword, war. [3] For there will be five in a house: there will be three against two and two against three, father against son and son against father, [4] and they will stand alone."

On the basis of conventional wisdom, most people think Jesus comes to bring peace. Jesus, instead, teaches pictorial contrawisdom: he has come to bring conflicts in the form of fire, sword, and war. This contrawisdom is present in Q tradition:

Gos. Thom. 16:1–4	Luke 12:51–53	Matt 10:34–49
Conventional Wisdom: [1] Perhaps people think that I have come to cast peace upon the world.		*Conventional Wisdom:* [34a] "Do not think that I have come to bring peace to the earth;

Gos. Thom. 16:1–4	Luke 12:51–53	Matt 10:34–49
Contrawisdom (Rule): ² They do not know that I have come to cast conflicts upon the earth: fire, sword, war.	*Contrawisdom (Rule):* ⁴⁹ "I came to bring fire to the earth, and how I wish it were already kindled! ⁵⁰ I have a baptism with which to be baptized, and what stress I am under until it is completed! ⁵¹ Do you think that I have come to bring peace to the earth? No, I tell you, but rather division!	*Contrawisdom (Rule):* ³⁴ᵇ I have not come to bring peace, but a sword.
[*Unstated Case:* This conflict will have its effect on households.]	[*Unstated Case:* This conflict will have its effect on households.]	[*Unstated Case:* This conflict will have its effect on households.]
Description (Result): ³ For there will be five in a house: there will be three against two and two against three, father against son and son against father,	*Description (Result):* ⁵² From now on five in one household will be divided, three against two and two against three; ⁵³ they will be divided: father against son and son against father, mother against daughter and daughter against mother, mother-in-law against her daughter-in- law and daughter-in-law against mother-in-law."	*Description (Result):* ³⁵ For I have come to set a man against his father, and a daughter against her mother, and a daughter-in-law against her mother-in-law; ³⁶ and one's foes will be members of one's own household.
Implication: ⁴ and they will stand alone.		*Implication:* ³⁷ Whoever loves father or mother more than me is not worthy of me; and whoever loves son or daughter more than me is not worthy of me; ³⁸ and whoever does not take up the cross and follow me is not worthy of me. ³⁹ Those who find their life will lose it, and who lose their life for my sake will find it.

Both Luke and Matthew have an expanded form of the Q/*Thomas* tradition. Luke contains an amplification in the form of a soliloquy by Jesus on the baptism with which he has been baptized. Also it contains an amplified version of the divisions in the household, not only speaking of fathers and sons but speaking of mothers, daughters, mothers-in-law, and daughters-in-law. The Matthean version does not speak of fathers, mothers, and mothers-in-law being set against their sons, daughters, and daughters-in-law. In addition, Matthew contains an extended implication about people who love family members more than Jesus and are not willing to take up their cross and follow Jesus. The statement in *Thomas* that "they will stand alone" appears to be a Thomasine way of referring to the lack of relationship with Jesus that is also spoken about in Matt 10:37–39. Again we find the variation characteristic of Q/Thomasine tradition. In this instance, the contrawisdom exists in the Q tradition itself and the *Gospel of Thomas* simply includes it without amplification.

Gospel of Thomas 18:1–3

This enthymematic logion reasons further about the relation of disciples to Jesus, which is a topic in *Gos. Thom.* 16:4 and Matthew 10:37–39. In *Thomas*, instead of Jesus being the one who takes up a cross, he is the beginning. If disciples have discovered the beginning they will know their end, since their end is to return to the beginning.

> The disciples said to Jesus, "Tell us how our end will be." [2] Jesus said, "Have you discovered the beginning, then, that you are seeking after the end? For where the beginning is, the end will be. [3] Blessed is one who stands at the beginning: That one will know the end and will not taste death."

Once again the reader encounters contrawisdom in the *Gospel of Thomas*. The reasoning in the logion is as follows:

> [*Unexpressed Wisdom*: The one who knows the end will not taste death.] *Contrawisdom (Warrant/Rule)*: Where the beginning is, the end will be.
>
> *Abductive Description (Case joined with Result)*: Have you discovered the beginning, then, that you are seeking after the end? [If you have discovered the beginning, then you are standing where the end will be!]
>
> *Explanation (Result)*: Blessed is one who stands at the beginning: That one will know the end and will not taste death.

Once again the reader encounters abductive reasoning. Straightforward reasoning from the contrawisdom would suggest that (Case) if one has discovered the beginning, (Result) then one has discovered the end. When this case and result are joined together, the insight emerges that when they have found the beginning (in the presence of Jesus) they are standing at the end as well as the beginning! This produces a new result, namely that one is blessed who stands at the beginning, since that one also knows the end and will not taste death.

Gospel of Thomas 19:1–4

Gos. Thom. 19 also contains a beatitude, but this one occurs at the beginning of the logion:

> Jesus said, "Blessed is one who came into being before coming into being. ²If you become my disciples and hearken to my sayings, these stones will serve you. ³ For there are five trees in Paradise for you; they do not change, summer or winter, and their leaves do not fall. ⁴ Whoever knows them will not taste death."

Again the reader encounters a logion built upon contrawisdom. The final statement in the logion suggests that *Gos. Thom.* 19 is building on the insight of *Gos. Thom.* 18. If it is accepted wisdom that the person who knows the beginning is blessed and will not taste death, then one can extend this reasoning even further to "coming into being before coming into being." The reasoning in this logion appears to contain an inner mode of reasoning as follows:

> *Rule*: Whoever discovers the interpretation of these sayings will not taste death (*Gos. Thom.* 1).
>
> *Case*: If you become my disciples and hearken to my sayings,
>
> *Result*: these stones will serve you!

This logion would appear to be the conclusion of a long introduction to the *Gospel of Thomas* that builds an argument on the basis of the initial logion about listening carefully to Jesus' sayings (which means becoming his disciple), interpreting the sayings to find their meaning, and, as a result, not tasting death. This inner reasoning has become an environment for abductive discovery of information that extends far beyond conventional wisdom. If the reasoning in the logion is introducing the major premise in its initial statement, the reasoning proceeds as follows:

> *Contrawisdom (Rule)*: Blessed is one who came into being before coming into being.
>
> *Joining of Case and Result from Gos. Thom. 1 and 19*: If you become my disciples and hearken to my sayings, you will discover the interpretation of these sayings and not taste death, and these stones will serve you.
>
> *Result*: There are five trees in Paradise for you; they do not change, summer or winter, and their leaves do not fall. Whoever knows them will not taste death.

The reader now has entered fully into the domain of contrawisdom. The initial contrawisdom appears to be based on "a myth of an already existent being entering the mundane world."[36] Jesus, an example of such a being, stands before disciples with sayings that can lead them to understand that they also are such beings. This leads to the case/result (abductive reasoning) that if they become Jesus' disciples, they will discover the interpretation that leads them to this knowledge about themselves, and they will not taste death. "These stones will serve you" may mean that objects in the phenomenal world will become the things that at first hide true insight but then become the objects that (through searching and reflecting) lead a person into true knowledge. Perhaps the five trees in Paradise are a matter of finding both the pictorial beginning (Garden of Eden) and the pictorial end (Paradise). Since, as is stated in *Gos. Thom.* 18, true knowledge takes one both to the beginning and the end, one who becomes a true disciple comes to know "the five trees in Paradise." One wonders if these trees are in some way related to the tree of the knowledge of good and evil in the Garden of Eden. Valantasis is perceptive when he says:

> The knowledge of the mythology developed here that organizes a hierarchy of beings and posits the existence of a paradise with five unchanging trees confers the same benefit as the discovery of the interpretations of the sayings (Saying 1) and the standing at the beginning and knowing the end (Saying 18) since all of these sayings present the seeker as "not tast(ing) death." The immortal status of the seeker may be achieved through a number of different enterprises (interpretative, intellectual, and mythological).[37]

Gos. Thom. 19 joins insights in the initial sayings in the *Gospel of Thomas* with interpretative, intellectual, and mythological knowledge that the seeking listener acquires through engagement with the first nineteen logia, which form an extended introduction. As we have seen above,

---

[36] Valantasis, *Thomas*, 88.
[37] Valantasis, *Thomas*, 89–90.

these sayings contain a combination of deductive, inductive, and abductive reasoning. In certain instances the reasoning builds on conventional, pictorial wisdom; in other instances the reasoning builds on contrawisdom in Q/synoptic tradition; in still other instances, like *Gos. Thom.* 18–19, the reader sees glimpses of a world that looks more like the world of the Gospel of John than the synoptic gospels.

3. *Concluding Remarks*

This essay has presented a beginning place for future analysis. Some sayings in the gospel tradition present conventional wisdom. Others present contrawisdom. It will be important in the future to identify the topics that various arenas of tradition develop according to conventional knowledge and contrawisdom. The preliminary analysis presented in this essay shows that Q/synoptic tradition contains both conventional wisdom and contrawisdom. Only future analysis can tell us the proportions of conventional and contrawisdom in this tradition. It appears that the *Gospel of Thomas* features more contrawisdom than conventional wisdom as it builds its system of thought through the logia attributed to Jesus. Future analysis also can display the proportions and kinds of deductive, inductive, and abductive reasoning in all the canonical gospels as well as throughout the *Gospel of Thomas*.[38] This initial study has given only a glimpse of an analysis of ten logia in the *Gospel of Thomas*.

There are many remaining tasks in this kind of study. One thinks of investigation of all the enthymematic logia in Q, the canonical gospels, and the *Gospel of Thomas*. One also thinks of interactive comparison of the enthymematic texture not only of all the gospels with one another but with other Mediterranean wisdom discourse and with wisdom discourse in other geographical and cultural regions of the world. The wisdom of this world is not confined simply to the Bible or to accepted and marginal Christians during the first centuries of the emergence of Christianity. It is important for us to develop practices of analysis and interpretation that can move not only beyond the confines of our treasured canons in our own religious traditions but beyond the confines of the Mediterranean world into other traditions throughout the world.

---

[38] See Vernon K. Robbins, "From Enthymeme to Theology," 191–214. Cf. *idem*, "Argumentative Textures," 27–65.

CHAPTER NINE

THE PORTRAIT OF JESUS IN THE *GOSPEL OF THOMAS*

Antti Marjanen

1. *Introduction*

When Philip Sellew presented his paper "The Construction of Jesus in the Gospel of Thomas" at the 1993 SBL Annual Meeting in Washington, he led off by saying: "One of the several issues still outstanding in interpreting it [the *Gospel of Thomas*] is how to explain its view of Jesus and his role." In ten years the situation has not altered very much. With few exceptions,[1] recent studies on the significance of Jesus in the *Gospel of Thomas* have not dealt so much with *Thomas'* view of Jesus, but have rather concentrated more on questions of what and how the writing contributes to our understanding of the historical Jesus. The present article does not pose those questions. Instead, it seeks to delineate *Thomas'* own christological emphases and to place *Thomas'* portrait of Jesus within the context of early Christianity. I shall try to sketch what the *Gospel of Thomas* says about Jesus' origin, his nature and being, and his mission, and at the same time I shall ask how *Thomas'* notion of Jesus is related to other approximately contemporary understandings of Jesus, such as those of the Pauline letters, the Gospel of John, Valentinian Christians and some other second- and third-century Christian currents.

The fact that the *Gospel of Thomas* is a collection of originally more or less independent logia does not mean that those who were responsible for the composition of this gospel did not follow certain principles while choosing and editing their material.[2] It is thus assumed

---

[1] Besides Sellew's unpublished paper, *Thomas'* view of Jesus has been treated before him by Stevan L. Davies, "The Christology and Protology of the *Gospel of Thomas*," *JBL* 111 (1992): 663–82. Other studies which include discussions about the characterization of Jesus in the *Gospel of Thomas* are Majella Franzmann, *Jesus in the Nag Hammadi Writings* (Edinburgh: Clark, 1996), 28, 78–81, 103, 107–8, 114; Thomas Zöckler, *Jesu Lehren im Thomasevangelium* (NHMS 47; Leiden: Brill, 1999), 244–52.

[2] So also Richard Valantasis, *The Gospel of Thomas* (New Testament Readings;

in this article that, as far as *Thomas'* view of Jesus is concerned, it
also presents a sufficiently coherent picture to differentiate it from
other early Christologies.[3] This does not rule out the possibility that
the Christology presented in the *Gospel of Thomas* might have under-
gone some development in the process of composition, which may
very well have taken a longer period of time.

It is almost a scholarly axiom to say that *Thomas'* Jesus is a preexistent heavenly figure who comes down to earth to reveal the saving secrets to the elect.[4] As a general presentation of the Thomasine
Jesus, this holds good. Yet it does not bring out well enough the
specific characteristics of *Thomas'* view of Jesus and thus does not
help us to locate the gospel. Therefore, I shall try to present a more
nuanced picture of the Thomasine Jesus, and I believe this can be
done by comparing what the gospel says about Jesus to what it says
about the elect, that is, those who will find the kingdom (49).

2. *The Origin and Being of Jesus*

In light of the fact that *Thomas'* Jesus is so often characterized as a
heavenly preexistent figure, it is surprising how little the writer of
the gospel really speaks about that. Unlike the prologue of John, for
example, there is actually no single logion which explicitly states that
Jesus was with the Father before he came to proclaim his message.
There are logia, however, which imply this. The incarnation language of logion 28 makes it obvious that Jesus is assumed to have
existed prior to his appearance in a human form.[5] The same is pre-

London and New York, NY: Routledge, 1997), 6–8. A different view was proposed
by Stevan L. Davies in his paper "The Oracles of the *Gospel of Thomas*" presented
at the Annual Meeting of the SBL, Chicago, IL, November 19–22, 1994. Davies
argued that the *Gospel of Thomas* was a random collection of enigmatic words which
were used as oracular sayings of divination but which did not represent coherent
ideology. In his previous studies, however, Davies (see note 1, for example) can presuppose a *Thomas'* view of Jesus although he emphasizes that the author was not
actually interested in Christology per se, since "Jesus is not himself an essential element in salvation" (Davies, "Christology," 664).

[3] For the purposes of this article, the *Gospel of Thomas* refers to that Greek text
which lies back of the Coptic translation, a copy of which has been preserved in
the Nag Hammadi Library.

[4] Valantasis (*Gospel of Thomas*, 9) has rightly called the Thomasine Jesus "a mys-
tagogue (Saying 17), a revealer of sacred knowledge to seekers, who discloses the
mysteries to those who are worthy (Saying 62)."

[5] Cf. Valantasis, *Gospel of Thomas*, 102.

supposed by logion 77, which suggests that the all, ⲡⲧⲏⲣϥ, whether it is taken to refer to the created cosmos or to the elect of the Living Father mentioned in logion 50,[6] gained its beginning from the pre-existent Jesus. With its understanding of Jesus as a preexistent heavenly figure who is incarnated in a human body, the *Gospel of Thomas* resembles those christological texts of the New Testament, such as the pre-Pauline hymn in Paul's letter to the Philippians[7] and the Gospel of John,[8] which are conventionally thought to be proponents of wisdom or preexistence Christology.

The nature and being of the Thomasine Jesus is also reflected in those sayings which deal with the relationship between the Father and Jesus. When Salome asks Jesus about his origin in logion 61, Jesus appears to claim, in his somewhat cryptic answer, that he not only has his origin in ⲡⲉⲧϣⲏϣ, which, whatever it means exactly,[9] obviously refers to the Father, but that he has also been given "some of the things of (his) Father." The statement seems to indicate that Jesus shares some of the divine qualities with his Father. Taking this into account, it is not surprising that Jesus is not only called the Son of the Living One (37) but often given the common attribute of the Father, "living" (3; 37; 50), as well (prologue; 52; 59; 111).[10] All this

---

[6] For the ambiguity of logion 77, see Antti Marjanen, "Is *Thomas* a Gnostic Gospel?" in *Thomas at the Crossroads: Essays on the Gospel of Thomas* (ed. Risto Uro; Studies of the New Testament and Its World; Edinburgh: Clark, 1998), 107–39, esp. 121–24.

[7] Cf. Phil 2:6–7. It is less clear whether Paul himself is advocating a preexistence Christology. To be sure, in 2 Cor 8:9 Paul comes close to that when he states that Jesus "even though he was rich made himself poor." Unlike the hymn in the Epistle of Paul to the Philippians, the incarnation language is not explicitly associated with a reference to the preexistence of Jesus. Yet, if the allusion to the richness of Jesus in 2 Cor 8:9 is tantamount to Jesus being "in the form of God" in Phil. 2:6 then Paul can also be regarded as representing a similar Christological understanding. Christopher Tuckett has also pointed out that some Pauline passages which speak about Christ employ the language used of various aspects of the preexistent Wisdom (Rom 8:3; 10:6–7; 1 Cor 8:6; 10:4,9; Gal 4:4) and thus suggest that Paul wants to imply "an equation between Jesus and the figure of Wisdom (*Christology and the New Testament: Jesus and His Earliest Followers* [Louisville, KY: Westminster John Knox, 2001], 62–64)."

[8] John 1:1; 17:5.

[9] The most likely interpretation of the word ⲡⲉⲧϣⲏϣ is the "One who is equal (to himself)"; for interpretations of this word, see Hans-Martin Schenke, "On the Compositional History of the *Gospel of Thomas*," *Forum* 10:1–2 (1994): 14 n. 13; Ismo Dunderberg, "Thomas' I-sayings and the Gospel of John," in *Thomas at the Crossroads: Essays on the Gospel of Thomas* (ed. Risto Uro; Studies of the New Testament and Its World; Edinburgh: Clark, 1998), 49–51; Antti Marjanen, "Women Disciples in the *Gospel of Thomas*," in Uro, *Thomas at the Crossroads*, 91.

[10] This is pointed out by Franzmann, *Jesus*, 78. It is to be noted, however, that the term "the one who lives" can be used in a derivative sense of a Thomasine Christian as well (111; cf. also 4).

suggests that Jesus in the *Gospel of Thomas* is seen both as a preexistent
and as a divine heavenly being. In its emphasis on the divine nature
of Jesus, *Thomas* again comes close to Paul and John. Although both
Paul and John clearly distinguish between the Father and Jesus, both
attribute the divine sonship to Jesus (Rom 1:3; Gal 4:4; John 11:27;
20:31), and John can even go so far as to call Jesus himself "God"
(John 1:1,18; 20:28).[11]

That the Thomasine Jesus is viewed as a preexistent, divine heavenly figure has led some scholars to conclude that his appearance
on the earth has to be interpreted in terms of gnostic docetic
Christology.[12] This conclusion is usually drawn on the basis of Jesus'
phrase ⲀⲈⲓⲟⲨⲱⲚϨ ⲈⲂⲞⲖ ⲚⲀⲨ ϨⲚ ⲤⲀⲣϮ ("I appeared/was revealed
to them in flesh") in logion 28.[13] However, if this phrase is perceived
to be a docetic formulation, the author of the christological hymn
in 1 Tim 3:16 has to be an advocate of docetism as well. As Ismo
Dunderberg has convincingly pointed out in a recent article, the
phrase ὃς ἐφανερώθη ἐν σαρκί ("who appeared in flesh") in 1 Tim
3:16 is fully tantamount to the Thomasine ⲀⲈⲓⲟⲨⲱⲚϨ ⲈⲂⲞⲖ ⲚⲀⲨ
ϨⲚ ⲤⲀⲣϮ in log. 28.[14] Or if we consider the writings of Paul and
John, to which I earlier compared *Thomas'* christological views, there
is no essential difference between the incarnation language in *Gos.
Thom.* 28, in Rom 8:3 (ὁ θεὸς τὸν ἑαυτοῦ υἱὸν πέμψας ἐν ὁμοιώματι
σαρκὸς ἁμαρτίας; "God sent his son in the likeness of sinful flesh"),

---

[11] If "God" in Rom 9:5 can be taken to refer to Jesus Paul also uses that title
of him. This is not certain, however; cf. James D. G. Dunn, "Christology (NT),"
ABD 1:984; Tuckett, *Christology and the New Testament*, 64–65.

[12] So, e.g., Bertil Gärtner, *Ett nytt evangelium? Thomas hemliga Jesusord* (Stockholm:
Diakonistyrelsens bokförlag, 1960), 128–29; Jacques-É. Ménard, *L'évangile selon Thomas*
(NHS 5; Leiden: Brill, 1975), 123.

[13] Valantasis (*The Gospel of Thomas*, 102–3) makes an exception. For him the
appearance of Jesus "in flesh" is not to be interpreted in terms of a gnostic docetic
motif. Instead, Valantasis thinks that the description of the people among whom
Jesus enters as drunk and disoriented, blind and empty gives this logion a gnostic
tone. To be sure, blindness and drunkenness are certainly features which are used
to characterize the disorientation of the human beings in the world in gnostic texts
as Hans Jonas (*The Gnostic Religion* [2d ed.; London: Routledge, 1963], 48–97), to
whom Valantasis refers, has demonstrated. Since the same imagery is also employed
in other early Christian texts (cf., e.g., 1 Thess 5:6–8; *Teach. Silv.* 88.22–29; 94.19–22)
it does not necessarily, however, substantiate gnostic influence.

[14] Dunderberg, "Thomas' I-sayings and the Gospel of John," 47–48. So also Bo
Frid and Jesper Svartvik, *Thomasevangeliet* (Lund: Arcus, 2002), 172. It is noteworthy
that the Greek version of *Gos. Thom.* 28 (P. Oxy. 1) has a wording nearly equivalent
to that of 1 Tim 3:16: καὶ ἐν σαρκὶ ὤφθην αὐτοῖε ("and I appeared to them in flesh").

and in John 1:14 (ὁ λόγος σὰρξ ἐγένετο; "the word became flesh"). Examined in relation to the classical examples of docetic Christology, according to which Christ was either never really "involved in the material and human realities of this creation" (e.g., the docetic opponents of the Letters of John and the Letters of Ignatius; 1 John 4:2–3; 2 John 7; Ign. *Smyrn.* 2.1; *Trall.* 10) or he avoids all suffering by leaving the earthly Jesus before his crucifixion (e.g., Basilides; *Treat. Seth* 55.10–56.19),[15] none of these texts can really be styled as docetic.[16]

So far I have argued that as far as the origin and nature of Jesus is concerned *Thomas*' characterization of Jesus is practically the same as that of Paul and John. Thus, from that perspective *Thomas* can be regarded as a representative of a relatively advanced Christology among early Christian writers. Nevertheless, this does not mean that *Thomas*', Paul's, and John's Christologies would be identical in every way. Jesus' mission, for example his soteriological role, is interpreted very differently by each. But that is not all. There is a conspicuous difference among them also in the way they comprehend the relationship of the heavenly preexistent Jesus to the believers or, to use the Thomasine terminology, to the elect.

For Paul and John, the fact that Jesus is a preexistent divine figure means that he is in every way unique compared with the rest of humanity. For *Thomas* the situation is different. Jesus is by no means the only one who is of heavenly origin and who belongs to the realm of light. According to logia 49 and 50, the elect are also from the kingdom and from the light, and there they will return. The beginning of Jesus' statement in logion 19 actually implies that the preexistence of the elect is a presupposition for salvation: "Blessed is he who was, before he came into being."

---

[15] For this two-dimensional definition of docetic Christology among second- and third-century Christian thinkers, see Michael Slusser, "Docetism: A Historical Definition," *SecCent* 1 (1981): 163–71. For other non-docetic Christologies among the writings of the Nag Hammadi Library, see Antti Marjanen, "The Suffering of One Who Is a Stranger to Suffering: The Crucifixion of Jesus in the Letter of Peter to Philip," in *Fair Play: Diversity and Conflicts in Early Christianity: Essays in Honour of Heikki Räisänen* (ed. Ismo Dunderberg, Kari Syreeni and Christopher Tuckett; NovTSup 103; Leiden: Brill, 2002), 487–98.

[16] In his recent characterization of the Thomasine Christology, Gerd Theissen (*The Religion of the Earliest Churches: Creating a Symbolic World* [trans. John Bowden; Minneapolis, MN: Fortress, 1999], 284) has stated similarly: "nowhere does it (i.e., the *Gospel of Thomas*) advocate a docetic Christology."

The essential difference between Jesus and the elect is that while Jesus appears on the earth he is aware of his heavenly origin. All the others, including the elect, are spiritually drunk and blind, having a need to be made conscious of their real origin and nature (3; 28). This takes us a step further in *Thomas'* characterization of Jesus. Next we address the question about the mission of Jesus.

2. *The Mission of Jesus*

It is of course not news to anybody who has read the *Gospel of Thomas* that the death and resurrection of Jesus play no role in the work. Jesus' mission is not to die for anybody, as for example in Paul and John, but his task is to reveal the saving message to the elect. Thus Jesus is described as a teacher, as the form of the work already demonstrates.

Very often *Thomas'* Jesus is characterized as the teacher of wisdom, and this is certainly a correct designation in many ways. To be more exact, however, the Thomasine Jesus should be seen as the teacher who invites people to seek after knowledge (3; 18; 19; 56; 67; 69; 80; 91; 111). And it is important to realize that it is not actually Jesus whom the elect are supposed to come to know. In fact, the right understanding or definition of Jesus need not be sought (43; 91). Instead, it is crucial for the disciples of Jesus to find the knowledge of themselves, or more precisely, the knowledge of the kingdom of light which can be found within them (3; 24; 70; 111). Stevan Davies has expressed this very succinctly when he says: "Jesus' message about the kingdom of God is Thomas's concern, not Jesus' message about Jesus."[17] At this point *Thomas'* Christology clearly diverges from that of Paul and John. The faith in Jesus as a savior is a totally foreign idea for *Thomas*. As a matter of fact, in logion 91 the request of the disciples, "Tell us who you are so that we may believe in you," seems to reflect a complete misunderstanding.

In view of *Thomas'* emphasis on the self-knowledge of the disciples, Jesus' relationship to the disciples is portrayed in a somewhat surprising way. On the one hand, Jesus is certainly the one who invites and even chooses the disciples to listen to his message (19; 23; 62). He is also the one who presents or actually sets the prerequisites for discipleship (3; 55; 94; 101). There is no doubt that

---

[17] Davies, "Christology," 674.

through his teaching he is understood to be instrumental in bringing the possibility of salvation to the elect. And yet, he is not awarded
any honorific christological titles which would demonstrate his specific
value and role, and which would also indicate a clear hierarchical
difference between him and his disciples.[18]

In fact, when two disciples, Peter and Matthew, try to define, in
logion 13, the significance of Jesus by employing the titular expressions "a just messenger/angel" and "a wise philosopher," their attempts
prove to be less acceptable than the apostle Thomas' inability to
describe Jesus in any way. There has been some discussion as to
why Peter's and Matthew's confessions are not approved. Two solutions have been suggested. Some scholars have thought that logion
13 is to be taken as polemic against such christological views the
author of the gospel deemed to be wrong. It is especially Peter's
angel Christology which has inspired scholars to make this inference;[19]
the conclusion is bolstered by the fact that neither angels nor Peter
are treated favorably elsewhere in the gospel (88; 114). Another way
to look at logion 13 is to regard Peter's and Matthew's answers not
as wrong but as inadequate.[20]

I think both solutions miss the point of the logion. It is neither
right nor adequate titular confessions which are sought in the text.[21]

---

[18] Apart from three instances (47; 73; 74), the word ⲍⲟⲉⲓⲥ, for example, is never
used in a titular sense ("Lord") but always with a secular meaning "master" or
"owner" (21; 64; 65). In logia 47, 73, and 74 it is unlikely that Jesus is meant; in
logia 73 and 74 the word probably refers to God, and the same is apparently true
with logion 47, if indeed an exact correspondence need or can be identified behind
the metaphorical use of the word. The Thomasine Jesus speaks once about his
ⲙⲛ̄ⲧⲍⲟⲉⲓⲥ (90), but even there it is not his superiority but rather the mildness of
his "mastership" which is emphasized. The christological titles ⲥⲱⲧⲏⲣ ("Savior")
and the "Son of God" do not appear at all in the *Gospel of Thomas*, and the "Son
of Man" occurs only once (86) but it is very questionable whether it is used as a
christological title. In any case, the "sons of man" can be employed to refer to the
elect as well (106). To be sure, Jesus' divine sonship is introduced in two logia (37;
44), but it is relativized by the fact that the elect can also be called the "sons of
the Living Father" (3).
[19] So, e.g., Loren T. Stuckenbruck, *Angel Veneration and Christology: A Study in Early
Judaism and in the Christology of the Apocalypse* (WUNT, 2. Reihe 70; Tübingen: Mohr,
1995), 139 n. 239.
[20] So, e.g., Eckhard Rau, "Jenseits von Raum, Zeit und Gemeinschaft: 'Christ-
Sein' nach dem Thomasevangelium," *NovT* 45 (2003): 142.
[21] So also Stephen J. Patterson, "Understanding the *Gospel of Thomas* Today," in
The Fifth Gospel: The Gospel of Thomas Comes of Age (ed. Stephen J. Patterson, James
M. Robinson and Hans-Gebhard Bethge; Harrisburgh, PA: Trinity Press International,
1998), 57.

This is confirmed by the fact that even the address of the apostle Thomas, ΠϹΔϨ ("teacher"/"master"), is not endorsed. The point the author of the text wants to make is: there should be no barrier between Jesus and his disciples or the elect, whether it be that of a title, or that of power or position. As I have argued elsewhere, along with logion 13 a new ideal of discipleship is presented in the gospel. It can be characterized as "masterless" or "Jesus-like."[22] Whereas in logion 12 Jesus still exhorts his disciples to obey James as their leader instead of himself, in logion 13 Jesus says to Thomas, who has drunk and become intoxicated at the bubbling spring: "I am not your master." The same theme is repeated in logion 108, in which Jesus states: "Whoever will drink from my mouth will become like me. I myself will become he and what is hidden will be revealed to him."

The idea of a "masterless" or "Jesus-like" discipleship fits well with the christological tendency found already in connection with those sayings which speak about the common origin and nature of Jesus and the elect. Although *Thomas'* view of Jesus can, together with that of Paul and John, be placed among those early Christian writers who represent a relatively advanced wisdom Christology and who from that perspective distinguish Jesus from the rest of humanity, simultaneously it has a kind of egalitarian vein. To be sure, compared with the elect, Jesus has a special function, since he, as the only one being aware of the light within himself, is also able to make the saving message available to the others. In that sense Jesus functions as the "spiritual guide"[23] of the elect (cf. also 114).[24] But as far as one's origin, nature and position with regard to one's salvation are concerned, the elect and Jesus do not differ in any way.[25]

---

[22] Marjanen, "Women Disciples in the *Gospel of Thomas*," 90–91; see also Antti Marjanen, *The Woman Jesus Loved: Mary Magdalene in Nag Hammadi Library and Related Documents* (NHMS 40; Leiden: Brill, 1996), 40–41. A similar view is presented by Zöckler, *Jesu Lehren*, 245–47.

[23] The characterization derives from Valantasis, *Gospel of Thomas*, 76.

[24] Although logion 114 may be part of the latest redaction of the *Gospel of Thomas* (see Marjanen, "Women Disciples," 103) it is well aligned with the Thomasine ideology and thus provides a good illustration of the relationship between Jesus and the elect. It is Jesus who by disclosing the secret wisdom leads Mary (and other women disciples) "to become a living spirit resembling . . . males" but it is Mary and other women who, by making themselves males, prove to be worthy of the kingdom of heaven.

[25] A similar conclusion is reached by Risto Uro, *Thomas: Seeking the Historical Context of the Gospel of Thomas* (London: Clark, 2003), 23, 45.

4. Thomas' *Christology within the Context of Early Christianity*

Where are we to place the kind of Christology represented by *Thomas* within the context of early Christianity? We have already recognized the similarities between *Thomas*, Paul and John as to their views of Jesus' preexistent heavenly origin and his divine nature. Yet this does not constitute the whole portrait of Jesus in the *Gospel of Thomas*. It is the egalitarian vein in *Thomas'* Christology, the possibility to become Christ granted to all the elect, which is its most characteristic feature and which also sets it apart from the other more advanced early Christologies of Paul and John. Whereas John and perhaps also Paul accepted the idea of a preexistent heavenly soul, found in the Hellenistic-Jewish wisdom thought (e.g., Wis 8:19–20), but applied it only to Jesus, *Thomas* sees the soul or the divine light in everybody, or at least in all the elect.

The process of salvation is also perceived differently in the *Gospel of Thomas*. The role of the savior which is assigned to Jesus by many early Christian authors is in a way attributed to the elect themselves in *Thomas*. Certainly, Jesus is still the one who invites the elect to take part in the saving knowledge, but he is not the savior in terms of Pauline or Johannine Christology and soteriology. For *Thomas*, the final outcome of a human being's attempt to be saved does not depend on any act of Jesus, but on something which a human being has in him/herself (70). Therefore, it is natural that the author develops an idea of a masterless disciple who, after having found the interpretation of the secret teaching imparted by Jesus, can dispense with him.

The *Gospel of Thomas* is not the only example of early Christian interest in an egalitarian type of Christology according to which there is no substantial or hierarchical difference between Christ and those who receive his revelatory message. In the Syrian *Odes of Solomon* 3:7 a writer depicts his union with Christ in a way that closely recalls *Gos. Thom.* 108: "I have been united to him because the lover has found the beloved, and because I love him that is the son, I have become a son." In the *Apocryphon of James* the Risen Lord comforts his oppressed disciples by promising that if they do the will of God, God will not only love them but also "make them equal!" with Jesus (5.2–3). Neither of these works can be regarded as Valentinian or Gnostic, but both clearly connect closely with the christological tendency found in the *Gospel of Thomas*. The points of contact in terms of Christology between

the *Gospel of Thomas* and the *Odes of Solomon* may well be explained
by their common geographical origin.[26] The connections between the
Gospel of Thomas and the *Apocryphon of James* are not so obvious and
require further study.

There are also some gnostic texts in which the Thomasine type
of egalitarian Christology has gained a foothold. In some excerpts
from the Valentinian *Gospel of Philip* we are told that a person who has
received an unction "is no longer a Christian but a Christ" (67.23–27),
and a person who has seen Christ has become Christ him/herself
(61.30–31). Despite terminological similarities, the emphases of the
Gospel of Thomas and the *Gospel of Philip* are not completely identical.
In the *Gospel of Thomas* a disciple becomes a Christ when the secret
teachings are disclosed to him or her (108), whereas in the *Gospel of
Philip* the transformation into a Christ-like existence seems to be a
result of a ritual, probably an unction accompanying a baptism or
a sacrament of bridal chamber (67.9–27;[27] cf. also 74.12–22).[28]

A similar christological and soteriological tendency can be observed
in other gnostic texts as well. The third-century *Pistis Sophia* contains
a speech in which the Savior affirms that "everybody who will receive
the mystery of the Ineffable and is completed in all its types and all
its patterns . . . is superior to all the angels. . . . This person is I and
I am this person" (230.3–231.15).[29] Just as in the *Gospel of Thomas* it
is the reception of the secret revelation which gives a person a status
equal to that of Jesus himself. The same motif is found among the
so-called Carpocratians. According to Irenaeus, they think that their
soul "is like that of Christ" and therefore they "declare themselves

---

[26] The location of both texts is usually placed in Syria; cf., e.g., Uro, *Thomas*, 26–30.

[27] For a ritual context of this text as well as that of *Gos. Phil.* 61.30–31, see
Hans-Martin Schenke, *Das Philippusevangelium (Nag-Hammadi-Codex II,3)* (Berlin: Akademie
Verlag, 1997), 304–6, 378–80.

[28] Stevan L. Davies (*The Gospel of Thomas and Christian Wisdom* [New York, NY:
Seabury, 1983], 133–36) argues that *Gos. Thom.* 108 has to be understood in a baptismal context since drinking from Christ recalls drinking from the one Spirit which
for Paul stands for baptism (1 Cor 12:12–14). This is hardly likely because both *Gos.
Thom.* 13 and *Gos. Thom.* 108 clearly indicate that drinking from the bubbling spring
or the mouth of Jesus has to do with the reception of hidden teachings. Besides,
in neither case is there any allusion to baptism or any other ritual whatsoever.

[29] For the edition of the text, see *Pistis Sophia* (ed. Carl Schmidt; translation and
notes Violet Macdermot; NHS 9; Leiden: Brill, 1978). In the present article the
reference to *Pistis Sophia* is made according to that edition. The first number gives
the page number of the Coptic text, the second number refers to the line of the
Coptic text. The translation is Macdermot's with some modifications.

similar to Jesus."[30] A modification of the Thomasine type of Christology is provided by Irenaeus' account of a Marcosian meeting during which the prophet Marcus, a gnostic teacher who, according to Irenaeus, "boasts himself as having improved upon his master,"[31] invites his women followers to prophesy by saying: "Adorn thyself as a bride who is expecting her bridegroom, that *thou mayest be what I am, and I what thou art*" (*Haer.* 1.13.3; italics mine).

The fact that the Thomasine Christology and soteriology contain such features which find their way into Valentinian and gnostic thought does not of course mean that the *Gospel of Thomas* itself has to be defined as Valentinian or gnostic. Rather, it is more likely that it is *Thomas* which has given an impetus to or at least shares in a trajectory which eventually leads to Valentinian or gnostic thinking. Thus, the Thomasine Christology, partly resembling that of the Gospel of John and the Pauline letters, but partly also radically differing from them, exerts influence both locally in Syrian traditions and crosses the geographical borders into Valentinian and gnostic traditions.

---

[30] *Haer.* 1.25.2 (*ANF* 1:350).
[31] *Haer.* 1.13.1 (*ANF* 1:334).

CHAPTER TEN

FROM THOMAS TO VALENTINUS: GENESIS EXEGESIS IN FRAGMENT 4 OF VALENTINUS AND ITS RELATIONSHIP TO THE *GOSPEL OF THOMAS*

Ismo Dunderberg

The few extant fragments of Valentinus contain a short excerpt from a sermon, in which he addresses his audience as those who are "immortal from the beginning" and "rule over the creation and the entire corruption." This fragment 4 of Valentinus[1] in the *Stromateis* of Clement of Alexandria (*Strom.* 4.89.1–3) has been subject to lively discussions in recent years. Above all, scholars have debated whether it betrays gnostic tendencies or not. Efforts have also been made to bring to light affinities between Valentinus' teaching about immortality and Jewish Wisdom literature, Paul and the Gospel of John. It has even been noted in passing that the fragment can be understood as an interpretation of Genesis.

What has not been taken sufficiently into account thus far is that there are close parallels to this fragment of Valentinus in the *Gospel of Thomas*. It is, in fact, surprising that so little attention has been paid to them, for the importance of Genesis traditions in the *Gospel of Thomas* has already been highlighted by many specialists.[2] Most recently, Elaine Pagels has argued that *Thomas* makes extensive use of Genesis 1:26–27 "to show that the divine image implanted at creation enables humankind to find . . . the way back to its origin in the

---

[1] I prefer Walther Völker's traditional numbering of the fragments of Valentinus to the alternative system created by Bentley Layton. See Völker, ed., *Quellen zur Geschichte der christlichen Gnosis* (SAQ, n.F. 5; Tübingen: Mohr, 1932) and Layton, *The Gnostic Scriptures: A New Translation with Annotations and Introductions* (New York, NY: Doubleday, 1987), 229–49. In Layton's system, this fragment runs as "Fragment F (VFrF)" (*ibid.*, 240–41).

[2] E.g., Stevan L. Davies, "Christology and Protology of the *Gospel of Thomas*," *JBL* 111 (1992): 663–82, esp. 663–74; Margaretha Lelyveld, *Les logia de la vie dans l'Évangile selon Thomas: À la recherche d'une tradition et d'une rédaction* (NHS 34; Leiden: Brill, 1987). The latter study shows, among other things, that a number of Jewish views about Adam can be traced in *Thomas* (pp. 27–30, 38–43, 49–54).

mystery of the primordial creation."³ I will argue in this article that
Valentinus' fragment 4 presupposes a tradition of Genesis exegesis
that is very similar to that traced in *Thomas* by Pagels. This raises the
question whether Valentinus might have been familiar with Thomasine
traditions. Bentley Layton not only made this proposal in *The Gnostic
Scriptures*⁴ but also arranged his entire collection of translations in
accordance with it. Nevertheless, he did not provide any detailed
argumentation for his suggestion. My article can be understood as
a case study pointing in the same direction as Layton's hypothesis,
although at the same time I remain very much aware that no far-
reaching conclusions are possible on the basis of one small excerpt
from Valentinus' teachings.

Before turning to specific affinities between Valentinus and the *Gospel
of Thomas*, I will discuss the interpretation of the relevant fragment
itself, which has been subject to considerable disagreement in recent
studies. I will also take up a number of other possible analogies to
Valentinus' teaching about immortality in order to show that he and
Thomas are indeed especially close to each other in this respect.

1. *Fragment 4 of Valentinus*

Fragment 4 of Valentinus runs in its entirety as follows:⁵

Οὐαλεντῖνος δὲ ἔν τινι ὁμιλίᾳ κατὰ λέξιν γράφει· ἀπ' ἀρχῆς ἀθάνατοί ἐστε
καὶ τέκνα ζωῆς ἐστε αἰωνίας καὶ τὸν θάνατον ἠθέλετε μερίσασθαι εἰς ἑαυτούς,
ἵνα δαπανήσητε αὐτὸν καὶ ἀναλώσητε, καὶ ἀποθάνῃ ὁ θάνατος ἐν ὑμῖν καὶ
δι' ὑμῶν. ὅταν γὰρ τὸν μὲν κόσμον λύητε, ὑμεῖς δὲ μὴ καταλύησθε, κυριεύετε
τῆς κτίσεως καὶ τῆς φθορᾶς ἁπάσης.

Valentinus writes in some sermon word for word: "You are immortal
from the beginning, and you are children of eternal life. You wanted
death to be divided to yourselves in order to use it up and waste it,
so that death would die in and through you. For when you, on the
one hand, nullify the world, but, on the other, will not be dissolved,
you rule over the creation and the entire corruption."

³ Elaine H. Pagels, "Exegesis of Genesis 1 in the Gospels of Thomas and John,"
JBL 118 (1999): 477–96, esp. 488. Her view builds upon Hans-Martin Schenke, *Der
Gott "Mensch" in der Gnosis: Ein religionsgeschichtlicher Beitrag zur Diskussion über die paulinische
Anschauung von der Kirche als Leib Christi* (Göttingen: Vandenhoeck & Ruprecht, 1962).
⁴ Layton, *Gnostic Scriptures*, xv–xvi.
⁵ Clement of Alexandria, *Strom.* 4.89.1–3 (frag. F in Layton, *Gnostic Scriptures*,
240–41).

The fragment is characterized by a sublime style and very condensed way of expression.[6] This, connected with the lack of the original context, makes the interpretation of the fragment very difficult. Much is dependent on a scholar's choice of interpretive framework. Clement presented the fragment as part of a larger section describing Gnostic teachings against martyrdom. He also explained the fragment as reflecting two standard Valentinian ideas. In Clement's opinion, Valentinus speaks of the spiritual "race saved by nature" (φύσει... σωζόμενον γένος) that came from above to destroy death. Moreover, Clement explains the fragment by maintaining that Valentinus attributed the origin of death to the inferior creator God (*Strom.* 4.89.4).

We cannot be sure whether Clement's interpretation was based upon a further reading of Valentinus's sermon or on what he considered to be stock Valentinian ideas on the basis of other sources he knew. For the latter possibility speaks the fact that the "spiritual race" is not attested in other fragments of Valentinus, whereas it appears in other sources known to Clement.[7] In addition, though it is a standard accusation in patristic sources that Valentinians thought of themselves as being saved by nature, it remains unclear how many of them really held this idea.[8] For these reasons, I am inclined to believe that Clement's interpretation of the fragment is secondary.

The scholarly debate related to this fragment revolves, as was mentioned above, around the question of whether Valentinus takes a distinctly gnostic stance in it. Christoph Markschies resolutely denies this possibility and interprets the fragment in light of Pauline and Johannine views.[9] Yet there are two other German scholars who insist

---

[6] For these issues, see the meticulous analysis by Christoph Markschies, *Valentinus Gnosticus? Untersuchungen zur valentinianischen Gnosis mit einem Kommentar zu den Fragmenten Valentin* (WUNT 65; Tübingen: Mohr, 1992), 124–27.

[7] Cf. Markschies, *Valentinus*, 146–49. Among other things, Markschies points out that the term τὸ διάφορον γένος, which Clement employs in his commentary on fragment 4 of Valentinus, recalls the expression τὸ διάφερον σπέρμα, which was characteristic of Theodotus's teaching as documented in another work by Clement (*Exc. Theod.* 41.1–3).

[8] The claim of Valentinians as being those saved by nature goes back to Irenaeus (*Haer.* 1.6.1), whom other patristic authors usually follow on this point. Ansgar Wucherpfennig's recent study strengthens considerably the view that Heracleon did not subscribe to this opinion, but that it was read into his teaching by Origen, who interpreted that teaching in light of what he knew about Valentinianism from Irenaeus; cf. Ansgar Wucherpfennig, *Heracleon Philologus: Gnostische Johannesexegese im zweiten Jahrhundert* (WUNT 142; Tübingen: Mohr, 2002).

[9] Markschies, *Valentinus*, 131–36.

that the fragment does indeed reflect gnostic ideas. Jens Holzhausen
has argued that Valentinus really voices a critique of early Christian
views about martyrdom, as Clement suggests.[10] Yet Holzhausen builds
his case not on the context of this fragment in Clement's work, but
on fiscal imagery that he traces in the fragment itself.[11] The verbs
Valentinus employs for destruction (ἀναλοῦν, δαπανᾶν) are often used
for spending money for some purpose, and the verb μερίζεσθαι can
be employed for dividing money. Holzhausen contends that the fiscal
imagery was used by Valentinus for an ecclesiastical view that martyrdom is a price which must be paid for salvation. Accordingly,
Holzhausen paraphrases Valentinus's teaching as follows: "Although
human beings are already immortal, they want to use death as pay-
ment to inherit eternal life."[12] Paul Schüngel, in turn, has argued that
Valentinus speaks in the fragment against the Christian eucharist. While
Paul taught that Christians "proclaim the Lord's death" (1 Cor 11:26)
as they participate in the eucharist, Valentinus wanted to say, according to Schüngel, that they only divide (share) death with each other
in so doing.

The interpretations of Holzhausen and Schüngel remain, however,
in my opinion, less than convincing. To begin with, they presuppose
a reading of the fragment which I consider unlikely. In that reading, it is assumed that the original immortality of human beings and
their attempts to destroy death are played against each other in the
fragment ("you are immortal from the beginning, *but* you wanted
death to be divided to yourselves"). In my view, the logic in the
fragment goes the other way around. In the concluding part, a con-
sequence is drawn from what has been said earlier: "*For* (γάρ) when
you nullify the world, . . . you rule over creation and the entire corruption." In this conclusion, the sentence "when you nullify the
world" seems to be a summation of what Valentinus has said before
about consuming death and about its perdition "in you and through
you." The attempts of his addressees at spending up death are, therefore, not disqualified by him, but lead to a *positive* outcome. In my
reading of the fragment, death will perish, and the addressees will
become masters of creation as the *result* of these attempts.

---

[10] Jens Holzhausen, "Gnosis und Martyrium: Zu Valentins viertem Fragment,"
ZNW 85 (1994): 116–31.
[11] Also Layton, *Gnostic Scriptures*, 241, interprets Valentinus's usage of the above
mentioned verbs in terms of fiscal imagery.
[12] Holzhausen, "Gnosis und Martyrium," 123.

I also fail to see clear connections between the fragment and early Christian texts praising martyrdom quoted by Holzhausen in support of his view,[13] nor does the fragment contain clear terminological affinities to the eucharist in general, or to Paul's view about it in particular, not to speak of polemics against the latter, as Schüngel has maintained. Schüngel's view is, moreover, at odds with the evidence suggesting that Valentinians usually took the eucharist for granted. It would be difficult to account for their unanimous acceptance of the eucharist, if Valentinus took a totally different attitude in this matter.[14] We could also expect clearer signs of Valentinus' rejection of the eucharist in patristic writings, for this would have been useful in their anti-Valentinian polemics. The lack of such evidence, therefore, speaks strongly against Schüngel's interpretation.

In my view, we can be quite sure that the fragment can be understood in terms of Genesis exegesis. The sentence "you wanted death to be divided to yourselves" (καὶ τὸν θάνατον ἠθέλετε μερίσασθαι εἰς ἑαυτούς) in the fragment suggests a reflection of the account of Adam and Eve in Genesis 2–3, in which death is allocated to Adam and Eve first as a threat and then, after the fall, as a punishment (Gen 2:17; 3:19). If so, Valentinus applies the story of Adam and Eve to his audience: this is what *you* used to do,[15] it is *you* who wanted death to be divided to you.[16] Valentinus's interpretation may seem odd at

---

[13] Cf. Holzhausen, "Gnosis und Martyrium," 123–27. The most concrete affinity offered by Holzhausen is that between the expression λαβεῖν μέρος in the *Martyrdom of St. Polycarp* 14:2 and the verb μερίζεσθαι used by Valentinus. Yet even this parallel remains remote. In addition, it is unlikely that the former expression would have been, as such, a *terminus technicus* for Christian martyrdom. In *Mart. Pol.* 14:2, this aspect becomes visible only in the larger phrase of which λαβεῖν μέρος is a part (τοῦ λαβεῖν μέρος ἐν ἀριθμῷ τῶν μαρτύρων, "to have a share among the number of martyrs," trans. Musurillo). It would be far-fetched to assume that the use of the verb μερίζεσθαι indicates Valentinus's knowledge of this whole phrase in the *Martyrdom of St. Polycarp*.

[14] I am grateful to Elaine Pagels for reminding me about this point in her comments on an earlier draft of this article. For evidence, see, e.g., *Gos. Phil.* pp. 55 (§ 15); 57 (§ 23); 63 (§ 53); 67 (§ 68); *Euch. A* and *Euch. B* (liturgical attachments to *Val. Exp.*).

[15] I take the imperfect form of the verb θελεῖν used by Valentinus as denoting customary, or continuing, past action. It could also be understood as conative, denoting "an action attempted, intended, or expected in the past" (H. W. Smyth, *Greek Grammar* [Cambridge, MA: Harvard University Press, 1956] § 1895; cf. Markschies, *Valentinus*, 137). The latter meaning could also be used of *futile* attempts (e.g., Luke 1:59), but this does not seem to be the case in the fragment of Valentinus.

[16] I find it unlikely that Valentinus's sermon, from which this fragment stems, could be understood as addressed to Adam and Eve. For this interpretation, see Markschies, *Valentinus*, 146.

first sight, but it finds support from other Jewish and early Christian interpretations of Genesis to be discussed below.

The fragment also contains several other allusions to Genesis. The opening words "you are immortal *from the beginning*" indicate an interpretation of the original state of humankind described in Genesis.[17] Notably, the expression ἀπ᾽ ἀρχῆς used in the fragment appears also in the Gospel of Matthew, which Valentinus certainly knew,[18] as referring to the creation of human beings (Matt 19:4).[19] Moreover, Valentinus's statement at the end of the fragment that his addressees will rule over the creation is most likely associated with the dominion of humankind over animals affirmed in Gen 1:26–28.

What seems surprising in Valentinus's interpretation of Genesis is the positive value attached to the distribution of death among human beings. As was argued above, the sentence "you wanted death to be divided to yourselves" should not be opposed to original immortality mentioned at the beginning. The distribution of death among human beings ultimately leads not to their perdition, but to that of *death*. Moreover, Valentinus employs in this connection a passive expression "to be divided (μερίσασθαι) to yourselves," which can be understood as a *passivum divinum*. Already Clement seems to have taken the passive in this sense, as he read from the fragment that Valentinus attributed the origin of death to the creator God, although this God is not directly mentioned in the fragment itself.[20]

Given the positive purpose attached to death in this fragment, however, the passive could also be referred to the *supreme God*. This would be consistent with Valentinus's description of death as serving positive goals for his addressees. Death exists only in order to be

---

[17] Cf. Markschies, *Valentinus*, 127–28.

[18] Valentinus no doubt alludes to Matt 5:8 and 19:17 in fragment 2; cf. Markschies, *Valentinus*, 58–59.

[19] Also in Sir. 16:26 ἀπ᾽ ἀρχῆς is used in a portrayal of God's creation of the world ("When the Lord judged [LXX] his works from the beginning, and in making them, determined their boundaries"). Cf. Jacob Jervell, *Imago Dei: Gen. 1,26f. im Spätjudentum, in der Gnosis und in den paulinischen Briefen* (FRLANT 58; Göttingen: Vandenhoeck & Ruprecht, 1960), 30. For other references, see Markschies, *Valentinus*, 127–28.

[20] Clement adds to his commentary on Valentinus's fragment another passage that seems to be a quotation rather than Clement's own inference from his teaching (*Strom.* 4.89.5): "Therefore he (Valentinus) understands the scripture 'No one will see God's face and live' (Exod 33:20) as if (God is) responsible for death (θανάτου αἴτιος)." This may have contributed to Clement's interpretation of μερίσασθαι in terms of *passivum divinum* referring to the Demiurge. Markschies, *Valentinus*, 149–52, discusses the possibility whether this passage could be an authentic fragment of Valentinus, but ends up with the conclusion that it is more likely an opinion of his student that Clement refers to here.

"wasted" by them. When they do this, they also annihilate death. Valentinus's argument implies that there is a paedagogical reason for the existence of death. His addressees are originally immortal, but they need to be in the world to deal with death, destroy it and bring the world to naught. This is the way they become masters of the creation.[21] If this is the underlying presupposition of Valentinus's teaching, a link can be seen between it and the strong emphasis placed on paedagogy by later Valentinians. For they considered the visible world as a place of education, to which the believers must descend from the divine realm before they can reach their final salvation on the latter.[22]

In the fragment of Valentinus, attempts at destroying death and at nullifying the world appear as parallel expressions for one and the same thing. There is no indication that Valentinus would have been speaking of a post-mortem state of his addressees, nor do I find it likely that the nullification of the world would denote a concrete destruction. It seems more likely that Valentinus encourages his audience to take towards the *present world* an attitude that makes them masters of it. That Valentinus speaks of "nullification" in this context indicates that the attitude he recommends to his audience involves detachment from the world. It remains open, however, what kind of detachment Valentinus was exactly thinking of. The no longer extant parts of his sermon may or may not have contained a further exposition on this issue. Detachment from the world did not necessarily require or mean radical asceticism, nor a complete withdrawal from society, as Philo shows. Despite his appreciation of the ascetic life style, he himself approved of wealth, public honours, drinking and eating— given that the right attitude towards them was involved.[23] It may be that Valentinus was no more demanding in this respect than Philo.[24]

---

[21] For a similar interpretation of this fragment, see Holger Strutwolf, *Gnosis als System: Zur Rezeption der valentinianischen Gnosis bei Origenes* (Forschungen zur Kirchen- und Dogmengeschichte 56; Göttingen: Vandenhoeck & Ruprecht, 1993), 129: "They are completely superior to death, indeed, their coming into this reality of death appears as a voluntary action, the goal of which is to overcome death." Yet I am not convinced by Strutwolf's contention that Valentinus addresses this teaching to the group of pneumatics only.

[22] E.g., Irenaeus, *Haer.* 1.6.1, 1.7.5; *Tri. Trac.* 104, 123, 126–27; *Val. Exp.* 37; cf., Strutwolf, *Gnosis als System*, 132, 204; Einar Thomassen, *Le Traite Tripartite (NH I, 5)* (BCNH Textes 19; Quebec: Les Presses de l'Université Laval, 1989), 402.

[23] Philo, *Fug.* 24–32; cf. Gerhard Sellin, *Der Streit um die Auferstehung der Toten: Eine religionsgeschichtliche und exegetische Untersuchung von 1 Korinther 15* (FRLANT 138; Göttingen: Vandenhoeck & Ruprecht, 1986), 155.

[24] Ptolemy's *Letter to Flora* (33.5.13–14) bears witness to ascetic practices among

2. *Hellenistic Jewish and Early Christian*
Background to Valentinus's views

Valentinus no doubt conceives of immortality as being part of the original state of humankind, as he affirms that "you *are* immortal from the beginning." This is different from what is said in Genesis, but is in line with a number of Jewish interpretations of the first chapters of Genesis. In Genesis itself, the Yahwist "nowhere says that Adam, before his disobedience, was immortal, was never going to die." In Genesis, thus, "the problem that Adam's disobedience created . . . was not that he brought death into the world but that he brought near to himself the distant possibility of immortality."[25] The Yahwist's story is not about the origin of death, as it became understood later. In this story, rather, God's warning that Adam shall die *on the day* he eats from the tree of the knowledge of good and evil (Gen 2:17) should be understood as a threat of his instant and premature death.[26]

Nevertheless, Hellenistic Jewish authors already tended to read out from this account in Genesis that immortality belonged to the original human state created by God. For example, it is said in Wis 2:23–24: "God created us for incorruption, and made us in the image of his own eternity, but through the devil's envy death entered the world and those who belong to his company experience it."[27] A similar view lies in the background of the book of Sirach, in which the origin of death is attributed to Eve and her fall (Sir 25:24). Also Paul thought that death came into existence only after, and because of, Adam's fall (Rom 5:12; 6:23; 1 Cor 15:21).

It may seem more unusual that Valentinus speaks of immortality as a present quality ("you *are* immortal," ἀθάνατοί ἐστε), while the authors of the books of Wisdom and Sirach as well as Paul presupposed that immortality was lost in the fall. Yet Justin Martyr,

---

later Valentinians. These practices, however, remain very moderate. The fact that Ptolemy mentions them only in passing suggests, in addition, that no special emphasis was put on these practices among Valentinians.

[25] Both quotations are from James Barr, *The Garden of Eden and the Hope of Immortality* (Minneapolis, MN: Fortress, 1993), 5–6.

[26] Cf. Barr, *Garden of Eden*, 10, who points out a similarity between God's warning to Adam in Gen 2:17 and that of Solomon to Shimei in 1 Kings 2:37, 42.

[27] This view also recurs in Rabbinic writings, cf., e.g., *Genesis Rabbah* 21.5 (Adam "was not meant to experience death"); *Numeri Rabbah* 16.24.

who was roughly contemporary with Valentinus, also reckoned with the possibility that each person can be immortal in the same way Adam and Eve were in the beginning. Justin argued that people created in the image of God are immortal and free from suffering like God, but they *have become* like Adam and Eve and bring death upon themselves.[28] A similar view is attested also in a rabbinic midrash: "I said: 'You are godlike beings (Ps 82:6)' but you have ruined yourselves like Adam, and so, 'indeed, you shall die like Adam.'"[29] Another midrash explains Psalm 82:6 as demonstrating that human beings were originally "like the ministering angels, who are immortal," but adds: "Yet, after all this greatness, *you* wanted to die!"[30] The latter sentence bears a striking similarity in phrasing to what Valentinus says ("you wanted death to be divided to you . . ."). Yet the rabbinic passage is clearly concerned with the negative consequences of death, whereas Valentinus attached a positive value to it.

Justin and the two rabbinic passages share with each other the idea that an option to immortality was not only offered to Adam and Eve but is also offered to all other human beings as well, though each of them has failed just like Adam and Eve did. This idea becomes more understandable, if one takes into account that, in Jewish Wisdom literature, immortality is often dealt with from an ethical point of view. Immortality is connected to the keeping of the law (Wis 6:18).[31] Death brings all people together (Sir 14:17; 17:2; 40:1–2; Wis 7:1), but human beings can also choose between death and life (Sir 15:17; cf. Wis 1:12). Death is associated with the ungodly, who "by their words and deeds summoned death" (Wis 1:16). The hope of the godly is, in contrast, "full of immortality" (Wis 3:4). This does not exclude their physical death (Wis 4:16), but this death is merely ostensible: "In the eyes of the foolish they seem to have died" (Wis 3:1).[32]

---

[28] Justin, *Dial.* 124.4; cf. Markschies, *Valentinus*, 129–30.

[29] *Exodus Rabbah* 23.1 (trans. Lehrman in H. Freedman and Maurice Simon, *Midrash Rabbah* [10 vols; London: Soncino, 1939–51]).

[30] *Numeri Rabbah* 16.24 (trans. Slotki in Freedman and Simon, *Midrash Rabbah*). For the two midrash interpretations mentioned above, see Jervell, *Imago Dei*, 88, 118.

[31] For a similar view in rabbinic writings, see Jervell, *Imago Dei*, 91, who sums up their view by saying that those keeping God's commands "will live forever in this world and in that to come."

[32] For views about death and immortality in the books of Sirach and Wisdom, see John J. Collins, "The Root of Immortality: Death in the Context of Jewish Wisdom," *HTR* 71 (1978): 177–2, and Michael Kolarcik, *The Ambiguity of Death in the Book of Wisdom 1–6: A Study of Literary Structure and Interpretation* (AnBib 127; Rome: Pontifical Biblical Institute, 1991).

In Jewish Wisdom literature, the hope of immortality is also connected with ruling over nations. In the Book of Wisdom, this expectation is associated with God's future judgement of the ungodly: "Love righteousness, you judges of the earth" (Wis 1:1).[33] The godly will receive from God signs of royal power (Wis 5:16), and they will reign together with God, as the ungodly and the nations will be condemned (Wis 3:8; 4:16). Paul has taken this idea up in 1 Corinthians (6:2–3). Nevertheless, he speaks only with sweeping irony of those who already "have been kings" (ἐβασιλεύσατε, 1 Cor 4:8). It is striking that in fragment 4 of Valentinus the future aspect associated with the believers' ruling over creation in this tradition is entirely lacking.

Valentinus was no doubt a representative of the Alexandrian exegetical tradition.[34] Therefore, it is also necessary to take into account Philo's views about immortality,[35] which are closely related to his interpretation of Genesis. Philo distinguishes between the human being made of clay (Gen 2:7), who is "by nature mortal," and the one made after the divine image (Gen 1:27), who is "by nature incorruptible." The divine breath is the soul supplied by the Father of all that makes the human being made out of clay alive. Hence Philo concludes that "the human being is the borderland between mortal and immortal nature, . . . mortal as to the body, but immortal as to the mind (κατὰ δὲ τὴν διάνοιαν)."[36]

In *Legum allegoriae*, Philo paints a more complex and dualistic picture of the human mind.[37] He identifies the earthly Adam not with the body, but with the mind (νοῦς) that is "made out of matter" (1.42). This "material" *nous* is "earthly and perishable" (1.90), and ignorant of itself (1.32). Hence, it would not understand the nature of God, "had not God himself drawn it up to himself" (1.38). The earthly *nous* needs to be made a living soul by means of God's breath. Philo's phrasing is notable at this point: "But this mind is earthly and in reality corruptible, *if* God would not breathe (εἰ μὴ ὁ θεός

---

[33] The RSV translation of οἱ κρίνοντες in Wis 1:1 as "rulers" is misleading.
[34] Cf. Markschies, *Valentinus*, 404.
[35] For Philo's views on death and immortality, see Erwin R. Goodenough, "Philo on Immortality," *HTR* 39 (1946): 85–108; Hans C. C. Cavallin, *An Enquiry into the Jewish Background* (vol. 1 of *Life after Death: Paul's Argument for the Resurrection of the Dead in 1 Cor 15*; ConBNT 7:1; Lund: Gleerup, 1974), 135–40; Sellin, *Streit*, 101–14, 135–36.
[36] *Opif.* 134–35.
[37] For this important difference between Philo's *Opif.* and *Leg.* see, especially, Sellin, *Streit* 99–101.

ἐμπνεύσειεν) into it the power of true life" (1.32). The latter sentence shows that Philo regards God's breathing as potential. He "does not speak here at all or not only about creation in the past but inspiration that is always possible . . . the human being (more exactly the nous) is immortal only insofar as it is inspired by pneuma."[38]

Philo's understanding of life and death is also ethically oriented. He associates immortality with a certain lifestyle rather than with a post-mortem state of human beings. Philo distinguishes "the death of the human being," which is "the separation of the soul from the body," from "the death of the soul," which is "the decay of virtue."[39] The latter is far more important to Philo than the former. Philo can also maintain that the servants of God "live immortal life" already, and the ungodly are likewise already dead in their souls.[40]

Immortality also means to Philo that invisible things are preferred to the visible ones.[41] Thus, immortal life involves detachment from the world and visible things through ascetic behavior, heavenly ascent of the *nous*, and pneumatic inspiration.[42] The most concrete example of Philo's view about how immortality can already be obtained in this life on earth is his idealizing account of the Jewish group of Therapeutae.[43] They "considered their mortal life already ended" (τετελευτηκέναι νομίζοντες ἤδη τὸν θνητὸν βίον). What this meant in practice can be seen in the fact that they abandoned their property, which they left to their children and relatives.[44] They preferred a life in simplicity,[45] and withdrew themselves from big cities, their families, kin and home countries in order to seek wisdom in solitude and to praise God in weekly gatherings of the like-minded.[46]

---

[38] Sellin, *Streit*, 104–5 (my trans.).
[39] *Leg.* 1.106; cf. Sellin, *Streit*, 135–36.
[40] *Spec.* 1.345.
[41] This recalls Plato's view about the philosopher's role (e.g., *Phaed.* 67e; 114de); cf. Goodenough, "Philo on Immortality," 93, 106.
[42] Sellin, *Streit*, 137–55.
[43] For the relationship of Philo's Therapeutae to the Essenes, which has been a debated issue, see Geza Vermes and Martin D. Goodman, eds., *The Essenes According to Classical Sources* (Sheffield: Sheffield Academic Press, 1989), 15–17. Their conclusion is (p. 17): "the available evidence does not justify a complete identification of the Therapeutae and the Essenes/Qumran sectaries. The most likely conclusion is that the former represented an Egyptian off-shoot of the Palestinian ascetic movement of the Essenes."
[44] *Contempl.* 13.
[45] *Contempl.* 37–39.
[46] *Contempl.* 18–20, 30ff.

Valentinus is most likely closer to Philo's understanding of immortality than to some early Christian views about it. Valentinus does not hint at a concrete hope of immortality linked with the expectation of Jesus' immediate parousia, which is implied by Paul's correspondence with the Thessalonian Christians. It seems that they had expected Jesus' return to take place in so a near future that they did not reckon with the possibility that some members of their community would die before it came to pass (1 Thess 4:12–15). A similar expectation becomes visible also in the tradition of Jesus' sayings: "Truly I tell you, there are some standing here who will not taste death until they see that the kingdom of God has come with power" (Mark 9:1, RSV).[47]

The fragment of Valentinus does not contain clear allusions to sacraments either, although though they were associated with immortality by other early Christians. This understanding took the most concrete form in the teaching of Menander, who maintained that his baptism granted to his followers eternal youth and immunity from death.[48] Similar tendencies are visible in the baptismal teaching of deutero-Pauline authors. Already Paul drew an analogy between baptism and the death of Christ (Rom 6:4), but was careful not to claim that resurrection had already taken place in baptism. Instead, he emphasized an ethical linkage between resurrection and the Christian way of living.[49] The author of Colossians, however, argues that the believers not only have been buried with Christ in baptism, but also have been raised with him by God (Col 2:12). In a similar manner, the author of Ephesians maintains that believers have already been raised up with Christ (Eph 2:6; cf. 5:14).[50]

---

[47] Mark 9:1 does not necessarily imply a complete avoidance of death; it can also be understood in terms of prolongation of earthly life characteristic of the descriptions of the Messianic age already in prophetic books (e.g., Isa 65:20, 22). The saying was, in any case, subject to reinterpretation. Its placement at the beginning of the story of Jesus' transfiguration in Mark (9:2–9) suggests that the author of this gospel saw already in this story the fulfillment of Jesus' promise.

[48] Cf. Markschies, *Valentinus*, 131. For Menander, see Justin, *1 Apol.* 26.4; Irenaeus, *Haer.* 1.23.5; Tertullian, *An.* 50. Menander's baptism effecting immortality is, however, not mentioned by Justin, who offers the earliest account of him, but only in later accounts by Irenaeus and Tertullian. Yet Menander's promise that his followers will not suffer death at all appears already in Justin.

[49] For Paul's view about baptism, see especially A. J. M. Wedderburn, *Baptism and Resurrection: Studies in Pauline Theology against Its Graeco-Roman Background* (WUNT 44; Tübingen: Mohr, 1987). Markschies, *Valentinus*, 132, takes Rom 6:4 into account, but ignores Colossians and Ephesians at this point.

[50] The polemic in 2 Tim 2:18 levelled against those teaching that "the resurrection has already taken place" shows that this was a matter of debate among the followers of Paul.

In the Gospel of John, immortality is connected to the eucharist
(6:51–58). This view was shared by Ignatius, who considers the
eucharist to be a "medicine of immortality, a remedy preventing
dying (φάρμακον ἀθανασίας, ἀντίδοτος τοῦ μὴ ἀποθανεῖν)."[51] In John,
however, the sacramental association appears only in the aforemen-
tioned passage dealing with the eucharist. More prominent in John
is the affirmation that the believer already has "life" (10:10; 20:31)
or "eternal life" (3:15–16, 36; 5:24; 6:40, 47, 54). In addition, immortality is associated in John with believing in Jesus and keeping his
words. The Johannine view, therefore, has in common with Jewish
Wisdom literature and Philo the strong emphasis on the ethical aspect
associated with immortality. The Johannine Jesus promises that "whoever keeps my word will never see death" (8:51), and that "everyone who lives and believes in me will never die" (11:26).

Valentinus certainly knew Pauline letters, and he may have known
the Gospel of John as well. Nevertheless, he does not make any use
of the idea visible in them that sacraments, either baptism or eucharist,
provide immortality. It is possible, however, that the Johannine teaching of immortality that can be acquired already in one's lifetime
could have contributed to Valentinus's teaching. Yet the Gospel of
John does not bear witness to the original immortality of humankind,
which Valentinus presupposes. This gospel speaks, rather, of a transformation of the believer "from death to life" (5:24) that results from
hearing and believing in Jesus.

3. *Valentinus's Fragment and the* Gospel of Thomas

After this survey of other evidence, it is now time to turn to affinities
between Valentinus's fragment 4 and the *Gospel of Thomas*. Pagels has
argued that the bottom line of Genesis exegesis in the latter is that
the divine image given at creation is present in, and enables salvation
for, humankind. In *Thomas*, this interpretation involves a striking contrast between Adam and the recipients of the gospel. The description
of a person who after seeking and finding will "rule over all things"
(*Gos. Thom.* 2) recalls, says Pagels, "the birthright of Adam" described
in Gen 1:26–28. Nevertheless, it is said of Adam himself (*Gos. Thom.*
85) that "Adam came from great power and great wealth, but he

[51] Ignatius, *Eph.* 20.2.

was not worthy of you. For had he been worthy, [he would] not [have tasted] death."[52] While Adam got rid of his original immortality, it is promised to those who discover "the interpretation of these sayings" that they "will not taste death" (*Gos. Thom.* 1).[53]

The promise of immortality brings together Valentinus's fragment 4 and the *Gospel of Thomas*. In addition, in both cases the promise is followed by a similar affirmation that the addressees of their teaching will rule over either "all things" (*Gos. Thom.* 2) or "the world, the entire corruption" (Valentinus). Futhermore, immortality is also considered a present state in *Thomas*: "The dead are not alive, and the living will not die" (*Gos. Thom.* 11).[54] It is also noteworthy that Valentinus links immortality with "the beginning," while in *Thomas* immortality results from the discovery of the beginning (*Gos. Thom.* 18–19). Most importantly, however, Valentinus's interpretation is consistent with the idea in *Thomas* that the divine image was not lost in the fall but is still present in humankind. This idea is presupposed in Valentinus's insistence that his recipients *are* "immortal from the beginning" and "children of eternal life." Valentinus does not, apparently, discuss a mythic *Urmensch* here. His point is, rather, that all human beings (or at least the implied audience of his sermon) stem from the eternal realm. Also this point concurs with the Genesis exegesis of the *Gospel of Thomas* outlined above.

In fact, one could even consider the possibility whether Valentinus knew the *Gospel of Thomas*, for there seems to be an "argument of order": immortality and ruling over all things or over creation are affirmed in the same order by Valentinus and in *Gos. Thom.* 1–2. Yet this hypothesis cannot be proven with any certainty. The textual basis is too narrow, and there are not enough verbal agreements

---

[52] Translation from Marvin W. Meyer, *The Gospel of Thomas: The Hidden Sayings of Jesus* (San Francisco, CA: Harper, 1992).

[53] Cf. Pagels, "Exegesis of Genesis 1," 482. I find unlikely Stephen Johnson's suggestion that the expression "taste death" in John 8:52 indicates a Johannine reaction against the *Gospel of Thomas*; cf. Stephen R. Johnson, "The *Gospel of Thomas* 76:3 and Canonical Parallels: Three Segments in the Tradition History of the Saying," in *The Nag Hammadi Library after Fifty Years: Proceedings of the 1995 Society of Biblical Literature Commemoration* (ed. John D. Turner and Anne McGuire; NHMS 44; Leiden: Brill, 1997), 308–26. The expression seems to me too common to admit of any specific conclusions about the relationship between John and *Thomas* (cf. Mark 9:1; Heb 2:9; 4 Ezra 6:26; *C.H.* 10.8); cf. Jacques-É. Menard, *L'Évangile selon Thomas* (NHS 5; Leiden: Brill, 1975), 77.

[54] Trans. from Meyer, *Gospel of Thomas*.

between Valentinus and *Gos. Thom.* 1–2 that could lend additional support for this possibility. Nevertheless, it seems clear that Valentinus and *Thomas* drew upon similar traditions of Genesis exegesis. For even if we take into account other evidence from Hellenistic Jewish and early Christian writings discussed above, the interpretation of Genesis in *Thomas* offers by far the closest parallel to Valentinus' teaching of immortality in his fragment 4.

4. *Conclusion*

I have argued above that fragment 4 of Valentinus deals with the ideal relationship of his addressees to present reality rather than with contempt for martyrdom or for the eucharist, as Holzhausen and Schüngel have suggested respectively. Moreover, I have suggested that the fragment may reflect a view of the world as a place of education for those originally immortal, a view characteristic of Valentinus's followers. The fragment also implies detachment from the world, but it remains unclear whether Valentinus recommended to his audience any radical change in life style.

Fragment 4 of Valentinus offers an interpretation of Genesis that is strikingly similar to that in *Thomas*. Valentinus was, however, more inclined than *Thomas* to "gnostic" tendencies in his Genesis exegesis. We find no equivalent in *Thomas* to an idea attested in another fragment of Valentinus that the creator angels were hostile towards Adam. In this fragment, Valentinus argues that the angels tried to destroy (or hide) Adam, as they became aware of the superior essence deposited in him without their knowledge.[55] The fragment does not show what according to Valentinus happened to Adam's divine essence after the malevolent intervention of the creator angels. I think that there are basically two alternatives, if we take into account also what Valentinus says about immortality in fragment 4, as discussed above. Either it should be assumed that the angels could not deprive Adam of his divine essence, or that they managed to destroy Adam, but his loss was *not* inherited by later generations of humankind. The

---

[55] Valentinus, frag. 1 (Clement, *Strom.* 4.89.6–4.90.1; frag. C in Layton, *Gnostic Scriptures*, 234–35). I discuss this fragment and its affinities with the *Apocryphon of John* in my article "Valentinian Views about Adam's Creation: Valentinus and the *Gospel of Philip*" in *Lux Humana, Lux Aeterna* (FS Lars Aejmelaeus; ed. Antti Mustakallio, Heikki Leppä and Heikki Räisänen; Publications of the Finnish Exegetical Society 89; Helsinki: The Finnish Exegetical Society, 2005), 509–27.

latter alternative would be in line with the view discussed above that
each human being has personally "chosen" to become like Adam
and is now subject to death not because of Adam but because of
his or her own choice. In addition to the passages in Justin and rabbinic writings mentioned above, this view is implicated also in *Thomas's*
contention that Adam was "not worthy of you" (*Gos. Thom.* 85).

The idea that most clearly connected the interpretations of Genesis
of Valentinus and *Thomas* to each other was that of dominion over
all things. This idea was linked with Gen 1:26–28 already in Jewish
Wisdom literature.[56] The dominion of humankind over animals in
paradise is recalled, for example, in Sir 17:4 and Wis 9:2. In Wis 10:2,
this passage is already understood in the sense that Wisdom gave Adam
"strength to rule over all things (κρατῆσαι ἁπάντων)." Nevertheless,
neither *Thomas* nor Valentinus explains the dominion over all things
in terms of the believers' co-reigning with God at the final judgement, as was done in the Book of Wisdom.[57] I find it likely that
they subscribe, rather, to a well-known philosophical tradi-tion that
a sage is the real ruler of all things. This tradition was also embraced
by Philo: "the sage alone is a ruler and king, and virtue a rule and
a kingship whose authority is final."[58] His interpretation of Gen 12:1
("Now the Lord said to Abraham, 'Go from your land and your
kindred and your father's house'") shows nicely that what is at stake
in this tradition is human beings' control over themselves:[59]

> Make yourself a stranger to them (body, sense perception, and speech)
> in judgement and purpose; let none of them cling to you; rise supe-
> rior to them all; they are your subjects, never treat them as sovereign
> lords; you are a king, school yourself once and for all to rule, not to
> be ruled; evermore be coming to know yourself.

"Ruling" is, hence, understood by Philo in terms of one's escape from
the body and its pleasures, from reliance on the senses, and from
uttered speech.[60] This understanding of dominion as self-control goes
back to Plato,[61] and was common coin in antiquity.[62]

---

[56] Cf. Jervell, *Imago Dei*, 24–26.
[57] See above p. 230.
[58] *Somn.* 2.244; cf. Burton L. Mack, "The Kingdom Sayings in Mark," *Forum* 3:1
(1987): 3–47, esp. 12–13.
[59] *Migr.* 7–8; cf. Sellin, *Streit*, 155.
[60] *Migr.* 9–12.
[61] *Res.* 580cd.
[62] For this idea in antiquity, see Michel Foucault, *The Use of Pleasure* (vol. 2 of

For Philo, being a ruler over all things involves first and foremost escape "from pleasures and desires (ἡδονὰς καὶ ἐπιθυμίας) that act as (the body's) jailers."[63] Liberation from emotions is, thus, one possible framework against which ancient educated readers could have understood the promise in *Thomas* of dominion over all things. It is not far-fetched to think that this was how Valentinians conceived of ruling over all things, for the idea of the extirpation of emotions is well attested for them. Valentinus himself thought that the Son must cleanse the human heart from "improper desires" (ἐπιθυμίαις οὐ προσηκούσαις) by which evil spirits torture it.[64] It may be guessed, therefore, that Valentinus's futher exposition of what the dominion "over the entire corruption" means included a discussion of emotions and their extirpation. This guess, however, goes far beyond what we can really know on the basis of our very limited access to Valentinus' teachings. In any case, this is certainly one of the ways the followers of Valentinus may have understood his teaching of immortality. For the way they elaborated the myth of Sophia shows their keen interest in contemporary philosophical school opinions about emotions and their extirpation.[65]

The History of Sexuality; trans. R. Hurley; London: Penguin, 1992), 78–82. One example of this idea is Epictetus's distinction between the things "under our control" and those "not under our control"; the former consist of "moral purpose," while the latter includes the body, possessions, family, and country (*Diatr.* 1.22.10). For a discussion of this passage and its relationship to *Thomas*, see Risto Uro, *Thomas: Seeking the Historical Context of the Gospel of Thomas* (London: Clark, 2003), 54–79.

[63] *Migr.* 9.

[64] Valentinus, frag. 2 (Clement, *Strom.* 2.114.3–6; frag. H in Layton, *Gnostic Scriptures*, 244–45).

[65] This aspect looms large in the Valentinian myth of Sophia, as can be seen, e.g., in Irenaeus, *Haer.* 1.4.1–2, 1.4.5.

CHAPTER ELEVEN

THE ROLE AND SIGNIFICANCE OF THE CHARACTER OF THOMAS IN THE *ACTS OF THOMAS*

PATRICK J. HARTIN

This study approaches the *Acts of Thomas* as a literary text by analyzing it from a narrative critical perspective.[1] The author of the *Acts of Thomas* has chosen the literary genre of a narrative over that of other possible genres to communicate a specific understanding of the Christian message. This examination focuses on the distinctive character of Thomas within the *Acts of Thomas*. Two aspects form the center of this consideration: the role that Thomas plays in the narrative and his self-awareness. In particular, I wish to draw out the implications this examination has for the reader in order to show how this narrative contributes toward the reader's self-understanding of Jesus, the source of divine inspiration; and of God, the Father of all.

1. *The Genre and Function of the* Acts of Thomas

The classification of a writing as a literary genre is not an end in itself. It is a heuristic tool that is used in order to make sense of a text through a comparison with other writings of a similar nature. The identification of a work's genre helps to understand its message more

---

[1] In studies on the apocryphal acts, attention has focused largely on issues related to the texts of the documents; to their connection with tradition; to an examination of their social world; to their reception over time; and to their intertextuality. See for example, the excellent articles in Dennis Ronald MacDonald, Jr., ed., *The Apocryphal Acts of Apostles* (Semeia 38; Atlanta, GA: Scholars Press, 1986) and Robert F. Stoops Jr. and Dennis R. MacDonald, Jr., eds., *The Apocryphal Acts of the Apostles in Intertextual Perspectives* (Semeia 80; Atlanta, GA: Scholars Press, 1997). One of the characteristics of the *Acts of Thomas* (as well as that of most of the other Acts) is that they are self-contained texts. See François Bovon and Eric Junod, "Reading the Apocryphal Acts of the Apostles," in MacDonald, *The Apocryphal Acts of Apostles*, 171. The world of the text is self explanatory and self-referential. Therefore, it is important to examine the text in itself and to allow the text to speak for itself.

clearly since a writer deliberately selects a specific structure to facil-
itate the intended purpose of this communication. As Luke Timothy
Johnson has argued in his commentary on the letter of James, "function follows form."[2] In fact, form, content and function are deter-
minative for any specific genre.[3]

The study of the canonical gospels has shown that in choosing
the literary genre of a narrative, the authors utilized the *form* of a
narrative (containing the ingredients of characters, plot, and setting)
to express a *content* that focuses upon the traditions related to the
person and message of and about Jesus of Nazareth,[4] for the *purpose*
of communicating to readers an understanding of their own life and
faith seen against the background of this narrative.[5] Their function
is not to provide a journalistic account of the life and ministry of
Jesus of Nazareth. Rather, the function is orientated toward illuminating
and challenging the faith commitment of a community of readers.

In an analogous way, we can speak about the genre of the *Acts
of Thomas* as that of a narrative. As such, *form, content and function* contribute toward a correct understanding of its genre. The *Acts of Thomas*
conforms to the form of a narrative in that its overarching structure
embraces the elements of a story-line where characters and setting
all interact in the communication process. The content of the narrative focuses on the interpretation of materials and traditions related
to the apostle Thomas. As in the case of the canonical gospels, the
narrative aims at providing instructions for the readers of the *Acts
of Thomas* with direction for their own life and faith situations. The
function is not to provide a diary of the life and deeds of the apostle Thomas. Instead, it intends to illuminate the reader's discipleship
through a reflection on the discipleship of the apostle Thomas.

---

[2] Luke Timothy Johnson, *The Letter of James: A New Translation with Introduction and
Commentary* (AB 37A; New York, NY: Doubleday, 1995), 16.

[3] As John J. Collins has observed ("Introduction: Towards the Morphology of a
Genre," in *Apocalypse: The Morphology of a Genre* [ed. Adela Yarbro Collins; Semeia
14; Missoula, MT: Scholars Press, 1979], 1–20). See also Adela Yarbro Collins,
"Introduction: Early Christian Apocalypticism," in *Early Christian Apocalypticism: Genre
and Social Setting* (ed. Adela Yarbro Collins; Semeia 36; Atlanta, GA: Scholars Press,
1986), 1–11.

[4] See Helmut Koester, *Ancient Christian Gospels: Their History and Development* (Philadelphia, PA: Trinity Press International, 1990), 46.

[5] For example, the Gospel of John articulates its function in this way: these things
"are written so that you may come to believe that Jesus is the Messiah, the Son
of God, and that through believing you may have life in his name" (John 20:31).

This function also helps the reader understand why the author of this narrative includes not just the usual narrative characteristics, but also includes other secondary forms such as sermons, prayers, speeches, hymns and liturgical elements.[6] These sub-forms illuminate the function or purpose of the narrative more fully. Through sermons and prayers, in particular, the author is able to develop a consciousness of certain important themes.[7] Without doubt this adds further support to the view that this writing is not intended to be read in a one-dimensional way as a simple account of the trials and joys of the deeds of the apostle Thomas. Instead, the narrative functions much in the manner of an allegory whereby the faith and life of a community of readers are instructed more deeply and fully.[8] While the main function of this work teaches and calls readers to an awareness and implementation of certain values, it does so through the ability that every narrative has to entertain.[9] However, the entertainment value is not the main and exclusive function of the *Acts of Thomas*, as some commentators have been accustomed to argue, when they have categorized it as "popular literature."[10]

The *Acts of Thomas*, as with the other apocryphal Acts of that period, are not to be viewed as peripheral writings, but as ones that had a significant importance and influence on the religious thought and action of the communities for whom they were composed. The *Acts* gave direction and shape to the lives of their Christian readers.[11]

---

[6] Harold W. Attridge, "Intertextuality in the *Acts of Thomas*," in Stoops and MacDonald, *The Apocryphal Acts of The Apostles*, 88.

[7] See Michael LaFargue, *Language and Gnosis: The Opening Scenes of the Acts of Thomas* (HDR 8; Philadelphia, PA: Fortress, 1985), 58.

[8] I am indebted for this insight to LaFargue (*Language and Gnosis*, 214).

[9] "The *Acts of Thomas* is literature that seeks to instruct and inculcate values while it entertains," Harold W. Attridge, "Paul and the Domestication of Thomas," in *Theology and Ethics: Paul and His Interpreters* (ed. Eugene H. Lovering; Nashville, TN: Abingdon, 1996), 225.

[10] As H. J. W. Drijvers explains: "It therefore does not seem justified to describe the ATh—as is widely done—as popular literature, in which we can recognize motifs of the ancient novel in a popular and crude form. Rather they came into being in a learned milieu, to which symbolism and typology were familiar and in which a certain form of biblical exegesis had already developed, which comes to light also in other writings from the same area in space and time" ("The *Acts of Thomas*," in *Writings Relating to the Apostles; Apocalypses and Related Subjects* [vol. 2 of *New Testament Apocrypha*; revised ed. by Wilhelm Schneemelcher; English trans. R. McL. Wilson; Louisville, KY: Westminster John Knox, 1992], 322–23).

[11] As Averil Cameron says: "They provided for Christians a set of texts in which the Christian self was expounded, first in narrative terms and then in terms of

In the brief examination of the character of Thomas that follows, the intention is to illuminate how the function of this narrative shapes the lives of the readers out of which it arises and for whom it is written.

2. *The Character of Thomas*

The Role That the Character of Thomas Plays in the Narrative

The apostle's role is predominantly that of an agent for the transcendent God. His task is to reveal Christ and to carry out God's plan of salvation. His role illustrates what it means to be a disciple and how this discipleship is carried out in practice. He exercises his role through what he says (particularly through his prayers) and what he does (his miracles). His deeds culminate in a death that is described in terms reminiscent of the death of Jesus.

Judas Thomas (also called Didymus) is first introduced in the narrative as an apostle. In the opening "vocational scene"[12] Thomas is chosen by lot to go to India. He is very reluctant and raises a number of objections. He remarks: "Wherever you wish to send me, send me, but elsewhere. For I am not going to the Indians" (*Acts Thom.* 1).[13] This is reminiscent of the vocational scenes of Moses in his encounter with God at the burning bush (Exodus 3) or perhaps more directly that of Jonah (1:1–17) where objections are raised to the mission God had entrusted to them.

Judas Thomas is, then, sold by Jesus to the merchant Abban. In this sale the reader comes to discover one of the central motifs of the entire writing: as the slave of Jesus, who purchased him by his death on the cross,[14] Thomas' task is to do Jesus' will. Three themes emerge from this idea of being the slave or servant of Jesus.

---

asceticism; the writing of Christian texts would shape Christian lives" (*Christianity and the Rhetoric of Empire: The Development of Christian Discourse* [Sather Classical Lectures 55; Berkeley, CA: The University of California Press, 1991], 116).

[12] LaFargue, *Language and Gnosis*, 65.

[13] The translation of the *Acts of Thomas* that is quoted here (unless otherwise noted) is that of John K. Elliott, "The *Acts of Thomas*," in *The Apocryphal New Testament* (ed. J. K. Elliott; Oxford: Clarendon, 1993), 439–511.

[14] See *Acts Thom.* 72: "Jesus, who has taken a form and become like a man and appeared to all of us in order not to separate us from your love; Lord, you are he

It shows, first of all, that the life of the apostle is *under the control and direction of the Lord*: his will accomplishes everything.[15] True riches emanate from his relationship with Jesus. This contributes to a sense of alienation from the world and shows that his ascetic message, particularly in relation to sexuality and marriage, has as its foundation his union with the Lord. This serves as an illustration for all Christians in their vision of the world: they are to "Become passers-by" as the *Gospel of Thomas* expresses it.[16] Thomas leads a life[17] that demonstrates a basic detachment from all things earthly. His asceticism first emerges in the context of the wedding celebration in Act One where he refrains from eating and drinking. This asceticism derives from his understanding of the relation between the heavenly and earthly realms (*Acts Thom.* 5–7). In the first act the bridal couple is led to understand that they are in a heavenly marriage with Christ. This explains why intercourse is to be shunned for it is a renunciation of one's union with Christ.[18] Every person is called to return to the original

---

who has given himself for us and has bought us with a price by his blood, as a precious possession. But what have we, Lord, to offer in exchange for your life which you have given for us? For what we have is your gift."

[15] As Thomas continues to pray: "You are he who from my youth gave me patience in temptation and sowed in me life and preserved me from corruption; you are he who brought me into the poverty of this world and filled me with the true riches; you are he who showed me that I was yours: wherefore I was never joined to a wife, that the temple worthy of you might not be found in pollution" (*Acts Thom.* 144). This gives a specific focus to the *Acts of Thomas*: Jesus has brought him into this world and protects him from the world's evil assaults.

[16] *Gos. Thom.* 42. The translation of the *Gospel of Thomas* that is quoted in this article is from Stephen J. Patterson, James M. Robinson and Hans-Gebhard Bethge, *The Fifth Gospel: The Gospel of Thomas Comes of Age* (Harrisburg, PA: Trinity Press International, 1998).

[17] As the servant of Jesus, Thomas' task is to make God and Christ known in the world. Jesus is the one who initiates this revelatory process (as is seen in the initial sale of Thomas). He is the one who works through Thomas in his miracles and in his prayers and speeches. And, ultimately, Jesus is the one who is made known. This emerges clearly in the opening scene where Thomas sets off with the merchant, Abban: "And he went to the merchant, Abban, carrying nothing at all with him, but only his price. For the Lord had given it to him, saying, 'Let your worth also be with you along with my grace, wherever you may go'" (*Acts Thom.* 3). Jesus' gift of the purchase price to Thomas is connected with the grace Jesus bestows on Thomas that enables him to make Jesus known. Jesus grants Thomas that power and grace to overcome his initial fear of being a foreigner, preaching in a strange land. As LaFargue says: "Jesus is giving Thomas the status, the authority which will later enable him to actually exert power in Andrapolis rather than remain a vulnerable foreigner" (*Language and Gnosis*, 179).

[18] Thomas expresses this thought well when he says later of Mygdonia in the narrative: "If the Lord has truly and indeed risen in her soul and she has received

state of union with Christ. At the beginning of the human condition human beings were in union with God. The secret of life is to
become again what one once was.[19]

Secondly, as servant of the Lord, Thomas sees his entire existence
as devoted *to doing the will of his master*. Despite previous objections
to his mission to India, Thomas ultimately submits and accepts Jesus'
will: "I go wherever you wish, O Lord Jesus, your will be done"
(*Acts Thom.* 3). As Harold Attridge has noted,[20] a type of *inclusio* is
created at the end of the narrative when chapter 144 returns to the
theme of doing God's will. There Thomas prays the Our Father and
concludes with the statement: "I pray your prayer and bring your
will to fulfilment: be with me to the end." When he comes to the
wedding banquet, the apostle explains why he is not eating or drinking
at the meal: "For something greater than food or even drink have I
come here, that I might accomplish the will of the king" (*Acts Thom.* 5).
This same theme of doing the will of the Lord occurs over and over
again as a reminder to the reader of what the follower of Jesus is
called to do.[21] This is the essence of Thomas' life, and by implication that of every follower of Jesus, namely to do the will of the one
who called and sent him.

Thirdly, as servant of the Lord Jesus, the life of Thomas takes on
a life of *imitation of the life of his master*. *Preaching* (for example, his
preaching to the crowds after the healing of the young man bitten
by a serpent [*Acts Thom.* 37]), *teaching* (his instruction of Mygdonia
to refrain from intercourse in the Ninth Act [*Acts Thom.* 82–118]),
miracles (for example, the healing of the young man who had been
bitten by a serpent [*Acts Thom.* 33]), *death*: these are all elements that
reflect this imitation.[22] Like Jesus in Paul's hymn in Phil 2:7, Thomas
has taken on the form of a slave, and like Jesus, Thomas gives his
life to bring freedom to those to whom he ministers.

---

the sown seed, she will neither care for this earthly life nor fear death, nor will
Charisius be able to harm her in any way. For he whom she has received into her
soul is greater, if indeed she has truly received him" (*Acts Thom.* 93).

[19] See Drijvers, *Acts of Thomas*, 329.

[20] Attridge, "Intertextuality in the *Acts of Thomas*," 114.

[21] As the wild asses prophesy: "This man is his apostle, the revealer of truth. It
is he who does the will of him who sent him" (*Acts Thom.* 79).

[22] The colt of an ass draws attention to this when addressing Thomas: "Fellow
worker of the Son of God, who though free, has been a servant, and being sold,
has brought many to freedom" (*Acts Thom.* 39).

While Thomas' words bear special efficacy, so do his deeds—they demonstrate God's power working through him. Especially in his death Thomas carries out his imitation of Jesus to the full. The opening scene of the *Acts of Thomas* gives a premonition of what is to occur. His sale into captivity was a reminder of the sale of Jesus through Judas's betrayal. The roles are now reversed since the Lord sells Judas Thomas into captivity and gives him his purchase price. The reference to Thomas as Judas here shows perhaps that an allusion to Judas Iscariot is intended. There is also possibly an allusion to Genesis 37 where Joseph was sold into slavery by his brothers.[23] Like Jesus, Thomas prays before his death (*Acts Thom.* 144–148) and welcomes death as an acceptance of Christ's will for him.[24] The narrative continues to describe Thomas' death as an imitation of that of Jesus by setting his death outside the city where he is speared to death: "He therefore took him and went out of the city, and armed soldiers also went with him" (*Acts Thom.* 164). This would have reminded the readers of the occasion when the Roman soldier pierced the side of Jesus. Finally, like Jesus, Thomas appears to his followers Siphor and Vazan and tells them that he has ascended.[25]

The role that the character of Thomas plays in the narrative brings the reader to an awareness that what is being described in the story is more than simply a record of the adventures of Thomas in foreign lands. While the narrative reads like a novel, it contains many allusions that call for an understanding that moves beyond the literal. The contrast is drawn between life in this world, which is subject to death, sexuality and the desires that bring frustration and conflict, and the spiritual, heavenly, immortal existence. God originally created human nature as immortal. Thomas' preaching and activity aim at restoring humanity to that original condition. This is achieved through the process of an asceticism that aims at rediscovering and rekindling

---

[23] The reference to Egypt is introduced here for the first time. The theme of slavery and salvation connected with Egypt will return later in the *Hymn of the Pearl*. See Drijvers, "*Acts of Thomas*," 326–27.

[24] "I do accomplish his will. For if I had willed not to die, I know in Christ that I am able; but this which is called death is not death, but a setting free from the body; wherefore I receive gladly this setting free from the body, that I may depart and see him . . . for I have endured much toil in his service and have laboured for his grace that is come upon me and does not depart from me" (*Acts Thom.* 160).

[25] "Why do you sit here and keep watch over me? I am not here but I have gone up and received all that I was promised. But rise up and go down hence; for after a little time you also shall be gathered to me" (*Acts Thom.* 169).

that original situation.[26] On the basic level, Christian life is understood as an eschatological journey on which the Lord Jesus accompanies his servants in this dangerous world. As Thomas prays: "My
Lord and my God, who accompanies his servants, guide and leader
of those who believe in him . . ." (*Acts Thom.* 10). I think LaFargue's
insight into the "allegorical nature of Thomas' journey" is to endorsed.[27]
The world in which the apostle moves is hostile not just to him but
also to God. Human beings in this world have become slaves of sin.
The journey of Thomas challenges the reader to return to that union
with God symbolized metaphorically by the image of a marriage.
This heavenly marriage restores the original status and liberates one
from the world.[28] The *Hymn of the Pearl*, as I shall indicate below,
gives further expression to this interpretation of the *Acts of Thomas*.

Thomas' Self-Awareness

Thomas' self-awareness emerges through an examination of his relationship with Jesus. Thomas is presented as the twin of Jesus, similar
in appearance (*Acts Thom.* 11; 34), who shares in Jesus' work of salvation (*Acts Thom.* 39). Thomas is the earthly representative of Jesus
in heaven—in this way he is Jesus' alter ego: "He saw the Lord
Jesus talking with the bride. He had the appearance of Judas Thomas,
the apostle" (*Acts Thom.* 11). As the twin of Jesus,[29] Thomas' experiences
are similar to those of Jesus and even his words quote Jesus' sayings:[30]

---

[26] See Drijvers, "*Acts of Thomas*," 328.

[27] LaFargue, *Language and Gnosis*, 89.

[28] As Mygdonia says to her husband Charisius: "You are a bridegroom who
passes away and is destroyed, but Jesus is the true bridegroom, remaining immortal in eternity. That bridal gift was treasures and garments which grow old; this,
however, is living words which never pass away" (*Acts Thom.* 124).

[29] While Thomas never refers to himself as the twin of Jesus, this is the way in
which others come to recognize him: "Twin brother of Christ, apostle of the Most
High" (*Acts Thom.* 39). Even Jesus speaks of Thomas as his brother: "I am not Judas
Thomas, I am his brother. . . . Remember, my children, what my brother said to you,
and to whom he commended you" (*Acts Thom.* 11–12). On a number of occasions
Jesus changes into Thomas (*Acts Thom.* 11, 54, 55, 57, 118, 151). This gives further
support for the tradition within Syriac Christianity that their disciple, Thomas, was
the Twin of Jesus. As A. F. J. Klijn says: "It is however, quite clear that Thomas
is identical with Christ as far as both of them are able to preach the new preaching
of life. The conquest of the devil, was something which could only be done by Christ.
Therefore it was necessary to say that Thomas was not Christ (65, 100)" (*The Acts
of Thomas: Introduction—Text—Commentary* [NovTSup 5; Leiden: Brill, 1962], 37).

[30] In a scene reminiscent of the disciples sending people away (Luke 18:15), the

"And to the multitudes he said, 'He who has ears to hear, let him hear;' and 'Come to me all who labour and are heavy laden, and I will give you rest'" (*Acts Thom.* 82). As the twin of Jesus, Thomas understands that he is able to speak on Jesus' behalf and to make promises that reflect Jesus' mind: "And the apostle said to her, 'Even if I go away, I shall not leave you alone, but Jesus will be with you because of his compassion'" (*Acts Thom.* 88).

Thomas is also the recipient of special revelations and secret knowledge as well as the transmitter of this knowledge (*Acts Thom.* 10; 39; 47; and 78).[31] This picture of Jesus communicating secret knowledge to Thomas also lies at the heart of the *Gospel of Thomas* as the prologue to that sayings collection reveals.[32] *The Book of Thomas the Contender* also shows the same relationship of Thomas to Jesus as the recipient of special revelation.[33] Without doubt this understanding of the figure of Thomas is one that is at the heart of all the Thomasine literature.

From the above, we can deduce the following regarding Thomas' self-awareness. He is conscious of his origin, his mission and his destiny. As the slave of Jesus, he knows that he is in a special relationship with Jesus. However, by being sold into slavery in this world, he experiences a separation from the heavenly realm. He maintains his union with Jesus through his asceticism. His task is to act in the

---

Acts of Thomas says: "Why do you make those go away who come to hear the word and show willingness for it? You wish to be near me, whereas you are far off—as it has been said of the people who came to the Lord: 'Having eyes you see not, and having ears you hear not'" (*Acts Thom.* 82).

[31] See, for example, *Acts Thom.* 47: "Jesus, hidden mystery which has been revealed to us; you are he who made known to us many secrets, who separated me from all my companions and told me three words with which I am inflamed, but which I cannot communicate to others." Here the *Acts of Thomas* alludes to the three words that Jesus spoke to Thomas in the *Gospel of Thomas*: "Jesus took him (Thomas), (and) withdrew, (and) he said three words to him. But when Thomas came back to his companions, they asked him: 'What did Jesus say to you?' Thomas said to them, 'If I tell you one of the words he said to me, you will pick up stones and throw them at me, and fire will come out of the stones (and) burn you up'" (*Gos. Thom.* 13).

[32] "These are the hidden words that the living Jesus spoke. And Didymos Judas Thomas wrote them down" (*Gos. Thom., Incipit*).

[33] The prologue of the *Book of Thomas the Contender* introduces the writing in this way: "The secret words that the savior spoke to Judas Thomas which I, even I Mathaias, wrote down, while I was walking, listening to them speak with one another" (John D. Turner, trans., "The Book of Thomas the Contender," in *The Origin of the World, Expository Treatise, On the Soul, Book of Thomas the Contender* [vol. 2 of *Nag Hammadi Codex II, 2–7 together with XIII, 2*, Brit. Lib. Or. 4926(1), and P. Oxy. 1, 654, 655*; ed. Bentley Layton; NHS 21; Leiden: Brill, 1989], 181).

manner of his brother, as his representative in bringing humanity to
an awareness of the heavenly realm to which they are called and to
challenge his readers to act in this world in an ascetical way that
will regain that union. He is in a unique relation with Jesus as the
recipient of a special knowledge. His destiny is to suffer in the manner in which Jesus suffers and ultimately to return to union with
Jesus in the heavenly realm.

St. Ephrem shows how this twinship was understood in the context
of the Syriac Church.[34] It was viewed not as an ontological or physical twinship, but as a twinship that derives from action and spiritual
grace in which the apostle acts in an identical way to that of Jesus.
"I could do it indeed through the name of Jesus" (*Acts Thom.* 41).[35]

The *Gospel of Thomas* contains a saying that expresses the concept
of a heavenly likeness that reflects one's true likeness: "Jesus says:
'When you see your likeness you are full of joy. But when you see
your likenesses that came into existence before you—they neither die
nor become manifest—how much you will bear?'" (*Gos. Thom.* 84).
The concept of twinship gives expression to the understanding that
in the earthly realm humanity is separated from its divine origin and
that human beings must return to that true source in order to be
fully human. On earth Thomas is the visible representation of Jesus.
He is aware of his bondage to the Lord and seeks to carry out fully
the will of Jesus. Symbolically, being sold into slavery to Abban represents his entry into the human world and his separation from the
divine. His journeys lead people to discover their divine origin and
destiny. Ultimately, when Thomas returns to the Lord in his ascension, he is reunited with the divine.[36]

The relationship between Thomas and Jesus as his twin has a particular relevance for the readers of this narrative in the context of
the world of Syriac Christianity. In an allegorical way through a
reflection on the life of the apostle the writer shows them what their
own origin and mission are and where their destiny lies.[37]

---

[34] See Joseph Kallarangatt, "The *Acts of Thomas* Deserves More Theological and
Ecclesiological Attention," *Christian Orient* 17 (1986): 9.

[35] His double names also place him in the same category of those apostles who
also have bilingual names such as Simon Peter, Saul Paul and John Mark. As such
he holds an importance within the body of Christian apostles.

[36] "Why do you sit here and keep watch over me? I am not here but I have
gone up and received all that I was promised" (*Acts Thom.* 169).

[37] "What was thought and written in this milieu is the property of a spiritual

The Hymn of the Pearl

At the heart of this narrative lies the *Hymn of the Pearl*. Although scholars argue about many aspects such as its independent existence[38] and its interpretation, nevertheless its present position in the context of the *Acts of Thomas* provides a wonderful commentary and illustration of the basic message of the *Acts of Thomas*. Just as Thomas calls for an awareness of one's origin, mission and destiny, so too this hymn provides a poetic and imaginative illustration of the discovery of one's true self. Its importance lies in the fact that it provides an allegory for the life journey of Thomas and of every believer.[39]

A key to interpreting the allegorical meaning of this hymn is found in lines 75 through 78:

> But I could not recall my splendour,
> For it had been when I was still a child and quite young that I had
>   left it behind in my father's palace.
> But, when suddenly I saw my garment reflected as in a mirror,
> I perceived in it my whole self as well
> And through it I knew and saw myself.
> For though we originated from the one and the same we were partially
>   divided,
> Then again we were one, with a single form.

The focus in this hymn rests on the robe and not on the pearl. The beautiful robe reflects the prince's true self: it is his "mirror image."[40]

---

elite which was conversant with contemporary culture and found an answer of its own to the questions of human existence. The apostle Judas Thomas, his deeds and his teaching, are a part of the answer, a symbolic and religious composition about the divine Spirit which is the twin brother of man, and with whom he must unite in order to become fully man again" (Drijvers, "*Acts of Thomas*," 337).

[38] Bentley Layton, *The Gnostic Scriptures: A New Translation with Annotations and Introductions* (Garden City; NY: Doubleday 1987), 367–69.

[39] The hymn (*Acts Thom.* 108–13) presents an allegorical "folktale" (Layton, *Gnostic Scriptures*, 369) about salvation. It tells the story of a king's son who was sent from his parent's home to Egypt to bring back a pearl that was being guarded by a serpent. He has to leave behind him a beautiful robe that his parents promise he will inherit on his return. During the course of his trip to Egypt, he forgets his royal heritage and his mission. His parents, aware of what has happened, send him a letter to remind him of his origin, his mission and his destiny. He then completes his mission and returns home from Egypt with the pearl. His parents send him the robe to meet him on his return journey. In this robe he recognizes his true self. Clothed in this robe that bore the "image of the King of Kings" (line 86) he enters the court of his father.

[40] See Patrick J. Hartin, "The Search for the True Self in the *Gospel of Thomas*, the *Book of Thomas* and the *Hymn of the Pearl*," *HvTSt* 55 (1999): 1015.

It gives expression to the basic notion of the *Acts of Thomas* that one's earthly self is related to a heavenly counterpart, a heavenly double or twin. At death, one is reunited with this heavenly counterpart. This allegorical story symbolizes the search for one's true self. It describes how one is separated from one's true nature and how one regains this union. This theme is very similar to that of the *Acts of Thomas*: the separation of oneself from one's true being, one's entry into this hostile world, and ultimately one's triumph over the forces of this world whereby one returns to the heavenly abode and union with one's true self. As Drijvers expresses it: "The main theme of the Hymn of the Pearl is exactly that of the ATh, man's return from the demonic world to that condition in which God created him, and his reunion with his brother Christ, with whom he will be heir in the kingdom (lines 15, 48, 78)."[41]

The description of the prince clothed in his robe and his entry into heaven could very easily be a description of Thomas' return and reunion with his twin, Jesus:

> And I covered myself completely with my royal robe over it.
> When I had put it on I ascended to the land of peace and homage.
> And I lowered my head and prostrated myself before the splendour of
>   the father who had sent it to me.
> For it was I who had obeyed his commands
> And it was I who had also kept the promise,
> And I mingled at the doors of his ancient royal building.
> He took delight in me and received me in his palace (lines 97–102).

Both the *Acts of Thomas* and the *Hymn of the Pearl* reflect a common understanding that in this earthly existence one experiences a sense of alienation from this world and separation from one's true self, the heavenly image or counterpart with whom the self will be reunited after death. The character of Thomas and the figure of the prince in the hymn are both allegorical examples for all believers: they live in this world with a feeling of alienation and they strive to attain the heavenly world where they will be reunited with their heavenly image.

---

[41] Drijvers, "*Acts of Thomas*," 332.

3. *Relevance for the Reader*

How does this understanding of the role and the self-awareness of the character of Thomas relate to the reader? The allegorical function of the narrative brings readers to an awareness of their own practical discipleship. In this way the narrative helps to shape readers' lives.[42] From the narrative of the deeds and words of the apostle Thomas, the reader is led to an awareness of a number of important attitudes that determine his or her life. As LaFargue says: "Specifically, the thought expressed in the *Acts Thom.* is interesting as a 'hermeneutics of experience.' It advocates a certain way of interpreting and making sense of human experience generally."[43]

The following are among the most important insights that I see the *Acts of Thomas* expressing for the reader.[44] First, the relationship with Christ is to be valued above all things. The believer is united to Christ in an inseparable bond (*Acts Thom.* 12, 14, 61, 98, 158). This union is expressed through the imagery of a heavenly marriage with Christ (*Acts Thom.* 98). The whole criticism against sexual intercourse stems from this intimate awareness of union with Jesus—a union that must not be broken. This union shapes one's entire existence. The type of life that the apostle Thomas leads embraces a detachment from all earthly things and shows how this alienation can be overcome through asceticism. The reader has learned from Christ, as well as Thomas, that the way in which the evils of earthly existence can be overcome is through aceticism.[45]

Secondly, the Christian life is experienced as an eschatological journey on which one is accompanied by the Lord. This union with Christ is already evident in the earthly realm, but will flower forth into something greater in the world to come. The narratives always have a vision into the world that is to come.[46]

---

[42] See Cameron, *Christianity and the Rhetoric of Empire*, 116.

[43] LaFargue, *Language and Gnosis*, 206–7.

[44] As LaFargue, (*Language and Gnosis*, 214) notes, these attitudes are not to be seen as new ideas or themes of which the community who reads this narrative are unaware. Rather, these attitudes give concrete expression to attitudes and themes that they already hold as sacred.

[45] "Remember, my children, what my brother said to you, and to whom he commended you; and know that if you refrain from this filthy intercourse you become temples holy and pure, being released from afflictions and troubles, known and unknown, and you will not be involved in the cares of life and of children, whose end is destruction" (*Acts Thom.* 12; see also 28; 85; 86).

[46] Kallarangatt, "*Acts of Thomas*," 18.

Thirdly, twinship provides the theological motif for the relationship of the individual Christian to the inner divine source of the living Jesus. The concept of twinship, as well as the allegorical understanding of the *Hymn of the Pearl*, illustrate for the reader that in this earthly realm one experiences a separation from the divine source and origin, and that one is called to return to be reunited with the divine after death.

Fourthly, since Christians have been purchased through the blood of Jesus (*Acts Thom.* 72),[47] they, like Thomas, are slaves of Christ. The life of every believer must be led by the desire to do the will of the Lord. The believer responds out of gratitude by doing the Lord's will. After Jesus' ascension, his followers continue his work. They are to do exactly what Jesus came to do, namely, to show humanity's "real destination and descendance."[48]

Finally, The *Acts of Thomas* presents a clear awareness of the individual's threefold relationship.[49] It brings the believer to a realization of his or her true self that has an origin in the divine and is not at home in this world but is alienated from it. It communicates a true sense of the self's dependence upon Jesus who has saved one from the forces of evil and gives one the power and the grace to overcome the hostilities of this world. The self is called to experience that union with Jesus and to treasure that bond over all else. Finally, the self becomes aware of a true destiny: to be reunited with the divine and to return to the Father of all.

The great value of the *Acts of Thomas*, as well as other Acts of a similar nature, was that they gave expression to the religious and cultural horizons in which Christians of the third century lived. They present a way of looking at reality and conceiving the universe, and show how to live within that reality. They did not construct this symbolic universe afresh—rather they gave expression to the way in

---

[47] "Jesus, who have taken a form and become like a man and appeared to all of us in order not to separate us from your love; Lord, you are he who has given himself for us and has bought us with a price by his blood, as a precious possession. But what have we, Lord, to offer in exchange for your life which you have given for us?" (*Acts Thom.* 72).

[48] Klijn, *Acts of Thomas*, 37.

[49] "Belief in the identity of these three—the individual self, the inner source of divine inspiration (Jesus) and god in the most universal sense (the father)—links the Thomas literature with other bodies of scripture in this book, especially the writings of Valentinus (GTr) and his school (TRs)" (Layton, *Gnostic Scriptures*, 360).

which Syrian Christians experienced their universe and their particular place within it. While the *Acts of Thomas* reflected the cultural and symbolic universe of the communities among whom it was read and handed on, at the same time the narrative helped to shape the lives of those who read it.[50] Through the example of the character of Thomas, the apostle that was held in the greatest esteem in their tradition, Syrian Christians were challenged to embrace his understanding of reality, his relationship to the world and to Christ, and ultimately his understanding of the destiny to which they are called. Writings such as the *Acts of Thomas* helped form the imagination and lives of Christians of the third century by giving them a specific identity, a clear understanding of their origin and destination, and above all a way of living in this world as one called to union with Christ.[51]

---

[50] See Cameron, *Christianity and the Rhetoric of Empire*, 116.

[51] As Cameron says: "Like these Christian Lives in the fourth century and later, the stories in the apocryphal Acts had an important part to play in the creation of a Christian universe of myth, which would be both totalizing in itself and capable of development at different intellectual and literary levels" (*Christianity and the Rhetoric of Empire*, 113).

CHAPTER TWELVE

"BE PASSERSBY":
GOSPEL OF THOMAS 42, JESUS TRADITIONS, AND ISLAMIC LITERATURE

MARVIN MEYER

Pound for pound and word for word, *Gos. Thom.* 42 is the most beguiling saying in the *Gospel of Thomas*. Composed of a quotation formula plus two Coptic words, this saying has prompted scholars to scramble in an effort to provide satisfactory interpretations of the saying. In this essay I seek to join the scholarly scramble by examining the Coptic of *Gos. Thom.* 42 and reconstructions of the saying in other languages, evaluating attempts to translate and interpret the saying, and exploring similar themes in literature useful for our study of sayings of Jesus in the *Gospel of Thomas*, particularly Islamic literature. At the end of all this I shall venture to propose a trajectory of transmission and development of the saying and themes connected to the saying.[1]

1. *Coptic and Other Languages*

Gos. Thom. 42 occupies the entirety of line 19 on page 40 of Nag Hammadi Codex II: ⲡⲉϫⲉ ⲓ̅ⲥ̅ ϫⲉ ϣⲱⲡⲉ ⲉⲧⲉⲧⲛ̅ⲣ̅ⲡⲁⲣⲁⲅⲉ. The Coptic grammatical forms in the line are not difficult to identify. After a conventional quotation formula, the saying itself consists of the imperative ϣⲱⲡⲉ followed by the second person plural circumstantial ⲉⲧⲉⲧⲛ̅ⲣ̅ⲡⲁⲣⲁⲅⲉ. The circumstantial (ⲉ-) employs the auxiliary ⲣ̅- (from ⲉⲓⲣⲉ) with the pronominal ⲧⲉⲧⲛ̅-, as is common with a verb of Greek derivation (here, ⲡⲁⲣⲁⲅⲉ, from παράγω).

The Coptic grammatical forms of *Gos. Thom.* 42 are clear enough, but the translation and interpretation are not. Part of the difficulty

---

[1] In this essay the English translations of ancient and late antique sources are my own, unless otherwise indicated. Translations of the sayings in the *Gospel of Thomas* are taken from my edition, *The Gospel of Thomas: The Hidden Sayings of Jesus* (San Francisco, CA: HarperSanFrancisco, 1992).

of translation stems from disagreement about the understanding of the syntactical construction of the saying. The most straightforward understanding of the syntax seems to me to be that it is to be identified as a periphrastic imperative, in this case ϣⲱⲡⲉ with the circumstantial. Bentley Layton gives several examples of this construction, for example 1 Pet 1:16: ϣⲱⲡⲉ ⲉⲧⲉⲧⲛ̄ⲟⲩⲁⲁⲃ, "be holy" (Greek ἅγιοι ἔσεσθε, with variant readings for the imperative, γίνεσθε and γένεσθε). Such an understanding of the syntax suggests the following sort of translation of *Gos. Thom.* 42: "Be passersby," "Become passersby," or simply "Pass by."[2]

Conversely, a few translators of *Gos. Thom.* 42 have understood the syntactical construction as the imperative ϣⲱⲡⲉ with a circumstantial indicating simultaneity of action. This understanding of the syntax is certainly possible, but it may be a more difficult grammatical analysis in a text like the *Gospel of Thomas* that often uses ϣⲱⲡⲉ (or the equivalent) with an element of specification to indicate transformation: a person will become a single one, the lion will become human, the female will become male, Jesus will become the person who drinks from Jesus' mouth, and so on.[3] Nonetheless, this understanding of the syntax, if accepted, suggests a translation of *Gos. Thom.* 42 like the following: "Come into being as you pass away," "Come to be as you pass by," or "Come to be and pass by."[4]

Some scholars have gone further in attempting to understand the language of *Gos. Thom.* 42 and have tried to recover an earlier Greek or Semitic version of the saying. Inspired either by the verb of Greek derivation in *Gos. Thom.* 42 or by the likelihood of a Greek *Vorlage* to the Coptic *Gospel of Thomas*, a number of scholars have reconstructed a Greek version of saying 42. Most obvious may be γίνεσθε παράγοντες.[5] We might observe that variations on the Greek imper-

---

[2] See Bentley Layton, *A Coptic Grammar, with Chrestomathy and Glossary, Sahidic Dialect* (Porta Linguarum Orientalium, NS 20; Wiesbaden: Harrassowitz, 2000), 294.

[3] On transformation in the *Gospel of Thomas*, see Marvin Meyer, "Albert Schweitzer and the Image of Jesus in the *Gospel of Thomas*," in *Jesus Then and Now: Images of Jesus in History and Christology* (ed. Marvin Meyer and Charles Hughes; Harrisburg, PA: Trinity Press International, 2001), 82–83 (also in Marvin Meyer, *Secret Gospels: Essays on Thomas and the Secret Gospel of Mark* [Harrisburg, PA: Trinity Press International, 2003], 28–30).

[4] See the discussion in Tjitze Baarda, "Jesus Said: Be Passers-By; On the Meaning and Origin of Logion 42 of the *Gospel of Thomas*," in *Early Transmission of Words of Jesus: Thomas, Tatian and the Text of the New Testament* (ed. J. Helderman and S. J. Noorda; Amsterdam: VU Boekhandel/Uitgeverij, 1983), 180–81.

[5] So, among others, Joachim Jeremias, *Unbekannte Jesusworte* (3rd ed.; Gütersloh: Mohn, 1963), 107.

ative are possible (γένεσθε or ἔσεσθε, as with 1 Pet 1:16, above), and perhaps we might even consider a simple Greek imperative for the clause (παράγετε). Other suggestions have included ἔστε παρερχόμενοι[6] and γίνεσθε περαταί;[7] in an aside Tjitze Baarda also mentions γίνεσθε παροδῖται (compare the *Acts of John*) or γίνεσθε παρίοντες or γίνεσθε διοδεύοντες (compare Epictetus).[8] According to the evidence of Greek sources and Coptic translations of Greek sources, all these versions are possible reconstructions of a Greek version of *Gos. Thom.* 42.

Baarda goes beyond this point of reconstruction of a Greek version of saying 42, as do Joachim Jeremias and Gilles Quispel, and all three have attempted to reconstruct what they assume to be a Semitic—Aramaic or Hebrew—original version of *Gos. Thom.* 42. For the second word, after the imperative, Jeremias and Quispel have suggested a form derived from עבר, understood as "wanderer" or "wandering teacher," and Baarda has suggested עברי, "Hebrew."[9]

We shall discuss these proposed Semitic versions more fully later, but here we consider the possible implications of an assumed Semitic original version for the organization of the sayings in the *Gospel of Thomas*, particularly in the thinking of Baarda. The question of the sequence of sayings in the *Gospel of Thomas* has proved to be a vexing one to scholars for a long time, and to date no overall organizational scheme has proved convincing. While there may be clusters of sayings—parables, for instance—most helpful for understanding the sequence of the *Gospel of Thomas* have been proposals regarding *Stichwörter*, catchwords that may connect one *Thomas* saying to another in a series. Ordinarily the possible catchword connections in the *Gospel of Thomas* have been discussed on the level of Coptic and Greek words.[10]

Baarda uses his supposition of a Semitic original and his reconstruction of a Semitic word for "Hebrews" to suggest an organized sequence of two (or more) sayings in the middle of the *Gospel of Thomas*. Baarda first recollects a comment by Rodolphe Kasser concerning a possible relationship between *Gos. Thom.* 42 and 43, and then he refers to a scholarly attempt to identify *Gos. Thom.* 37–42 and 43–50

---

[6] Rodolphe Kasser, *L'Évangile selon Thomas: Présentation et commentaire théologique* (Bibliothèque théologique; Neuchâtel: Delachaux & Niestlé, 1961), 71.

[7] Baarda, "Be Passers-By," 193–94.

[8] *Ibid.*, 192.

[9] Discussion in Baarda, "Jesus Said: Be Passers-By," 194–95.

[10] See Stephen J. Patterson, *The Gospel of Thomas and Jesus* (FF: Reference Series; Sonoma, CA: Polebridge Press, 1993), 94–110.

as clusters of sayings. On the basis of the Semitic original he believes
he has recovered, Baarda can provide the connection that Kasser sought
and—voilà—a sequence of sayings emerges in the *Gospel of Thomas*.
According to Baarda, sayings 42 and 43 are very closely related:
"together these two sayings comprise a dialogue between Jesus and
his disciples. On this view, the dialogue runs as follows:

> Jesus said: 'Be (*šōpe*) Hebrews.'
> His disciples said to Him: 'Who are you,
> that you say *that* to us?'
> (Jesus said:) 'Through what I say to you,
> do you not recognise who I am?
> But you have become (-*šōpe*) *as the Jews*,
> for they love the tree and hate its fruit,
> and they love the fruit and hate the tree.' "[11]

Baarda's bold solution to questions raised by *Gos. Thom.* 42, fascinating as that solution is, is as strong—or as precarious—as his
assumption of a Semitic original for saying 42 and his understanding of passersby as "Hebrews."

2. *Multiple Translations and Interpretations*

There are three basic translations and interpretations of *Gos. Thom.* 42,
and they are based on understandings of the Coptic and other texts
associated with the Coptic. We shall consider these three seriatim.

First, "Come into being as you pass away," with variations. As
noted, this interpretation is based upon a feasible but somewhat
difficult understanding of the Coptic of the *Gospel of Thomas*. It has
been advocated largely by earlier interpreters of the *Gospel of Thomas*,
such as Bertil Gärtner, Robert M. Grant and David Noel Freedman
with William R. Schoedel, Johannes Leipoldt, and others.[12] Baarda
accepts the grammatical legitimacy and defensibility of this translation and interpretation, though he himself ends up taking a differ-

[11] Baarda, "Jesus Said: Be Passers-By," 196.
[12] Bertil Gärtner, *The Theology of the Gospel according to Thomas* (trans. Eric J. Sharpe;
New York, NY: Harper, 1961); Robert M. Grant and David Noel Freedman, *The
Secret Sayings of Jesus* (with an English Translation of the Gospel of Thomas by
William R. Schoedel; Garden City, NY: Doubleday, 1960); Johannes Leipoldt, *Das
Evangelium nach Thomas: Koptisch und deutsch* (TU 101; Berlin: Akademie-Verlag, 1967).

ent approach.[13] According to this translation and interpretation, the saying communicates a powerful, paradoxical message: embrace existence and also nonexistence, being and also nonbeing, life and also death. And the imperative is simply but emphatically put: ϢⲰⲠⲈ, "become," "be."

There are plenty of other texts from antiquity and late antiquity that communicate a similar message, and in similar words. In the New Testament, 1 Cor 7:31 and other texts use the same Greek verb with the meaning "pass away," and 2 Cor 4:16 offers what may be taken to be a similar message in different words ("Though our outer person is wasting away, our inner one is being renewed day by day"). *Acts John* 76 contains the same sort of message with nearly as dramatic a delivery as the *Gospel of Thomas*: ἀπόθανε ἵνα ζήσῃς, "die that you may live." The Mithras Liturgy likewise includes paradoxical lines in its words to be uttered by the initiate: "Lord, having been born again, I am passing away (ἀπογίγνομαι); growing and having grown, I am dying; having been born from a life-producing birth, I am passing on (πορεύομαι), released to death" (*PGM* IV,718–22). And, Gärtner emphasizes, *Gos. Thom.* 11 also has the verb ⲠⲀⲢⲀⲦⲈ (twice), with the same meaning proposed by Gärtner and friends for saying 42.[14]

Thus understood, *Gos. Thom.* 42 may be poignant and potent, but, Stephen Patterson objects, it does not cohere with the overall message of the *Gospel of Thomas*. He points out that Thomasine Christians do not come into being, because they already exist (saying 19), and they do not pass away, because they are immortal (sayings 1, 11, 18, 19, 85, 111).[15] Quispel critiques Grant in a similar vein, only more sharply, for being enamored of the gnostic hypothesis and a gnosticizing translation. He states that Grant, "épris de l'hypothèse gnostique, découvre dans ces mots les profondeurs de la gnose naasénienne," and so Grant (or Schoedel) translates saying 42 as he does—to which Quispel adds, "C'est d'autant plus profond que c'est incompréhensible. Mais il faut se souvenir que ὁ παράγων est un substantif grec qui veut dire 'le passant.'"[16]

---

[13] Baarda, "Jesus Said: Be Passers-By," 180–81.
[14] Gärtner, *Theology*, 244.
[15] Patterson, *Gospel of Thomas*, 129.
[16] Gilles Quispel, "L'Évangile selon Thomas et les origines de l'ascèse chrétienne," in *idem, Gnostic Studies II* (Nederlands Historisch-Archaeologisch Instituut te Istanbul 34:2; Istanbul: Nederlands Historisch-Archaeologisch Instituut te Istanbul, 1975), 104.

These are powerful critiques of *Gos. Thom.* 42 interpreted as "Come into being as you pass away," but the book should not be closed on this interpretation just yet. For what if some interpreter from antiquity or late antiquity is in fact a gnostic or mystic who reads the saying in this way?

Second, "Be Hebrews." In his quest for an original Semitic version of *Gos. Thom.* 42, Baarda proposes that the Coptic may derive from the Greek γίνεσθε περαταί, where a περατής is a traveler or wanderer like Abraham, and that περαταί may reflect עברים, "Hebrews." He observes that the Septuagint of Gen 14:13 translates העברי, "the Hebrew" (as in Abram the Hebrew), with τῷ περάτῃ (Symmachus later translates with τῷ Ἑβραίῳ). Baarda goes on to show how Philo allegorizes the word "Hebrew" to indicate a περατής in *De migratione Abrahami*, how Origen understands the meaning of "Hebrews" to be περατικοί, and how Hippolytus calls a second-century gnostic group Peratae.[17] This evidence leads Baarda to understand *Gos. Thom.* 42 originally to employ the Semitic for "Hebrews."

So Baarda seeks and finds a Semitic original lurking behind a Greek version of a Coptic saying. The original, which might reflect "the earliest periods of (Palestinian?) transmission," may then be reconstructed: הוו עבריין (Aramaic) or היו עברים (Hebrew).[18]

At the conclusion of his article Baarda raises questions to help explain what is at stake in his translation and interpretation of *Gos. Thom.* 42: "Is it possible that here Thomas is taking us back to a phase in history when the church, or a particular community or group within it, set itself up against the Jews as the new Israel, in which the shibboleth was no longer the law but being a child of Abraham? Was there a time when the followers of Jesus distanced themselves as the true *Hebrews* from their fellow countrymen, who to them were only *Jews*, who to their mind were only playing off the law against Jesus? It is tempting to reflect on this possibility but, ultimately, one should not dwell too long on the saying in the Coptic Gospel of Thomas, 'Be passers-by.' "[19]

Indeed, is it possible? And indeed, one should not reflect too long on such anti-Jewish sentiments. Baarda's interpretation is learned and brilliant. It is an ingenious and subtle reading of *Gos. Thom.* 42, but

---

[17] Baarda, "Jesus Said: Be Passers-By," 193–95.
[18] *Ibid.*, 195.
[19] *Ibid.*, 197.

it may be too ingenious and subtle for its own good. It is founded upon an uncertain assumption of a Semitic original supported with a tenuous understanding of obscure texts in several languages. At the end of the day this understanding does not fully persuade. Still, the general point that Baarda substantiates—and that Jeremias and Quispel substantiated before him, with their similar concern for a Semitic original—namely, that themes reminiscent of *Gos. Thom.* 42 are at home in a Semitic context, may prove quite helpful.

Third, "Be passersby," with variations that massage the meaning and interpret the precise nuance of the saying. This translation or one very much like it is usually used these days by scholars, yet the disarmingly simple wording leaves ample room for speculation about what exactly is meant. Just what is one to pass or pass by?

In *The Gnostic Scriptures* Bentley Layton opts for this translation and refers to epitaphs on tombstones: "Epitaphs on Greek tombstones of the period often salute the 'stranger' or 'passerby' (usually called *ksenos* or *parodites*), as though in the words of the corpse buried in the tomb."[20] Layton then mentions *Gos. Thom.* 56, with the world described as a carcass or corpse.[21]

A couple examples of such epitaphs on tombstones may be given. One tombstone has an epitaph that directly addresses one passing by: "Hello, passerby (παροδεῖτα). . . . Then hear, stranger (ξεῖνα), my country and name. . . ."[22] Another has an epitaph that quotes what the tombstone, or the one buried by the tombstone, says: "the tombstone calls to all passing by (παρερχομένοις): here lies the body of Makaria, always remembered."[23]

For Layton and others, *Gos. Thom.* 42 may call upon one to pass by the world, in fairly general terms (as, for Layton, one passes by a

---

[20] Bentley Layton, *The Gnostic Scriptures: A New Translation with Annotations and Introductions* (Garden City, NY: Doubleday, 1987), 387.

[21] Compare also *Gos. Thom.* 80, with reference to the body (ⲡⲥⲱⲙⲁ) rather than a corpse (ⲡⲧⲱⲙⲁ); see Meyer, *Gospel of Thomas*, 91, note to saying 56, on the Aramaic word פֿגרא as either "body" or "corpse." Perhaps compare the Greek Platonic (and Orphic) identification of σῶμα and σῆμα.

[22] G. H. R. Horsley, *New Documents Illustrating Early Christianity: A Review of Greek Inscriptions and Papyri Published in 1977* (North Ryde: Ancient History Documentary Research Centre, Macquarie University, 1982), 55. For further examples, see Philip Sellew, "Jesus and the Voice from beyond the Grave: The *Gospel of Thomas* in the Context of Funerary Epigraphy" (Chapter 3 in this volume).

[23] G. H. R. Horsley, *New Documents Illustrating Early Christianity: A Review of Greek Inscriptions and Papyri Published in 1978* (North Ryde: Ancient History Documentary Research Centre, Macquarie University, 1983), 107.

tombstone and a corpse). Passing by or overcoming the world is a theme well attested in the *Gospel of Thomas*, and not only in saying 56 (and saying 80). Saying 27, for example, makes use of the image of fasting from the world (and perhaps observing a sabbath from the world) to proclaim the importance of abstaining from the world: "If you do not fast from the world, you will not find the kingdom. If you do not observe the sabbath as a sabbath, you will not see the father."

In his brief discussion of *Gos. Thom.* 42 Layton alludes to another way of understanding what it means to pass by. When he states that saying 42 may also be understood as recommending the wandering life of one like Thomas himself as presented in the *Acts of Thomas*,[24] he introduces the theme of itinerancy, particularly within the context of Syrian Christianity. Others have followed the same basic approach, including Jeremias and Quispel, who also see the life of the wanderer in the Hebrew word עבר in the Hebrew Scriptures and the Talmud (*b. Sanh.* 70a; 103b).[25] Quispel translates saying 42, "Werdet Wanderer!" and he goes on to observe, "Wahrscheinlich bezieht sich das Wort auf die judenchristlichen Wanderlehrer und Wanderpropheten, welche das Wort Gottes verkündeten. Allerdings betrachten die pseudo-klementinischen *Recognitiones* alle Christen als Reisende auf dem Wege zur Gottesstadt."[26] Quispel then traces the theme of itinerancy within Syrian Christian sources, including, in addition to the *Acts of Thomas*, Addai, Ephrem Syrus, Macarius, and the *Liber Graduum*. He concludes, "So enthüllt das *Thomasevangelium* die Zusammenhänge zwischen den palästinensischen Wanderlehrern und den Wandermönchen der gesamten syrischen Christenheit."[27]

Recently Stephen Patterson has suggested the translation "Become itinerants" for *Gos. Thom.* 42,[28] and Arthur Dewey, in a somewhat similar vein, has brought forward "Be (or become) transient (or transients)"; Dewey also allows for more fluid translations: "Get going," "Be on the way."[29] Patterson's interpretation follows rather closely the contributions of Jeremias and Quispel. According to Patterson,

---

[24] Compare the *Acts of Thomas* in general, and *Acts Thom.* 4 and 109 on being a stranger in a foreign land.

[25] Jeremias, *Unbekannte Jesusworte*, 110; Quispel, *Makarius, das Thomasevangelium und das Lied von der Perle* (NovTSup 15; Leiden: Brill, 1967), 20–21.

[26] Quispel, *Makarius*, 21.

[27] *Ibid.*, 22.

[28] Patterson, *Gospel of Thomas*, 131.

[29] Arthur J. Dewey, "A Passing Remark: Thomas 42," *Forum* 10:1–2 (1994): 83–84.

Thomas Christians are social radicals who pass by the world literally and concretely, wandering from place to place and living the radical life of the homeless itinerant. *Gos. Thom.* 42 then is consonant with saying 14: "When you go into any region and walk through the countryside (ⲈⲦⲈⲦⲚ̅ϢⲀⲚⲂⲰⲔ ⲈϨⲞⲨⲚ ⲈⲔⲀϨ ⲚⲒⲘ ⲀⲨⲰ Ⲛ̅ⲦⲈⲦⲘ̅ⲘⲞⲞϢⲈ ϨⲚ̅ Ⲛ̅ⲬⲰⲢⲀ), when people receive you, eat what they serve you and heal the sick among them. For what goes into your mouth will not defile you; rather, it is what comes out of your mouth that will defile you." Like Quispel in the passage quoted above, Patterson places the *Gospel of Thomas* within the broader world of Palestinian and Syrian itinerancy, with Q, the *Didache*, the Pseudo-Clementines, and additional Syrian Christian sources, and he sees a saying like *Gos. Thom.* 42 as showing a continuation of the itinerant lifestyle of the Jesus movement.[30]

Dewey presses *Gos. Thom.* 42 even more vigorously, not so much to explore the meaning of Palestinian and Syrian itinerancy, but rather to argue that the saying may go back to the historical Jesus with a more aphoristic and ambiguous meaning.

Initially Dewey wonders whether the saying might simply reflect the mission instructions in Q (Q 10:2–16), where Jesus is presented explaining how the disciples are to go forth as wandering missionaries. Discreetly, in a footnote, Dewey asks whether ὑπάγετε, "Be on the way," of Luke 10:3, may be from Q and not from Luke, and then he speculates about whether ὑπάγετε could be the Greek *Vorlage* for *Gos. Thom.* 42. There is nothing inherently profound about this Greek word, however, since ὑπάγετε is a common expression in ancient literature, and ὑπάγετε and other forms of ὑπάγω are used extensively in early Christian literature. He also notes that Matt 10:16b, Matthew's addition to the Q mission instructions, makes use of the imperative of γίνομαι with an adjective, in a manner that is somewhat like the form of *Gos. Thom.* 42: "So be shrewd (γίνεσθε οὖν φρόνιμοι) as snakes and innocent as doves."[31] We may compare

---

[30] Patterson, *Gospel of Thomas*, 158–70. On the possibility of a Common Tradition or Common Sayings Tradition behind Q and the *Gospel of Thomas*, see Patterson, "Wisdom in Q and Thomas," in *In Search of Wisdom: Essays in Memory of John G. Gammie* (ed. Leo G. Perdue, Bernard Brandon Scott, and William Johnston Wiseman; Louisville, KY: Westminster John Knox, 1993), 187–221; John Dominic Crossan, *The Birth of Christianity: Discovering What Happened in the Years Immediately After the Execution of Jesus* (San Francisco, CA: HarperSanFrancisco, 1998).

[31] Dewey, "A Passing Remark," 81.

this Greek version with the Coptic of *Gos. Thom.* 39, which uses the Coptic imperative: ϣⲱⲡⲉ ⲙ̄ⲫⲣⲟⲛⲓⲙⲟⲥ.

The appearance of the edition of Q from the International Q Project confirms that ὑπάγετε most likely is from Q. In *The Critical Edition of Q*, the text of Q 10:3 is given as follows: [ὑπάγετε·] ἰδοὺ ἀποστέλλω ὑμᾶς ὡς (πρόβατα) ἐν μέσῳ λύκων, where square brackets around ὑπάγετε indicate that only the Lukan text is represented here.[32] Dewey admits that he is tempted by ὑπάγετε, but he does not yield to the temptation. He admits that the saying of *Gos. Thom.* 42 might come from some common, everyday utterance, but he believes it may be a common, everyday utterance of Jesus and not simply a saying like that found in the mission instructions in Q.

Thus, in general Dewey joins his voice to the chorus of scholars who maintain that the historical Jesus preached and practiced a life of passing by for God and God's kingdom. After all, in one, itinerant sense of passing by, Jesus says in *Thomas*, "[Foxes have] their dens and birds have their nests, but the child of humankind has no place to lay his head and rest." Jesus says essentially the same thing in Q, the synoptic gospels, and, we shall see, Islamic sources.[33]

But Dewey's real contribution to the discussion of *Gos. Thom.* 42 may lie in the spin he places upon the saying as an aphorism of the historical Jesus with, as he puts it, "an ambiguous edge."[34] He states, "I submit that the saying may well be invitational—in an aphoristic sense, that is, without full scale plans or institutionalized context. This saying would reflect the open drive of Jesus' experiment, expressing an invitation to enter into this unfinished revisioning of life style and society."[35] To the voting fellows of the Jesus Seminar, to whom his article is addressed, Dewey recommends a red vote for *Gos. Thom.* 42. He can recommend attribution of a saying to the historical Jesus with no greater conviction than that.

---

[32] James M. Robinson, Paul Hoffmann, and John S. Kloppenborg, eds., *The Critical Edition of Q* (Hermeneia Supplement; Philadelphia, PA: Fortress, 2000), 162–63.

[33] *Gos. Thom.* 86; compare Matt 8:20 (Q); Luke 9:58 (Q); more discussion below and in Meyer, *The Gospel of Thomas*, 101, with a reference to Plutarch's *Life of Tiberius Gracchus* 9.4–5.

[34] Dewey, "A Passing Remark," 84.

[35] *Ibid.*, 81–82. Dewey adds that such an ambiguous aphoristic saying of Jesus fits well within the world of Jewish wisdom and the world of Cynic traditions, and thus he relates his interpretation in part to the controversial theories regarding Jesus, Q, and the Cynics as expounded, e.g., in Burton L. Mack, *A Myth of Innocence: Mark and Christian Origins* (Philadelphia, PA: Fortress, 1988); Leif E. Vaage, *Galilean Upstarts: Jesus' First Followers according to Q* (Harrisburg, PA: Trinity Press International, 1994).

Dewey admits that as a saying of Jesus *Gos. Thom.* 42 is ambiguous, and I believe he is right—perhaps more so than he himself realizes. For that ambiguity, I suggest, may extend both to the hermeneutic of the *Gospel of Thomas* and to the rhetoric of the historical Jesus. I have argued elsewhere that a hermeneutical ambiguity characterizes the sayings—ⲚϢⲀⲜⲈ ⲈⲐⲎⲠ, hidden sayings, secret sayings—in the *Gospel of Thomas,* and that these sayings are presented as obscure sayings that need the interpretive engagement of the readers.[36] The hermeneutical principle articulated at the opening of the *Gospel of Thomas* implies an interactive hermeneutic and a way of salvation through wisdom and understanding: "Whoever discovers the interpretation (ⲐⲈⲢⲘⲎⲚⲈⲒⲀ) of these sayings will not taste death." Readers and interpreters are encouraged to find a hermeneutical key to unlock the meaning of the sayings, and, depending on the approaches of the readers and interpreters, a variety of interpretations may emerge from their creative encounter with the sayings. I agree with the approach of Richard Valantasis, who calls the theology of the *Gospel of Thomas* a performative theology. This theology, Valantasis affirms, emerges from the active response of readers and interpreters to the sayings of Jesus in the *Gospel of Thomas,* as these readers "construct their own narrative and theology linking the individual sayings into a cohesive text."[37] Hence, there may be no single authoritative interpretation of *Gos. Thom.* 42. Readers of the *Gospel of Thomas* are to discover for themselves what it means to be passersby. As *Thomas* says, ϢⲒⲚⲈ ⲀⲨⲰ ⲦⲈⲦⲚⲀϬⲒⲚⲈ ("Seek and you will find," *Gos. Thom.* 92).

But a deliberate and even playful ambiguity may also characterize the rhetorical approach of the historical Jesus.[38] To state it succinctly: I suggest Jesus was an itinerant Jewish preacher of wisdom who proclaimed the kingdom or reign of God in terms that left much to the creative imagination, who told open-ended kingdom

---

[36] See Meyer, "Albert Schweitzer and the Image of Jesus" 77–78 (also in *Secret Gospels,* 22–24); idem, *"Gospel of Thomas* Logion 114 Revisited," in *For the Children, Perfect Instruction: Studies in Honor of Hans-Martin Schenke on the Occasion of the Berliner Arbeitskreis für koptisch-gnostische Schriften's Thirtieth Year* (ed. Hans-Gebhard Bethge et al.; NHMS 54; Leiden: Brill, 2002), 101–11 (also in Marvin Meyer, *Secret Gospels,* 96–106).
[37] Richard Valantasis, *The Gospel of Thomas* (New Testament Readings; London and New York, NY: Routledge, 1997), 196.
[38] For discussion about the *Gospel of Thomas* and the historical Jesus, and references, see Dewey, "A Passing Remark"; Meyer, "Albert Schweitzer and the Image of Jesus"; Patterson, *Gospel of Thomas.*

stories and parables and expected listeners to draw their own conclusions, who asked interlocutors to look at a coin and decide for
themselves to whom it belongs, who practiced an alternative lifestyle,
called the hungry, the thirsty, and the disenfranchised fortunate, and
encouraged love for all, even enemies. That sort of historical Jesus
could have said "Be passersby" in a way that might make people
pause, think, and respond. Dewey states he prefers the translation "Be
transients" (or the like) for *Gos. Thom.* 42, "because it catches the
ambiguity of the Coptic and quite likely that of the original. A double sense of finitude and movement/mission is present in both."[39]
Whatever we think of Dewey's exact formulation, we may appreciate
his concerns. The historical Jesus, too, may have said, "Seek and you
will find," and when the *Gospel of Thomas* presented these words as
words of Jesus, it may have understood Jesus quite well. *The Gospel
of Thomas* took the rhetoric of a preacher of wisdom and made it
into a salvific hermeneutic: "Let one who seeks not stop seeking until
one finds. When one finds, one will be troubled. When one is troubled,
one will marvel and will reign over all."[40] This, for *Thomas*, is the
kingdom or reign of God.

3. *Islamic Texts and* Thomas

In his discussion of *Gos. Thom.* 42, Jeremias compared it to a saying
known from Islamic tradition, and thus he addressed an issue that
is potentially of great value for the study of sayings of Jesus and the
Gospel of Thomas. That issue is the use of Islamic literature, particularly
Islamic texts with sayings of Jesus, in the study of such documents
as the *Gospel of Thomas*—and in the present essay, *Gos. Thom.* 42.

In the Qur'an and other Islamic texts, Jesus (in Arabic, *'Isa*) appears
in a large number of passages, especially as a speaker of wise sayings.
Although previously some scholars have published studies of these
sayings,[41] the appearance of Tarif Khalidi's book, *The Muslim Jesus*,

---

[39] Dewey, "A Passing Remark," 83.

[40] *Gos. Thom.* 2; P. Oxy. 654.5–9 adds the stage of rest to the process of seeking and finding: "and [having reigned], one will [rest] (κα[ὶ βασιλεύσας
ἐπαναπα]ήσεται)." Compare the *Gospel of the Hebrews* and the *Book of Thomas*, and
see below on rest.

[41] See Michael Asin y Palacios, *Logia et Agrapha Domini Jesu apud Moslemicos Scriptores*
(Paris: Didot, 1919, 1926; repr. Turnhout: Brepols, 1974), PO 13.3, 335–431; 19.4,

has made many sayings and stories of Jesus in Islamic literature readily available.[42]

In his introduction Khalidi surveys the impact of eastern Christianity and the biblical and extracanonical texts of eastern Christianity upon the formation of Islam and the image of prophet Jesus within Islam. He describes the process by which this impact occurred as one of encounter and emanation: "the overall process by which the Muslim gospel came into being must be thought of not as a birth but more as an emanation, a seepage of one religious tradition into another by means textual and nontextual alike. The overwhelming Christian presence in central Islamic regions such as Syria, Iraq, and Egypt in the first three centuries of Islam meant intimate encounters with a living Christianity suffused with rich and diverse images of Jesus. Doubtless the slow but steady increase in the number of converts from Christianity played an important intermediary role, as witnessed in the *isnad* ["transmission"] of some sayings and stories as well as in the putative Christian origin of several transmitters, which is revealed in their personal names. But the Qur'anic fascination with Jesus must also have been a powerful stimulus in the assembly and diffusion of the gospel in the Muslim environment."[43]

One of the texts of eastern Christianity, especially Syrian (and perhaps Egyptian) Christianity, that may have impacted Islam is the *Gospel of Thomas*, and so it comes as no surprise that there are parallels between sayings of Jesus in the *Gospel of Thomas* and sayings of Jesus in Islamic literature. These parallels deserve careful attention, but here we can only cite examples.

531–624; Roderic Dunkerley, *Beyond the Gospels* (Middlesex: Penguin, 1957); Jeremias, *Unbekannte Jesusworte*; D. S. Margoliouth, "Christ in Islam: Sayings Attributed to Christ by Mohammedan Writers," *ExpTim* 5 (1893–94): 59, 107, 177–78, 503–4, 561; Marvin Meyer, "Did Jesus Drink from a Cup? The Equipment of Jesus and His Followers in Q and al-Ghazzali," in *From Quest to Q ; Festschrift James M. Robinson* (ed. Jon Ma. Asgeirsson, Kristin De Troyer, and Marvin Meyer; BETL 146; Leuven: Peeters & Leuven University Press, 2000), 143–56; *idem, The Unknown Sayings of Jesus* (San Francisco, CA: HarperSanFrancisco, 1998); William G. Morrice, *Hidden Sayings of Jesus: Words Attributed to Jesus outside the Four Gospels* (Peabody, MA: Hendrickson, 1997); Muhammad 'Ata ur-Rahim, *Jesus, Prophet of Islam* (Elmhurst: Tahrike Tarsile Qur'an, 1991); James Robson, *Christ in Islam* (New York, NY: Dutton, 1930); James Hardy Ropes, "Agrapha," in *A Dictionary of the Bible* (ed. James Hastings; New York, NY & Edinburgh: Scripners & Clark, 1904), extra vol., 343–52.

[42] Tarif Khalidi, ed., *The Muslim Jesus: Sayings and Stories in Islamic Literature* (Convergences: Inventories of the Present; Cambridge, MA: Harvard University Press, 2001).

[43] *Ibid.*, 29–30.

Abu Hamid Muhammad al-Ghazali was an eleventh to twelfth-century Muslim professor, theologian, and mystic who collected say-ings of Jesus and had them published in the greatest of his literary works, *Ihya' 'ulum al-din, The Revival of the Religious Sciences*. In this work he includes a partially familiar story and saying of Jesus. Seeking shelter, Jesus finds a tent occupied by a woman and a cave inhab-ited by a lion, and he says, "My God, you have given everything a resting place, but to me have you given none." God replies, "Your resting place is in the house of my mercy."[44] While this saying resem-bles Q 9:58 (Matt 8:20; Luke 9:58), it also recalls the version in *Gos. Thom.* 86 (cited above), with its modest allusion to rest.[45] Furthermore, if the versions of the saying in Q (Matthew and Luke) and *Thomas* make use of "child of humankind" ("son of man," using the Semitic idiom) as a general reference to a person, and probably in this case to Jesus himself, the version in al-Ghazali has Jesus simply speak of himself directly in the first person singular.

Again, al-Ghazali also has this saying of Jesus: "Jesus said, 'Evil scholars are like a rock that has fallen at the mouth of a brook: it does not drink the water, nor does it let the water flow to the plants. And evil scholars are like the drainpipe of a latrine that is plastered outside but filthy inside; or like graves that are decorated outside but contain dead people's bones inside.'"[46] Here the reference to the drainpipe and the graves recalls Q 11:44 (Matt 23:27–28; Luke 11:44). The image of the rock at the mouth of the brook is similar in sentiment to Q 11:52 (Matt 23:13; Luke 11:52) and *Gos. Thom.* 39, but a more vivid parallel is to be located in folk stories about grouchy dogs in mangers full of hay, as in Aesop and Lucian—and *Gos. Thom.* 102.[47]

In Islamic texts there are also passages that shed light on *Gos. Thom.* 42. In some Islamic texts Jesus describes himself as a home-less wanderer, an itinerant in the service of wisdom. In al-Ghazali

---

[44] For the translations of Islamic texts, I have consulted the Arabic and Latin of Michael Asin y Palacios, *Logia et Agrapha Domini Jesu apud Moslemicos Scriptores*, along with other translations, and I have been assisted by Ra'id Faraj. For the present passage in al-Ghazali, see Meyer, *Unknown Sayings of Jesus*, 153.

[45] On rest compare also the addition to *Gos. Thom.* 2 in P. Oxy. 654.5–9 (cited above), and *Gos. Thom.* 50; 51; 60; 61; and 90.

[46] Meyer, *Unknown Sayings of Jesus*, 148.

[47] Compare the note on Aesop, Lucian, and Thomas 102 in Meyer, *Gospel of Thomas*, 105.

(above), Jesus says he has no resting place; he also says, "My seasoning is hunger, my undergarment is fear of God, my outer garment is wool, my fire in winter is the sun's rays, my lamp is the moon, my riding beast is my feet, and my food and fruit are what the earth produces. At night I have nothing and in the morning I have nothing, yet there is no one on earth richer than I."[48] Other sayings place Jesus on the road, walking about and commenting on what he passes on the way. Again in al-Ghazali, Jesus passes by a pig and gives greetings, and he passes by the stinking carcass of a dog. In the latter instance it is said, "One day Jesus was walking with his disciples, and they passed by the carcass of a dog. The disciples said, 'How this dog stinks!' But Jesus said, 'How white are its teeth!' "[49]

A goodly number of sayings of Jesus in Islamic texts have him assume a critical stance toward the world and the pleasures of the world. In Abu Talib al-Makki, Jesus renounces the world and calls it a pig, without the friendliness of the previous porcine greeting.[50] In Abu Bakr ibn Abi al-Dunya, Jesus tells his disciples to renounce the world and its pleasures, as ascetics, and then they will pass through the world and they will not be anxious.[51]

The language of passing by the world and passing through the world is also reflected in a famous Islamic saying of Jesus, the very saying that attracted the attention of Jeremias. This is an inscription from a mosque in Fatehpur Sikri, India, dating from the time of the Grand Mogul Akbar: "Jesus said, 'This world is a bridge. Pass over it, but do not build your dwelling there.' "[52] This saying has been commented on by scholars, recently by Khalidi, who mentions several attestations and versions of the saying. A few scholars, such as Asin, Baarda, and Jeremias, have traced the saying back to the very beginnings of Islam. Some have compared the structure of the saying to another Semitic saying, *Pirke Avot* 4:21, about this world as a vestibule for the world to come. Jeremias suggests that the saying about the bridge may be pre-Islamic, and Baarda agrees.[53]

---

[48] Meyer, *Unknown Sayings of Jesus*, 154.
[49] *Ibid.*, 152.
[50] Khalidi, *Muslim Jesus*, 138–39.
[51] *Ibid.*, 117.
[52] See Meyer, *Unknown Sayings of Jesus*, 156, with the note on p. 178, for discussion and additional parallels to this saying in Islamic texts.
[53] See Baarda, "Be Passers-By," 188.

This saying is also to be found in the *Disciplina clericalis* of Petrus Alphonsi, in Latin: *seculum est quasi pons, transi ergo, ne hospiteris*. Petrus Alphonsi is known to have gathered much of his wisdom from sources from the east, and he attributes this saying to a philosopher. Baarda observes, "It is very likely that Petrus Alphonsi borrowed the metaphor from Arabic literature."[54]

It is conceivable, then, as some scholars have intimated, that the motif of passing by in the *Gospel of Thomas* may be connected to motifs of passing, particularly passing over the bridge of the world, in Islamic literature.[55]

4. A Passing Trajectory

I trust this essay indicates, at least in a small way, the significance of Islamic literature and sayings of Jesus preserved in Islamic texts for the study of Jesus traditions. With regard to *Gos. Thom.* 42, it may be possible to suggest, here at the end of the essay, a trajectory of transmission and development for themes linked to *Gos. Thom.* 42. Such a suggestion must be tentative. Yet, on the basis of the observations in the previous pages, I propose a reasonable case can be made for the identification of five historical moments in the development of themes of passing by.

First, I suggest, like Dewey, that the historical Jesus spoke of passing by in aphorism, though the precise form of the aphorism has proved to be elusive. He not only spoke of passing by, he also lived in those terms, as a Jewish preacher of wisdom with an itinerant lifestyle and a challenging rhetorical style. He spoke and lived in this way within a Jewish heritage that offered reflections, we have seen, on passing by. Jesus encouraged listeners to encounter his words creatively, so that a call to passing by could entail a fundamental challenge to various aspects of everyday life.

Second, Q people assumed an itinerant lifestyle, and they incorporated a mandate for itinerancy into the mission instructions of Q. Their interest in itinerancy was expressed in continuity with the lifestyle of Jesus. The opening of the mission instructions has Jesus

---

[54] *Ibid.*, 189.
[55] *Ibid.*, 190, with references.

commissioning the disciples in a manner that almost anticipates *Gos. Thom.* 42, in one way of understanding it: "Be on the way. Look, I am sending you like sheep in the middle of wolves. Take no money, no bag, no sandals, no staff. Do not greet anyone on the road" (Q 12:3–4).

Third, a cryptic saying attributed to Jesus, "Be passersby," was incorporated into the *Gospel of Thomas*, most likely in Syria, as a saying to be interpreted by those who would seek and find and live. The *Gospel of Thomas* presents an interactive hermeneutic that is in some respects reminiscent of the rhetorical style of Jesus, but in the *Gospel of Thomas* it is presented as a means of salvation. While such a hermeneutic allows for a number of different interpretations of *Gos. Thom.* 42, even "Come into being as you pass away," one interpretation may well have understood Jesus to be proclaiming that readers of *Thomas* should pass by the world and renounce the world.

Fourth, as early as the time of Muhammad, or even before, themes of passing by, as in the *Gospel of Thomas*, passed from Christian sources in Syria or Egypt into the world of prophet Muhammad and Islam. These themes were incorporated into the traditions of Islam, and Jesus became a prophet preaching about renouncing, passing by, and passing over the world.

Fifth, in his research for his book of quotable quotes and sermon illustrations, Petrus Alphonsi learned about the Islamic saying that the world is a bridge to be passed over, and he added this saying to his collection as the wisdom not of Jesus but of a philosopher.

That was Spain, in the twelfth century, and that was the first time that we know of that the saying, variously at home in the world of the middle east, made its way to Europe. Finally it has made its way to the desks of scholars and into bookshops—hopefully not the evil scholars exposed in the *Gospel of Thomas* and Islamic texts—and now it is up to us to interpret what it means to be passersby.

BIBLIOGRAPHY

Allen, R. E. *Plato's Euthyphro and the Earlier Theory of Forms*. New York, NY: Oxford University Press, 1970.

Anderson, John G., Franz Cumont, and Henri Grégoire, eds. *Studia Pontica III: Recueil des inscriptions grecques et latines du Pont et de l'Arménie*. Brussels: Lamertin, 1910.

The Ante-Nicene Fathers. Edited by Alexander Roberts and James Donaldson. 1885–1887. Repr. Peabody, MA: Hendrickson, 1995.

Arnal, William E. "The Rhetoric of Marginality: Apocalypticism, Gnosticism, and Sayings Gospels." *Harvard Theological Review* 88 (1995): 471–94.

———. *Jesus and the Village Scribes: Galilean Conflicts and the Setting of Q*. Minneapolis, MN: Fortress, 2001.

Asgeirsson, Jon Ma. "Arguments and Audience(s) in the *Gospel of Thomas* (Part I)." Pages 47–85 in the *SBL Seminar Papers, 1997*. Society of Biblical Literature Seminar Papers 36. Atlanta, GA: Scholars Press, 1997.

———. "Arguments and Audience(s) in the *Gospel of Thomas* (Part II)." Pages 352–42 of volume 1 of the *SBL Seminar Papers, 1998*. 2 vols. Society of Biblical Literature Seminar Papers 37. Atlanta, GA: Scholars Press, 1998.

———. "Doublets and Strata: Towards a Rhetorical Approach to the *Gospel of Thomas*." Ph.D. diss., Claremont Graduate University, 1998.

———. "The *Gospel of Thomas*: The Original Scent of Christianity [In Icelandic]." *Gangleri* 76 (2002): 17–20.

Asin y Palacios, Michael. *Logia et Agrapha Domini Jesu apud Moslemicos Scriptores*. Patrologia Orientalis 13:3, 335–431; 19:4, 531–624. Paris: Firmin-Didot, 1919, 1926; repr. Turnhout: Brepols, 1974.

Attridge, Harold W. "The Greek Fragments [of the *Gospel of Thomas*]." Pages 95–128 in *Gospel According to Thomas, Gospel According to Philip, Hypostasis of the Archons, and Indexes*. Vol. 1 of *Nag Hammadi Codex II, 2–7 together with XIII, 2*, Brit. Lib. Or. 4926(1), and P. Oxy. 1, 654, 655*. Edited by Bentley Layton. Nag Hammadi Studies 20. Leiden: Brill, 1989.

———. "Paul and the Domestication of Thomas." Pages 218–31 in *Theology and Ethics: Paul and His Interpreters*. Edited by Eugene H. Lovering. Nashville, TN: Abingdon, 1996.

———. "Intertextuality in the *Acts of Thomas*." Pages 87–124 in *The Apocryphal Acts of the Apostles in Intertextual Perspectives*. Edited by Robert F. Stoops, Jr. and Dennis R. MacDonald, Jr. Semeia 80. Atlanta, GA: Scholars Press, 1997.

Aune, David E. *The New Testament in Its Literary Environment*. Philadelphia, PA: Westminster, 1987.

———. "Heracles and Christ: Heracles Imagery in the Christology of Early Christianity." Pages 3–19 in *Greeks, Romans, and Christians: Essays in Honor of Abraham J. Malherbe*. Edited by David L. Balch, Everett Ferguson, and Wayne A. Meeks. Minneapolis, MN: Fortress, 1990.

———. "Luke 20:34–36: A 'Gnosticized' Logion of Jesus?" Pages 187–202 in *Geschichte—Tradition—Reflexion: Festschrift für Martin Hengel zum 70. Geburtstag*. Edited by Hubert Cancik, Hermann Lichtenberger, and Peter Schäfer. Tübingen: Mohr, 1996.

Baarda, Tjitze. *Early Transmission of Words of Jesus: Thomas, Tatian and the Text of the New Testament*. A collection of studies selected and edited by J. Helderman and S. J. Noorda. Amsterdam: VU Boekhandel/Uitgeverij, 1983.

———. "'Jesus Said: Be Passers-by:' On the Meaning and Origin of Logion 42 of the Gospel of Thomas." Pages 179–205 in *Early Transmission of Words of Jesus: Thomas, Tatian and the Text of the New Testament*. A collection of studies selected and edited by J. Helderman and S. J. Noorda. Amsterdam: VU Boekhandel/Uitgeverij, 1983.

Barr, James. *The Garden of Eden and the Hope of Immortality*. Minneapolis, MN: Fortress, 1993.

Bateson, Gregory, and Mary C. Bateson. *Angels Fear: Towards an Epistemology of the Sacred*. New York, NY: Macmillan, 1987.

Bauer, Johannes B. "Das Thomas-Evangelium in der neuesten Forschung." Pages 182–205 in *Geheime Worte Jesu: Das Thomas-Evangelium*. Edited by R. Grant and D. Freedman. Frankfurt: Scheffler, 1960.

———. "The Synoptic Tradition in the Gospel of Thomas." Pages 314–17 in *Studia Evangelica* 3/Texte und Untersuchungen 88. Berlin: Akademie Verlag, 1964.

Bauer, Walter. *Orthodoxy and Heresy in Earliest Christianity*. Edited by Robert Kraft and Gerhard Krodel. Translated by the Philadelphia Seminar on Christian Origin. Philadelphia, PA: Fortress, 1971.

Beckwith, Roger. *The Old Testament Canon of the New Testament Church and Its Background in Early Judaism*. Grand Rapids, MI: Eerdmans, 1985.

Bellinzoni, Arthur J. *The Sayings of Jesus in the Writings of Justin Martyr*. Novum Testamentum Supplements 17. Leiden: Brill, 1967.

Berchman, Robert M. *From Philo to Origen: Middle Platonism in Transition*. Brown Judaic Studies 69. Chico, CA: Scholars Press, 1984.

Berger, Peter L., and Thomas Luckman. *The Social Construction of Reality: A Treatise in the Sociology of Knowledge*. London: Lane, 1967.

Bloomquist, L. Gregory. "A Possible Direction for Providing Programmatic Correlation of Textures in Socio-Rhetorical Analysis." Pages 74–95 in *Rhetorical Criticism and the Bible*. Edited by S. E. Porter and D. L. Stamps. Journal for the Study of the New Testament Supplement Series 195. Sheffield: Sheffield Academic Press, 2002.

Bos, Abraham P. "'Aristotelian' and 'Platonic' Dualism in Hellenistic and Early Christian Philosophy and in Gnosticism." *Vigiliae Christianae* 56 (2002): 273–91.

Bousset, Wilhelm. "Die Himmelsreise der Seele." *Archiv für Religionswissenschaft* 4 (1901): 136–69, 229–73.

Bovon, Francois and Eric Junod. "Reading the Apocryphal Acts of the Apostles." Pages 161–71 in *The Apocryphal Acts of Apostles*. Edited by Dennis Ronald MacDonald, Jr. Semeia 38. Atlanta, GA: Scholars Press,1986.

Bowra, Cecil Maurice. *Early Greek Elegists*. Cambridge, MA: Harvard University Press, 1938.

Bowra, Cecil Maurice, ed. *Pindari carmina cum fragmentis*. 2nd ed. Oxford: Clarendon, 1947.

Branham, Robert Bracht, and Marie-Odile Goulet-Cazé. "Introduction." Pages 1–27 in *The Cynics: The Cynic Movement in Antiquity and Its Legacy*. Edited by R. Bracht Branham and M.-O. Goulet-Cazé. Berkeley, CA: University of California Press, 1996.

Bronkhorst, Johannes. "Asceticism, Religion, and Biological Evolution." *Method and Theory in the Study of Religion* 13 (2001): 374–418.

Bruss, Jon S. "Hidden Presences: Monuments, Gravesites, and Corpses in Greek Funerary Epigram." Ph.D. diss., University of Minnesota, 2000.

Bultmann, Rudolf. "Zur Geschichte der Lichtsymbolik im Altertum." Pages 323–55 in *Exegetica: Aufsätze zur Erforschung des Neuen Testaments*. Edited by Erich Dinkler. Tübingen: Mohr, 1967. [Published originally in *Philologus* 97 (1947): 1–36.]

Burkert, Walter. *Greek Religion*. Translated by John Raffan. Cambridge, MA: Harvard Universtity Press, 1985 [1977].

———. *Ancient Mystery Cults*. Cambridge, MA: Harvard University Press, 1987.

Burridge, Richard A. *What Are the Gospels? A Comparison with Graeco-Roman Biography*. Society for New Testament Studies Monograph Series 70. Cambridge, MA: Cambridge University Press, 1992.

Butts, James. "The 'Progymnasmata' of Theon: A New Text with Translation and Commentary." Ph.D. diss., The Claremont Graduate School, 1987.

Cameron, Averil. *Christianity and the Rhetoric of Empire: The Development of Christian Discourse.* Sather Classical Lectures 55. Berkeley, CA: University of California Press, 1991.

Cameron, Ron. *The Other Gospels: Non-Canonical Gospel Texts.* Philadelphia, PA: Westminster, 1982.

——. "The Gospel of the Hebrews." Pages 333–35 in *The Other Bible.* Edited by W. Barnstone. San Francisco, CA: HarperCollins, 1984.

——. "Parable and Interpretation in the Gospel of Thomas." *Forum* 2:2 (1986): 13–39.

——. "The *Gospel of Thomas* and Christian Origins." Pages 381–92 in *The Future of Early Christianity: Essays in Honor of Helmut Koester.* Edited by B. Pearson in Collaboration with A. Thomas Kraabel, George W. E. Nickelsburg and Norman R. Petersen. Minneapolis, MN: Fortress, 1991.

——. "Alternate Beginnings—Different Ends: Eusebius, Thomas, and the Construction of Christians Origins." Pages 501–25 in *Religious Propaganda and Missionary Competition in the New Testament World: Essays Honoring Dieter Georgi.* Edited by Lukas Bormann, Kelly Del Tredici and Angela Standhartinger. Novum Testamentum Supplements 74. Leiden: Brill, 1994.

Campbell, David A. *Greek Lyric Poetry: A Selection of Early Greek Lyric, Elegiac and Iambic Poetry.* London: Macmillan, 1967.

Cavallin, Hans C. C. *An Enquiry into the Jewish Background.* Vol. 1 of *Life after Death: Paul's Argument for the Resurrection of the Death in 1 Cor 15.* Coniectanea Biblica: New Testament Series 7:1. Lund: Gleerup, 1974.

Cerfaux, Lucien, and Gérard Garitte. "Les paraboles du Royaume dans L'Évangile de Thomas." *Muséon* 70 (1957): 307–27.

Clairmont, Christoph. *Gravestone and Epigram: Greek Memorials from the Archaic and Classical Period.* Mainz: Zabern, 1970.

Collins, John J. "The Root of Immortality: Death in the Context of Jewish Wisdom." *Harvard Theological Review* 71 (1978): 177–92.

——. "Introduction: Towards the Morphology of a Genre." Pages 1–20 in *Apocalypse: The Morphology of a Genre.* Edited by Adela Yarbro Collins. Semeia 14. Missoula, MT: Scholars Press, 1979.

Corley, Kathleen E. *Women and the Historical Jesus: Feminist Myths of Christian Origins.* Santa Rosa, CA: Polebridge Press, 2002.

Cornélis, E. "Quelques éléments pour une comparison entre l'Évangile de Thomas et la notice d'Hippolyte sur les Naassènes." *Vigiliae Christianae* 15 (1961): 83–104.

Crossan, John Dominic. *In Parables: The Challenge of the Historical Jesus.* New York, NY: Harper, 1973.

——. *In Fragments: The Aphorisms of Jesus.* San Francisco, CA: Harper & Row, 1983.

Crossan, John Dominic. *Four Other Gospels: Shadows on the Contours of Canon.* Minneapolis, MN: Seabury, 1984. Repr., Sonoma, CA: Polebridge Press, 1992.

——. *The Historical Jesus: The Life of a Mediterranean Jewish Peasant.* New York, NY: HarperCollins, 1991.

——. *The Birth of Christianity: Discovering What Happened in the Years Immediately after the Execution of Jesus.* New York, NY: HarperCollins, 1998.

Crum, Walter E. *A Coptic Dictionary.* Oxford: Oxford University Press, 1939.

Cullmann, O. "Das Thomasevengelium und die Frage nach dem Alter in ihm enthaltenen Tradition." *Theologische Literaturzeitung* 85 (1960): 321–34.

Daniels, Jon. "The Egerton Gospel: Its place in Early Christianity." Ph.D. diss., The Claremont Graduate School, 1989.

Davies, Stevan L. *The Gospel of Thomas and Christian Wisdom.* New York, NY: Seabury, 1983.

——. "The Christology and Protology of the *Gospel of Thomas.*" *Journal of Biblical Literature* 111 (1992): 663–82.

——. "The Oracles of the Gospel of Thomas." Paper Presented at the annual meeting of the Society of Biblical Literature. Chicago, IL, Nov. 19–22, 1994.

Day, Joseph W. "Rituals in Stone: Early Greek Grave Epigrams and Monuments." *Journal of Hellenic Studies* 109 (1989): 16–28.

DeConick, April D. *Seek to See Him: Ascent and Vision Mysticism in the Gospel of Thomas.* Supplements to Vigiliae Christianae 33. Leiden: Brill, 1996.

——. *Voices of the Mystics: Early Christian Discourse in the Gospels of John and Thomas and Other Ancient Christian Literature.* Journal for the Study of the New Testament. Supplement Series 157. Sheffield: Sheffield Academic Press, 2001.

——. "The Original *Gospel of Thomas*." *Vigiliae Christianae* 56 (2002): 167–99.

——. *Recovering the Original Gospel of Thomas: A History of the Gospel and Its Growth.* Journal for the Study of the New Testament: Supplement Series 286. London: T & T Clark International, 2005.

Dewey, Arthur J. "A Passing Remark: Thomas 42." *Forum* 10:1–2 (1994): 69–85.

Dibelius, Martin. *Die Formgeschichte des Evangeliums.* 4th ed. With a foreword by G. Bornkamm. Tübingen: Mohr, 1961 [1919].

Döring, Klaus. *Exemplum Socratis: Studien zur Sokratesnachwirkung in der kynisch-stoischen Popularphilosophie der frühen Kaiserzeit und im frühen Christentum.* Hermes 42. Wiesbaden: Steiner, 1979.

Douglas, Mary. *Natural Symbols: Explorations in Cosmology.* 2nd ed. London: Barrie & Jenkins, 1973 [1970].

Downing, F. Gerald. "Ethical Pagan Theism and the Speeches in Acts." *New Testament Studies* 27 (1981): 544–63.

——. "Common Ground with Paganism in Luke and in Josephus." *New Testament Studies* 28 (1982): 546–59.

——. *Cynics and Christian Origins.* Edinburgh: Clark, 1992.

Drijvers, Han J. W. "The *Acts of Thomas*." Pages 322–339 in *Writings Relating to the Apostles; Apocalypses and Related Subjects.* Vol. 2 of *New Testament Apocrypha.* Edited by Wilhelm Schneemelcher. English translation edited by R. McL. Wilson; Louisville, KY: Westminster John Knox, 1992.

Drijvers, Han J. W., and G. J. Reinink. "Taufe und Licht: Tatian, Ebionäerevangelium und Thomasakten." Pages 91–110 in *Text and Testimony: Essays in Honour of A. F. J. Klijn.* Edited by T. Baarda, A. Hilhorst, G. P. Luttikhuizen, and A. S. van der Wonde. Kampen: Kok, 1988. Repr. in Han J. W. Drijvers, *History and Religion in Late Antique Syria.* Aldershot: Variorum, 1994.

Dudley, Ronald R. *A History of Cynicism: From Diogenes to the 6th Century A.D.* Repr., Chicago, IL: Ares, 1980 [1937].

Dunderberg, Ismo. "Thomas' I—sayings and the Gospel of John." Pages 33–64 in *Thomas at the Crossroads: Essays on the Gospel of Thomas.* Edited by Risto Uro. Studies of the New Testament and Its World. Edinburgh: Clark, 1998.

——. "Thomas and the Beloved Disciple." Pages 65–88 in *Thomas at the Crossroads: Essays on the Gospel of Thomas.* Edited by Risto Uro. Studies of the New Testament and Its World. Edinburgh: Clark, 1998.

——. "Valentinian Views about Adam's Creation: Valentinus and the *Gospel of Philip*." Pages 509–27 in *Lux Humana, Lux Aeterna.* FS Lars Aejmelaeus. Edited by Antti Mustakallio, Heikki Leppä and Heikki Räisänen. Publications of the Finnish Exegetical Society 89. Helsinki: The Finnish Exegetical Society, 2005.

Dunkerley, Roderic. *Beyond the Gospels.* Middlesex: Penguin, 1957.

Dunn, James D. G. "Christology (NT)." Pages 979–91 in volume 1 of *The Anchor Bible Dictionary.* Edited by David Noel Freedman. 6 vols. New York, NY: Doubleday, 1992.

Elliott, John K. "The *Acts of Thomas*." Pages 439–511 in *The Apocryphal New Testament.* Edited by J. K. Elliott. Oxford: Clarendon, 1993.

Elliot, John H. "Social-Scientific Criticism of the New Testament: More on Methods and Models." Pages 1–33 in *Social-Scientific Criticism of the New Testament and Its Social World.* Edited by John H. Elliott. Semeia 35. Decatur, GA: Scholars Press, 1986.

Emmel, Stephen. "Indexes of Words, Catalogues of Grammatical Forms." Pages 262–336 in *Gospel According to Thomas, Gospel According to Philip, Hypostasis of the Archons, and Indexes*. Vol. 1 of *Nag Hammadi Codex II, 2–7 together with XIII,2*, Brit. Lib. Or. 4926(1), and P. Oxy. 1, 654, 655*. Edited by Bentley Layton. Nag Hammadi Studies 20. Leiden: Brill, 1989.

Engberg-Pedersen, Troels. *Paul and the Stoics*. Louisville, KY: Westminster John Knox, 2000.

Epictetus. Translated by W. A. Oldfather. 2 vols. Loeb Classical Library. Cambridge, MA: Harvard University Press, 1925–28.

Eriksson, Anders. *Traditions as Rhetorical Proof: Pauline Argumentation in 1 Corinthians*. Coniectanea Biblica: New Testament Series 29. Stockholm: Almquist & Wiksell International, 1998.

Erskine, Andrew. *The Hellenistic Stoa: Political Thought and Action*. Ithaca, NY: Cornell University Press, 1990.

Fallon, Francis T., and Ron Cameron. "The Gospel of Thomas: A Forschungsbericht and Analysis." *Aufstieg und Niedergang der römischen Welt* 25.6: 4195–251. Part 2, Principat 25.6. Edited by H. Temporini and W. Haase. Berlin: De Gruyter, 1988.

Fieger, Michael. *Das Thomasevangelium: Einleitung, Kommentar und Systematik*. Neutestamentliche Abhandlungen, n.F. 22. Münster: Aschendorff, 1991.

Finley, Moses I. *The Ancient Economy*. 2nd ed. London: Penguin, 1992.

Fischel, H. A. "Prolegomenon." Pages xii–xxiv in *Essays in Graeco-Roman and Related Talmudic Literature*. Selected by H. A. Fischel. Edited by H. M. Orlinsky. New York, NY: KTAV, 1977.

Fitzmyer, Joseph A. "The Oxyrhynchus Logoi of Jesus and the Coptic Gospel according to Thomas." Pages 355–433 in *Essays on the Semitic Background of the New Testament*. London: Geoffrey Chapman, 1971.

Foley, Helene P., ed. *The Homeric Hymn to Demeter: Translation, Commentary, and Interpretive Essays*. Princeton, NJ: Princeton University Press, 1994.

Fossum, Jarl. "Jewish-Christian Christology and Jewish Mysticism." *Vigiliae Christianae* 37 (1983): 260–87.

———. "*Kyrios Jesus* and the Angel of the Lord in Jude 5–7." *New Testament Studies* 33 (1987): 226–43.

———. "Colossians 1.15–18a in the Light of Jewish Mysticism and Gnosticism." *New Testament Studies* 35 (1989): 183–201.

Foucault, Michel. *The Use of Pleasure*. Vol. 2 of *The History of Sexuality*. Translated by R. Hurley. London: Penguin, 1992.

Francis, James A. *Subversive Virtue: Asceticism and Authority in the Second Century Pagan World*. University Park, PA: The Pennsylvania State University Press, 1995.

Franzmann, Majella. *Jesus in the Nag Hammadi Writings*. Edinburgh: Clark, 1996.

Freedman, H., and Maurice Simon, *Midrash Rabbah*. 10 vols. London: Soncino, 1939–51.

Frend, William Hugh Clifford. "The Gospel of Thomas: Is Rehabilitation Possible." *Journal of Theological Studies* 18 (1967): 13–26.

Frid, Bo, and Jesper Svartvik. *Thomasevangeliet*. Lund: Arcus, 2002.

Funk, Robert W. *John and the Other Gospels*. Vol. 2 of *New Gospel Parallels*. Edited by Robert W. Funk. Philadelphia, PA: Fortress, 1985.

———. *Honest to Jesus*. New York, NY: Harper Collins, 1996.

Gager, John G. *Moses in Greco-Roman Paganism*. Society of Biblical Literature Monograph Series 16. Nashville, TN: Abingdon, 1972.

Galletier, Édouard. *Étude sur la poésie funéraire romaine d'après les inscriptions*. Paris: Hachette, 1922.

Gärtner, Bertil. *Ett nytt evangelium? Thomasevangeliets hemliga Jesusord*. Stockholm: Diakonistyrelsens bokförlag, 1960. English Translation: Gärtner, Bertil. *Theology of the Gospel of Thomas*. Translated by Eric J. Sharpe. London: Collins, 1961. New York, NY: Harper.

Garland, Robert. *The Greek Way of Death*. 2nd ed. Ithaca, NY: Cornell University Press, 2001.

Geffcken, Johannes. *Griechische Epigramme*. Heidelberg: Winter, 1916.

Georgi, Dieter. *The Opponents of Paul in Second Corinthians*. Philadelphia, PA: Fortress, 1986.

Glockmann, Günter. *Homer in der frühchristlichen Literatur bis Justinus*. Texte und Untersuchungen zur Geschichte der altchristlichen Literatur 105. Berlin: Akademie-Verlag, 1968.

Goodenough, Erwin R. "Philo on Immortality." *Harvard Theological Review* 39 (1946): 85–108.

Graf, Fritz. *Eleusis und die orphische Dichtung Athens in vorhellenistischer Zeit*. Religionsgeschichtliche Versuche und Vorarbeiten 33. Berlin: De Gruyter, 1974.

Grant, Robert M. "Notes on the Gospel of Thomas." *Vigilae christianae* 13 (1959): 170–80.

Grant, Robert M., and David Noel Freedman. *The Secret Sayings of Jesus*. With an English Translation of the Gospel of Thomas by William R. Schoedel. Garden City, NY: Doubleday, 1960. London: Collins, 1960.

Griffin, Jasper. *Homer on Life and Death*. Oxford: Clarendon, 1980.

Griffith, Mark. "Man and the Leaves: A Study of Mimnermus fr. 2." *California Studies in Classical Antiquity* 8 (1976): 73–88.

Grobel, Kendrick. "How Gnostic is the *Gospel of Thomas*?" *New Testament Studies* 8 (1961–62): 367–73.

Gruen, Erich S. *Heritage and Hellenism: The Reinvention of Jewish Tradition*. Berkeley, CA: University of California Press, 1998.

Haenchen, Ernst. *Die Botschaft des Thomas-Evangeliums*. Theologische Bibliothek Töpelmann 6. Berlin: Töpelmann, 1961.

———. "Literatur zum Thomasevangelium." *Theologische Rundschau*, n.F. 27 (1961–62): 147–78, 306–38.

Hamilton, Edith, and Huntington Cairns, eds. *Plato: The Collected Dialogues including the Letters*. With Introduction and Prefatory Notes. Bollingen Series 71. Princeton, NJ: Princeton University Press, 1961.

Handmann, Rudolf. *Hebräer-Evangelium: Ein Beitrag zur Geschichte und Kritik des Hebräischen Matthäus*. Leipzig: Hinrichs, 1888.

Hansen, Peter Allan. *Carmina epigraphica graeca*. Berlin: De Gruyter, 1983.

Harrington, Daniel J. S.J., *The Gospel of Matthew*. Sacra Pagina 1. Collegeville, MN: The Liturgical Press, 1991.

Harris, J. Rendel. *Boanerges*. Cambridge, MA: Cambridge University Press, 1913.

Hartin, Patrick J. "The Search for the True Self in the *Gospel of Thomas*, the *Book of Thomas* and the *Hymn of the Pearl*." *Hervormde teologiese studies* 55 (1999): 1001–21.

Hellermann, Joseph H. *The Ancient Church as Family*. Minneapolis, MN: Fortress, 2001.

Henderson, John B. *Scripture, Canon, and Commentary: A Comparison of Confucian and Western Exegesis*. Princeton, NJ: Princeton University Press, 1991.

Hicks, Edward L., Charles T. Newton, Gustav Hirshfeld, and F. H. Marshall, eds. *The Collection of Ancient Greek Inscriptions in the British Museum*. 4 vols. Oxford: Clarendon, 1874–1916. Repr., Milan: Cisalpino, 1977–79.

Hock, Ronald F., and Edward N. O'Neil, eds. *The Progymnasmata*. Vol. 1 of *The Chreia in Ancient Rhetoric*. Society of Biblical Literature Texts and Translations 27: Graeco-Roman Religion Series 9. Atlanta, GA: Scholars Press, 1986.

Hock, Ronald F. "Homer in Greco-Roman Education," Pages 56–77 in *Mimesis and Intertextuality in Antiquity and Christianity*. Edited by Dennis R. MacDonald. Studies in Antiquity and Christianity. Harrisburg, PA: Trinity Press International, 2001.

Hoffmann, Paul. *Studien zur Theologie der Logienquelle*. Neutestamentliche Abhandlungen 8. Münster: Aschendorf, 1972.

Holman, Susan R. "Healing the Social Leper in Gregory of Nyssa's and Gregory of Nazianzus's 'περὶ φιλοπτωχίας'." *Harvard Theological Review* 92 (1999): 283–309.

Holmberg, Bengt. *Sociology and the New Testament: An Appraisal*. Minneapolis, MN: Fortress, 1990.

Holmes, Michael W., ed. *The Apostolic Fathers: Greek Texts and English Translations.* Grand Rapids, MI: Baker, 1999.

Holzhausen, Jens. "Gnosis und Martyrium: Zu Valentins viertem Fragment." *Zeitschrift für die neutestamentliche Wissenschaft und die Kunde der älteren Kirche* 85 (1994): 116–31.

Horrell, David G. *The Social Ethos of the Corinthian Correspondence: Interests and Ideology from 1 Corinthians to 1 Clement.* Studies of the New Testament and Its World. Edinburgh: Clark, 1996.

Horsley, G. H. R. *New Documents Illustrating Early Christianity: A Review of Greek Inscriptions and Papyri Published in 1977.* North Ryde: Ancient History Documentary Research Centre, Macquarie University, 1982.

———. *New Documents Illustrating Early Christianity: A Review of Greek Inscriptions and Papyri Published in 1978.* North Ryde: Ancient History Documentary Research Centre, Macquarie University, 1983.

Horsley, Richard A. *Sociology and the Jesus Movement.* New York, NY: Crossroad, 1989.

Horsley, Richard A., and Jonathan A. Draper. *Whoever Hears You Hears Me: Prophets, Performance, and Tradition in Q.* Harrisburg, PA: Trinity Press International, 1999.

Humphreys, Sally C. "Family Tombs and Tomb Cult in Ancient Athens: Tradition or Traditionalism?" *Journal of Hellenic Studies* 100 (1980): 96–126.

Hurley, Patrick J. *A Concise Introduction to Logic.* 2nd ed. Belmont: Wadsworth, 1985.

Jackson, Howard M. *The Lion Becomes Man: The Gnostic Leontomorphic Creator and the Platonic Tradition.* Society of Biblical Literature Dissertation Series 81. Atlanta, GA: Scholars Press, 1983.

Jacobson, Arland D. "Jesus against the Family: The Dissolution of Family Ties in the Gospel Tradition." Pages 189–218 in *From Quest to Q: Festschrift James M. Robinson.* Edited by Jon Ma. Asgeirsson, Kristin de Toyer and Marvin W. Meyer. Bibliotheca Ephemeridum Theologicarum Lovaniensium 146. Leuven: Peeters & Leuven University Press, 2000.

Jaeger, Werner. *Early Christianity and Greek Paideia.* Cambridge, MA: Harvard University Press, 1962.

Jeffery, Lilian H. "The Inscribed Gravestones of Archaic Attica." *Annual of the British School at Athens* 57 (1962): 115–53.

Jeremias, Joachim. *Unbekannte Jesuworte.* 3rd. ed. Gütersloh: Mohn, 1963.

———. *The Parables of Jesus.* 2nd ed. New York, NY: Scribners, 1972.

Jervell, Jacob. *Imago Dei: Gen. 1,26f. im Spätjudentum, in der Gnosis und in den paulinischen Briefen.* Forschungen zur Religion und Litteratur des Alten und Neuen Testament 58. Göttingen: Vandenhoeck & Ruprecht, 1960.

Johansen, K. Friis. *The Attic Grave—Reliefs of the Classical Period: An Essay in Interpretation.* Copenhagen: Munksgaard, 1951.

Johnson, Luke Timothy. *The Letter of James: A New Translation with Introduction and Commentary.* The Anchor Bible 37A. New York, NY: Doubleday, 1995.

Johnston, Sarah Iles. *Restless Dead: Encounters between the Living and the Dead in Ancient Greece.* Berkeley, CA: University of California Press, 1999.

Johnson, Stephen R. "The *Gospel of Thomas* 76:3 and Canonical Parallels: Three Segments in the Tradition History of the Saying." Pages 308–26 in *The Nag Hammadi Library after Fifty Years: Proceedings of the 1995 Society of Biblical Literature Commemoration.* Edited by John D. Turner and Anne McGuire. Nag Hammadi and Manichaean Studies 44. Leiden: Brill, 1997.

Jonas, Hans. *The Gnostic Religion.* 2nd ed. London: Routledge, 1963.

Jones, F. Stanley. *An Ancient Jewish Christian Source on the History of Christianity: Pseudo-Clementine Recognitions 1.27–71.* Society of Biblical Literature Texts and Translations 37. Atlanta, GA: Scholars Press, 1995.

Kaibel, Georg. *Epigrammata graeca ex lapidibus conlecta.* Berlin, 1878. Repr., Hildesheim: Olms, 1965.

Kallarangatt, Joseph. "The *Acts of Thomas* Deserves More Theological and Ecclesiological Attention." *Christian Orient* 17 (1986): 3–18.

Kasser, Rodolphe. *L'Évangile selon Thomas: Présentation et commentaire théologique*. Bibliothèque théologique. Neuchâtel: Delachaux & Niestlé, 1961.

Kennedy, George A. *New Testament Interpretation through Rhetorical Criticism*. Chapel Hill: University of North Carolina Press, 1984.

——. *Aristotle On Rhetoric: A Theory of Civic Discourse*. New York, NY: Oxford University Press, 1991.

Khalidi, Tarif, ed. and trans. *The Muslim Jesus: Sayings and Stories in Islamic Literature*. Convergences: Inventories of the Present. Cambridge, MA: Harvard University Press, 2001.

Klijn, A. F. J. *The Acts of Thomas: Introduction—Text—Commentary*. Novum Testamentum Supplements 5. Leiden: Brill, 1962.

——. "Jewish-Christianity in Egypt." Pages 161–75 in *The Roots of Egyptian Jewish Christianity*. Studies in Antiquity and Christianity. Edited by Birger A. Pearson and James E. Goehring. Philadelphia, PA: Fortress, 1986.

——. *Jewish-Christian Gospel Tradition*. Supplements to Vigiliae Christianae 17. Leiden: Brill, 1992.

Klijn, A. F. J., and. G. J. Reinink. *Patristic Evidence for Jewish-Christian Sects*. Novum Testamentum Supplements 36. Leiden: Brill, 1973.

Kline, Leslie L. *The Sayings of Jesus in the Pseudo-Clementine Homilies*. Society of Bibilical Literature Dissertation Series 14. Missoula, MT: Scholars Press, 1975.

Kloppenborg, John S. *The Formation of Q: Trajectories in Ancient Wisdom Collections*. Studies in Antiquity and Christianity. Philadelphia, PA: Fortress, 1987.

——. "Nomos and Ethos in Q," Pages 35–48 in *Gospel Origins and Christian Beginnings: In Honor of James M. Robinson*. Edited by James E. Goehring Charles W. Hedrick, Jack T. Sanders with Hans Dieter Betz. Forum Fascicles 1. Sonoma, CA: Polebridge Press, 1990.

——. "Literary Convention, Self–Evidence, and the Social History of the Q People." Pages 77–102 in. *Early Christianity, Q, and Jesus*. Edited by John Kloppenborg and Leif Vaage. Semeia 55. Atlanta, GA: Scholars Press, 1992.

Kloppenborg Verbin, John S. "A Dog among the Pigeons." Pages 73–80 in *From Quest to Q: Festschrift James M. Robinson*. Edited by Jon Ma. Asgeirsson, Kristine De Troyer, and Marvin Meyer. Bibliotheca Ephemeridum Theologicarum Lovaniensium 146. Leuven: Peeters & Leuven University Press, 2000.

Koester, Helmut. *Synoptische Überlieferung bei den apostolischen Vätern*. Texte und Untersuchungen 65. Berlin: Akademie-Verlag, 1957.

——. "One Jesus and Four Primitive Gospels." *Harvard Theological Review* 61 (1968): 203–47. Repr. pages 158–204 in James M. Robinson and Helmut Koester, *Trajectories through Early Christianity*. Philadelphia, PA: Fortress, 1971.

——. "GNOMAI DIAPHOROI: The Origin and Nature of Diversification in the History of Early Christianity." Pages 114–57 in James M. Robinson and Helmut Koester, *Trajectories through Early Christianity*. Philadelphia, PA: Fortress, 1971.

——. "Apocryphal and Canonical Gospels." *Harvard Theological Review* 73 (1980): 105–130.

——. *Introduction to the New Testament: History and Literature of Early Christianity*. 2 vols. Hermeneia: Foundations and Facets. Philadelphia, PA: Fortress, 1982.

——. "Three Thomas Parables." Pages 195–203 in *The New Testament and Gnosis*. Edited by A. H. B. Logan and A. J. M. Wedderburn. Edinburgh: Clark, 1983.

——. "Introduction" [to the *Gospel According to Thomas*]. Pages 38–49 in *Gospel According to Thomas, Gospel According to Philip, Hypostasis of the Archons, and Indexes*. Vol. 1 of *Nag Hammadi Codex II, 2–7 together with XIII, 2*, Brit. Lib. Or. 4926(1), and P. Oxy. 1, 654, 655*. Edited by B. Layton. Nag Hammadi Studies 20. Leiden: Brill, 1989.

——. *Ancient Christian Gospels: Their History and Development*. Philadelphia, PA: Trinity Press International, 1990.

——. "Q and Its Relatives," Pages 49–63 in *Gospel Origins and Christian Beginnings:*

In Honor of James M. Robinson. Forum Fascicles 1. Edited by James E. Goehring, Charles W. Hedrick, Jack T. Sanders with Hans Dieter Betz. Sonoma, CA: Polebridge Press, 1990.

Kolarcik, Michael. *The Ambiguity of Death in the Book of Wisdom 1–6: A Study of Literary Structure and Interpretation*. Analecta Biblica 127. Rome: Pontificial Biblical Institute, 1991.

Kretschmar, Georg. "Ein Beiträg zur Frage nach dem Ursprung frühchristlichen Askese." *Zeitschrift für Theologie und Kirche* 61 (1964): 27–67.

Kurtz, Donna C., and John Boardman. *Greek Burial Customs*. Ithaca, NY: Cornell University Press, 1971.

LaFargue, Michael. *Language and Gnosis: The Opening Scenes of the Acts of Thomas*. Harvard Dissertation in Religion 18. Philadelphia, PA: Fortress, 1985.

Lambdin, Thomas. "The *Gospel According to Thomas*" [English translation]. Pages 53–93 in *Gospel According to Thomas, Gospel According to Philip, Hypostasis of the Archons, and Indexes*. Vol. 1 of *Nag Hammadi Codex II, 2–7 together with XIII,2*, Brit. Lib. Or. 4926(1), and P. Oxy. 1, 654, 655*. Edited by Bentley Layton. Nag Hammadi Studies 20. Leiden: Brill, 1989.

Lanigan, Richard L. "From Enthymeme to Abduction: The Classical Law of Logic and the Postmodern Rule of Rhetoric." Pages 49–70 in *Recovering Pragmatism's Voice: The Classical Tradition, Rorty, and the Philosophy of Communication*. Edited by L. Langsdorf and A. R. Smith. Albany, NY: SUNY, 1995.

Lattimore, Richmond. *Themes in Greek and Latin Epitaphs*. Illinois Studies in Language and Literature 28:1–2. Urbana, IL: University of Illinois Press 1942.

———. *The Odes of Pindar*. 2nd ed. Chicago, IL: University of Chicago Press, 1976.

Latyshev, Basilius, *Inscriptiones orae septentionalis Ponti Euxini graecae et latinae*. St. Petersburg: Societas Archaeologica Imperii Russici, 1885–1916. Repr. Hildesheim: Olms, 1965.

Layton, Bentley. *The Gnostic Scriptures: A New Translation with Annotations and Introductions*. Garden City, NY: Doubleday, 1987.

———, ed. *Gospel According to Thomas, Gospel According to Philip, Hypostasis of the Archons, and Indexes*. Vol. 1 of *Nag Hammadi Codex II, 2–7 together with XIII, 2*, Brit. Lib. Or. 4926(1), and P. Oxy. 1, 654, 655*. Nag Hammadi Studies 20. Leiden: Brill, 1989.

———. *A Coptic Grammar, with Chrestomathy and Glossary, Sahidic Dialect*. Porta Linguarum Orientalium, NS, 20. Wiesbaden: Harrassowitz, 2000.

Leipoldt, Johannes. "Ein neues Evangelium? Das koptische Thomasevangelium übersetz und bescprochen." *Teologische Literaturzeitung* 83 (1958): 482–96.

———. *Das Evangelium nach Thomas: Koptisch und Deutsch*. Texte und Untersuchungen 101. Berlin: Akademie-Verlag, 1967.

Lelyveld, Margaretha. *Les logia de la vie dans l'Évangile selon Thomas: Á la recherche d'une tradition et d'une rédaction*. Nag Hammadi Studies 34. Leiden: Brill, 1987.

Lentz, Tony M. *Orality and Literacy in Hellenic Greece*. Carbondale: Southern Illinois University Press, 1989.

Lesky, Albin. *Geschichte der griechischen Literatur*. 3rd ed. Bern & Munich: Francke Verlag, 1971 [1957–1958].

Liddell, H. G., and R. Scott. *Greek-English Lexicon*. London: Clarendon, 1973.

Lier, Bruno. "Topica carminum sepulcralium latinorum." *Philologus* 62 (1903): 445–77.

Logan, Alastair H. B. *Gnostic Truth and Christian Heresy*. Edinburgh: Clark, 1996.

Lowry, Eddie R., Jr. "Glaucus, the Leaves, and the Heroic Boast of *Iliad* 6.146–211." Pages 193–211 in *The Ages of Homer: A Tribute to Emily T. Vermeule*. Edited by Jane B. Carter and Sarah P. Morris. Austin, TX: University of Texas Press, 1995.

Luomanen, Petri. "Where Did Another Rich Man Come From? The Jewish-Christian Profile of the Story about the Rich Man in the 'Gospel of the Hebrews' (Origen, *Comm. in Matth.* 15.14)." *Vigiliae Christianae* 57 (2003): 243–75.

Luz, Ulrich. *Das Evangelium nach Matthäus, Mt 8–17*. Evangelisch-katholischer Kommentar zum Neuen Testament 1:2. Zürich: Benziger Verlag, 1990.

——. *Das Evangelium nach Matthäus, Mt 18–25.* Evangelisch-katholischer Kommentar zum Neuen Testament 1:3. Zürich: Benziger Verlag, 1997.

MacDonald, Dennis Ronald Jr., ed. *The Apocryphal Acts of Apostles.* Semeia 38. Atlanta, GA: Scholars Press, 1986.

MacDonald, Dennis Ronald. *There is No Male and Female: The Fate of a Dominical Saying in Paul and Gnosticism.* Philadelphia, PA: Fortress, 1987.

——, ed. *Christianizing Homer: The Odyssey, Plato and the Acts of Andrew.* New York, NY: Oxford University Press, 1994.

——. *The Homeric Epics and the Gospel of Mark.* New Haven: Yale University Press, 2000.

McGuire, Anne. "Virginity and Subversion: Norea Against the Powers in the *Hypostasis of the Archons.*" Pages 239–58 in *Images of the Feminine in Gnosticism.* Edited by K. L. King. Studies in Antiquity and Christianity. Philadelphia, PA: Fortress, 1988.

Mack, Burton L. "The Kingdom Sayings in Mark." *Forum* 3:1 (1987): 3–47.

——. "The Kingdom That Didn't Come." Pages 620–21 in the *SBL Seminar Papers, 1988.* Society of Biblical Literature Seminar Papers 27. Atlanta, GA: Scholars Press, 1988.

——. *A Myth of Innocence: Mark and Christian Origins.* Philadelphia, PA: Fortress, 1988.

——. *Rhetoric and the New Testament.* Guides to Biblical Scholarship. Minneapolis, MN: Fortress, 1990.

——. *The Lost Gospel: The Book of Q and Christian Origins.* San Francisco, CA: HarperSanFrancisco, 1993.

——. *Who Wrote the New Testament: The Making of the Christian Myth.* San Francisco, CA: HarperSanFrancisco, 1995.

Mack, Burton L., and Edward N. O'Neil. "The Chreia Discussion of Hermogenes of Tarsus: Introduction, Translation and Comments." Pages 153–81 in vol. 1 of *The Chreia in Ancient Rhetoric.* Edited by Ronald F. Hock and Edward N. O'Neil. Society of Biblical Literature Texts and Translations 27: Graeco-Roman Religion Series 9. Atlanta, GA: Scholars Press, 1986.

Mack, Burton L., and Vernon K. Robbins. *Patterns of Persuasion in the Gospels.* Foundations & Facets: Literary Facets. Sonoma, CA: Polebridge Press, 1989.

Malherbe, Abraham J. *The Cynic Epistles.* A Study Edition. Society of Biblical Literature Sources for Biblical Study 12. Atlanta, GA: Scholars Press, 1977.

——. *Paul and the Popular Philosophers.* Minneapolis, MN: Fortress, 1989.

Marcus, Joel. *The Mystery of the Kingdom of God.* Society of Biblical Literature Dissertation Series 90. Atlanta, GA: Scholars Press, 1986.

Margoliouth, David Samuel. "Christ in Islam: Sayings Attributed to Christ by Mohammedan Writers." *The Expository Times* 5 (1893–94): 59, 107, 177–78, 503–4, 561.

Marjanen, Antti. *The Woman Jesus Loved: Mary Magdalene in Nag Hammadi Library and Related Documents.* Nag Hammadi and Manichaean Studies 40; Leiden: Brill, 1996.

——. "Women Disciples in the *Gospel of Thomas.*" Pages 89–106 in *Thomas at the Crossroads. Essays on the Gospel of Thomas.* Edited by R. Uro. Edinburgh: Clark, 1998.

——. "Is *Thomas* a Gnostic Gospel?" Pages 107–39 in *Thomas at the Crossroads: Essays on the Gospel of Thomas.* Edited by R. Uro. Studies of the New Testament and Its World. Edinburgh: Clark, 1998.

——. "*Thomas* and Jewish Religious Practices." Pages 163–82 in *Thomas at the Crossroads: Essays on the Gospel of Thomas.* Edited by R. Uro. Studies of the New Testament and Its World. Edinburgh: Clark, 1998.

——. "The Suffering of One Who Is a Stranger to Suffering: The Crucifixion of Jesus in the Letter of Peter to Philip." Pages 487–98 in *Fair Play: Diversity and Conflicts in Early Christianity: Essays in Honour of Heikki Räisänen.* Edited by Ismo Dunderberg, Kari Syreeni and Christopher Tuckett. Novum Testamentum Supplements 103. Leiden: Brill, 2002.

Markschies, Christoph. *Valentinus Gnosticus? Untersuchungen zur valentinianischen Gnosis mit einem Kommentar zu den Fragmenten Valentin*. Wissenschaftliche Untersuchungen zum Neuen Testament 65. Tübingen: Mohr, 1992.

Martin, Dale B. *The Corinthian Body*. New Haven, CT: Yale University Press, 1995.

May, Herbert G., and Bruce M. Metzger, eds. *The New Oxford Annotated Bible with the Apocrypha: Revised Standard Version*. Containing the Second Edition of the New Testament and an Expanded Edition of the Apocrypha. An Ecumenical Study Bible. New York, NY: Oxford University Press, 1977.

Mayeda, Goro. *Das Leben—Jesu—Fragment Papyrus Egerton 2 und seine Stellung in der urchristlichen Literaturgeschichte*. Bern: Haupt, 1946.

Meeks, Wayne A. "The Man From Heaven in Johannine Sectarianism." *Journal of Biblical Literature* 91 (1972): 44–72.

Ménard, Jacques É. *L'Évangile selon Thomas*. Nag Hammadi Studies 5. Leiden: Brill, 1975.

Meyer, Marvin W. *The Gospel of Thomas: The Hidden Sayings of Jesus*. San Francisco, CA: Harper, 1992.

——. *The Unknown Sayings of Jesus*. San Francisco, CA: HarperSanFrancisco, 1998.

——. "Did Jesus Drink from a Cup? The Equipment of Jesus and His Followers in Q and al-Ghazzali." Pages 143–56 in *From Quest to Q; Festschrift James M. Robinson*. Edited by Jon Ma. Asgeirsson, Kristin De Troyer, and Marvin Meyer. Bibliotheca Ephemeridum Theologicarum Lovaniensium 146. Leuven: Peeters & Leuven University Press, 2000.

——. "Albert Schweitzer and the Image of Jesus in the *Gospel of Thomas*." Pages 72–90 in *Jesus Then and Now: Images of Jesus in History and Christology*. Edited by Marvin Meyer and Charles Hughes. Harrisburg, PA: Trinity Press International, 2001.

——. *Gospel of Thomas* Logion 114 Revisited." Pages 101–11 in *For the Children, Perfect Instruction: Studies in Honor of Hans-Martin Schenke on the Occasion of the Berliner Arbeitskreis für koptisch-gnostische Schriften's Thirtieth Year*. Edited by Hans-Gebhard Bethge, Stephen Emmel, Karen L. King and Imke Schletterer. Nag Hammadi and Manichaean Studies 54. Leiden: Brill, 2002. Repr. pages 96–106 in *Secret Gospels*.

——. *Secret Gospels: Essays on Thomas and the Secret Gospel of Mark*. Harrisburg, PA, Trinity Press International, 2003.

Miles, Jack. *God: A Biography*. New York, NY: Vintage Books, 1996.

Miller, Robert J., ed. *The Complete Gospels*. Annotated Scholars Version. Rev. and exp. ed. Sonoma, CA: Polebridge Press, 1994.

Mimouni, Simon Claude. *Le judéo-christianisme ancien: essais historiques*. Paris: Cerf, 1998.

Minette de Tillesse, Gaetan. *Le secret messianique dans l'Évangile de Marc*. Paris: Cerf, 1968.

Montefiore, Hugh. "A Comparison of the Parables of the Gospel According to Thomas and of the Synoptic Gospels." *New Testament Studies* 7 (1960–61): 220–48.

Morray-Jones, Christopher R. A. "Paradise Revisited (2 Cor 12:1–12): The Jewish Mystical Background of Paul's Apostolate, Part 1: The Jewish Sources." *Harvard Theological Review* 86 (1993): 177–217.

——. "Paradise Revisited (2 Cor 12:1–12): The Jewish Mystical Background of Paul's Apostolate, Part 2: Paul's Heavenly Ascent and Its Significance." *Harvard Theological Review* 86 (1993): 265–92.

Morrice, William G. *Hidden Sayings of Jesus: Words Attributed to Jesus outside the Four Gospels*. Peabody, MA: Hendrickson, 1997.

Morris, Ian. *Burial and Society: The Rise of the Greek City-State*. Cambridge, MA: Cambridge University Press, 1987.

——. *Death-Ritual and Social Structure in Classical Antiquity*. Cambridge, MA: Cambridge University Press, 1992.

Muir, J. V. "Religion and the New Education: The Challenge of the Sophists." Pages

191–218 in *Greek Religion and Society*. Edited by P. E. Easterling and J. V. Muir. With a Foreword by Sir Moses Finley. London: Cambridge University Press, 1985.

Murphy, Nancey C. *Reasoning & Rhetoric in Religion*. Valley Forge, PA: Trinity Press International, 1994.

Neyrey, Jerome H. *Honor and Shame in the Gospel of Matthew*. Louisville, KY: Westminster John Knox, 1998.

Nortwick, Thomas van. *Somewhere I have Never Travelled: The Second Self and the Hero's Journey in Ancient Epic*. New York, NY: Oxford University Press, 1992.

Novum Testamentum Graece. Post Ebehard et Erwin Nestle editione vicesima septima revisa communiter ediderunt Barbara et Kurt Aland, Johannes Karavidopoulos, Carlo M. Martini, Bruce M. Metzger. Stuttgart: Deutsche Bibelgesellschaft, 1993.

Pagels, Elaine H. *The Johannine Gospel in Gnostic Exegesis*. Nashville, TN: Abingdon, 1973.

——. "Exegesis of Genesis 1 in the *Gospels of Thomas* and John." *Journal of Biblical Literature* 118 (1999): 477–96.

Parisinou, Eva. *The Light of the Greek Gods: The Role of Light in Archaic and Classical Greek Cult*. London: Duckworth, 2000.

Parker, Robert. *Miasma: Pollution and Purification in Early Greek Religion*. Oxford: Clarendon, 1983.

Patterson, Stephen J. "*The Gospel of Thomas:* Introduction." Pages 77–123 in John S. Kloppenborg, Marvin W. Meyer, Stephen J. Patterson and Michael G. Steinhauser. *Q Thomas Reader*. Sonoma, CA: Polebridge Press, 1990.

——. "The *Gospel of Thomas* and the Synoptic Tradition: A Forschungsbericht and Critique." *Forum* 8:1–2 (1992): 45–97.

——. *The Gospel of Thomas and Jesus*. Foundations & Facets: Reference Series. Sonoma, CA: Polebridge Press, 1993.

——. "Wisdom in Q and *Thomas*." Pages 187–221 in *In Search of Wisdom: Essays in Memory of John G. Gammie*. Edited by Leo G. Perdue, Bernard Brandon Scott, and William Johnston Wiseman. Louisville, KY: Westminster John Knox, 1993.

——. "Understanding the *Gospel of Thomas* Today." Pages 33–75 in *The Fifth Gospel: The Gospel of Thomas Comes of Age*. Edited by Stephen J. Patterson, James M. Robinson and Hans-Gebhard Bethge. Harrisburg, PA: Trinity Press International, 1998.

——. "*Askesis* and the Early Jesus Tradition." Pages 49–70 in *Asceticism and the New Testament*. Edited by Leif E. Vaage and Vincent Wimbush. New York, NY and London: Routledge, 1999.

Patterson, Stephen J., James M. Robinson, and Hans-Gebhard Bethge. *The Fifth Gospel: The Gospel of Thomas Comes of Age*. Harrisburg, PA: Trinity Press International, 1998.

Pearson, Birger A., and James E. Goehring. *The Roots of Egyptian Jewish Christianity*. Studies in Antiquity and Christianaity. Philadelphia, PA: Fortress, 1986.

Peek, Werner. *Griechische Vers-Inschriften, I: Grab-Epigramme*. Berlin: Akademie-Verlag, 1955.

Perkins, Judith. *The Suffering Self: Pain and Narrative Representation in the Early Christian Era*. London: Routledge, 1995.

Perrin, Nicholas. *Thomas and Tatian: The Relationship Between the Gospel of Thomas and the Diatessaron*. Academia Biblica 5. Atlanta, GA: Society of Biblical Literature, 2002.

Perrin, Norman. *Rediscovering the Teaching of Jesus*. New York, NY: Harper, 1967.

Petersen, Norman R. *The Gospel of John and the Sociology of Light: Language and Characterization in the Fourth Gospel*. Valley Forge, PA: Trinity Press International, 1993.

Petersen, William L. *Tatian's Diatessaron: Its Creation, Dissemination, Significance and History in Scholarship*. Supplements to Vigiliae Christianae 25. Leiden: Brill, 1994.

Peterson, Erik. "Einige Beobachtungen zu den Anfängen der christlichen Askese." Pages 209–20 in *Frühkirche, Judentum, und Gnosis: Studien und Untersuchungen*. Freiburg: Herder, 1959.

Petrucci, Armando. *Writing the Dead: Death and Writing Strategies in the Western Tradition*. Translated by Michael Sullivan. Stanford, CA: Stanford University Press, 1998.

Philo. Translated by F. H. Colson and G. H. Whitaker. 10 Vols. Loeb Classical Library. Cambridge, MA: Harvard University Press, 1927–62.

Pitre, B. J. "Blessing the Barren and Warning the Fecund: Jesus' Message for Women Concerning Pregnancy and Childbirth." *Journal for the Study of the New Testament* 81 (2001): 59–80.

Pohlenz, Max. *Die Stoa: Geschichte einer geistigen Bewegung.* 2 vols. Göttingen: Vandenhoeck & Ruprecht, 1948–1949.

Potthoff, Stephen E. "Refreshment and Reunion in the Garden of Light." Ph.D. diss., University of Minnesota, 2000.

Powell, Mark Allan. *What is Narrative Criticism? A New Approach to the Bible.* London: SPCK, 1993.

Price, Simon. *Religions of the Ancient Greeks.* Cambridge, MA: Cambridge University Press, 1999.

Pritz, R. A. *Nazarene Jewish Christianity: From the End of the New Testament Period Until Its Disappearance in the Fourth Century.* Leiden: Brill, 1988.

Pyysiäinen, Ilkka. *How Religion Works: Towards a New Cognitive Science of Religion.* Cognition and Culture Book Series 1. Leiden: Brill, 2001.

Quispel, Gilles. " 'The *Gospel of Thomas*' and the 'Gospel of the Hebrews.' " *New Testament Studies* 12 (1965–66): 371–82.

——. *Makarius, das Thomasevangeliums und das Lied von der Perle.* Supplements to Novum Testamentum 15. Leiden: Brill, 1967.

——. "Gnosticism and the New Testament." Pages 196–212 in *Gnostic Studies I.* Nederlands historisch-archaeologisch Instituut te Istanbul 34. Istanbul: Nederlands Historisch-Archaeologisch Instituut te Istanbul, 1974.

——. "The *Gospel of Thomas* and the New Testament." Pages 3–16 in *Gnostic Studies II.* Nederlands Historisch-Archaeologisch Instituut te Istanbul 34. Istanbul: Nederlands Historisch-Arachaeologisch Instituut te Istanbul, 1975.

——. "L'Evangile selon Thomas et les Clementines." Pages 17–29 in *Gnostic Studies II.* Nederlands Historisch-Archaeologisch Instituut te Istanbul 34. Istanbul: Nederlands Historisch-Arachaeologisch Instituut te Istanbul, 1975.

——. "L'Évangile selon Thomas et les origines de l'ascèse chrétienne." Pages 98–112 in *Gnostic Studies II.* Nederlands Historisch-Archaeologisch Instituut te Istanbul 34:2. Istanbul: Nederlands Historisch-Archaeologisch Instituut te Istanbul, 1975.

——. "The Discussion of Judaic Christianity." Pages 146–158 in *Gnostic Studies II.* Nederlands Historisch-Archaeologisch Instituut te Istanbul 34. Istanbul: Nederlands Historisch-Archaeologisch Instituut te Istanbul, 1975.

——. "Gnosis and the New Sayings of Jesus. Pages 180–209 in *Gnostic Studies II.* Nederlands Historisch-Archaeologisch Instituut te Istanbul 34. Istanbul: Nederlands Historisch-Archaeologisch Instituut te Istanbul, 1975.

——. "The *Gospel of Thomas* Revisited." Pages 245–54 in *Colloque International sur Les Textes de Nag Hammadi, Québec, 22–25 août 1978.* Edited by B. Barc. Bibliothèque copte de Nag Hammadi 1. Louvain: Peeters, 1981.

Radice, Roberto. "Observations on the Theory of the Ideas as the Thoughts of God in Philo of Alexandria." Pages 127–34 in *Heirs of the Septuagint: Philo, Hellenistic Judaism and Early Christianity: Festschrift for Earle Hilgert.* Edited by David T. Runia. Studia Philonica 3. Atlanta, GA: Scholars Press, 1991.

Räisänen, Heikki. *Das "Messiasgeheimnis" im Markusevangelium.* Helsinki: The Finnish Exegetical Society, 1976. English translation: *The "Messianic Secret" in Mark's Gospel.* Translated by C. M. Tuckett. Edinburgh: Clark, 1990.

Ur-Rahim, Muhammad 'Ata. *Jesus, Prophet of Islam.* Elmhurst: Tahrike Tarsile Qur'an, 1991.

Rau, Eckhard. "Jenseits von Raum, Zeit und Gemeinschaft: 'Christ-Sein' nach dem Thomasevangelium." *Novum Testamentum* 45 (2003): 138–59.

Raubitschek, Antony Erik. "Das Denkmal-Epigramm." *L'Epigramme grecque: Fondation*

Hardt 14 (1968): 3–36. Repr. pages 245–65 in *The School of Hellas*. New York, NY: Oxford University Press, 1991.

Rebenich, Stefan. "Jerome: The 'Vir Trilinguis' and the 'Hebraica Veritas.'" *Vigiliae Christianae* 47 (1993): 50–77.

Rehm, Bernhard. *Homilien*. Vol. 1 of *Die Pseudoklementinen*. Edited by B. Rehm. Die griechischen christlichen Schriftstelle der ersten Jahrhunderte 42. Berlin: Akademie-Verlag, 1953.

Reiser, Marcus. *Jesus and Judgment: The Eschatological Proclamation in Its Jewish Context*. Translated by L. Maloney. Minneapolis, MN: Fortress, 1997.

Rice, David G., and John E. Stambaugh. *Sources for the Study of Greek Religion*. Society of Biblical Literature Sources for Biblical Study 14. Missoula, MT: Scholars Press, 1979.

Ricoeur, Paul. "Naming God." *Union Seminary Quarterly Review* (1979): 215–27.

Riley, Gregory J. "Thomas Traditions and the *Acts of Thomas*." Pages 533–42 in the *SBL Seminar Papers, 1993*. Society of Biblical Literature Seminar Papers 30. Atlanta, GA: Scholars Press.

—. "Thomas Christianity." Paper presented at the annual meeting of the Society of Biblical Literature. Washington, DC, Nov. 20–23, 1993.

———. "The *Gospel of Thomas* in Recent Scholarship." *Currents in Research: Biblical Studies* 2 (1994): 227–52.

———. *Resurrection Reconsidered: Thomas and John in Controversy*. Minneapolis, MN: Fortress, 1995.

———. *One Jesus, Many Christs: How Jesus Inspired Not One True Christianity, But Many*. New York, NY: HarperCollins, 1997.

———. "Mimesis of Classical Ideals in the Second Christian Century." Pages 91–103 in *Mimesis and Intertextuality in Antiquity and Christianity*. Edited by Dennis R. MacDonald. Studies in Antiquity and Christianity. Harrisburg, PA: Trinity Press International, 2001.

Robbins, Vernon K. "Pragmatic Relations as a Criterion for Authentic Sayings." *Forum* 1:3 (1985): 35–63.

———. "Rhetorical Argument about Lamps and Light in Early Christian Gospels." Pages 177–95 in *Context: Festskrift til Peder Johan Borgen*. Edited by P. W. Böckman and R. E. Kristiansen. Relief. Publikasjoner utgitt av Religionsvitenskapelig institutt, Universitetet i Trondheim 24. Trondheim: Tapir, 1987.

———. "The Chreia." Pages 13–16 in *Greco-Roman Literature and the New Testament: Selected Forms and Genres*. Edited by David E. Aune. Society of Biblical Literature Sources in Biblical Study 21. Atlanta, GA: Scholars Press, 1988.

———. "Writing as a Rhetorical Act in Plutarch and the Gospels." Pages 142–168 in *Persuasive Artistry: Studies in New Testament Rhetoric in Honor of George A. Kennedy*. Edited by D. F. Watson. Journal for the Study of the New Testament Supplement Series 50. Sheffield: Sheffield Academic Press, 1991.

———. "Progymnastic Rhetorical Composition and Pre-Gospel Traditions: A New Approach." Pages 116–121 in *The Synoptic Gospels: Source Criticism and the New Literary Criticism*. Edited by C. Focant. Bibliotheca Ephemeridum Theologicarum Lovaniensium 110. Leuven: Peeters & Leuven University Press, 1993.

———. "Social-Scientific Criticism and Literary Studies: Prospects for Cooperation in Biblical Interpretation." Pages 274–89 in *Modelling Early Christianity: Social-Scientific Studies of the New Testament and Its Context*. Edited by Philip F. Esler. London: Routledge, 1995.

———. *The Tapestry of Early Christian Discourse: Rhetoric, Society and Ideology*. London: Routledge, 1996.

———. *Exploring the Texture of Texts: A Guide to Socio-Rhetorical Interpretation*. Valley Forge, PA: Trinity Press International, 1996.

———. "Rhetorical Composition and Sources in the *Gospel of Thomas*." Pages 86–114 in the *SBL Seminar Papers, 1997*. Society of Biblical Literature Seminar Papers 36. Atlanta, GA: Scholars Press, 1997.

———. "From Enthymeme to Theology in Luke 11:1–13." Pages 191–214 in *Literary Studies in Luke-Acts: A Collection of Essays in Honor of Joseph B. Tyson*. Edited by R. P. Thompson and T. E. Phillips. Macon, GA: Mercer University Press, 1998. Online: http://www.emory.edu/COLLEGE/RELIGION/faculty/robbins/Theology/theology191.html

———. "Enthymemic Texture in the *Gospel of Thomas*." Pages 343–66 in volume 1 of the *SBL Seminar Papers, 1998*. 2 vols. Society of Biblical Literature Seminar Papers 37. Atlanta, GA: Scholars Press, 1998.

———. "Argumentative Textures in Socio–Rhetorical Interpretation." Pages 27–65 in *Rhetorical Argumentation in Biblical Texts: Essays from the Lund 2000 Conference*. Edited by A. Eriksson, T. H. Olbricht, and W. Übelacker. Emory Studies in Early Christianity. Harrisburg, PA: Trinity Press International, 2002.

———. "The Intertexture of Apocalyptic Discourse in the Gospel of Mark." Pages 11–15 in *The Intertexture of Apocalyptic Discourse in the New Testament*. Edited by Duane F. Watson. SBL Symposium 14. Atlanta, GA: Society of Biblical Literature, 2002.

———. "A Comparison of Mishnah Gittin 1:1–2:2 and James 2:1–13 from a Perspective of Greco-Roman Rhetorical Elaboration." Pages 201–16 in *Mishnah and the Social Formation of the Early Rabbinic Guild: A Socio-Rhetorical Approach*. Edited by Jack N. Lightstone. Studies in Christianity and Judaism/Études sur le christianisme et le judaïsme 11. Waterloo: Wilfrid Laurier University Press for the Canadian Corporation for Studies in Religion/Corporation Canadienne des Sciences Religieuses, 2002.

Robinson, James M. "Gnosticism and the New Testament." Pages 125–43 in *Gnosis: Festschrift für Hans Jonas*. Edited by Barbara Aland. Göttingen: Vandenhoeck & Ruprecht, 1978.

———. "On Bridging the Gulf from Q to the *Gospel of Thomas* (or Vice Versa)." Pages 127–75 in *Nag Hammadi, Gnosticism, and Early Christianity*. Edited by Charles W. Hedrick and Robert Hodgson, Jr. Peabody, MA: Hendrickson, 1986.

———, ed. *The Nag Hammadi Library*. Rev. ed. The Definitive New Translation of the Gnostic Scriptures. Complete in One Volume. San Francisco, CA: Harper & Row, 1988.

———. *The Jesus of the Sayings Gospel Q*. Occasional Papers of the Institute for Antiquity and Christianity. Claremont, CA: Institute for Antiquity and Christianity, 1993.

Robinson, James M., Paul Hoffmann, and John S. Kloppenborg, eds. *The Critical Edition of Q*. Hermeneia Supplement. Philadelphia, PA: Fortress, 2000. Leuven: Peeters, 2000.

Robinson, James M., and Helmut Koester. *Trajectories through Early Christianity*. Philadelphia, PA: Fortress, 1971.

Robson, James. *Christ in Islam*. New York, NY: Dutton, 1930.

Rohrbaugh, Richard. " 'Social Location of Thought' as Heuristic Construct in New Testament Study." *Journal for the Study of the New Testament* 30 (1987): 103–19.

Ropes, James Hardy. "Agrapha." Pages 343–52 in the extra vol. of *A Dictionary of the Bible*. Edited by James Hastings. New York, NY: Scribners. Edinburgh: Clark, 1904.

Roques, René. "Gnosticisme et Christianisme: L'Évangile selon Thomas." *Irénikon* 33 (1960): 29–40.

———. " 'L'Évangile selon Thomas': Son édition critique et son identification." *Revue de l'historie des religios* 157 (1960): 187–218.

Ross, William David. *Plato's Theory of Ideas*. Oxford: Oxford University Press, 1976.

Rowland, Christopher. *The Open Heaven: A Study of Apocalyptic in Judaism and Early Christianity*. New York, NY: Crossroads, 1982.

Rudhardt, J. "À propos de l'hymne homérique à Déméter." *Museum Helveticum* 35 (1978): 1–17.

Sabre, Ru Michael. "Peirce's Abductive Argument and the Enthymeme." *Transactions of the Charles S. Peirce Society* 36, no. 3 (1990): 365–69.

Säve-Söderbergh, Torgny. "Gnostic and Canonical Gospel Traditions (with special reference to the *Gospel of Thomas*)." Pages 552–62 in *Le origini dello gnosticismo: colloquio di Messina, 13–18 aprile, 1966: Testi e discussioni*. Edited by U. Bianchi. Studies in the History of Religions 12. Leiden: Brill, 1967.

Schenke, Hans-Martin. *Der Gott "Mensch" in der Gnosis: Ein religionsgeschichtlicher Beitrag zur Diskussion über die paulinische Anschauung von der Kirche als Leib Christi*. Göttingen: Vandenhoeck & Ruprecht, l962.

———. "On the Compositional History of the *Gospel of Thomas*." *Forum* 10:1–2 (1994): 9–30.

———. *Das Philippusevangelium (Nag-Hammadi-Codex II,3)*. Berlin: Akademie Verlag, 1997.

Schimanowski, Gottfried. *Die himmlische Liturgie in der Apocalypse des Johannes*. Wissenscaftliche Untersuchungen zum Neuen Testament 2. Tübingen: Mohr, 2002.

Schmidt, Karl, ed. *Pistis Sophia*. Translation and Notes Violet Macdermot. Nag Hammadi Studies 9. Leiden: Brill, 1978.

Schmidtke, Alfred *Neue Fragmente und Unterschungen zu den Judenchristliche Evangelien: Ein beitrag zur Literatur und Geschichte der Judenchristen*. Texte und Untersuchungen 37:1. Leipzig: Hinrichs, 1911.

Schneemelcher, Wilhelm, ed. *New Testament Apocrypha*. English translation edited by Robert McL. Wilson. 2 vols. Louisville, KY: Westminster John Knox, 1991–1992.

Schoedel, William R. "Naassene Themes in the Coptic *Gospel of Thomas*." *Vigiliae Christianae* 14 (1960): 225–234.

Schottroff, Luise. *Lydia's Impatient Sisters: A Feminist Social History of Early Christianity*. Translated by Barbara and Martin Rumscheidt. Louisville, KY: Westminster John Knox, 1995.

Schrage, Wolfgang. *Das Verhältnis des Thomas-Evangeliums zur synoptischen Tradition und zu den koptischen Evangelienübersetzungen: Zugleich ein Beitrag zur gnostischen Synoptikerdeutung*. Beihefte zur Zeitschrift für die neutestamentliche Wissenschaft 29. Berlin: Töpelmann, 1964.

Schröter, Jens. *Erinnerung an Jesu Worte: Studien zur Rezeption der Logienueberlieferung in Markus, Q und Thomas*. Wissenschaftliche Monographien zum Alten und Neuen Testament 76. Neukirchen-Vluyn: Neukirchener Verlag, 1997.

Schüssler Fiorenza, Elisabeth. *In Memory of Her: A Feminist Theological Reconstruction of Christian Origins*. New York, NY: Crossroad, 1988.

Scott, Bernard Brandon. *Hear Then the Parable: A Commentary on the Parables of Jesus*. Minneapolis, MN: Fortress, 1989.

Seaford, Richard. *Reciprocity and Ritual: Homer and Tragedy in the Developing City-State*. Oxford: Clarendon, 1994.

Segal, Alan F. *Paul the Convert: The Apostolate and Apostasy of Saul the Pharisee*. New Haven, CT: Yale University Press, 1990.

Segovia, Fernando F. *The Farewell of the Word: The Johannine Call to Abide*. Minneapolis, MN: Fortress, 1991.

Sellew, Philip. "Early Collections of Jesus' Words." Th.D. diss., Harvard University, 1986.

———. "The Construction of Jesus in the *Gospel of Thomas*." Paper Presented at the annual meeting of the Society of Biblical Literature. Washington, DC, Nov. 20–23, 1993.

———. "Pious Practice and Social Formation in the *Gospel of Thomas*." *Forum* 10:1–2 (1994): 47–56.

———. "Death, the Body, and the World in the *Gospel of Thomas*." Pages 530–34 in *Proceedings of the XII International Patristics Conference, Oxford, 1995*. Edited by E. A. Livingstone. Studia Patristica 31. Leuven: Peeters, 1996.

———. "The *Gospel of Thomas*: Prospects for Future Research." Pages 237–46 in *The*

Nag Hammadi Library after Fifty Years: Proceedings of the 1995 Society of Biblical Literature Commemoration. Edited by John D. Turner and Anne McGuire. Nag Hammadi and Manichaean Studies 44. Leiden: Brill, 1997.

——. "Thomas Christianity: Scholars in Search of Community." Pages 11–35 in *The Apocryphal Acts of Thomas.* Edited by Jan N. Bremmer. Leuven: Peeters, 2001.

Sellin, Gerhard. *Der Streit um die Auferstehung der Toten: Eine religionsgeschichtliche und exegetische Untersuchung von 1 Korinther 15.* Forschungen zur Religion und Literatur des Alten und Neuen Testaments 138. Göttingen: Vandenhoeck & Ruprecht, 1985.

Sextus Empiricus. *Outlines of Pyrrhonism.* Translated by G. R. Bury. Great Books in Philosophy. Buffalo, NY: Prometheus, 1990.

Sieber, J. H. "A Redactional Analysis of the Synoptic Gospels with regard to the Question of the Sources of the Gospel According to Thomas." Ph.D. diss. The Claremont Graduate School, 1965.

Sivertsev, Alexei. "The *Gospel of Thomas* and the Early Stages in the Development of the Christian Wisdom Literature." *Journal of Early Christian Studies* 8 (2000): 319–40.

Slusser, Michael. "Docetism: A Historical Definition." *Second Century* 1 (1981): 163–71.

Smith, Jonathan Z. "The Garments of Shame." *History of Religions* 5 (1965–66): 217–38.

——. "The Social Description of Early Christianity." *Religion Studies Review* 1 (1975): 19–25.

Smyth, H. W. *Greek Grammar.* Cambridge, MA: Harvard University Press, 1956.

Smyth, K. "Gnosticism in 'The Gospel according to Thomas'." *Heythrop Journal* 1 (1960): 189–198.

Snodgrass, Klyne. "The *Gospel of Thomas*: A Secondary Gospel." *The Second Century* 7 (1989–90): 19–38.

Sourvinou-Inwood, Christiane. *"Reading" Greek Death.* Oxford: Clarendon, 1995.

Sperber, Dan. *Rethinking Symbolism.* Translated by A. L. Morton. Cambridge, MA: Cambridge University Press, 1975.

Stegemann, Ekkehard W., and Wolfgang Stegemann. *The Jesus Movement: A Social History of Its First Century.* Translated by O. C. Dean. Minneapolis, MN: Fortress, 1999.

Stendahl, Krister. *The School of St. Matthew and Its Use of the Old Testament.* 2nd ed. Philadelphia, PA: Fortress, 1968.

Stoops, Robert F., Jr. and Dennis R. MacDonald, Jr., eds. *The Apocryphal Acts of the Apostles in Intertextual Perspectives.* Semeia 80. Atlanta, GA: Scholars Press, 1997.

Stroumsa, Gedaliahu. "Forms of God: Some Notes on Metatron and Christ." *Harvard Theological Review* 76 (1985): 269–88.

Strubbe, J. H. M. "'Cursed Be He that Moves My Bones.'" Pages 33–59 in *Magika Hiera: Ancient Greek Magic and Religion.* Edited by Christopher A. Faraone and Dirk Obbink. New York, NY: Oxford University Press, 1991.

Strutwolf, Holger. *Gnosis als System: Zur Rezeption der valentinianischen Gnosis bei Origines.* Forschungen zur Kirchen- und Dogmengeschichte 56. Göttingen: Vandenhoeck & Ruprecht, 1993.

Stuckenbruck, Loren T. *Angel Veneration and Christology: A Study in Early Judaism and in the Christology of the Apocalypse.* Wissenschaftliche Untersuchungen zum Neuen Testament 2. Reihe 70. Tübingen: Mohr, 1995.

Syreeni, Kari. "Wonderlands: A Beginner's Guide to Three Worlds." *Svensk exegetisk årsbok* 64 (1999): 33–46.

Tabor, James. *Things Unutterable: Paul's Ascent to Paradise in its Greco-Roman, Judaic, and Early Christian Contexts.* Lanham, MD: University Press of America, 1986.

Theissen, Gerd. "Wanderradikalismus: Literatursoziologische Aspekte der Über-lieferung von Worten Jesu im Urchristentum." *Zeitschrift für Theologie und Kirche* 70 (1973): 245–71.

——. *Soziologie der Jesusbewegung: Ein Beitrag zur Entstehungsgeschichte des Urchristentums.*

Theologische Existenz heute 194. Munich: Kaiser, 1977. English translation: Gerd. *The First Followers of Jesus: A Sociological Analysis of the Earliest Christianity*. Translated by John Bowden. London: SCM, 1978. *Sociology of Early Palestinian Christianity*. Philadelphia, PA: Fortress, 1978.

——. *Studien zur Soziologie des Urchristentums*. 2nd edition. Wissenschaftliche Untersuchungen zum Neuen Testament 19. Tübingen: Mohr, 1983.

——. "The Wandering Radicals: Light Shed by the Sociology of Literature on the Early Transmission of Jesus' Sayings." Pages 33–59 in *Social Reality and the Early Christians*. Translated by M. Kohl. Minneapolis, MN: Fortress, 1992.

——. *The Religion of the Earliest Churches: Creating a Symbolic World*. Translated by John Bowden. Minneapolis, MN: Fortress, 1999.

Theissen, Gerd, and Annette Merz. *The Historical Jesus: A Comprehensive Guide*. Translated by John Bowden. London: SCM, 1998.

Thomassen, Einar. *Le Traite Tripartite (NH I, 5)*. Bibliothèque copte de Nag Hammadi Textes 19. Quebec: Les Presses de l'Université Laval, 1989.

Tolbert, Mary Ann. "Asceticism and Mark's Gospel." Pages 29–48 in *Asceticism and the New Testament*. Edited by Leif E. Vaage and Vincent L. Wimbush. New York, NY: Routledge, 1999.

Tolman, Judson Allen, Jr. *A Study of the Sepulchral Inscriptions in Buecheler's "Carmina Epigraphica Latina."* Chicago, IL: The University of Chicago Press, 1910.

Tuckett, Christopher. *Christology and the New Testament: Jesus and His Earliest Followers*. Louisville, KY: Westminster John Knox, 2001.

Turner, H. E. W., and Hugh Montefiore. *Thomas and the Evangelists*. Studies in Biblical Theology 35. London: SCM, 1962.

Turner, John D. "The Book of Thomas the Contender" [English translation]. Pages 180–205 in *On the Origin of the World, Expository Treatise, On the Soul, Book of Thomas the Contender*. Vol 2 of *Nag Hammadi Codex II, 2–7 together with XIII, 2*, Brit. Lib. Or. 4926(1), and P. Oxy. 1, 654, 655*. Edited by Bentley Layton. Nag Hammadi Studies 21. Leiden: Brill, 1989.

Uro, Risto. *Sheep among the Wolves: A Study of the Mission Instructions of Q*. Annales Academiae Scientiarum Fennicae: Dissertationes humanarum litterarum 47. Helsinki: Academia Scientiarum Fennica, 1987.

——. "'Secondary Orality' in the *Gospel of Thomas*? Logion 14 as a Test Case." *Forum* 9:3–4 (1993): 305–29. Repr. with the title "*Thomas* and the Oral Gospel Tradition" pages 8–32 in *Thomas at the Crossroads: Essays on the Gospel of Thomas*. Edited by Risto Uro. Studies of the New Testament and Its World. Edinburgh: Clark, 1998.

——, ed. *Thomas at the Crossroads: Essays on the Gospel of Thomas*. Studies of the New Testament and Its World. Edinburgh: Clark, 1998.

——. "Is *Thomas* an Encratite Gospel?" Pages 140–62 in *Thomas at the Crossroads*. Edited by R. Uro. Studies of the New Testament and Its World. Edinburgh: Clark, 1998.

——. "'Who Will Be Our Leader?' Authority and Autonomy in the *Gospel of Thomas*." Pages 457–85 in *Fair Play: Diversity and Conflicts in Early Christianity: Essays in Honour of Heikki Räisänen*. Edited by Ismo Dunderberg, Kari Syreeni, and Christopher Tuckett. Supplements to Novum Testamentum 103. Leiden: Brill, 2002. Repr. pages 80–105 in Risto Uro. *Thomas: Seeking the Historical Context of the Gospel of Thomas*. Edinburgh: Clark, 2003.

——. *Thomas: Seeking the Historical Context of the Gospel of Thomas*. London: Clark, 2003.

Vaage, Leif E. *Galilean Upstarts: Jesus' First Followers According to Q*. Valley Forge, PA: Trinity Press International, 1994.

Valantasis, Richard. *Spiritual Guides of the Third Century: A Semiotic Study of the Guide—Disciple Relationship in Christianity, Neoplatonism, Hermetism, and Gnosticism*. Harvard Dissertations in Religion 27. Minneapolis, MN: Fortress, 1991.

——. "Constructions of Power in Asceticism." *Journal of the American Academy of Religion* 63 (1995): 775–821.

——. "A Theory of the Social Function of Asceticism." Pages 544–52 in *Asceticism*. Edited by Vincent L. Wimbush and Richard Valantasis. New York, NY: Oxford University Press, 1995.

——. *The Gospel of Thomas*. New Testament Readings. London: Routledge, 1997.

——. "Is the *Gospel of Thomas* Ascetical? Revisiting an Old Problem with a New Theory." *Journal of Early Christian Studies* 7 (1999): 55–81.

Vermes, Geza, and Martin D. Goodman, eds. *The Essenes According to Classical Sources*. Sheffield: Sheffield Academic Press, 1989.

Vermeule, Emily. *Aspects of Death in Early Greek Art and Poetry*. Sather Classical Lectures 46. Berkeley, CA: University of California Press, 1979.

Vernant, Jean-Pierre. *Mortals and Immortals: Collected Essays*. Edited by Froma I. Zeitlin. Princeton, NJ: Princeton University Press, 1991.

Vielhauer, Philipp, and Gerhard Strecker. "Jewish-Christian Gospels." Pages 134–78 in *Gospels and Related writings*. Vol. 1 of *New Testament Apocrypha*. Revised edition edited by W. Schneemelcher. English translation edited by Robert McL. Wilson. Cambridge, MA: James Clarke, 1991.

Völker, Walther, ed. *Quellen zur Geschichte der christlichen Gnosis*. Sammlung ausgewählter kirchen- und dogmengeschichtlichen Quellenschriften n.F. 5. Tübingen: Mohr, 1932.

Vööbus, Arthur. *History of Asceticism in the Syrian Orient*. Vol. 1. Leuven: Corpus scriptorum christianorum orientalium 148. Leuven: van den Bempt, 1958.

Walsh, George B. "Callimachean Passages: The Rhetoric of Epitaph in Epigram." *Arethusa* 24 (1991): 77–105.

Walker, Jeffrey. *Rhetoric and Poetics in Antiquity*. New York, NY: Oxford University Press, 2000.

Wedderburn, A. J. M. *Baptism and Resurrection: Studies in Pauline Theology against Its Graeco-Roman Background*. Wissenschaftliche Untersuchungen zum Neuen Testament 44. Tübingen: Mohr, 1987.

West, Martin L. *The Orphic Poems*. Oxford: Clarendon, 1983.

——. *Iambi et elegi graeci ante Alexandrum cantati*. 2 vols. 2nd ed. Oxford: Clarendon, 1989.

Wiles, Maurice F. *The Spiritual Gospel: The Interpretation of the Fourth Gospel in the Early Church*. Cambridge, MA: Cambridge University Press, 1960.

Williams, Francis E. "The Apocryphon of James." Pages 13–53 in *Introductions, Texts, Translations, Indices*. Vol. 1 of *Nag Hammadi Codex I*. Edited by H. W. Attridge. Nag Hammadi Studies 22. Leiden: Brill, 1985.

Williams, James G., ed. *René Girard: The Girard Reader*. New York, NY: Crossroad, 1996.

Williams, Michael A. *Rethinking Gnosticism: An Argument for Dismantling a Dubious Category*. Princeton, NJ: Princeton University Press, 1996.

Wilson, Robert McL. "The Coptic '*Gospel of Thomas*'." *New Testament Studies* 5 (1958–59): 273–76.

——. "Thomas and the Growth of the Gospels." *Harvard Theological Review* 53 (1960): 231–250.

——. *Studies in the Gospel of Thomas*. London: Mowbray, 1960.

Winter, Bruce W. *Philo and Paul among the Sophists: Alexandrian and Corinthian Responses to a Julio-Claudian Movement*. 2nd ed. Foreword by G. W. Bowersock. Grand Rapids, MI: Eerdmans, 2002 [1997].

Wrede, William. *Das Messiasgeheimnis in den Evangelien*. Göttingen: Vandenhoeck & Ruprecht, 1901.

Wucherpfennig, Ansgar. *Heracleon Philologus: Gnostische Johannesexegese im zweiten Jahrhundert*. Wissenschaftliche Untersuchungen zum Neuen Testament 142. Tübingen: Mohr, 2002.

Yarbro Collins, Adela. "Introduction: Early Christian Apocalypticism." Pages 1–11 in *Early Christian Apocalypticism: Genre and Social Setting*. Semeia 36. Edited by Adela Yarbro Collins. Atlanta, GA: Scholars Press.

Zöckler, Thomas. *Jesu Lehren im Thomasevangelium*. Nag Hammadi and Manichaean Studies 47. Leiden: Brill, 1999.

Zuntz, Günther. *Persephone: Three Essays on Religion and Thought in Magna Graecia*. Oxford: Clarendon, 1971.

MODERN AUTHOR INDEX

SCRIPTURAL INDEX